PERSONALITY DEVELOPMENT IN TWO CULTURES

*A Cross-Cultural Longitudinal Study of School Children in Mexico and the United States*

*The Hogg Foundation Research Series*

WAYNE H. HOLTZMAN, EDITOR

Published for the Hogg Foundation for Mental Health

# Personality Development in Two Cultures

*A Cross-Cultural Longitudinal Study of School Children in Mexico and the United States*

Wayne H. Holtzman
Rogelio Díaz-Guerrero
Jon D. Swartz

*in collaboration with*

Luis Lara-Tapia
Luis M. Laosa
María Luisa Morales
Isabel Reyes Lagunes
Donald B. Witzke

UNIVERSITY OF TEXAS PRESS • AUSTIN AND LONDON

Library of Congress Cataloging in Publication Data

Holtzman, Wayne H
 Personality development in two cultures.

 (The Hogg Foundation research series)
 Bibliography: p.
 Includes index.
 1. Personality and culture. 2. Children in Mexico.
3. Children in the United States. I. Díaz-Guerrero,
Rogelio, joint author. II. Swartz, Jon David, joint
author. III. Title. IV. Series.
BF698.9.C8H57      155.2'34      74-30178
ISBN 0-292-77512-1

# CONTENTS

Appendices

# TABLES

# FIGURES

# PREFACE

When a multivariate longitudinal study is carried out satisfactorily, the help of many people and organizations is necessary. When, in addition, such a study is carried out in two cultures simultaneously and involves cross-national, linguistic, and subcultural factors as well, the number of people and agencies involved is increased algebraically.

First and foremost, we wish to thank both the United States Public Health Service and the Foundations Fund for Research in Psychiatry, whose generous support of the projects in the United States and Mexico, respectively, was indispensable to the successful completion of such a large-scale endeavor. The National University of Mexico and the University of Texas provided facilities and administrative support for the research program. During the last few years of the project, additional support was provided by the Hogg Foundation for Mental Health and by a Spencer Fellowship awarded to Jon D. Swartz by the National Academy of Education.

In the early years of the study, in addition to the authors, those who participated in the research program as examiners, interviewers, and assistants consisted of the following: Marion Bishop, Charles Brasfield, John Breeskin, Shirley Cone, Sara Currie, David Dávila, Paul Diamond, Kay Dreisbach, Moira Dunton, Bobby Farrow, Kathleen Fleming, Gail Gordon, Mary Hudspeth, Ruth Isely, Connie Kitley, Daniel Klein, Don Laird, Arthur Landy, David Lynch, Thomas Mandeville, Rodney McGinnis, Jonelle McLemore, Mary Moran, Kenneth Parker, Billy Pester, Alvan Rosenthal, Jeffrey Sanders, Stephen Seaquist, Roberta Shaw, Karen Spivey, Jane Stitt, Carol Swartz, and Charlene Williams at the University of Texas; and René Ahumada, Piedad Aladro Lubel, Elda Alicia Alba Canto, Guiliana de Astis Arlotta, María Eugenia Díaz Martín, María de la Luz Fernández, Gustavo Fernández, Dyrna Gladys

García, Isabel Jaidar Matalobos, Eric Lizt, Alejandro Lugo, Martha Eugenia Peña Ledesma, Brenda Marcela Re, Angel San Román, Elena Sommer, and Dalila Yussif of the National University of Mexico. Special thanks are due Joseph S. Thorpe of the University of Missouri, Columbia, for major assistance during the early stages of this project when he was closely associated with it as a faculty member at the University of Texas.

More recently, assistants on the project in both cultures have included the following: Hilda Anguiano, Lilia Ayala, Marta Barbiaux, Keith Bell, Raúl Bianchi, Enriqueta Bolaños, Betty Bremond, John Cooney, Estela Cordero, Graciela Díaz Guerrero, Pedro Díaz Guerrero, Silvia Díaz Guerrero, Susan Eisner, Michael Faubion, María Eugenia Flores, Rocio Gary, Gilda Gómez, Suzanne Gray, María Lucina Gutiérrez, Carmen Guillén, Angel Islas, James Holtzman, Alice Isbell, Marie Kluckhohm, Elena Krinsky, José Antonio Mantilla, Nahum Martínez, Maureen McGavern, Gloria Morales, Blanca Nualart, Richard Palmer, Sharon Parker, Rufus Parsons, Mary Raleigh, Marie Dolores Rodríguez, Michael Selman, Susan Sullivan, Raúl Tenorio, Alicia Velázquez, María de Jesús Villalpando, María Enedina Villegas, and Carl White.

The entire manuscript was reviewed by Herman Witkin, who offered many helpful suggestions for its improvement. Sections of the manuscript were also read by Jerome Kagan. We wish to thank these individuals for their helpful criticisms concerning the manuscript. Early drafts of the manuscript, as well as the final version, were typed by Mrs. Pearl Gardner, a service for which we are most grateful.

Appreciation is expressed to the staff of the Austin Independent School District and to the Secretary of Public Education in Mexico for their assistance in securing the cooperation of the schools that provided subjects for the study and to the superintendents, principals, and teachers of all the schools in both countries; to the parents who consented to interviews and to the participation of their children in the study; and to the children themselves who served as willing subjects for six consecutive years of testing.

In what we believe is a unique event in publishing history, this book is being published simultaneously in two different countries in the respective languages of those countries. In Mexico the book is being published by Editorial Trillas, Mexico City, and in the

United States by the University of Texas Press, Austin, Texas. Only by publishing the results of our cross-cultural investigation in this fashion can the long-standing and truly cooperative collaboration of the psychologists in both countries be presented adequately. The study was conducted both in English and in Spanish, and its results are being presented in both of these languages.

W. H. H.

R. D.-G.

J. D. S.

# PART ONE

## Background of the Study

---

Those who know no culture other than their own cannot know
their own.

Ralph Linton

*The Cultural Background of Personality*

---

# 1. Introduction

One of the most significant developments in contemporary psychology is the rapid growth of cross-cultural research on a scale unheard of a decade ago. The widening search for cultural variation, the growing realization of parochial limitations in American psychology, the increased communication among behavioral scientists across many disciplines as well as different nations, and the development of technology and resources that make it feasible to undertake large-scale research all contribute greatly to this new kind of comparative psychology—a comparative psychology of human behavior in markedly different natural settings rather than a comparative psychology dealing with different animal species.

Cross-cultural, comparative approaches are particularly appealing for the study of sociocultural factors in any aspect of human development. Different patterns of child rearing, variations in family life style, contrasting value systems, sociolinguistic variations, and different social orders and their political or economic systems are but a few of the major environmental influences upon human development that require a cross-cultural approach if one is to study them under real-life conditions. In spite of the obvious appeal of cross-cultural approaches to human development, conceptual and

methodological difficulties encountered in such research have been
so forbidding that until recently psychologists have generally left
the field to anthropologists and social theorists.

According to J. W. M. Whiting (1954), the cross-cultural method first was used by E. B. Tylor (1889) who presented a paper,
"On a Method of Investigating the Development of Institutions;
Applied to Laws of Marriage and Descent," at the meetings of the
Royal Anthropological Institute of Great Britain. The intent of this
study was to support Tylor's view of cultural evolution, but its
ultimate importance was that in the paper—and in the discussions
of it that followed—most of the basic assumptions of cross-cultural
research were touched upon.

Twenty-five years later—again to test evolutionary theory—the
method was employed once more: L. T. Hobhouse, G. C. Wheeler,
and M. Ginsberg (1915) published a monograph in which the frequency of occurrence of certain social institutions was determined
for each stage of economic development from lower hunters to advanced agriculturalists. While these early uses of "the cross-
cultural method" are interesting and useful as anchor points in
gaining historical perspective, the true beginning of modern cross-
cultural research generally is attributed to Margaret Mead's work
in the South Seas (1928; 1930), Bronislaw Malinowski's *Sex and
Repression in Savage Society* (1927), and Edward Sapir's writings
on psychiatry and anthropology (1927; 1932; 1934) almost fifty
years ago. These early studies of child development and family patterns created quite a sensation throughout the world because of
their dramatic implications for psychoanalytic theory. In the en-
suing years numerous anthropologists undertook similar psychodynamic case studies of personality development in exotic cultures.
Many of these investigators employed the Rorschach or a variation
of the Thematic Apperception Test (TAT) to probe the depths of
the aborigine psyche in the manner of a clinician, hoping thereby
to gain insight into the modal personality of a given culture. Bert
Kaplan (1961) estimated that over 150 studies in seventy-five societies had employed projective techniques in the 1940–1960 period
alone. The net outcome of these cross-cultural personality studies
employing projective techniques, however, has been disappointing.
In his excellent survey of projective techniques and cross-cultural
research, Gardner Lindzey (1961) goes still further in discussing a

dozen unsettled issues of a methodological nature and a number of major flaws that continue to plague attempts to use the Rorschach, the Thematic Apperception Test, and similar materials for assessing personality in nonwestern cultures. While many of these anthropological studies using projective techniques tell us much about the limitations of the techniques, clearly the net outcome for understanding personality development is very small indeed.

J. W. M. Whiting and Irvin L. Child (1953) have pointed out that most studies concerned with culture and personality are intensive case studies of a single society, rather than cross-cultural investigations in the real sense of the word. Starting with George P. Murdock's (1949) classification of about two hundred societies as a universe from which to draw appropriate samples representing wide cultural variation, J. W. M. Whiting and his colleagues have conducted a series of truly comparative studies that constitute one of the most significant advances to date, methodologically speaking, on cultural factors in personality development. Data from countless ethnographic studies are scanned and coded for one or two key cultural variables, such as the degree of over-all infant indulgence and the type of household structure. Correlations are computed between two variables across many cultures, using whole societies as sampling units; and generalizations are made on the basis of statistical inference. The general method is one with which psychologists feel very much at home, although the basic raw data may be unfamiliar. The facts that Whiting and his colleagues addressed themselves to important psychological problems and that they used familiar methods account for the wide recognition given their work by psychologists. At the same time many anthropologists only reluctantly concede that the approach has some merit.

The striking correlations obtained in many of the cross-cultural studies of the Whiting and Child type cannot be easily dismissed, in spite of the obvious crudity of measurement, the uneven quality of the original data, and the difficulty of interpreting the meaning of the obtained correlations because of possible confounding of variables. Representing the first attempt at truly pancultural research design, these studies, based largely on the Human Relations Area Files, point the way to important additional empirical investigations that are necessary to fill in the cultural gaps due to missing and inadequate data.

Recognizing the limitations of using ethnographic data gathered by other anthropologists for quite different purposes, John W. and Beatrice B. Whiting in 1963 formed a group of social scientists at Harvard, Yale, and Cornell universities to embark on new systematic field studies on child-rearing practices and personality development (Whiting, ed. 1963). Six different cultures were chosen, ranging from a village in New England to an African tribe in Kenya. Each team of field workers selected a sample of twenty-four mothers and twenty-four children who were studied intensively. Particular attention was paid to patterns of aggression, dependency, and internalization of various mechanisms of behavior control. Similar methods of observation and rating were employed in all six cultures. These six were seen as the first of what might eventually be as many as one hundred societies examined in a standard manner to facilitate cross-cultural comparison. In spite of this laudable objective, however, it is unlikely that many more such studies will be made following the same standard methods because of the great expense and the relatively low yield.

From a psychologist's point of view, the studies of child rearing in six cultures by the Whitings, Child, and Lambert (Whiting, ed. 1963) do not add a great deal to our present knowledge of personality development. Taken by themselves, the studies of six cultures are analogous to six extensive, detailed case studies of interesting individuals, such as those that might be reported by a skilled clinical psychologist. Rich in its complexity and faithful in the registering of qualitative detail, the six-culture project is certainly a major improvement over the highly variable, uneven ethnographies typically obtained by anthropologists working independently of each other. Yet the net product leaves much to be desired. The basic data are essentially naturalistic, at the level of observation and interview, and the problem of calibrating the human observer still remains.

Perhaps we are expecting too much from such anthropological studies with respect to psychological problems of personality development. While the central concerns of anthropologists and psychologists may be the same, there are major differences in the ways these concerns are viewed. The anthropologist is preoccupied with mastering the language and customs of an unfamiliar society and with identifying the major aspects of culture that are essential from his point of view. Indeed, considering the present state of development of psychological techniques for personality assessment in our own culture, it is rather premature to expect much to be gained from the application of these techniques in a nonliterate society. If the psychologist wishes to investigate certain sociocultural factors in personality development, he must himself develop cross-cultural settings for his research, rather than counting on the hard-pressed anthropologist to do it for him. What, then, are the prospects for the psychologist in the cross-cultural study of personality development?

## Cross-Cultural Research in Psychology

Most cross-cultural studies by American psychologists consist of unsystematic replication of American research in another literate society, usually one that is Western European in culture. Techniques for measuring social attitudes or assessing personality are translated into French, German, or another appropriate language so that they can be easily applied in countries other than the United States or the British Commonwealth. Problems of sampling, linguistic equivalence of meaning, examiner variability, and cultural variation in response set are usually lightly dismissed or completely ignored. Moreover, the theoretical rationale for undertaking the cross-cultural study in the first place is often conspicuously absent.

While many of these same problems arise in conducting research within a single culture, the deliberate introduction of a cultural variable as part of the research design complicates the research greatly.

## Measurement and Control of Cross-Cultural Variables

To have any meaning as a cross-cultural study, a plan for research must deal first with the fundamental questions of what cultural variables are present and why they are important. The most ambitious use of cultural variables is a pancultural design in which a sample of many societies is selected from the universe of different societies existent in the world today. If the purpose of the cross-cultural study is to deal with biological, interpersonal, or environmental universals—that is, concepts that are appropriately applied to nearly any human culture—and if both variety and replication of cultural variables are essential for reaching a generalization, then the design must be pancultural. The cross-cultural surveys by Whiting and Child are excellent examples of this approach. Robert R. Sears (1961) has suggested that three motivational variables are probably transcultural in nature and maintain fairly well their conceptual equivalence across many cultures—aggression, dependency, and competition. Child (1954), in his universal behavior system, expands this list to nine personality traits, although it is unclear that all nine retain conceptual equivalence in every culture.

The main difficulty with pancultural psychological research is the frustrating lack of dependable data on a large and representative sample of world cultures. Reliance upon data already collected for other purposes severely limits the kinds of questions that can be asked. Although Whiting, Child, and Lambert have attempted to correct this deficiency in their six-cultures project, the outcome thus far is disappointing from a psychological point of view, for reasons already suggested.

More realistic than the pancultural approach is one in which a limited sample of cultures is drawn from the world universe; cultures that maximize desired variation with regard to a dimension of special interest. The studies of children's moral values undertaken by Harold H. and Gladys L. Anderson (1961; 1962) in nine different countries of Western Europe and the Americas is an example of this approach. Questionnaire data were collected from large numbers of children in metropolitan centers within each nation, using the Anderson Incomplete Stories to elicit fantasy material, and the data were coded for such themes as honesty, responsibility, anxiety, and guilt. The countries were then ranked according to their presumed degree of authoritarian versus democratic political-social structure. While these studies can be criticized for certain weaknesses, such as the use of a projective technique of unknown reliability and validity, such matters are of incidental concern here. Of greater importance is the validity of the major hypothesis concerning authoritarian versus democratic societies. Unfortunately, the particular countries selected by the Andersons differ on many dimensions, not just one. Even if the techniques for assessing child personality are valid in each nation, and even if the samples are large and truly representative of metropolitan school children, how do we know that the obtained differences in mean scores across nations are really due to the hypothesized cultural dimension, and not to any number of other dimensions confounded with it? The Achilles' heel in such research is the fact that in the last analysis we simply do not know, and we cannot really defend such a proposition. Although there is little doubt that the international differences obtained by the Andersons are statistically significant, the reasons for such differences must remain in the realm of speculation and unproven hypothesis.

Kenneth W. Terhune (1963), a student of the Andersons at Michigan State University, made a noteworthy attempt to overcome this difficulty in the original Anderson studies by including other key demographic variables in a cross-national study. In addition to country, the primary variables of sex, religion, and socioeconomic status were used in a nonorthogonal analysis of variance. Controlling for sex, religion, and socioeconomic status in the cross-national comparison is a major improvement that increases considerably the power of the design. Yet what can be said about all the other potentially confounded variables still uncontrolled?

The most common type of cross-cultural study involves only two cultures, usually the United States and one other country. Here the possibilities for misinterpretation of the cultural variables are even greater. As Donald T. Campbell (1961) has pointed out, comparisons between two cultures are generally uninterpretable because many cultural differences are operating which might provide alternate explanations of the findings and which cannot be ruled out.

Typical of such bicultural studies is one by Albert I. Rabin (1959) comparing American and Israeli children by means of a sentence-completion technique. Rabin tried to equate the two samples on several potentially confounding variables by drawing children of comparable age and intelligence, and by using rural regions in both countries. The Israeli and American children differed, however, in many other important respects that could not be adequately controlled. The obtained differences in response to sentence-completion items were tentatively attributed to differences in the social structure of the two societies. Early in life Israeli children assume certain functions within the family that are continuous with adult roles. As soon as he is physically able, for example, the Israeli child begins to participate in the operation of the family farm. By contrast the role of a child in rural Michigan is discon-

tinuous with adult activities. The Israeli child's greater participation in adult activities is seen by Rabin as resulting in a more realistic appraisal of the family than occurs in the American child.
This argument is used as a post hoc explanation of why Israeli
children give fewer positive or favorable responses in the completion of sentences dealing with family and mother. But, as Rabin
himself is quick to point out, such interpretations are highly tentative at best. Although the obtained differences between Israeli and
American children are undeniable, the meaning of these differences
is completely unclear because of the many sociocultural and linguistic differences between the two societies.

The picture presented above with respect to the control, delinea-
tion, and replication of cultural factors in the study of personality
development is depressing. If the investigator adopts the strategy
of Whiting and Child and increases the number and variety of
cultures sufficiently to draw generalizations based on statistical
inference, he runs the risk of including questionable, second-hand
data. He limits himself, furthermore, to a very small number of
obvious personality variables, and he ends up with only a handful
of rather unstable correlations, the interpretation of which is con-
troversial. On the other hand, if the investigator narrows his focus
to only two cultures, the cultural factors per se may be completely
uninterpretable in spite of the fact that real differences in personality may have been demonstrated in the two cultures. Is there any
middle ground to which the investigator can retreat?

The answer is probably no, if one is interested in the rigorous
testing of hypotheses regarding the influence of specified cultural
patterns upon personality development. Such a test concerns general
laws of culture and personality and requires a nomothetic approach
in which each culture is but one sampling unit within the universe
of known cultures. However, if one is content with something less
than the rigorous testing of universal hypotheses, several plausible
alternatives are available.

The situation is roughly analogous to the controversy in psychology between nomothetic methods, on the one hand, which involve
the individual as a sampling unit from which generalizations are
made to a universe of individuals, and idiographic methods, on the
other hand, which involve repeated measures on a single person,
using a variety of techniques aimed at understanding the person as

a functioning organism. A great deal can be learned about the interplay of culture and personality development by repeated measurement using a variety of methods and adequate sampling of individuals within a single culture. By repeating the entire study in a second, a third, and even a fourth culture, cultures selected because of contrasting features of particular interest, the knowledge gained about sociocultural factors in personality development within one society can be critically re-examined again and again. While universal hypotheses about culture and personality cannot be tested in any rigorous sense by such a research strategy, just as it is difficult to generalize from results obtained in the intensive study of single individuals, limited hypotheses about subcultural variation and social factors within culture can be adequately tested.

## *Systematic Use of Subcultural Variation*

Considerable subcultural variation exists within every large society. Indeed, most recent studies reveal much greater cultural variation within the urban centers of different nations than across nations. While the same is certainly not true of the more isolated, exotic societies characteristically studied by anthropologists, most of the sociocultural variables of particular interest to psychologists are well represented in the majority of world nations.

Bernard C. Rosen (1964) attempted to make the most of such cultural variation in studies of achievement motivation among children in selected areas of Brazil and the United States. The major sociocultural variables examined were social class and type of community, in addition to the obvious linguistic and cultural differences across the two nations. Several hundred boys aged nine to eleven in two Brazilian and two American cities were given four TAT cards that were later scored for need-achievement as proposed by David C. McClelland and others (1953). A large number of mothers were also interviewed to obtain information concerning family structure and concerning values related to the achievement syndrome.

The major subcultural results in terms of family variables, social class, and degree of urbanization as they relate to achievement motivation were roughly similar in both Brazil and the United States. In addition, Brazilian children generally received much lower need-achievement scores than did the Americans, a finding that is interpreted by Rosen as due to the observed differences in family values and child-rearing practices. Though plausible and provocative, this cross-cultural comparison is weak from a logical point of view for reasons cited earlier. But the striking correlations found consistently within both cultures—the interactions between social class, age of mastery training, and family values that appear in a similar manner in both cultures—provide a fairly sound basis for important conclusions about a particular kind of achievement motivation and the sociocultural factors that influence it.

Rabin's work (1961) on kibbutz children and nonkibbutz children in Israel is an excellent example of how subcultural variation, when experimentally introduced, can be effectively employed to study culture and personality development. Using a variety of projective methods and carefully selected samples of adolescents, Rabin found consistent differences in motivation and attitudes between the peer-group orientation of the kibbutz children and the family orientation of the nonkibbutz children.

A third example of subcultural variation as an integral part of a cross-cultural design for the study of personality development is the work of S. B. Sarason and his colleagues at Yale. Having developed the Test Anxiety Scale for Children, I. Sarnoff, Seymour Sarason, and others (1958) obtained comparative data in England and the United States. The crisis of preparing for the "11-plus" examination in England provides a ready-made test-anxiety situation for English children, because their educational and occupational futures depend upon the outcome of that examination. Since language and general cultural differences between young children in the United States and England are minimal, the sociocultural factor of the "11-plus" examination constituted the major cross-cultural difference. Furthermore, an additional control was available in Sarason's general anxiety scale. Relationships between the Test Anxiety Scale for Children and such variables as age and sex were very similar in both cultures. The crucial finding, however, was the significantly greater *test* anxiety in English children than in Americans, coupled with the fact that no cross-cultural differences were found for *general* anxiety. This study illustrates the way in which a limited cross-cultural research design can be used for testing an important, though circumscribed, hypothesis about personality development.

*Achieving Semantic Equivalences of Techniques*

Problems of test translation and linguistic differences are relatively minor in Rabin's kibbutz study or the research by Sarnoff and his colleagues. In most cross-cultural research, however, the problem of achieving genuine semantic equivalence of psychological techniques in two different cultures is very troublesome. Given the best of translations, the semantic value of particular words and phrases may still differ appreciably across two cultures, leading to different response sets and interpretations of meaning. Robert F. Peck and Rogelio Díaz-Guerrero (1963) have illustrated this point very nicely in a series of studies dealing with the subtle meaning of such words as *love* and *respect* in Spanish and in English as the words are employed in communities ranging geographically from central Mexico to the southwestern United States. The traditional Mexican connotation of the word *respect* involves strong overtones of obedience, expectation of protection, and concern not to invade the respected one's rights. The over-all connotation is one of duty and deference to authority. By contrast, the modal American concept of respect emphasizes admiration without any feelings of subordination, a kind of democratic give-and-take while being considerate of the other person's feelings and ideas. It is obvious that such differences in meaning cross-culturally could easily lead to misinterpretation of verbal responses to psychological questionnaires.

An even more dramatic illustration of the dilemma created by the confounding of language differences and personality is the interesting study reported by Susan M. Ervin (1964). Sixty-four bilingual Frenchmen were given the Thematic Apperception Test on two different occasions, once in French and once in English. The response content and associated personality variables shifted significantly from one language to the other in ways that could be predicted from knowledge of French and English culture. Ervin's discovery raises an important question. Does an individual's personality look noticeably different when expressed in one language rather than in another? Until further work is done on this problem with additional samples of bilingual subjects, we have to qualify any cross-cultural interpretations of personality by admitting that the obtained cross-cultural differences could be the result of semantic variation, linguistic differences of expression, cultural variability in the meaning of examiner-subject interactions, or cultural differences in response set. Until these potentially confounding factors are more thoroughly understood and properly controlled, it is rather presumptuous to make bald assertions about cross-cultural differences in personality.

The several theoretical and methodological issues just described do not exhaust the problems encountered by the psychologist conducting cross-cultural research on personality development. In addition to the special issues peculiar to cross-cultural studies, there are the usual difficulties in measuring relevant aspects of personality, in obtaining an adequate sample of the desired behavior, functions, or traits, and in relating these in a meaningful way to known aspects of the child's environment.

When such difficulties are added to the major issues described above, one might well ask whether such research is really worth the effort. Granted that generalizations must be limited and tentative, pending further replications, and that rigorous cross-cultural designs can only be approximately implemented at best, the situation is not quite as discouraging as it may appear at first glance. Even in a bicultural study a great deal of insight can be gained into the role of specified cultural variables in human development, provided care is taken to include subcultural variations that can be matched cross-culturally, to employ well-trained native examiners who have been calibrated cross-culturally, to use only techniques that can be reasonably defended in both cultures, and, most important of all, to involve the close and continual collaboration of seasoned, native investigators who are fully sensitive to the above issues in both cultures.

## Brief History of the Austin–Mexico City Project

Until recently the study of personality through inkblot perception was handicapped by the psychometric limitations in the Rorschach that had been revealed by critical investigations in the late 1940's and early 1950's. While many of these investigations partially verified the underlying premises in the Rorschach as a projective technique, it soon became apparent that a rather fundamental and radical revision of the method was imperative if any substantial progress was to be made in this area. In 1955 an Austin research team embarked upon an extensive program of research

designed to overcome the limitations of the Rorschach by con-
structing a completely new set of inkblots on sound psychometric
principles.

After three years of developmental research, the two final parallel forms of the Holtzman Inkblot Technique (HIT) were completed, each consisting of forty-five matched inkblots of various
colors, forms, and shading nuances, together with two trial inkblots
common to both forms (Holtzman et al. 1961). Extending the
number of inkblots to forty-five and requiring only one response
per card results in a nearly constant number of responses. These
important innovations, in addition to a simple standardized inquiry
and objective scoring criteria, have yielded a number of scores
similar to those in the Rorschach but with much higher reliability,
better distribution characteristics, and clearer interpretability.
These improved psychometric properties have been achieved without loss of the rich symbolic quality of projective responses for
which the Rorschach has proved valuable.

With the assistance of a United States Public Health Service
(USPHS) Grant in 1959, a large-scale standardization program for
the individual and group versions of the HIT was completed and
published (Holtzman et al. 1961). The completion of this standardization program consisted of the following: (*a*) the validation and
refinement of variables in the individually administered version of
the HIT—including studies of reliability, intercorrelation and factor-matching studies, relationships between the Rorschach and
HIT, correlations with measures of cognition, correlations with
objective self-inventory personality measures, correlates of developmental level, intergroup comparisons involving twenty-two inkblot
variables on 1,642 individuals from fifteen different populations
ranging from five-year-old children to superior adults and including several abnormal groups, and multivariate statistical approaches to psychodiagnosis (Holtzman et al. 1961); (*b*) the development of a free-response group-administered version of the
HIT—including the standardization of a group method (Swartz
and Holtzman 1963), comparison of the group and individual versions (Holtzman et al. 1963), use of the group version in a study
of intellectual achievement-motivation (Herron 1962), and construction of a shortened version of the group method (Herron
1963); and (*c*) the development of machine methods for regular

and configural scoring analysis (Moseley 1963).

The availability for the first time of two parallel forms of a standardized inkblot test opened a new avenue of research in the assessment of personality through inkblot perception. Many of the theoretical and methodological problems in this area, which were attacked with little success using the Rorschach, now could be examined with real hope of significant results.

During the extensive standardization program for the twenty-two HIT variables, developmental trends across the different normative samples proved particularly interesting. Within the normal populations ranging from five-year-olds to superior adults, highly significant age trends were found for all but two of the twenty-two individual scores analyzed, as well as for most of the pattern scores derived from genetic-level indices of the Rorschach (Thorpe 1960; Thorpe and Swartz 1965). These cross-sectional results indicated a shift from the impulsive production of diffuse, undifferentiated responses, uncritical of form, to increasingly mature, well-organized perceptual and ideational activity. Other findings also substantiated similar studies with the Rorschach in a general way. Such cross-sectional comparisons, however, are subject to sampling biases and lack information regarding changes in individuals through time. The developmental correlates of inkblot scores, as well as other perceptual, cognitive, and personality variables, can only be determined in any rigorous sense by longitudinal studies involving relevant subcultural, family, peer-group, and other environmental measures.

The limitations inherent in any cross-sectional study when dealing with developmental trends led the University of Texas group in 1962, with the assistance of a renewal of a USPHS Grant, to undertake a major longitudinal study of large, representative samples of children with repeated measurement annually for six years.

Shortly after this program began, plans were completed for a cross-cultural replication of the entire study in Mexico City. The close proximity of Texas and Mexico has naturally resulted in considerable professional and scientific interaction over the years among psychologists and other behavioral scientists, particularly between those at the University of Texas and those at the National University of Mexico. The large proportion of Spanish-speaking people of Mexican descent in Texas and the heavy influx to Mexico City of North American ideas, products, tourists, scholars, and businessmen have sensitized both groups to the desirability of conducting cross-cultural research before further cultural diffusion and social changes occur.

Periodic exchanges, seminars, and workshops involving groups of psychologists from the National University and the University of Texas have been taking place since the Third Inter-American Congress of Psychology was held in Austin in 1955. Preliminary planning for collaboration on a major cross-cultural program of research actually began in 1959, when four Mexican psychologists led by Rogelio Díaz-Guerrero spent several months at the University of Texas working closely with American psychologists on the problems of conducting research on personality in the two countries. Considerable time was devoted to problems of standardization, translation, sampling, and examiner variability in the use of psychological techniques cross-culturally. In addition, the American psychologists concentrated on learning about variations of Mexican culture. During the next five years, over one hundred different Mexican psychology students participated in month-long workshops in Austin, where they had a firsthand look at American psychology, particularly techniques of test construction, personality measurement, and research design. A somewhat smaller group of American psychology students and research assistants attended a similar program in Mexico City, where they concentrated on learning ways to conceptualize relationships between culture and personality. This unusual degree of long-term collaboration and commitment to cross-cultural studies on the parts of both Mexican and American researchers has enabled members of the research teams in both countries to reach the level of mutual understanding and sophistication essential for collaboration in large-scale cross-cultural investigations.

An area of great interest to both Mexicans and Americans was personality development in children. As outlined above, the work of the research group in Austin on inkblot perception and personality already had shifted in this general direction, and the six-year longitudinal study had just begun. Unlike the research group in Austin, however, before their part of the study could begin, the Mexicans had to organize a research group, obtain major financial

18                                                    *Background of the Study*

support for a long-range operation, train psychological examiners, translate test materials, and conduct pilot studies of a statistical and sociological nature to determine demographic background data needed for obtaining samples of Mexican children comparable to those in Austin. In 1964 the Mexican research group received support for their part in the research program from the Foundations' Fund for Research in Psychiatry; from this point on, the major purpose of the research groups in both countries was to determine the relative importance of cultural factors, school environment, and characteristics of the family and home environment upon the development of cognitive, perceptual, and personality functioning in normal children from these two major, contrasting cultures.

While it is difficult to specify the major cultural dimensions on which Mexican and American societies differ, many informed observers have commented on this topic, and there is fairly good consensus about the dominant values, belief-systems, and styles of life characteristic of the two countries. Most Mexicans, particularly women, subscribe to the idea that life is to be endured rather than enjoyed, that it is better to be safe than sorry, and that it is better to proceed slowly than fast. The great majority of Americans, on the other hand, seem to believe just the opposite. This bipolar pattern of values and beliefs implicit in the two cultures has been developed in a series of studies by Díaz-Guerrero (1965) as the active and passive syndromes constituting a major part of the sociocultural premises underlying American and Mexican societies respectively.

This broad active-passive dimension appears clearly in the test results obtained during the first year of data collection in both cultures. As summarized earlier by Jon D. Swartz (1967), using only the results from the inkblot scores, the American child produced faster reaction times, used larger portions of the inkblots in giving his responses, gave more definite form to his responses, and was still able to integrate more parts of the inkblots while doing so. In addition, he incorporated other stimulus properties of the inkblots, such as color and shading, into his responses more often than the Mexican child, and elaborated his responses by ascribing more movement to his percepts. In attempting to deal with all aspects of the inkblots in such an active fashion, however, he failed more often than the Mexican child. This failure is indicated by the results for such variables as Form Appropriateness, Pathognomic Verbalization, Anxiety, and Hostility. The Mexican child gave responses with better form and less often produced responses that showed deviant thinking and anxious and hostile content. The cross-cultural results from the inkblots for the full six years of the study are given in Chapter 8.

That there are clear and major differences in the developmental trends for Mexican and American children is apparent. These differences are spelled out in the chapters that follow. Some of the most striking results are those that involve not single main effects, but rather complex interactions between culture, sex, and age.

In order to evaluate and interpret the results of the present cross-cultural research properly, it is important that the reader be familiar with the details of the research design, the various testing instruments employed, and the data domains common both to Mexico City and to Austin, Texas. The next two chapters of Part One were written to provide this background.

Part Two contains three chapters and is reserved for the methodological, psychometric, and intercorrelational studies carried out on selected test and interview variables *within* each culture that are relevant to cross-cultural comparisons. In Chapter 4 the most important of numerous studies of scoring, coding, and examiner reliability and the elaborate process of preparing massive amounts of data for analysis are presented. The test-retest stability over time of the principal measures employed, presented separately for each culture, makes up the contents of Chapter 5. In the last chapter in this section, Chapter 6, the relationships of test variables to other measures *within* each culture, using the complete U.S. and Mexican samples, are presented.

Part Three consists of five chapters that constitute the major portion of the cross-cultural results obtained. These results are based upon matched cross-cultural samples from the total set of U.S. and Mexican cases, controlled rigorously for the age, sex, and socioeconomic status of each child. Chapter 7 presents the results from the cognitive-perceptual measures employed, Chapter 8 the results from the Holtzman Inkblot Technique, and Chapter 9 the results from the various personality-attitudinal measures. The findings from parental and home variables and from the attitudes and values of the mothers interviewed are given in Chapters 10 and 11 respectively.

The concluding section of the book, Part Four, consists of three chapters. The many findings are integrated and discussed in Chapter 12. Some reflections on culture and personality pertaining to Mexico and the United States are presented in Chapter 13. And Chapter 14 provides a brief summary of the project.

---

In the next chapter, detailed descriptions of the research design employed, procedures for selecting the children who served as subjects in the United States and Mexico, and the criteria for test selection and continued inclusion in the test batteries are given. In addition, brief descriptions of the measures employed during the six years of the study are presented.

# 2. Basic Research Design and Descriptions of Tests Employed

In developmental psychology the *cross-sectional* research method involves the study of a large number of individuals (or variables) as they are at a particular point in time. Then comparisons of one age group (norm) with another can be made. By contrast, the *longitudinal* research method involves the study of the same individual over a relatively long period of time. Any comparisons made using data derived from this method are of the same individuals (or variables) with themselves at different points in time. In general, while superior in almost every respect over cross-sectional data (Hilton and Patrick 1970), longitudinal data are very costly and time-consuming to collect; and subject attrition is a serious problem. After considerable initial planning, the research design employed in the present investigation was selected to utilize the best features of both methods.

## Research Design and Subjects

An overlapping longitudinal design was employed so that a span of twelve years of development could be covered in only six calendar years of repeated testing. The basic design is presented in Table 2-1. The three-year overlap between groups makes it possible

Table 2-1
Overlapping Longitudinal Design for Six Years of Repeated Testing

| Group | Initial Age[a] | Number of Cases United States | Mexico | School Grades Covered |
|-------|---------|--------------|--------|----------------------|
| I | 6.7 | 133 | 150 | 1 2 3 4 5 6 |
| II | 9.7 | 142 | 143 | 4 5 6 7 8 9 |
| III | 12.7 | 142 | 150 | 7 8 9 10 11 12 |
|  | Total | 417 | 443 |  |

[a] The starting ages of 6.7, 9.7, and 12.7 years were chosen, since most children in the public schools of Texas reach these exact ages at some time during the school year, September 15–May 15. Actual time of testing took place within 30 days of the age as specified in the table.

to splice them together into one span of twelve years for determining developmental trends, while at the same time permitting replication and cross-validation of the perceptual-cognitive indices that are found related to different stages of development.

The relatively brief period of data collection and the size of the samples overcame to a great extent the problem of attrition. The inevitable loss of subjects with the passage of time was compensated for in part by the overlap of the three groups. For example, shrinkage in Group I during the last three years of data collection was partially compensated by the initially large size of Group II. It was expected that complete developmental data could be obtained for over six hundred children, three hundred in Austin and a comparable number in Mexico City. Thus, the final Ns of the three age groups would be sufficiently large to permit the application of multivariate analysis for the identification of specific as well as general principles of developmental change.

In Austin, children were mainly drawn from six elementary schools and one junior high school, representing a broad range of working-class, business, and professional families. The children of military personnel, university students, and legislators were eliminated from consideration because of the high likelihood they would move away before the end of the six-year period. The nature of the study was explained to the parents to secure their permission and cooperation for the repeated testing and interviewing. Only white, English-speaking families were used. The Austin sample probably can be characterized best as middle-class urban children from fairly stable families who represent the dominant values in American culture.

Defining the sample and selecting children in Mexico City proved to be more difficult, largely because little previous work had been done on the social characteristics of Mexican families and because the organization of education in Mexico is very different from that found in the United States. Preliminary pilot studies and demographic surveys had to be undertaken in Mexico City before a detailed sampling plan could be formulated. In addition, the Mexicans had to organize a research group, obtain major financial support for a long-range operation, train psychological examiners, and translate and adapt test materials before they could embark on the main longitudinal study. For these reasons there is a two-year lag in the collection of test data; the Austin project was in the middle of its third year of repeated testing when the first year of testing was begun in Mexico. At that time the academic year in Mexico City ran from January to October.

The preliminary sociological study in Mexico City was undertaken mainly in three school systems, two public and one private. The Sistema Oficial del Centro de la Ciudad (El Centro) is one of the oldest public school systems in Mexico City and is located near the center of the city. The area is similar in some ways to the Lower East Side of Manhattan; many current leaders in sports, entertainment, and public life have come out of its *vecindades* and *viviendas*. While most of the families in El Centro are lower class, they tend to be fairly stable. The Sistema Público Unidad Independencia school system is located away from the city in one of the fairly new public housing projects designed mainly for working-class people. The private school systems, which are usually run by the Catholic elite or clergy, cater mainly to middle-class families where the father is in business or one of the professions. Typical of the many such private schools in Mexico City, the system studied is most like the middle-class urban schools in the United States.

Considerable information about family structure, parental occupation and education, size and quality of the house, and possession of radio or television sets, automobiles, and refrigerators was obtained from interviews with the parents in the preliminary sociological survey. Only children whose parents were both born in

Mexico of Mexican parents were included in the sample for the cross-cultural study, in order to insure that the dominant Mexican value system and urban life style would be clearly present. The results of this survey indicated that the Mexican families in the private school system were very similiar in socioeconomic status to the American families in Austin. Consequently, twice as many children were drawn from the private school as from El Centro; and about one-third of the sample was drawn from Independencia. It was estimated that nearly two-thirds of the Mexican and Austin children could then be used for cross-cultural comparisons in which important subcultural variations would be matched across the two samples. The remaining one-third of the Mexicans would be too low socioeconomically, while the remaining third of the Americans would be too high.

*Tests and Related Measures*

In addition to the Holtzman Inkblot Technique, the basic test battery includes other selected cognitive, perceptual, and personality tests given individually to each child once a year on the anniversary date of the initial testing. Criteria employed in deciding whether or not to use a particular test consisted of the following: (*a*) suitability for individual administration under field conditions in a school; (*b*) demonstrated reliability and objectivity from previous studies; (*c*) appropriateness for use throughout the age span of six to seventeen years; (*d*) relevance to perceptual-cognitive development or importance as a measure of significant personality traits pertinent to developmental stages in children; and (*e*) feasibility for use in the Spanish and English languages within Mexican and American cultures respectively.

It was realized that some important psychological techniques might be suitable for administration once or twice; others would be appropriate for use with young children but inappropriate for older ones or vice versa; and still others might come to our attention as worthy of inclusion after a year of two of testing had been completed. Rather than adhere rigidly to a fixed set of measures to be applied uniformly in all six years and both samples, provision was made for distinguishing between the basic core battery, which was applied uniformly; the partial core battery, which was applied uniformly for all children in the second grade or above;

the supplementary repeated battery, consisting of tests employed two or more successive years though not uniformly; and other measures, which were used once or twice but not successively across years. A list of the techniques employed in these categories is presented in Table 2-2.

Both forms of the Holtzman Inkblot Technique (HIT) were used to insure a balanced design, alternating the two parallel forms in successive years. Unlike its predecessor, the Rorschach, the Holtzman Inkblot Technique consists of two parallel forms, A and B, each containing forty-five inkblots, to which the subject gives

Table 2-2
Psychological Test Batteries and Related Measures

---

Core Test Battery (All Subjects for 6 Years)

Holtzman Inkblot Technique
Human Figure Drawing
Vocabulary (WISC or WAIS)
Block Design (WISC or WAIS)

Partial Core Battery and Supplementary Repeated Battery

Test Anxiety Scale for Children
Time Estimation Test
Filled Time Estimation (Texas subjects, 4th, 5th, and 6th years)
Test Behavior Ratings
Object Sorting Test (first 3 years)
Embedded Figures Test (all subjects age 9.7 or older)
Stroop Color-Word Test (Texas subjects age 9.7 or older for 4 years)
Visual Fractionation Test (all subjects for 2 years)
Conceptual Styles Test (ages 7.7 and 8.7 only)
Perceptual Maturity Scale (last 3 years)
Word Association Test (last 3 years)
WISC or WAIS Arithmetic and Picture Completion (all subjects, 1st, 4th, 5th, and 6th years)

Other Measures

WISC remaining subtests (age 6.7)
Family and Home Ratings from interviews with mothers
Parental Attitude Scales (mother)
Academic Summary (school-record data)
Occupational Values Inventory (all subjects, 6th year)
Personality Research Form (all subjects, 6th year)
Survey of Study Habits and Attitudes (Texas subjects, age 17.7; Mexico subjects, 4th and 5th years)
Manuel's Reading Test (Mexico subjects, 4th and 5th years)
Views of Life and Sociocultural Premises (Mexico selected subjects, 6th year)

---

only one response per card. The total score on each of twenty-two variables is obtained by summing the individual scores across the forty-five cards. Previous studies using these total scores have indicated that, for the majority of these variables, uniformly high test-retest, inter-scorer, and split-half reliabilities are obtained. Additional studies have demonstrated that Forms A and B are strikingly similar, assuring their interchangeability as parallel forms for repeated testing. In the present research, Form A was given some subjects in the first year, while Form B was given others, alternating forms in subsequent years to yield a counterbalanced design. The Human Figure Drawing (HFD) was included because of the earlier work by Herman A. Witkin and others (1962), its ease of administration and scoring, and its extensive use previously in cross-cultural studies. Inspection of factor-analytic studies of standard intelligence scales suggested Vocabulary and Block Design in the Wechsler Intelligence Scale for Children (WISC) as the most appropriate subtests to be used repeatedly. For the last two years in Group III, the Vocabulary and Block Design subtests from the Wechsler Adult Intelligence Scale (WAIS) were substituted for the WISC.

In addition to the tests that constituted the basic core battery, a number of other instruments were employed in the first year. All of the first-grade children in Austin were given the complete WISC, while the fourth- and seventh-graders were given the Arithmetic and Picture Completion subtests. All the Mexican children were given the complete WISC because little is known about the factorial structure of intelligence in Mexican children. Minor adaptations of the Spanish WISC were necessary to produce semantic equivalence between the English and Spanish versions. A good discussion of the changes made to adapt the WISC for use in Mexico has been presented by Isabel R. de Ahumada, René Ahumada, and Díaz-Guerrero (1967).

Time Estimation is a short test given on three different occasions during the testing sessions. The child is simply requested to estimate the duration of one minute without counting or other external cues. The three estimates were separated in time by one or more tests. Previous studies of time sense (Levine et al. 1959; Spivak, Levine, and Sprigle 1959) have demonstrated a relationship between the ability to estimate the passage of time accurately and impulse inhibition and delay. Three scores were derived from each subject's time estimations: Delay, obtained by summing the three estimates; Inaccuracy, obtained by summing the absolute devia tion in seconds of each estimate from sixty seconds; and Inconsistency, the variance of the three estimates. This test was dropped for first-graders in the United States after it was discovered that many of them did not know what a minute was. During the fourth year of testing in Austin a "filled interval" time estimation task was added to the battery because of the findings of John Breeskin (1966) on "filled" versus "open" time intervals.

The Object Sorting Test (OST), a twelve-item form of the Embedded Figures Test (EFT), and the Stroop Color-Word Test (CWT) were also included in the first year in Austin, partly because of work suggesting that they provide important measures of "equivalence range," "field-articulation," and "constricted-flexible control."

The Object Sorting Test (OST), consisting of a total of sixty familiar objects chosen to maximize variations in material, color, size, shape, and content, was included partly because of the earlier work of Riley W. Gardner (1959) on measures of "equivalence range," or category width. All sixty objects were presented at once, in a random manner, by spreading them across the table in front of the child. After the objects had been spread out, the child was asked to examine them and inquire about any with which he was not familiar. Each unfamiliar object was listed on the OST record sheet and then was described as briefly as was sufficient to bring it into the child's realm of understanding. The child then was instructed to sort all of the objects into groups, stressing the following: (*a*) there is no correct answer to the test; (*b*) there may be as few or as many objects in each group as the child wishes; and (*c*) all of the objects should be sorted. As the child proceeded with the sorting, the examiner made notes on qualitative aspects of his performance (spontaneous comments, regroupings, questions). When the child indicated he was finished sorting the items, the reason or basis for each grouping was determined by asking, "Tell me, why do all these objects belong together?" The reason given by the child for each of his sorts then was recorded, as verbatim as possible. The OST results were scored, not only for number of categories, as advocated by Gardner (1959), but also according to

the open-closed and public-private dimensions developed by
Lawrence S. McGaughran and Louis J. Moran (1956). This latter
method yielded scores with significant inkblot correlates in an
earlier study of schizophrenic thought processes (Holtzman, Gorham, and Moran 1964).

The Embedded Figures Test (EFT) has been of major importance
in Witkin's work on individual differences in field dependence-independence (Witkin et al. 1962). A short, twelve-item form of
Witkin's technique (Witkin 1950) was used in the present study.
Each item in this test presents the subject with a complex, geometric,
variously colored figure in which he is to locate and trace a simple
figure that he has inspected previously. Successful performance
of the task requires selective attention only to relevant aspects of
the complex stimulus in order to avoid the effects of distracting
cues. From each subject's performance on the twelve items, four
scores were derived: number of re-exams, number of errors (incorrect tracings), total number of items correct, and reaction time
to correct solution averaged over the twelve items. Developmental
studies by Witkin and others (1962) have shown curvilinear
trends for the EFT across ages ten to seventeen, as well as interesting correlates with Rorschach scores.

First introduced in the United States by J. R. Stroop (1935), the
Stroop Color-Word Test has been used frequently as a measure
of susceptibility to distracting stimuli and has been demonstrated
to reflect the capacity to inhibit competing, irrelevant responses
elicited by the stimuli (Gardner et al. 1960; Jensen and Rohwer
1966). After practice both in pronouncing names of printed words
of colors (Part A), and in naming colors (Part B), the subject is required to identify the colors of inks in which a list of color-words
are printed (Part C). In each case the word is discrepant from the
color of the ink (e.g., the word *red* is printed in green ink). The
irrelevant cues cannot be screened out selectively; rather the subject must inhibit the competing and well-learned response of reading the word. An interference score, with the influence of reading
speed partialed out statistically, was obtained for each subject,
along with the total times for Parts B and C. The details of the
derivation of the interference score are given by Donald M. Broverman (1964). The Color-Word Test was not used in Mexico, since

such use would require a completely new standardization in another language.

Three new tests were employed in the second year: the Conceptual Styles Test, the Visual Fractionation Test, and the Test Anxiety Scale for Children.

The form of the Conceptual Styles Test (CST) used in the present cross-cultural research consists of nineteen sets of three line drawings each, the "best" from Jerome Kagan's original set of thirty (Kagan, Moss, and Siegel 1963). Each drawing is of a familiar object, and each is drawn so that an *analytic* concept competes with *relational* and *inferential-categorical* concepts as a basis for grouping. Usually the analytic concept is a much less obvious association to the stimuli than either the relational or the inferential-categorical. The nineteen sets of pictures are arranged in booklet form, and the subject is asked to select two drawings in each set of three "that are alike or go together in some way." Reaction time is recorded for the time of each selection, and each of the nineteen selections is scored for the number of analytical, relational, and inferential-categorical responses. An *analytic* response is one in which pictures are paired because of an objective attribute that is a differentiated part of the total stimulus. A *relational* response is one in which pictures are paired because of a functional relationship between them that is an obvious aspect of the total stimulus. An *inferential-categorical* response is one in which pictures are paired, not on similarity of differentiated parts, but on some inferred quality or language convention. In the event a subject gives a reason for his selection that involves more than one concept, the first concept given is the one scored.

Developed by Kagan (Kagan, Moss, and Siegel 1963), the Visual Fractionation Test (VFT) consists of four different designs, each containing three sets of components: elements, figure, and ground. The VFT measures the degree to which the subject attaches a new label to one of these three component parts of the total complex stimulus, while at the same time associating the new label to the whole stimulus. In the learning part of the task, twelve figures (with four different designs repeated three times in random sequence) are arranged in a booklet for individual administration. Each complex figure is printed on the front of a page, and a small card containing a three-letter nonsense syllable corresponding to the incorporated design is attached facedown to the back side of the previous page. The subject must learn the correct association between each design and its corresponding nonsense syllable. All figures are repeated either until (*a*) all associations are given correctly, or (*b*) five trials have been run. In the transfer part of the test, two drawings of each of the three parts—ground, figure, element—for each of the designs, or twenty-four items in all, are arranged in a booklet in a random sequence. The four nonsense syllables—WOM, FAM, SEP, and PUF—are printed on separate cards for use during this part of the test. Three kinds of scores are obtained: (*a*) number of trials to complete the learning task; (*b*) mean reaction times on the transfer trial for the eight items involving elements, the eight items involving figures, and the eight items involving grounds, as well as the over-all reaction time for all twenty-four items; and (*c*) number of items on the transfer trial that are correct for all items combined.

Sarason's Test Anxiety Scale for Children (TASC) (Sarason et al. 1960), is a thirty-item paper-and-pencil questionnaire designed to measure children's test anxiety as a convenient way of studying some of the properties of anxiety in general. Subsequent to the initial development of the TASC, additional items constituting a Lie Scale (eleven items) and a Defensiveness Scale for Children (DSC, twenty-seven items) were added to the items for the TASC, making a total of sixty-eight items given to each child in questionnaire form. The work of Sarason and his associates on the use of suppressor variables with the TASC led to the inclusion of both in the test battery in the third year of testing in Austin. Both scales were included in the Mexican TASC questionnaire for most of the children in the first year of testing as well as in every subsequent year.

In an attempt to characterize each child's reaction to the testing procedures, five five-point rating scales—Social Confidence, Self Confidence in Ability, Cooperation, General Anxiety Level, and Attention to Tasks—dealing with different aspects of the child's behavior and designated Test Behavior Ratings (TBR) were completed by the examiner immediately following each child's last testing session (beginning with the second year in Austin but employed all six years in Mexico City). Each scale had verbal labels describing each of the five points, and the examiner checked the appropriate point on each scale and noted and recorded any unusual behavior exhibited by the child but not covered by any of the scales.

In the third, fourth, and fifth years for the Austin sample, several additional techniques were employed. Most notable of these was the development and application of an extensive interview schedule and parental attitude questionnaire. Interviews lasting one to two hours were conducted with the mother of each child in the sample to determine important characteristics of the home environment and family life style. Special attention was given to intellectual stimulation and achievement press given the child by the family, in order to replicate and extend the work of Richard Wolf (1965) on home environment, intelligence, and school achievement. The sixty-eight-item attitude questionnaire was adapted from the work of Carl F. Hereford (1963) and is similar to other parental attitude scales. A few items of special relevance to cross-cultural attitudes were also included. Two new tests were added in the fourth year and repeated thereafter: Moran's Word Association Test and Robert L. Van de Castle's Perceptual Maturity Scale.

Moran's version of the free word-association experiment, for which there are both English (Moran 1966) and Spanish (Moran and Núñez 1967) versions, consists of an eighty-word list that is administered individually. The first forty-four words in the list have been equated on an adult sample for "compatibility" with the contrast-coordinate, synonym-superordinate, and functional sets. That is, the forty-four stimulus words evoked, from an adult sample, associates representative of these three sets with over-all equal frequency. The last thirty-six words in the list are spaced systematically such that every third word is maximally compatible with one set only, that is, has evoked from an adult sample predominantly one associate typical of a specific set. In this manner, the three sets are equally represented. Thus, the presence of an idiodynamic set might be inferred from the distribution of associates to the first forty-four stimulus words, then confirmed by differential predictions of responses to the last thirty-six words. The children were instructed to say the first word that came to mind when they heard each stimulus word. Variables routinely scored included predication, functional, synonym, superordinate, contrast, logical coordinate, faults, commonality, and reaction time per response. Later analysis involved the computation of three new scores more appropriate for cross-cultural analysis, two paradigmatic and one syntagmatic (Chapter 7).

The Perceptual Maturity Scale (PMS) of Van de Castle (1965) reflects perceptual style in the sense that the respondent is asked to choose the designs he prefers from among seventy-two matched pairs of items—one indicative of high perceptual maturity and one of low—drawn from the much larger pool of artistic and geometric figures in George S. Welsh's Figure Preference Test. In general, Van de Castle (1965) found that the simpler, asymmetrical geometric forms were developmentally lower on the age scale than were the more complicated and symmetrical figures.

Peer group sociometric ratings in the first year, teachers' ratings in the fourth year, and miscellaneous test and behavioral data in the school records complete the information available on the Austin sample through the fifth year of repeated testing.

During the sixth and final year of data collection two other new tests were administered to all three groups of subjects, the Occupational Values Inventory (OVI) and the Personality Research Form (PRF). In addition to these two individually administered instruments, data were collected in group settings for selected subjects on the Survey of Study Habits and Attitudes (SSHA); and an Academic Summary, containing school record data, was completed for those subjects on whom such data were available.

The OVI, developed for group administration in the Cross National Research Project (Díaz-Guerrero 1972*b*; Peck and associates, forthcoming) for the study of school children, originally involved the paired-comparison technique for fifteen different career value phrases ("Work in which you could lead other people," for example, represents a career value of "management"), producing a total of 105 forced-choice items representing the following values: altruism, aesthetics, independence, management, success and accomplishment, self-satisfaction, intellectual stimulation, creativity, security, prestige, economic returns, surroundings, associates, variety, and "follow father." The equivalence of the English and Spanish versions was assured by carrying out an independent back translation from Spanish to English after the original translation from English had been made. In the present cross-cultural study, the paired-comparison method was modified by having the children simply rank-order the fifteen career-value phrases in the individual testing sessions. The phrases were ranked in order from the most to the least valued, and the rank-order position of each career value constituted the score for analysis.

The PRF, developed by Douglas N. Jackson (1967), is a new paper-and-pencil self-report personality inventory for use within the normal range and currently is available in four standard forms. In the present study Form A was used in both cultures. The result of a research program whose purpose was to design a personality inventory with high reliability and validity, Form A of the PRF contains three hundred items that yield fourteen content scales—Achievement, Affiliation, Aggression, Autonomy, Dominance, Endurance, Exhibition, Harmavoidance, Impulsivity, Nurturance, Order, Play, Social Recognition, and Understanding—and one validity scale, Infrequency. The demonstrated validity of these PRF scales using ratings of the same traits as criteria in a multitrait-multimethod matrix (Jackson and Guthrie 1968), as well as the high reliability obtained in the standardization studies of the PRF, indicates the suitability of this particular inventory for the measurement of broadly relevant personality traits.

In addition to the tasks already discussed, the test battery in Mexico also included the EFT during the fourth and fifth years of data collection, the Brown-Holtzman SSHA (1967), and Manuel's Reading Test (1966). Moreover, selected children in the sixth year of Mexican data collection received Díaz-Guerrero's Views of Life Questionnaire and Sociocultural Premises (1972a). These last two measures deal with beliefs and values of the Mexican family and of Mexican culture. The conceptual realm with which they deal will be helpful in the interpretation of the over-all results of the study.

---

Chapter 3 explains how the different measures described in this chapter fall into four separate "data domains" for ease of exposition and interpretation.

# 3. Data Domains Common to
# Mexico City and Austin, Texas

The different types of data collected in the cross-cultural longitudinal study of school children in Mexico City and Austin, Texas, can be divided into four major categories: (a) performance data by children in testing sessions; (b) ratings of the child's behavior, personality, or other characteristics; (c) variables dealing with the family and home environment taken largely from interviews with the mothers and observations of the home; and (d) the attitudes toward child rearing and certain personal beliefs and values collected by questionnaire from the mother.

*Child's Performance on Tests*

*Cognitive/Mental Abilities.* The primary measures of mental abilities come from the Wechsler Intelligence Scale for Children and the Wechsler Adult Intelligence Scale, the latter given in the last stages of the longitudinal study to the oldest children. Vocabulary, Arithmetic, Block Design, and Picture Completion are available on all children in the initial year of testing in both populations. The Human Figure Drawing (and its variations in the form of the Draw-a-Man and the Draw-a-Person tests) is also often thought of as a cognitive or mental-abilities test. At least the primary developmental score, proposed by Florence Goodenough and refined and adapted by Dale B. Harris so that it would be appropriate for both male and female drawings, is clearly a cognitive measure. The Embedded Figures Test can also be thought of as a cognitive measure, although Witkin and others often refer to it as a cognitive style variable rather than an aspect of mental abilities. Nevertheless, most of the intercorrelations between the EFT and both cognitive and perceptual variables, going back to the early studies of Louis L. Thurstone, indicate a high loading on general cognitive ability. Kagan's Visual Fractionation Test can also be thought of as a cognitive task, since it involves certain measures of learning and transfer of a fairly traditional sort. So little has been done with this test that one cannot be sure of its psychometric characteristics and correlations with other measures of individual differences.

*Perceptual/Cognitive Style.* The Holtzman Inkblot Technique has a number of variables in it that are more properly categorized as measures of perceptual or cognitive style than as personality measures per se, even though many of the variables are admittedly personality measures. Such inkblot variables, for example, as Reaction Time, Rejection, Location, Form Definiteness, Form Appropriateness, Integration, and possibly even some of the content scales represent approaches to the study of personality through perceptual style (reliable individual differences in perception). The Time Estimation Test is clearly a measure of time perception under different circumstances. The Embedded Figures Test has a stylistic component as well as a direct cognitive one. The Perceptual Maturity Scale is designed specifically as a developmental measure of perceptual style. The Object Sorting Test yields a measure of equivalence range, a cognitive style variable studied extensively by Riley Gardner and others. Kagan's Conceptual Styles Test was designed specifically to get at certain cognitive style variables underlying the formation of concepts. Moran's Word Association Test can also be thought of as a cognitive style test as well as an indirect measure of certain personality variables. In a sense both perceptual and cognitive style variables by definition represent an approach to the study of personality through measures that are quite indirect, measures that have been termed by others as performance tests of personality or objective approaches to personality (See Cronbach 1970; Cattell and Warburton 1967).

*Personality/Attitudinal Variables.* The only direct personality measures of a comprehensive nature are those embedded in the Jackson Personality Research Form, which covers rather comprehensively most of the paper-and-pencil short-question type items, such as those that appear in other personality questionnaires. In addition, the Sarason Test Anxiety Scale for Children with its several subscales is a specialized form of personality questionnaire, as is the Brown-Holtzman Survey of Study Habits and Attitudes. The Occupational Values Inventory represents still another personality (attitudinal) instrument given directly to the child. Growing out of the earlier work in the cross-national study of Peck and associates (forthcoming), this measure was designed specifically for cross-cultural research with adolescent children. Most of the content variables—Pathognomic Verbalization, Popular, and, to some extent, the perceptual variables mentioned earlier from the Holtzman Inkblot Technique—can be thought of as personality measures. The last of the personality measures on each child comes from the Human Figure Drawing task in the expert ratings of masculinity-femininity characteristic of both the male and female drawings.

In addition to the above variables, which are common to both the Mexican and Texan samples, certain other tests and measures related to them are available for specialized populations within either the Mexican or the Texan sample but not in both. These are not mentioned in detail because of the emphasis here upon cross-cultural comparisons utilizing both samples.

### Ratings of the Child

*School Setting.* Most of the direct ratings of the child's behavior came from within the classroom or playground of the school attended by the child. The ratings that are common to both samples were made by the examiners at the time of testing. The Test Behavior Ratings were made on a five-point scale, ranging from 1, representing a low amount of the trait, to 5, representing the highest amount. The five traits rated by the examiner in each testing session were Social Confidence, Self-Confidence, Cooperation, General Anxiety, and Attention to Tasks. A problem in comparing these ratings across different examiners arises, due to the admittedly subjective nature of the ratings themselves. They probably have their greatest value where cases were judged by the same examiner. At the extremes of the rating scales it is quite likely that enough validity is present to justify comparisons across examiners within the same culture. A serious question arises, however, in cross-cultural comparisons, because of the different settings in the two countries where the examiners worked and possible subtle but important differences in adaptation level and semantic value of the traits employed, as far as the examiners were concerned. Further, more systematic studies across the different examiners at different times need to be done before any great reliance is placed upon the Test Behavior Ratings as measures of meaningful personality variables within the children rated. Among the children in Austin only, additional data of interest consist of the teacher-trait rating scales collected in Groups II and III, sociometric judgments from peer groups collected in Group I, adjustment ratings by the counselors in several high schools, and the high school academic records where grades or other ratings were available. In Mexico, data of a systematic nature that could be generalized across different Mexican schools were unavailable at the time.

*Home Setting.* Ratings of each child were made by the mother in the interview held with the mother about halfway through the six-year longitudinal study. Typical of the items in the interview schedule that constitute actual parental judgment of the child are items 2(A) and 2(B), dealing with the number and variety of special interests (activities, hobbies, pastimes, sports, etc.) of the child; item 14(A–D), in which the mother compared the child's performance with that of any siblings in the family and also compared the child's class rank in school with that of his classmates; item 22, recording the mother's judgment as to the extent to which the child read unassigned books; item 47, recording the mother's positive comments about the child; and item 49, in which the mother's negative comments about the child were recorded. These items, drawn from the interview schedule coding form (see Appendix C), differ from the other items in the parental interview by focusing directly upon the parent's judgment of the child. While there are too few such items to form any major scale, certain ones have a face validity sufficiently strong that they deserve systematic study in their own right. At least they indicate what the mother's perception of the child was at the time of the interview.

## Family Life Style and Home Environment Variables

Several of the items in the interview schedule were designed specifically to get at the most salient characteristics of the family's life style and to make possible the scaling of socioeconomic status or social class. Father's occupational level, father's educational level, and mother's educational level have been found in other studies to be the most reliable measures of socioeconomic status of the family. Father's occupation and father's education generally have the highest correlation of the three variables, particularly in Mexico, where mother's education tends to be somewhat independent of social class, since even among upper-class Mexican families many of the mothers are not educated beyond secondary school. For this reason the basic combined index of father's education and father's occupation represents the best single measure of socioeconomic status. Assigning a weight of 3 to father's educational level and a weight of 2 to father's occupational level yields an index of socioeconomic status ranging from 5 to 45.

Several other items within the interview schedule also play an important role in defining the family life style. The number, age, and sex of siblings; the number of other adults living in the home; religious affiliation of the father, the mother, and the child; the frequency of church attendance and the extent to which members of the family attend church; religious observances in the home; clubs to which the father, the mother, or both parents belong and the extent of their activity in such clubs; special interests of the parents, particularly those that are shared by both mother and father; the number of hours that the mother watches television; and the number of hours that the mother works outside the home are typical of items focusing specifically on family life style. While some of these items occur too rarely in both cultures to allow for very systematic cross-cultural comparison, others are sufficiently frequent in their occurrence to justify systematic statistical analysis. In any event, they provide information about the family that is useful when one wishes to select individual cases of a specific kind for special analysis. Very little of this type of analysis has been done as yet with the present data.

In addition to the items answered directly by the mother in the interview, ratings of the home environment are made by the examiner immediately following the interview on a number of factors: the amount of play space available for the child, the type of neighborhood in which the family lives, the condition of the house relative to others around it, the level of grammar and pronunciation, and the personal appearance of the mother. These also contribute heavily to a richer definition of family life style and social class than would otherwise be possible.

Much of the impetus for the development of special items in the interview schedule came from the doctoral dissertations by R. H. Dave (1964) and R. Wolf (1964), working under Benjamin Bloom at the University of Chicago. Dave and Wolf proposed to develop an instrument that would measure the home environment in terms of processes and forces. It was hypothesized that measurements of such processes would correlate more highly with measures of intelligence (Wolf) and achievement (Dave) than would "static" variables such as status indices derived from information concerning father's occupation and parents' education. The global ratings that form the cornerstone of the analyses by Dave and Wolf were possible to undertake only in the Austin sample because of their subjectivity and dubious cross-cultural validity when extended to an entirely different culture, as in Mexico. While many of the actual items are identical in the interview schedules used for both Mexico City and Austin, there appeared to be no conceivable way in which sufficiently high standardization of interviewers and coding judges could be obtained cross-culturally to justify the use of global ratings in both cultures. The analysis of global ratings was carried out thoroughly by Jane D. Stitt in her doctoral dissertation (1970) using only the Austin data. Her study of family and social background factors as they influence cognitive and perceptual development in children failed to reveal the high degree of relationship between the home environment scales and measures of intelligence and related cognitive variables among the children found by Dave and Wolf. While the Dave and Wolf sample was presumably more heterogeneous with regard to socioeconomic status, it is unlikely such heterogeneity alone could account for the much higher correlations (.75 to .80) between Dave's Index of Educational Environment and performance on either the Metropolitan Achievement Test or the Iowa Tests. Wolf's Index of Intellectual Environment was reported to correlate in the .60's with such measures as the Henmon-Nelson IQ scores, Grade 5, or the Differential Aptitude Test scores, Grade 9. The highest correlations obtained by Stitt in her replication of this study were .35 with WISC Vocabulary and .25 with Differential Aptitude Test scores.

A more recent study by Kevin Marjoribanks (1972) verifies the reasonably high relationship between press for achievement within the family and mental-ability test score (correlations of .66 for verbal and number ability). Since Marjoribanks worked with 185 eleven-year-old boys and their parents with extensive interviews in the home and with a variety of environmental characteristics similar to those used by Wolf and Dave, as well as those employed in the present study, it can be concluded that the subenvironmental approach in the form of constructs of environmental forces, as well as global environmental measures, represents a powerful means of studying the social context of intellectual performance.

In spite of the lack of comparable global ratings of environmental forces within the families of both the Mexican and the American children, a sufficient number of the individual items can be clearly classified as related to one or another important subenvironmental measure to justify systematic cross-cultural comparison. A number of the items in the interview schedule can be grouped into one of four major subenvironmental clusters: (*a*) degree of intellectual stimulation in the home; (*b*) parental aspirations for the child; (*c*) variety and richness of the home environment for social, cultural, artistic, and recreational development (socialization); and (*d*) degree of parental interest in academic progress of the child.

*Intellectual Stimulation.* Among those items that can be treated quantitatively are item 4(A), newspapers received regularly in the home; item 20, extent to which the mother or father read to the child before the child could read for himself; and possibly item 24(A), presence of a dictionary or encyclopedia or both within the home. Some other items bear only indirectly upon the degree of intellectual stimulation in the home, and it is best not to assume direct measurement, even though the number of items in this category is unusually small.

*Parental Aspirations for Child.* Item 38, the minimum amount of education that the parent feels the child *must* receive, is probably the best single indicator of parental aspiration for the child. Items 37 (how much education the parent would like the child to receive), 39 (type of work the parent would like to see the child do when grown), and 40 (type of work the parent would *not* like to see the child do when grown) are supporting items that are also of considerable interest in this cluster.

*Sociocultural, Artistic, and Recreational Development.* A number of items that do not deal with intellectual stimulation nevertheless are quite important in representing the extent to which the family provides a stimulating environment for sociocultural development and the development of certain artistic and recreational skills. These could be called important aspects of the child's early socialization within the family. Item 3(A), the number of the child's special lessons (ballet, sports, music, etc.); item 7(A), the number of recreational activities of the family; and item 9(A), the variety of places visited as a family unit, are among the best in this cluster. Of special interest are items 31(A) and 31(C), dealing with the extent to which the father and mother share activities with the child. These items show how actively and directly the parents have become involved in the socialization of the child. While it is possible that absence of any sharing does not reflect adversely upon such socialization, assertion by either parent that he or she spends a great deal of time sharing with the child is of special importance.

*Parental Interest in Academic Progress.* Three items in the interview schedule deal specifically and directly with the extent to which parents are interested in the child's progress in school. Item 12(A) measures the frequency with which the mother and father discuss together how the child gets along in school. Item 13(A) deals with the extent to which one of the parents discusses with the child the child's progress in school, and item 18(B) records the extent to which the child is helped by another family member with school work. There are other items or variations of the main stems of these items that also reflect the degree of parental interest in academic progress, but it is unlikely that much significant variance is left over when these three items are taken into account.

## Mother's Attitudes and Values

Heavy reliance was placed upon the five scales developed by Hereford (1963) and his colleagues in their studies of parental attitudes toward child rearing in Austin, Texas. His scales, in turn, were developed from early items in the Parent-Attitude Research Instrument by Earl Schaefer and Richard Bell, as well as other attitude scales that were available at the time. Two item characteristics from Hereford's original standardization were employed as possible criteria in selecting items for the Parent-Attitude Survey in the current study. First, since most of Hereford's items were phrased in a negative form (i.e., agreement with the statement produced a negative score on the scale), special efforts were made to salvage as many of the positive items as could be employed. The second criterion was the magnitude of the item-scale correlation in Hereford's original study. Because his sample essentially was the same population as the current Austin sample, it was believed that Hereford's original standardization results were especially pertinent to the current study. Fifty items were drawn from each of the five Hereford scales as follows: Confidence (nine items), Causation (eleven), Acceptance (ten), Understanding (ten), and Trust (ten).

Eight additional items were taken from the Cooperative Youth Study Scales (CYS) as reported by Bernice M. Moore and W. H. Holtzman in *Tomorrow's Parents* (1965), a study of nearly thirteen thousand high school youth throughout the state of Texas. Orientation to Society contributed four items, in which agreement with the statement represented a negative or pessimistic world outlook. Four items were also drawn from Authoritarian Discipline, a CYS scale that grew out of an earlier study of schizophrenogenic items in parental attitudes toward child rearing, a study by Lee Winder done in the early 1950's. Agreement with this scale represented acceptance of authoritarian practices in child rearing. The items with the highest item-scale correlation were selected to represent these two CYS scales.

Eight items were drawn from the work by Rosen (1964) in

studies of social attitudes among Brazilians. These items were modified to make them more appropriate for use in the United States and Mexico. Two additional items were taken from studies by Díaz-Guerrero in Mexico and are particularly appropriate for uncovering the sociocultural premises underlying the Mexican life style. It was believed that these two items would be especially useful in a cross-cultural study between the United States and Mexico because of the rapidly shifting culture from traditional to modern beliefs in Mexico City.

All sixty-eight items were placed in a single parent attitude survey with a five-choice response continuum ranging from *strongly agree* to *strongly disagree*, with *undecided* as the middle category. At the end of the sixty-eight items were placed fifteen traits identical to those used by R. S. Lynd and H. M. Lynd in their "Middletown" studies (1937) and repeated once again by Lois B. Murphy (1964) in her studies of parent attitudes and values in Kansas in the early 1950's. The mother was informed that the original study was done in a midwestern town in 1924 and that we were interested in finding out how parents felt about the importance of traits to be stressed in bringing up their children now as compared to the original work forty years ago. The mother was asked to mark the three traits considered most important with the letter *A*, the five traits next in importance with the letter *B*, any traits of third importance with the letter *C*, and the remaining traits, having no importance, with a zero.

Preliminary intercorrelation and item-analysis studies undertaken with the Austin samples of mothers prior to the cross-cultural study were rather disappointing in the lack of sufficient clustering of items to produce strong scales. Apparently, in the period of ten years between Hereford's original studies and our study of upper- and lower-middle-class mothers in Austin, there was a sufficiently marked shift in attitudes toward the more "liberal" or "modern" point of view to produce highly skewed items in many instances. None of Hereford's original scales proved strong enough to justify their use when considering only the Austin parents.

Nevertheless, the study was replicated in Mexico with exactly the same items. It was reasonable to assume that Mexican mothers were not as "modern" as the American mothers; in any event, a cross-cultural comparison could be made only if the items and procedures were exactly the same in both cultures. While some cross-cultural comparisons were made using clusters of items, such as the original Hereford scales, the CYS scales, and the Rosen scale, a complete cross-cultural item analysis was undertaken, one item at a time, to insure that no significant systematic variation was overlooked.

---

The three chapters in Part Two are concerned with methodological studies on selected measures within each culture that are particularly relevant to the larger cross-cultural study. In Chapter 4, for example, several studies related to scoring reliability are presented, particularly for those relatively new measures employed. In addition, reliability checks of examiners and test scorers and the extensive process of data preparation for analysis by computer are described.

# PART TWO

## Investigations within Each Culture Relevant to Cross-Cultural Comparisons

---

The psychology of personality as it exists today will be crushed and pulverized and a new creation made from the debris, not because of the wisdom inherent in criticisms of it but simply because in grappling with the problems of man it will be weighed in the balance and found wanting.

Gardner Murphy

*Personality: A Biosocial Approach to Origins and Structure*

---

# 4. Selected Methodological Studies

Many of the measures used in the cross-cultural longitudinal study are well known and have had a great deal of research conducted on them in the past. Others, however, are relatively new, at least as employed in cross-cultural personality assessment of young children. For this reason a number of minor methodological studies had to be undertaken before a clear understanding could be achieved of the psychometric characteristics of the measures for different age groups in both Mexico and the United States.

Scoring and coding studies had to be conducted for variables in the parental interview schedule, in the Parent-Attitude Survey, and in the interviewer's ratings of the home environment, as well as for several of the less well known psychological tests. Training and reliability checks on examiners as well as test scorers were essential to insure standardization of data across age groups, social classes, and cultures. Periodical checks of examiners and scorers were carried out throughout the six years of data collection. Elaborate procedures were also developed to prevent serious errors in the extensive process of preparing the massive amounts of data collected for statistical analysis by high-speed computer.

An analysis of dimensions present in the Parent-Attitude Survey was also undertaken in order to derive a small number of scores for further study. The normal attrition of cases over the six-year longitudinal study was examined systematically for any biases. Estimates of reliability based upon internal consistency measures were obtained for the Holtzman Inkblot Technique. And finally, the study of the consistency of repeated measures over time for various tests was carried out to determine the stability of measurement. These test-retest studies are reported in more detail in Chapter 5. Only the highlights of the other methodological studies can be presented here.

In the early stages of data collection, frequent meetings were held to discuss minor problems encountered by psychological examiners who were collecting test data on a standardized basis from children in the Austin schools. Examiners were checked out by observation behind one-way screens, and scoring was continuously checked and rechecked to insure a high degree of accuracy. Quality-control procedures were established for scoring the Holtzman Inkblot Technique to avoid having subtle biases creep into the test results. By the time the Mexican research team embarked upon its psychological-assessment program, two years after the beginning of the Austin study, the Mexican examiners had received thorough training in joint sessions with the American examiners. A number of the Mexican protocols were rescored independently by the supervisor of scoring for American protocols to insure a high degree of standardization across the two cultures.

A standard format for coding test data and other individual information was developed during the first year of data collection. The format was sufficiently flexible to permit the addition of new test data, as well as repeated application of the same tests in subsequent years. By the end of the six years of data collection as many as four hundred IBM cards had been punched with information for a typical subject. For the entire sample of children in both Mexico City and Austin, nearly a half-million IBM cards have been employed for initial storage of basic data, prior to transfer from cards to high-speed magnetic tape. Handling such massive amounts of data required continuous programming, editing, and cross-checking for internal consistency to prevent errors and to file the data in a form that could be made easily accessible.

*Development and Preliminary Analysis of the Interview Schedule*

Essential information about the family characteristics, life style, and home environment of each child in the study could be obtained only by interviewing the mother and observing actual conditions in the home. Such information was essential not only for proper classification of the children but also in its own right as sociological data highly relevant to each child's development. Building the interview schedule began with the collection of a pool of items and questions suggested by previous studies, including those of Dave (1964) and Wolf (1964). In a series of meetings involving research associates in both Mexico City and Austin, group consensus of judgment was employed in the initial selection and revision of items.

The first twenty-three items of the interview were demographic and factual in character: child's group and identification number; age, occupation, and education of parents; number of siblings and adults in the home; etc. There were fifty-five other questions aimed at family life style, particularly as it relates to the press for academic achievement. A copy of the interview schedule is included in Appendix A.

Following the open-ended questions of the interview was an attitude survey (Appendix B). Mothers were asked to mark one of five choices for each of sixty-eight statements concerning parents and children: Strongly Agree, Agree, Undecided, Disagree, Strongly Disagree. Fifty of the statements were taken from an instrument developed by Hereford (1963), comprising five scales: Confidence (in the parental role), Causation (of the child's behavior), Acceptance (of the child's behavior and feelings), Understanding, and Trust. Items were selected according to the strength of their item-scale correlation as reported by Hereford.

Eight additional items were selected from the Orientation to Society and Authoritarian Discipline scales of the Texas Cooperative Youth Study (Moore and Holtzman 1965). Two other items were suggested by the investigators who were replicating the study in Mexico, and eight were taken from Rosen's study of the "achievement syndrome" in Brazil and the United States (1964). The value orientations Rosen set out to study were activistic-passivistic, individualistic-familistic, and present-future. The items in the Parent-Attitude Survey of the present study are identified as to source in Appendix B.

At the end of the attitude survey, the mothers were asked to rate fifteen traits to be stressed in bringing up children: frankness in dealing with others; desire to make a name in the world; concentration; social concern; strict obedience; appreciation of art, music, and poetry; economy in money matters; loyalty to the church; knowledge of sex hygiene; tolerance; curiosity; patriotism; good manners; independence; and getting very good grades in school. The traits used were rated originally by "Middletown" mothers forty-five years ago (Lynd and Lynd 1937) and more recently by Topeka mothers (Murphy 1964).

Printed directions with the list of traits told of the previous study in 1924 and asked the mothers to mark the three traits considered most important with the letter *A*, the five traits next in importance with a *B*, any of third importance with a *C*, and those without importance with a zero. The directions used in Austin were taken verbatim from those used in Topeka. The rated traits were arranged in rank order for each of the three separate studies, assigning values of 3, 2, and 1 to ratings of *A*, *B*, and *C* respectively. It was hypothesized that the Topeka and Austin valuations would be quite similar because of temporal and geographical proximity and that both would differ from the "Middletown" ratings done forty years earlier.

The final data sheet of the interview contained ratings by the interviewer of the home and neighborhood and of the parent's appearance and language usage.

The interview was administered in trial form to seven mothers not in the sample and was coded and revised according to the need for more clarity in the questions or for more easily and reliably coded answers.

The building of the interview schedule was completed during the third year of testing in Austin, and a letter was sent asking for permission to interview the mother or surrogate mother of each child in the project. Only two mothers, both wives of medical doctors, declined to be interviewed. (They did allow their children to complete the six years of testing.) A total of 351 interviews were collected in Austin, representing all but eight of the children remaining in the testing program at the beginning of the third year. Of these interviews, 115 were conducted by one person, while the other 236 were done by another interviewer, a woman who had not been involved in the construction of the instrument. Both of the interviewers were women and were of approximately the same age as the mothers being interviewed. Nearly all of the interviews were conducted in the homes while the children were at school, and only rarely was anyone present other than the interviewer and the interviewee.

The interviewing was accomplished in both Austin and Mexico City over a period of approximately one year spread across the third and fourth years of testing. Since the program of data collection in Mexico was about two years behind that in Austin, the training of interviewers in Mexico City was carried out by the seasoned American interviewers in order to insure comparability across the two cultures.

Eight female research associates collected a total of 222 interviews from mothers in the Mexican sample. Their work was closely supervised by the Mexican coordinator of field studies. Only those cases likely to be included in the cross-cultural matched sample were interviewed because of limited funds. Collecting the interviews was more difficult in Mexico City than in Austin for several reasons. Households were scattered throughout a large metropolitan area in Mexico City. Eight interviewers were employed rather than only two, requiring more coordination. But the greatest problems were due to difficulties in making and keeping interview appointments. Many mothers, especially those with children in the private schools, were hard to contact, often requiring more than two visits to obtain the interview information.

Preparation of the interview data for statistical analysis involved the conversion of factual data and of answers to open-ended questions into ratings or numerical scores.

Some of the factual items were qualitative and binary, such as sex and interviewer, while others, such as number of siblings and father's age, were already numerical and did not require conversion. Other factual items required the establishment of categories appropriate to the information gathered. In some cases the categories were simply nominal (e.g., religious affiliation), while for such an item as father's occupation or father's education the categories were ordered so as to make possible ratings that repre-

sented a quantitative scale from less skilled to more skilled or
from less education to more education. Care was taken not to increase the number of points in a given scale beyond that warranted
by the fineness of the measurement.

The less factual items of information, consisting of such information as the mother's estimates of class rank and time spent on
homework, were handled in much the same way. Some answers
were recorded by the interviewer in precoded form.

The process of developing the final coding form found in Appendix C was a long one, with every effort made to use as much
of the interview material as could be reliably coded and put into an
appropriate form for statistical analysis. Trial tests of interjudge
reliability were made repeatedly on individual items before arriv-
ing at the final coding form.

From the interviews, 186 items of codifiable information were
finally extracted. Little in the way of decision was required on the
part of the judges in the coding of 130 items that either were precoded or were quite factual in content.

The remaining fifty-six items were somewhat more difficult to
judge, suggesting the need for a related study to test interjudge
reliability for the protocols collected in the Austin sample. Four
different judges, including one of the interviewers and the two students who coded all of the interviews, coded the fifty-six items on
each of thirty interview schedules. The four judges represented
two cultures, two generations, and both sexes—a heterogeneity
that assured a conservative estimate of interjudge reliability.
Product-moment correlation coefficients for the ratings assigned
the fifty-six items between all six possible pairs of judges were all
above .70 for thirty-three of these items and above .50 for nine
others. For the remaining fourteen items, at least one of the coefficients was below .50. Of the coefficients of concordance among
all four judges for the fifty-six difficult-to-code items, twenty were
above .85, thirty-eight were above .70, and all but five above .50,
indicating sufficiently high coding reliability to justify use of the
ratings for comparison with other data on each child.

For the American sample only, an effort was made to measure
"process variables"—twelve of Dave's twenty-one nine-point
scales, ranging from "parental aspirations for education of the
child" to "use of books and periodical literature." Global ratings

for each family were to be determined on the basis of the answers to a number of specified questions in the interview. After eight months of work to attain acceptable interjudge reliability on the global ratings and special efforts to arrive at scales that were indeed measuring different things, the number of scales was reduced to seven, and all but one of these were changed from nine-point to five-point scales. The seven final scales are as follows:

1. Parental aspirations for education of the child (five-point scale).
2. Parents' interest in academic progress of the child (five-point scale).
3. Knowledge of educational progress of the child (nine-point scale).
4. Opportunities provided by the family for intellectual stimulation, with emphasis on enlarging vocabulary and sentence patterns (five-point scale).
5. Extent and content of activities of the family in the home having educational value (five-point scale).
6. Extent and content of activities of the family outside the home having educational value (five-point scale).
7. Use of books and periodical literature (five-point scale).

Because of the subjective nature of the global ratings, it would have been impossible to achieve highly accurate ratings of a comparable nature in the Mexico City sample. Preliminary efforts to establish some kind of uniform scale failed because of subtle but important cultural differences in family life style, as well as the sociolinguistic differences in the interviewers themselves. For a full discussion of the global ratings, as well as a thorough analysis of the family and social background factors as they influence development in the American children, see the doctoral dissertation by Stitt (1970).

The frequency distributions of responses to the quantifiable items were examined by age group and were evaluated according to the number of points of the scale for a given item and the skewness or truncation of its distribution. Severe truncation or skewness resulted in the elimination of the item from further consideration unless the item content was of unusual interest.

A preliminary analysis was conducted on the Austin sample.

Intercorrelations were computed for eighty-three interview items in a matrix with the seven global ratings, four of the Middletown trait ratings, two preliminary factor scores derived from the attitude survey, and information as to age group, sex, coder, and interviewer—a total of one hundred variables. Since age-group differences in scores and frequencies did not appear to be significant, the three groups were combined for the intercorrelational analysis, and age group itself was used as a three-point variable. This analysis resulted in a further reduction in the number of items, only one item being selected to represent clusters of items that were highly intercorrelated. A principal-component factor analysis, with a normalized varimax rotation of the twenty factors obtained, aided in the reduction of variables.

Intercorrelations among the interview items for the Mexican sample were also computed. Examinations of the skewness and truncation of distributions in the two cultures, as well as a logical analysis of the probable reliability of parental response, provided a basis for further reduction in the number of variables that were believed to be valid for cross-cultural analysis. Over two hundred variables were finally retained for subsequent statistical cross-cultural analyses of variance in a special matched sample that was later formed for the major analyses presented in Chapters 7–11.

## Reliability Studies on the Holtzman Inkblot Technique

Internal consistency (split-half) reliability coefficients were routinely obtained for each variable in the Holtzman Inkblot Technique, using a standard program developed for this purpose. A study of interscorer agreement for the Holtzman Inkblot Technique was also carried out in Mexico. Only the highlights of these studies can be presented here to illustrate the results obtained.

Interscorer reliability for the American examiners and scorers had been well established by earlier methodological studies (Holtzman et al. 1961). Such data, however, were not yet available for use of the Holtzman Inkblot Technique in Mexico.

Ninety-eight Mexican children in Group I were selected for scoring twice on the HIT variables to determine the degree of agreement among independent scorers. A similar analysis was done for seventy-seven children in Group II and sixty children in Group III. Means, standard deviations, and intercorrelations of twenty-one HIT variables (omitting Popular) were computed across the two sets of independent scorers. The sex of the child was also coded into the analysis as a binary variable, making a total of forty-three variables for intercorrelation in each of the three groups.

No significant differences in means or standard deviations were discovered across the two sets of scores. Nor were there any differences that could be attributed to the sex of the child. Scoring agreement was unusually high in all three age groups. Interscorer-reliability coefficients in the high .90's were obtained uniformly for all of the variables except Space, Pathognomic Verbalization, Sex,

Table 4-1
Internal Consistency (Split-Half) Estimates of Reliability for
Seventeen Inkblot Variables in Year I

| Culture | Mexico | | | United States | | |
|---|---|---|---|---|---|---|
| Age Group | I | II | III | I | II | III |
| No. of Cases | 147 | 141 | 149 | 133 | 142 | 142 |
| RT | .94 | .94 | .96 | .92 | .97 | .97 |
| R | .95 | .87 | .91 | .90 | .93 | .88 |
| L | .94 | .95 | .95 | .95 | .97 | .95 |
| FD | .91 | .88 | .89 | .90 | .80 | .86 |
| FA | .90 | .82 | .77 | .86 | .81 | .67 |
| C | .94 | .84 | .78 | .93 | .83 | .85 |
| Sh | .61 | .55 | .58 | .74 | .58 | .78 |
| M | .84 | .83 | .85 | .86 | .87 | .88 |
| V | .86 | .52 | .87 | .90 | .76 | .79 |
| I | .57 | .69 | .77 | .58 | .85 | .82 |
| H | .84 | .81 | .79 | .82 | .81 | .83 |
| A | .92 | .83 | .71 | .80 | .73 | .72 |
| At | .83 | .86 | .75 | .91 | .80 | .69 |
| Ax | .92 | .73 | .70 | .78 | .68 | .80 |
| Hs | .95 | .63 | .66 | .88 | .72 | .78 |
| Br | .70 | .57 | .46 | .75 | .51 | .52 |
| Pn | .52 | .69 | .63 | .81 | .75 | .63 |

RT: Reaction Time
R: Rejection
L: Location
FD: Form Definiteness
FA: Form Appropriateness
C: Color
Sh: Shading
M: Movement
V: Pathognomic Verbalization

I: Integration
H: Human
A: Animal
At: Anatomy
Ax: Anxiety
Hs: Hostility
Br: Barrier
Pn: Penetration

and Abstract. Since Space, Sex, and Abstract occur very rarely, it is not surprising that interscorer reliability ranged from .56 to 1.00. For Pathognomic Verbalization, the interscorer agreement coefficients were .77, .88, and .97 for Groups I, II, and III respectively, values sufficiently high (with the possible exception of Group I) to justify complete confidence in the scoring procedures.

These results for the Mexican scorers of the HIT agree favorably with similar results for highly trained scorers in earlier studies of interscorer consistency using American samples.

Split-half reliability coefficients for HIT variables in the first year of data collection are presented separately for each of the three groups and two cultures in Table 4-1. The split-half reliability coefficients are uniformly very high for Reaction Time and Location. Coefficients in the high .80's and low .90's are also typically obtained in both cultures for Rejection, Form Definiteness, and Movement. Moderately high reliabilities in the low .80's were generally obtained for Form Appropriateness, Color, and Human. Reliabilities for the remaining variables vary somewhat across culture and age group. Only Barrier and Penetration show generally low reliabilities, ranging from .51 to .81. In general, these results are in line with similar results obtained for the standardization samples in earlier studies of the HIT. The reliabilities are sufficiently high to justify systematic analysis across cultures and age groups throughout the six years of study.

## Dimensions in the Parent-Attitude Survey

Most of the sixty-eight items in the Parent-Attitude Survey were drawn from an instrument developed by Hereford (1963), using items taken from earlier parental attitude studies as well as some items that were written specifically for his purposes. The five scales in the Hereford instrument were developed on a very similar population of mothers, a sample of housewives in Austin, fifteen years ago. For this reason it was thought that the scales would probably be more suitable than any other similar parental attitude scales currently available. The availability of high-speed computer programs for factor analysis on large numbers of variables made it possible to conduct dimensional studies on the sixty-eight items that would not have been practical fifteen years ago when the Hereford scales were first developed.

Inspection of the response distributions across the five possible choices for each item in the Austin sample of mothers indicated that distributions were highly skewed for over half of the items. Nevertheless, a preliminary intercorrelation analysis and principal-component factor analysis were carried out on 350 cases for which complete data were available. A total of twenty-one factors were extracted before the eigenvalues dropped below 1.00. A normalized varimax rotation was achieved by computer for the twenty-one factors. Inspection of the results indicated that no strong dimensions were present. Most of the factors appeared to reflect common ambiguities or structural components of the statements rather than clearly interpretable content similarities. None of the factors resembled the original five scales developed by Hereford.

A second, more conservative analysis was undertaken using Louis G. Guttman's image analysis as developed for factor analysis by Henry F. Kaiser (1963). While the number of factors was considerably smaller and a major portion of the variance was distributed on the first two factors, the over-all results were still less than satisfactory. Nevertheless, in some intercorrelational studies with other variables for the Austin sample, factor scores derived for the first two image-analysis factors were employed to reflect two dimensions within the Parent-Attitude Survey. Similar results carried out later with the Mexican sample alone yielded equally unsatisfactory dimensions.

A major problem with both samples when treated separately is the lack of sufficient variance in each item to yield correlations of any size. While there are clearly significant differences, item by item, between the Mexican and American samples, the American sample when considered alone has sharply skewed distributions on too many items. To overcome these deficiencies, a final analysis was carried out, using a combined sample of both Mexican and American parents. Cases in the two cultures were paired on socioeconomic status to yield a matched cross-cultural sample of 203 pairs, or 406 cases. Item intercorrelations for this combined sample were then factor-analyzed, using image-covariance analysis. A new procedure proposed by Donald J. Veldman (1974) was employed for determining the number of factors to be rotated. In this method, Kaiser's varimax criterion value, which can be inter-

preted as an index of the degree to which the rotation process has
approximated "simple structure," is computed after each rotation.
Veldman has demonstrated that choosing the solution that yields
the largest index of simple structure provides a rational conservative solution to determining the number of factors.

Three meaningful factors were revealed in this analysis of the
combined samples. In order to determine if these factors could be
obtained on each sample treated separately, a similar analysis was
performed independently for the 203 mothers in the Mexican
sample and for a similar number in the Austin sample. Each of
these independent factor analyses yielded four dimensions. Then
the samples were recombined and a final factor analysis was performed, in which four factors were extracted. This analysis appeared to produce the most meaningful set of dimensions for a
cross-cultural comparison between the Mexican and American
mothers.

The four-factor solutions for the American and Mexican samples were compared systematically, yielding high enough cosines
among the factor axes to indicate a common factor structure
present in both cultures. Consequently, factor scores were generated for each subject in each of the two cultures, using the
combined factor analysis as a basis for computation.

Items defining Factor 1 in the four-factor common solution are
presented in Table 4-2. Only those items are presented that have
loadings on Factor 1 above .35 while also having low loadings on
the other three factors. When considering only four factors, Factor
1 accounts for more of the variance (57 percent) than the other
three factors combined. Of the five Hereford scales, Causation has
more items defining Factor 1 than the other four Hereford scales
combined. In addition, seven of the eight items taken from the
Rosen scales have significant loadings on Factor 1. Disagreement
with these items results in a high score on Factor 1. A person with
such a high score is one who believes it is possible to mold a child's
character, personality, and intelligence by her own actions as a
parent. She is also future-oriented rather than oriented to the past
or present. She is likely to be optimistic and positive in her outlook
on life. A tentative name for Factor 1 is Internal Determinism.

Factor 2 accounts for about 27 percent of the variance in a
four-factor solution. Items with loadings above .35 on Factor 2 are

Table 4-2
Parent-Attitude Items Defining Factor I in the Combined Cross-Cultural Sample
of 406 Mothers

| Item No. | Item Statement | Factor Loading |
|---|---|---|
| 37 R | When a man is born the success he is going to have is already in the cards, so he might just as well accept it and not fight against it. | .62 |
| 24 T | It is hard to let children go and visit people because they might misbehave when parents aren't around. | .58 |
| 17 R | All a man should want out of life in the way of a career is a secure, not-too-difficult job, with enough pay to get by. | .57 |
| 7 Ca | With all a child hears at school and from friends, there's little a parent can do to influence him. | .55 |
| 52 Ca | A child is destined to be a certain kind of person no matter what the parents do. | .55 |
| 36 C | Few parents have to face the problems I find with my children. | .55 |
| 40 U | Most children's fears are so unreasonable it only makes things worse to let the child talk about them. | .54 |
| 59 Ca | A child that comes from bad stock doesn't have much chance of amounting to anything. | .54 |
| 2 Ca | When you come right down to it, a child is either good or bad and there's not much you can do about it. | .53 |
| 46 Ca | If a child is born bad, there's not much you can do about it. | .53 |
| 30 R | Planning only makes a person unhappy since your plans hardly ever work out anyway. | .52 |
| 10 U | If you let children talk about their troubles they end up complaining even more. | .51 |
| 23 R | Nothing is worth the sacrifice of moving away from one's parents. | .50 |
| 38 Ca | Psychologists now know that what a child is born with determines the kind of person he becomes. | .49 |
| 26 Ca | Some children are just naturally bad. | .49 |
| 49 R | Much of what a son does should be done to please his parents. | .48 |
| 19 C | I feel I am faced with more problems than most parents. | .48 |
| 55 O | It's hardly fair to bring children into the world with the way things look for the future. | .47 |
| 11 R | A good son would try to live near his parents even if it means giving up a good job in another part of the country. | .46 |
| 32 Ca | Some children are so naturally headstrong that a parent can't really do much about them. | .45 |
| 67 U | Family conferences which include the children don't usually accomplish much. | .44 |
| 62 O | When you get right down to it no one is going to care much what is going to happen to you. | .44 |
| 3 R | Nowadays with world conditions the way they are the wise person lives for today and lets tomorrow take care of itself. | .43 |
| 20 Ca | Most of the bad traits children have (like nervousness or bad temper) are inherited. | .43 |
| 39 A | When a boy is cowardly, he should be forced to try things he is afraid of. | .39 |

C:  item taken from Hereford's Confidence Scale
Ca: item taken from Hereford's Causation Scale
A:  item taken from Hereford's Acceptance Scale
U:  item taken from Hereford's Understanding Scale
T:  item taken from Hereford's Trust Scale
O:  item taken from CYS Orientation to Society Scale
R:  item adapted from Rosen's scales

presented in Table 4-3. With the exception of three items that are positively stated (9, 13, and 5), disagreement with the items in

Table 4-3
Parent-Attitude Items Defining Factor 2 in the Combined Sample

| Item No. | Item Statement | Factor Loading |
|---|---|---|
| 61 A | Children should be toilet-trained at the earliest possible time. | .57 |
| 21 A | A child who wants too much affection may become a "softie" if it is given to him. | .55 |
| 41 O | These days a person doesn't really know whom he can count on. | .52 |
| 60 C | Parents sacrifice most of their fun for their children. | .51 |
| 57 D | If a person doesn't always get much done but can enjoy life as he goes along, that is the best way. | .48 |
| 64 D | A boss should understand and not penalize a worker who sometimes without warning takes a little time off for fun. | .47 |
| 43 C | Children don't realize that it mainly takes suffering to be a good parent. | .45 |
| 27 A | One thing I cannot stand is a child's constantly wanting to be held. | .45 |
| 9 A | If you put too many restrictions on a child, you will stunt his personality. | −.44 |
| 15 U | Talking to a child about his fears most often makes the fear look more important than it is. | .44 |
| 66 T | Children must be told exactly what to do and how to do it or they will make mistakes. | .44 |
| 48 O | In spite of what most people say, the life for the average person is getting worse not better. | .43 |
| 13 Ca | Most all children are just the same at birth; it's what happens to them afterwards that is important. | −.43 |
| 6 T | Children have no right to keep anything from their parents. | .42 |
| 45 T | It is hard to know when to let boys and girls play together, when they can't be seen. | .41 |
| 16 Ca | Why children behave the way they do is too much for anyone to figure out. | .40 |
| 8 R | The secret of happiness is not expecting too much out of life and being content with what comes your way. | .40 |
| 5 U | Family life would be happier if parents made children feel they were free to say what they think about anything. | −.39 |
| 18 T | More parents should make it their job to know everything their child is doing. | .38 |

C: item taken from Hereford's Confidence Scale
Ca: item taken from Hereford's Causation Scale
A: item taken from Hereford's Acceptance Scale
U: item taken from Hereford's Understanding Scale
T: item taken from Hereford's Trust Scale
O: item taken from CYS Orientation to Society Scale
R: item adapted from Rosen's scales
D: item taken from Díaz-Guerrero's sociocultural premises studies in Mexico

Factor 2 would result in a high score, while the tendency to agree with the items would yield a low score on the dimension reflected in this factor. Of the Hereford scales, items from Acceptance tend to be stronger in defining Factor 2 than those from the other four scales. In addition, two items that were designed especially for this study by the Mexican team (57 and 64) have high loadings on this factor, as do several items from the CYS Orientation to Society scale (41 and 48). A person with a high score on Factor 2 is one who is accepting and trusting of children, who believes in giving the child freedom of a moderate amount, and who has a generally positive outlook on life. A tentative name for this factor might be Sophisticated Acceptance.

Factor 3 is a minor dimension best defined by the two items listed in Table 4-4. These two are the only items with loadings above .30 on Factor 3. Of the six items with loadings ranging from .20 to .30, three are also drawn from Hereford's Confidence Scale, suggesting that this factor is a fairly simple, minor dimension, reflecting parental anxiety and uncertainty at one end and parental confidence at the other. Since high scores on the factor result from disagreeing with the items, a person with a high score on Factor 3 tends to be one who has confidence in her child-rearing ability and feels she can cope adequately with problems that arise.

Factor 4 is also a minor dimension that is defined by four items with loadings of .30 or above, as listed in Table 4-5. Since three of these four items deal with authoritarian discipline versus a laissez-faire attitude in child rearing, a person with a high score on Factor 4 can be thought of as one who tends to be trusting and perhaps laissez-faire in dealing with children.

Factors 3 and 4 each account for only 7 percent of the common

Table 4-4
Parent-Attitude Items Defining Factor 3 in the Combined Sample

| Item No. | Item Statement | Factor Loading |
|---|---|---|
| 56 C | Raising children is a nerve-racking job. | .45 |
| 25 C | It's hard to know what to do when a child is afraid of something that won't hurt him. | .33 |

C: item taken from Hereford's Confidence Scale

Table 4-5
Parent-Attitude Items Defining Factor 4 in the Combined Sample

| Item No. | Item Statement | Factor Loading |
|---|---|---|
| 53 T | Children who are not watched will get in trouble. | .39 |
| 50 U | A child's ideas should be seriously considered in making family decisions. | .31 |
| 29 T | If rules are not closely enforced children will misbehave and get into trouble. | .31 |
| 65 AD | Strict discipline develops a fine strong character. | .30 |

T:   item taken from Hereford's Trust Scale
U:   item taken from Hereford's Understanding Scale
AD: item taken from CYS Authoritarian Discipline Scale

variance in the four-factor solution, indicating that they are of minor importance. The generally low loadings and lack of items defining these factors suggest that for most purposes the variations in parental attitudes are fairly well captured by the dimensions present in Factors 1 and 2. However, all four factors have been carried forward for additional correlational and variance analyses to determine the relationships between parental attitudes and other measures obtained directly from the children themselves (see Chapter 6) and to discover significant components of variance that can be attributed to culture, socioeconomic status, sex or age of the child, and interactions among these independent variables (see Chapter 10).

## Sample Bias as a Function of Normal Attrition through Time

In any longitudinal study that runs for a number of years, some loss of subjects is inevitable. Strenuous efforts were made in the present investigation to keep such attrition to a minimum. The number of children tested repeatedly for the six-year period is shown by age group, culture, and year tested in Table 4-6.

Most of the attrition in both the United States and Mexico occurred between years 1 and 2. The families likely to move to another town account for most of the cases lost in the early part of the study. The marked drop in number of cases between years 5 and 6 for Mexico is simply a result of the fact that only cases in the matched cross-cultural sample were tested in Mexico during the sixth year, because of lack of sufficient funds for the entire sample. From the second to the fifth year, the attrition in both cultures was extremely low.

The effects of attrition over the period of the study were determined by comparing test scores of children who remained in the study with test scores of those children who dropped out of the study before its completion. Comparisons were made on first-year test data only. Separate analyses were made for the Mexican and American samples. For the Mexican children, attrition was studied after the fifth year, omitting year 6, since only the cross-culturally matched cases of Mexicans were tested in the sixth year. All six years were used for the American children in defining those cases who dropped out or remained in.

A three-way analysis-of-variance design was employed with children classified by age, sex, and drop-out status. For the American sample, analyses were completed for twenty-two scores from the Holtzman Inkblot Technique, four subtest scores from the Wechsler Intelligence Scale for Children, and eleven scores from the Object Sorting Test. For the Mexican sample, Popular was omitted from the HIT scores. Since many hundreds of F-tests were made to determine the significance of main effects or interactions in the analysis-of-variance design, only those outcomes that proved to be significant beyond the .01 level involving the attrition factor will be reported.

In the analyses for the American children, only two of the variables yielded significant differences between the children who

Table 4-6
Number of Children Tested Repeatedly for Six Years

| Year | United States | | | Mexico | | |
|---|---|---|---|---|---|---|
| | I | II | III | I | II | III |
| 1 | 133 | 142 | 142 | 150 | 143 | 150 |
| 2 | 109 | 125 | 131 | 142 | 132 | 138 |
| 3 | 105 | 121 | 128 | 142 | 132 | 138 |
| 4 | 102 | 111 | 122 | 136 | 129 | 127 |
| 5 | 101 | 107 | 121 | 133 | 121 | 111 |
| 6 | 89 | 96 | 113 | 52[a] | 67[a] | 49[a] |

[a] Only cases in the matched cross-cultural sample were tested in Mexico during the sixth year.

stayed in the study throughout the six years and those who dropped out. For the Arithmetic subtest of the WISC, the retained children had a mean score of 9.6 in the first year of testing, while those who dropped out had a mean of 9.1, a difference significant beyond the .01 level. The interaction between attrition status and age group for Arithmetic was significant at the .02 level, indicating that the bias due to attrition was not equally spread across all three age groups. No mean differences were found for the youngest children in Group I; the means for Group II were 10.4 and 9.15 for the children who were retained and those who dropped out, respectively; and for Group III, the comparable means were 13.3 for those retained and 12.4 for those who dropped out. The only other significant score was Percent Public in the Object Sorting Test (and, of course, its mirror image, Percent Private). While the main effect was not significant, the interaction between age group and attrition status was significant beyond the .01 level. Further inspection of the differences between children who stayed in the study and those who dropped out according to each of the three age groups revealed that most of the interaction was due to a reversal of effect in Group II from what occurred in Group I. For the children in Group II, the mean scores on Percent Public were 45.7 for the retained children and 56.4 for those who dropped out. The comparable means in Group I were 64.4 for those who were retained and 55.6 for those who dropped out, just the reverse of the difference found in Group II. No differences were noted between the retained and dropped-out categories in Group III.

None of the variables analyzed for the Mexican children showed any significant biases due to normal attrition through the fifth year of the study. Whatever differences may have been associated with dropping out of the study were too minor to yield any statistically significant results in the analysis of variance of the first years' test scores.

In general, it can be concluded that the normal attrition processes in both the Mexican and the American samples failed to produce any serious biases that would affect the outcome of the longitudinal study. The slightly lower mean scores on Arithmetic for the Austin children in Groups II and III who dropped out of the study before the sixth year constitute the only bias discovered of any real consequence. And, even in this case, the bias is of insufficient magnitude to have a serious impact on the interpretation of other findings in the study.

---

In the next chapter the test-retest stability over time of the measures employed in two to six years is presented separately for each of the two cultures.

# 5. Test-Retest Stability over Time

The repeated testing of each child for a period of six years makes it possible to obtain important information on the stability of certain cognitive, perceptual, and personality measures over periods ranging from one to six years and during the period of child development when rapid growth occurs. While normal attrition, due to families' moving away, resulted in some loss in the number of cases, the sizes of the samples are still sufficiently large to justify extensive analysis and interpretation by each age group and each culture.

Computation of test-retest correlations was carried out for all measures that were obtained at least two years in a row. Repeated measures across the entire six years are available in all groups for the Holtzman Inkblot Technique, for Vocabulary and Block Design from the Wechsler scales, and for the Harris-Goodenough score on Human Figure Drawing. Six years of data are also available in most groups for the Time Estimation Test and the Arithmetic and Picture Completion subtests. Results for these tests will be presented first. Then those tests for which three, four, or five years of repeated testing are available will be analyzed and interpreted. And finally, test-retest correlations for measures obtained for only two years will be examined.

## Holtzman Inkblot Technique

For seventeen of the twenty-two variables in the Holtzman Inkblot Technique, the scores are sufficiently well distributed to permit the use of product-moment correlation coefficients. Tables 5-1 to 5-17 show the correlations across the six years separately for each age-group and culture, one inkblot score at a time.

The most stable of all the inkblot scores is Location. With the exception of the youngest children in the first year, the test-retest correlations for Location are high in both cultures, ranging into the .80's for the older children after several years of testing. Close behind Location in stability are Reaction Time, Form Definiteness, Movement, and Human. All of these variables deal with the cognitive-perceptual aspects of the child's performance.

Of the seventeen variables listed in Tables 5-1–5-17, Rejection, Form Appropriateness, Shading, Pathognomic Verbalization, Barrier, and Penetration tend to have generally low stability coefficients, ranging from insignicant values into the .40's and .50's, with an occasional value into the .60's and .70's. Four variables— Space, Sex, Abstract, and Balance—proved to be too infrequent in these samples of children to yield data amenable to treatment by

Table 5-1
HIT Reaction Time Test-Retest Correlations

| Years Correlated | Mexico | | | United States | | |
|---|---|---|---|---|---|---|
| | I | II | III | I | II | III |
| 1 & 2 | .23 | .31 | .41 | .48 | .63 | .67 |
| 1 & 3 | .29 | .37 | .38 | .43 | .51 | .56 |
| 1 & 4 | .17 | .40 | .21 | .31 | .51 | .40 |
| 1 & 5 | .25 | .27 | .34 | .27 | .44 | .44 |
| 1 & 6 | .37 | .34 | .25 | .22 | .21 | .36 |
| 2 & 3 | .33 | .34 | .74 | .41 | .68 | .69 |
| 2 & 4 | .36 | .42 | .52 | .38 | .58 | .58 |
| 2 & 5 | .35 | .36 | .49 | .19 | .58 | .62 |
| 2 & 6 | .24 | .37 | .36 | .24 | .33 | .56 |
| 3 & 4 | .54 | .45 | .76 | .59 | .68 | .78 |
| 3 & 5 | .65 | .47 | .70 | .56 | .69 | .71 |
| 3 & 6 | .32 | .44 | .42 | .46 | .63 | .63 |
| 4 & 5 | .47 | .52 | .81 | .56 | .72 | .80 |
| 4 & 6 | .36 | .62 | .55 | .44 | .58 | .68 |
| 5 & 6 | .33 | .58 | .77 | .56 | .73 | .85 |

NOTE: Table covers six years of repeated testing.

Table 5-2
HIT Rejection Test-Retest Correlations

| Years Correlated | Mexico | | | United States | | |
|---|---|---|---|---|---|---|
| | I | II | III | I | II | III |
| 1 & 2 | .28 | .21 | .30 | .51 | .34 | .37 |
| 1 & 3 | .16 | −.01 | .14 | .31 | .32 | .34 |
| 1 & 4 | .06 | .36 | .18 | .22 | .30 | .22 |
| 1 & 5 | .11 | .16 | .15 | .47 | .45 | .31 |
| 1 & 6 | .24 | .27 | .30 | .07 | .18 | .13 |
| 2 & 3 | .31 | .14 | .60 | .44 | .61 | .48 |
| 2 & 4 | .12 | .58 | .35 | .39 | .44 | .33 |
| 2 & 5 | .34 | .27 | .26 | .20 | .30 | .26 |
| 2 & 6 | .19 | .23 | .21 | .22 | .20 | .09 |
| 3 & 4 | .18 | .13 | .48 | .57 | .62 | .43 |
| 3 & 5 | .58 | .14 | .34 | .47 | .51 | .28 |
| 3 & 6 | .12 | .16 | .23 | .22 | .37 | .54 |
| 4 & 5 | .18 | .32 | .75 | .33 | .52 | .65 |
| 4 & 6 | .11 | .36 | .66 | .18 | .43 | .49 |
| 5 & 6 | .20 | .30 | .76 | .30 | .52 | .17 |

NOTE: Table covers six years of repeated testing.

Table 5-3
HIT Location Test-Retest Correlations

| Years Correlated | Mexico | | | United States | | |
|---|---|---|---|---|---|---|
| | I | II | III | I | II | III |
| 1 & 2 | .27 | .57 | .66 | .28 | .72 | .76 |
| 1 & 3 | .20 | .49 | .60 | .27 | .62 | .70 |
| 1 & 4 | .25 | .49 | .58 | .26 | .59 | .69 |
| 1 & 5 | .24 | .46 | .56 | .26 | .51 | .67 |
| 1 & 6 | .50 | .26 | .51 | .33 | .56 | .59 |
| 2 & 3 | .58 | .70 | .71 | .50 | .77 | .84 |
| 2 & 4 | .49 | .73 | .72 | .54 | .68 | .81 |
| 2 & 5 | .42 | .64 | .67 | .46 | .58 | .76 |
| 2 & 6 | .23 | .57 | .52 | .49 | .62 | .75 |
| 3 & 4 | .64 | .75 | .76 | .68 | .78 | .82 |
| 3 & 5 | .56 | .70 | .74 | .70 | .80 | .80 |
| 3 & 6 | .44 | .63 | .55 | .64 | .77 | .75 |
| 4 & 5 | .60 | .77 | .85 | .71 | .76 | .86 |
| 4 & 6 | .62 | .73 | .68 | .68 | .80 | .86 |
| 5 & 6 | .63 | .76 | .74 | .79 | .86 | .85 |

NOTE: Table covers six years of repeated testing.

Table 5-4
HIT Form Definiteness Test-Retest Correlations

| Years Correlated | Mexico | | | United States | | |
|---|---|---|---|---|---|---|
| | I | II | III | I | II | III |
| 1 & 2 | .40 | .55 | .51 | .28 | .40 | .58 |
| 1 & 3 | .34 | .49 | .46 | .32 | .40 | .47 |
| 1 & 4 | .18 | .46 | .45 | .36 | .27 | .51 |
| 1 & 5 | .22 | .40 | .37 | .42 | .38 | .52 |
| 1 & 6 | .18 | .35 | .44 | .36 | .33 | .41 |
| 2 & 3 | .48 | .56 | .60 | .36 | .40 | .66 |
| 2 & 4 | .43 | .54 | .56 | .55 | .44 | .69 |
| 2 & 5 | .27 | .54 | .51 | .32 | .39 | .62 |
| 2 & 6 | .15 | .26 | .58 | .44 | .36 | .56 |
| 3 & 4 | .53 | .63 | .78 | .48 | .50 | .72 |
| 3 & 5 | .40 | .56 | .69 | .35 | .63 | .68 |
| 3 & 6 | .48 | .37 | .59 | .32 | .39 | .56 |
| 4 & 5 | .59 | .67 | .75 | .57 | .65 | .69 |
| 4 & 6 | .63 | .56 | .70 | .58 | .56 | .71 |
| 5 & 6 | .69 | .60 | .74 | .65 | .49 | .75 |

NOTE: Table covers six years of repeated testing.

Table 5-5
HIT Form Appropriateness Test-Retest Correlations

| Years Correlated | Mexico | | | United States | | |
|---|---|---|---|---|---|---|
| | I | II | III | I | II | III |
| 1 & 2 | .34 | .19 | .25 | .34 | .34 | .38 |
| 1 & 3 | .27 | .30 | .41 | .30 | .43 | .38 |
| 1 & 4 | .25 | .18 | .23 | .23 | .10 | .22 |
| 1 & 5 | .10 | .12 | .40 | .24 | .32 | .21 |
| 1 & 6 | .22 | .17 | .26 | .10 | .14 | .30 |
| 2 & 3 | .50 | .34 | .52 | .37 | .38 | .35 |
| 2 & 4 | .36 | .55 | .42 | .34 | .41 | .44 |
| 2 & 5 | .38 | .36 | .35 | .29 | .51 | .47 |
| 2 & 6 | .36 | .12 | .29 | .26 | .13 | .40 |
| 3 & 4 | .57 | .35 | .28 | .62 | .10 | .46 |
| 3 & 5 | .39 | .34 | .37 | .39 | .32 | .43 |
| 3 & 6 | .23 | .26 | .30 | .36 | .32 | .40 |
| 4 & 5 | .43 | .41 | .43 | .38 | .35 | .58 |
| 4 & 6 | .49 | .17 | .27 | .39 | .34 | .55 |
| 5 & 6 | .40 | .26 | .39 | .23 | .32 | .58 |

NOTE: Table covers six years of repeated testing.

Table 5-6
HIT Color Test-Retest Correlations

| Years Correlated | Mexico | | | United States | | |
|---|---|---|---|---|---|---|
| | I | II | III | I | II | III |
| 1 & 2 | .20 | .25 | .28 | .17 | .56 | .66 |
| 1 & 3 | .23 | .26 | .31 | .30 | .52 | .48 |
| 1 & 4 | .16 | .27 | .34 | .34 | .26 | .26 |
| 1 & 5 | .01 | .08 | .50 | .30 | .25 | .23 |
| 1 & 6 | .14 | .43 | .32 | .06 | .17 | .37 |
| 2 & 3 | .49 | .39 | .49 | .30 | .56 | .54 |
| 2 & 4 | .38 | .28 | .40 | .41 | .35 | .41 |
| 2 & 5 | .15 | .12 | .36 | .22 | .30 | .27 |
| 2 & 6 | .39 | .34 | .32 | .08 | .36 | .48 |
| 3 & 4 | .42 | .43 | .76 | .52 | .58 | .37 |
| 3 & 5 | .27 | .19 | .52 | .44 | .49 | .25 |
| 3 & 6 | .35 | .07 | .54 | .45 | .44 | .38 |
| 4 & 5 | .45 | .49 | .65 | .45 | .50 | .47 |
| 4 & 6 | .45 | .40 | .62 | .31 | .63 | .52 |
| 5 & 6 | .58 | .67 | .57 | .42 | .68 | .65 |

NOTE: Table covers six years of repeated testing.

Table 5-7
HIT Shading Test-Retest Correlations

| Years Correlated | Mexico | | | United States | | |
|---|---|---|---|---|---|---|
| | I | II | III | I | II | III |
| 1 & 2 | .26 | .28 | .46 | .35 | .39 | .67 |
| 1 & 3 | .20 | .26 | .52 | .18 | .34 | .54 |
| 1 & 4 | .02 | .31 | .35 | .08 | .20 | .08 |
| 1 & 5 | .10 | .51 | .46 | .08 | .26 | .13 |
| 1 & 6 | .11 | .21 | .11 | .12 | .03 | .15 |
| 2 & 3 | .34 | .35 | .48 | .27 | .45 | .51 |
| 2 & 4 | .31 | .42 | .41 | .25 | .21 | .09 |
| 2 & 5 | .22 | .46 | .36 | .15 | .17 | .16 |
| 2 & 6 | —.01 | .25 | .23 | .21 | .16 | .23 |
| 3 & 4 | .22 | .34 | .58 | .30 | .21 | .23 |
| 3 & 5 | .20 | .42 | .67 | .36 | .27 | .28 |
| 3 & 6 | .28 | .26 | .45 | .18 | .42 | .26 |
| 4 & 5 | .37 | .50 | .61 | .29 | .41 | .51 |
| 4 & 6 | .14 | .38 | .67 | .39 | .29 | .44 |
| 5 & 6 | .15 | .53 | .66 | .34 | .46 | .41 |

NOTE: Table covers six years of repeated testing.

Table 5-8
HIT Movement Test-Retest Correlations

| Years Correlated | Mexico | | | United States | | |
|---|---|---|---|---|---|---|
| | I | II | III | I | II | III |
| 1 & 2 | .50 | .36 | .65 | .45 | .62 | .71 |
| 1 & 3 | .29 | .40 | .71 | .23 | .53 | .68 |
| 1 & 4 | .38 | .24 | .58 | .10 | .49 | .60 |
| 1 & 5 | .34 | .31 | .45 | .10 | .49 | .49 |
| 1 & 6 | .33 | .20 | .39 | .14 | .46 | .46 |
| 2 & 3 | .58 | .56 | .70 | .40 | .66 | .75 |
| 2 & 4 | .36 | .58 | .60 | .33 | .65 | .77 |
| 2 & 5 | .33 | .55 | .49 | .22 | .56 | .65 |
| 2 & 6 | .29 | .54 | .46 | .30 | .47 | .68 |
| 3 & 4 | .40 | .62 | .72 | .46 | .62 | .69 |
| 3 & 5 | .27 | .60 | .68 | .53 | .62 | .63 |
| 3 & 6 | .13 | .52 | .40 | .52 | .63 | .56 |
| 4 & 5 | .59 | .66 | .60 | .58 | .68 | .73 |
| 4 & 6 | .42 | .54 | .57 | .31 | .60 | .68 |
| 5 & 6 | .52 | .62 | .33 | .53 | .69 | .72 |

NOTE: Table covers six years of repeated testing.

Table 5-9
HIT Pathognomic Verbalization Test-Retest Correlations

| Years Correlated | Mexico | | | United States | | |
|---|---|---|---|---|---|---|
| | I | II | III | I | II | III |
| 1 & 2 | .41 | .10 | .39 | .19 | .32 | .33 |
| 1 & 3 | .39 | .09 | .54 | .02 | .32 | .25 |
| 1 & 4 | .39 | .07 | .13 | .00 | .28 | .22 |
| 1 & 5 | .44 | .02 | .02 | .03 | .21 | .06 |
| 1 & 6 | .08 | —.08 | .20 | .00 | .09 | .15 |
| 2 & 3 | .06 | .15 | .42 | .26 | .39 | .52 |
| 2 & 4 | .10 | .35 | .44 | .12 | .35 | .35 |
| 2 & 5 | .22 | .14 | .31 | .06 | .48 | .49 |
| 2 & 6 | —.05 | .02 | —.02 | .20 | .25 | .53 |
| 3 & 4 | .82 | —.06 | .08 | .61 | .33 | .26 |
| 3 & 5 | .78 | —.02 | .19 | .38 | .43 | .25 |
| 3 & 6 | —.04 | .00 | .00 | .40 | .38 | .37 |
| 4 & 5 | .75 | .17 | .36 | .45 | .49 | .43 |
| 4 & 6 | .57 | —.05 | .49 | .54 | .36 | .47 |
| 5 & 6 | .42 | .14 | .56 | .50 | .50 | .70 |

NOTE: Table covers six years of repeated testing.

Table 5-10
HIT Integration Test-Retest Correlations

| Years Correlated | Mexico | | | United States | | |
|---|---|---|---|---|---|---|
| | I | II | III | I | II | III |
| 1 & 2 | .36 | .36 | .52 | .04 | .58 | .60 |
| 1 & 3 | .06 | .20 | .24 | .06 | .54 | .47 |
| 1 & 4 | .30 | .12 | .37 | —.02 | .38 | .40 |
| 1 & 5 | .34 | .17 | .32 | .00 | .52 | .45 |
| 1 & 6 | .35 | .13 | .20 | —.05 | .35 | .39 |
| 2 & 3 | .08 | —.05 | .47 | .23 | .56 | .58 |
| 2 & 4 | .17 | .27 | .50 | .16 | .51 | .65 |
| 2 & 5 | .34 | .26 | .39 | .27 | .43 | .59 |
| 2 & 6 | .23 | .50 | .34 | .16 | .34 | .65 |
| 3 & 4 | —.02 | .00 | .33 | .25 | .49 | .59 |
| 3 & 5 | .16 | .10 | .18 | .32 | .50 | .58 |
| 3 & 6 | —.04 | .21 | —.07 | .22 | .38 | .55 |
| 4 & 5 | .35 | .59 | .47 | .34 | .60 | .65 |
| 4 & 6 | .45 | .37 | .29 | .09 | .58 | .67 |
| 5 & 6 | .38 | .45 | .37 | .58 | .69 | .78 |

NOTE: Table covers six years of repeated testing.

Table 5-11
HIT Human Test-Retest Correlations

| Years Correlated | Mexico | | | United States | | |
|---|---|---|---|---|---|---|
| | I | II | III | I | II | III |
| 1 & 2 | .40 | .43 | .64 | .27 | .35 | .59 |
| 1 & 3 | .44 | .38 | .52 | .36 | .48 | .60 |
| 1 & 4 | .26 | .42 | .60 | .34 | .37 | .52 |
| 1 & 5 | .29 | .31 | .42 | .34 | .48 | .52 |
| 1 & 6 | .03 | .24 | .18 | .34 | .39 | .50 |
| 2 & 3 | .41 | .51 | .59 | .39 | .43 | .62 |
| 2 & 4 | .32 | .62 | .63 | .44 | .51 | .70 |
| 2 & 5 | .22 | .37 | .47 | .20 | .42 | .61 |
| 2 & 6 | .03 | .17 | .45 | .25 | .39 | .68 |
| 3 & 4 | .46 | .62 | .73 | .43 | .58 | .69 |
| 3 & 5 | .47 | .55 | .69 | .46 | .53 | .64 |
| 3 & 6 | .18 | .26 | .54 | .39 | .49 | .52 |
| 4 & 5 | .55 | .58 | .65 | .49 | .55 | .67 |
| 4 & 6 | .33 | .36 | .68 | .45 | .52 | .64 |
| 5 & 6 | .54 | .43 | .65 | .66 | .68 | .69 |

NOTE: Table covers six years of repeated testing.

Table 5-12
HIT Animal Test-Retest Correlations

| Years Correlated | Mexico | | | United States | | |
|---|---|---|---|---|---|---|
| | I | II | III | I | II | III |
| 1 & 2 | .49 | .45 | .50 | .39 | .31 | .32 |
| 1 & 3 | .40 | .50 | .49 | .19 | .33 | .40 |
| 1 & 4 | .36 | .44 | .35 | .32 | .19 | .32 |
| 1 & 5 | .38 | .42 | .42 | .24 | .27 | .32 |
| 1 & 6 | .03 | .14 | .36 | .18 | .16 | .30 |
| 2 & 3 | .52 | .64 | .57 | .19 | .52 | .51 |
| 2 & 4 | .41 | .56 | .50 | .45 | .44 | .59 |
| 2 & 5 | .31 | .50 | .54 | .25 | .34 | .40 |
| 2 & 6 | .16 | .36 | .44 | .32 | .27 | .46 |
| 3 & 4 | .54 | .62 | .56 | .43 | .38 | .63 |
| 3 & 5 | .56 | .52 | .66 | .35 | .47 | .68 |
| 3 & 6 | .18 | .25 | .44 | .14 | .36 | .54 |
| 4 & 5 | .51 | .50 | .69 | .52 | .57 | .63 |
| 4 & 6 | .46 | .36 | .68 | .40 | .48 | .74 |
| 5 & 6 | .46 | .49 | .65 | .59 | .57 | .70 |

NOTE: Table covers six years of repeated testing.

Table 5-13
HIT Anatomy Test-Retest Correlations

| Years Correlated | Mexico | | | United States | | |
|---|---|---|---|---|---|---|
| | I | II | III | I | II | III |
| 1 & 2 | .48 | .52 | .42 | .53 | .35 | .39 |
| 1 & 3 | .38 | .59 | .51 | .44 | .12 | .56 |
| 1 & 4 | .19 | .39 | .48 | .53 | .23 | .21 |
| 1 & 5 | .28 | .50 | .25 | .36 | .28 | .50 |
| 1 & 6 | .16 | .30 | .40 | .21 | .21 | .17 |
| 2 & 3 | .63 | .67 | .65 | .46 | .54 | .53 |
| 2 & 4 | .35 | .56 | .47 | .39 | .56 | .38 |
| 2 & 5 | .39 | .43 | .56 | .22 | .52 | .33 |
| 2 & 6 | .24 | .54 | .72 | .18 | .37 | .32 |
| 3 & 4 | .48 | .54 | .66 | .65 | .64 | .29 |
| 3 & 5 | .38 | .48 | .58 | .49 | .66 | .58 |
| 3 & 6 | .17 | .59 | .68 | .17 | .38 | .34 |
| 4 & 5 | .50 | .45 | .64 | .60 | .65 | .38 |
| 4 & 6 | .67 | .52 | .75 | .35 | .55 | .52 |
| 5 & 6 | .74 | .33 | .61 | .44 | .49 | .25 |

NOTE: Table covers six years of repeated testing.

Table 5-14
HIT Anxiety Test-Retest Correlations

| Years Correlated | Mexico | | | United States | | |
|---|---|---|---|---|---|---|
| | I | II | III | I | II | III |
| 1 & 2 | .25 | .22 | .44 | .31 | .46 | .62 |
| 1 & 3 | .00 | .31 | .38 | .23 | .44 | .54 |
| 1 & 4 | .10 | .30 | .43 | .06 | .43 | .41 |
| 1 & 5 | .13 | .47 | .19 | .07 | .46 | .41 |
| 1 & 6 | —.04 | .07 | .40 | .13 | .29 | .30 |
| 2 & 3 | .37 | .52 | .26 | .34 | .54 | .54 |
| 2 & 4 | .26 | .47 | .33 | .16 | .57 | .39 |
| 2 & 5 | .13 | .38 | .37 | .11 | .40 | .42 |
| 2 & 6 | .24 | .40 | .37 | .15 | .52 | .44 |
| 3 & 4 | .16 | .48 | .49 | .39 | .51 | .32 |
| 3 & 5 | .23 | .45 | .46 | .53 | .50 | .44 |
| 3 & 6 | .31 | .40 | .37 | .30 | .47 | .39 |
| 4 & 5 | .62 | .53 | .49 | .42 | .54 | .48 |
| 4 & 6 | .30 | .55 | .42 | .34 | .57 | .42 |
| 5 & 6 | .29 | .35 | .36 | .39 | .55 | .46 |

NOTE: Table covers six years of repeated testing.

Table 5-15
HIT Hostility Test-Retest Correlations

| Years Correlated | Mexico | | | United States | | |
|---|---|---|---|---|---|---|
| | I | II | III | I | II | III |
| 1 & 2 | .30 | .34 | .34 | .32 | .65 | .65 |
| 1 & 3 | .26 | .45 | .32 | .29 | .47 | .61 |
| 1 & 4 | .35 | .34 | .31 | .14 | .50 | .45 |
| 1 & 5 | .33 | .24 | .16 | .19 | .54 | .44 |
| 1 & 6 | .02 | .12 | .32 | .21 | .40 | .27 |
| 2 & 3 | .60 | .50 | .38 | .38 | .51 | .65 |
| 2 & 4 | .46 | .55 | .40 | .36 | .64 | .65 |
| 2 & 5 | .43 | .54 | .23 | .25 | .60 | .58 |
| 2 & 6 | .25 | .57 | .42 | .18 | .48 | .56 |
| 3 & 4 | .48 | .51 | .42 | .48 | .57 | .53 |
| 3 & 5 | .42 | .53 | .34 | .54 | .59 | .51 |
| 3 & 6 | .14 | .35 | .35 | .36 | .41 | .37 |
| 4 & 5 | .66 | .52 | .36 | .58 | .61 | .65 |
| 4 & 6 | .14 | .53 | .27 | .40 | .49 | .56 |
| 5 & 6 | .33 | .55 | .07 | .37 | .54 | .58 |

NOTE: Table covers six years of repeated testing.

Table 5-16
HIT Barrier Test-Retest Correlations

| Years Correlated | Mexico I | II | III | United States I | II | III |
|---|---|---|---|---|---|---|
| 1 & 2 | .14 | .19 | .35 | .18 | .33 | .45 |
| 1 & 3 | .10 | .23 | .20 | .21 | .46 | .49 |
| 1 & 4 | .17 | .29 | .16 | .29 | .36 | .19 |
| 1 & 5 | .32 | .30 | .24 | .13 | .37 | .30 |
| 1 & 6 | .38 | .35 | .36 | .16 | .38 | .23 |
| 2 & 3 | —.09 | .01 | .18 | .21 | .29 | .56 |
| 2 & 4 | .24 | .31 | .39 | .34 | .36 | .45 |
| 2 & 5 | .18 | .46 | .45 | .14 | .31 | .45 |
| 2 & 6 | —.14 | .34 | .48 | .35 | .32 | .51 |
| 3 & 4 | .10 | .00 | —.05 | .30 | .49 | .50 |
| 3 & 5 | .17 | .12 | .10 | .16 | .51 | .46 |
| 3 & 6 | .10 | —.02 | .38 | .38 | .32 | .39 |
| 4 & 5 | .25 | .41 | .50 | .42 | .49 | .59 |
| 4 & 6 | .28 | .43 | .38 | .48 | .54 | .62 |
| 5 & 6 | .34 | .49 | .52 | .36 | .45 | .62 |

NOTE: Table covers six years of repeated testing.

Table 5-17
HIT Penetration Test-Retest Correlations

| Years Correlated | Mexico I | II | III | United States I | II | III |
|---|---|---|---|---|---|---|
| 1 & 2 | .44 | .43 | .39 | .34 | .25 | .52 |
| 1 & 3 | .24 | .36 | .30 | .21 | .15 | .43 |
| 1 & 4 | .24 | .42 | .43 | .14 | .12 | .41 |
| 1 & 5 | .37 | .25 | .30 | .13 | .12 | .21 |
| 1 & 6 | .09 | .04 | .16 | .02 | .06 | .28 |
| 2 & 3 | .15 | .54 | .24 | .36 | .27 | .45 |
| 2 & 4 | .32 | .55 | .37 | .20 | .30 | .45 |
| 2 & 5 | .30 | .46 | .42 | .17 | .37 | .37 |
| 2 & 6 | .10 | .08 | .22 | .10 | .26 | .43 |
| 3 & 4 | .2C | .64 | .33 | .30 | .33 | .30 |
| 3 & 5 | .23 | .08 | .32 | .26 | .38 | .34 |
| 3 & 6 | .19 | .15 | .18 | .26 | .36 | .30 |
| 4 & 5 | .41 | .51 | .49 | .51 | .41 | .35 |
| 4 & 6 | .18 | .32 | .40 | .30 | .37 | .51 |
| 5 & 6 | .21 | .27 | .61 | .34 | .40 | .42 |

NOTE: Table covers six years of repeated testing.

product-moment correlation coefficients. Because of their infrequency and truncation, no test-retest correlations are presented for
these four variables. The last of the inkblot variables, Popular,
was scored only in Austin and is not available for cross-cultural
comparison.

An inspection of the stability coefficients for inkblot variables
reveals several generalizations that are self-evident.

1. Test-retest stability is generally higher for the Austin children than for those in Mexico City, regardless of age group. This
cross-cultural difference is particularly marked for Integration,
Hostility, and Barrier. The higher stability coefficients for the Austin sample may be partly a function of the fact that the variance
for these three variables is larger in the Austin sample than in
the Mexican sample. For six of the inkblot variables—Rejection,
Form Definiteness, Form Appropriateness, Human, Animal, and
Penetration—there appear to be no significant differences between
the Mexican and American children in degree of test-retest stability.

2. Test-retest stability increases, generally, with an increase in
the age of the child. Those children in Group III tend to have the
highest degree of stability, and children in all three groups show
higher test-retest stability in the later years of the project than in
the initial years.

3. Correlations of scores for adjacent years ($r_{12}$, $r_{23}$, $r_{34}$, $r_{45}$, and
$r_{56}$) are generally higher than correlations where the interval between scores is two or more years. In fact the test-retest stability
drops off in a regular fashion with increasing size of interval
between tests, as shown in Table 5-24, where the average test-
retest stability is given for varying intervals between testing.

In summary, most of the inkblot variables show a sufficiently
high degree of stability across time to justify their use as predictors
of later behavior. At the same time, the test-retest correlations are
not so high as to suggest any kind of fixed traits that remain relatively invariant as the child grows older.

## WISC Vocabulary and Block Design

A striking cross-cultural difference in degree of stability for
Vocabulary is evident in the comparison between children in
Mexico City and those in Austin as presented in Table 5-18. The

American children show a high degree of stability in scores even across an interval of five years. The test-retest correlation coefficients generally range in the .60's and .70's even for the youngest children in Group I. By contrast, the children in Mexico City appear much less stable. Test-retest coefficients for the youngest children tend to be in the .20's and .30's, while those in Groups II and III are only slightly higher. In addition, the correlations fall off sharply after an interval of two or more years between tests.

The other Wechsler scale given throughout the six years of repeated testing to all children in both samples was Block Design. An inspection of the stability coefficients for Block Design in Table 5-19 shows only a slight cross-cultural difference. The American children show only slightly greater stability over time than do the Mexican children.

The instability of Vocabulary and the relative stability of Block Design for Mexican school children suggest that the school curriculum and environmental stimulation are much more variable in Mexican culture than among the American school children, where high stability for Vocabulary is the general rule. It remains

Table 5-18
WISC Vocabulary Test-Retest Correlations

| Years Correlated | Mexico | | | United States | | |
|---|---|---|---|---|---|---|
| | I | II | III | I | II | III |
| 1 & 2 | .36 | .47 | .51 | .68 | .55 | .78 |
| 1 & 3 | .28 | .61 | .55 | .72 | .57 | .73 |
| 1 & 4 | .35 | .54 | .47 | .56 | .58 | .70 |
| 1 & 5 | .24 | .40 | .46[a] | .64 | .57 | .67[a] |
| 1 & 6 | .20 | .43 | .26[a] | .45 | .55 | .64[a] |
| 2 & 3 | .52 | .53 | .56 | .68 | .71 | .81 |
| 2 & 4 | .40 | .55 | .56 | .57 | .61 | .80 |
| 2 & 5 | .31 | .53 | .38[a] | .65 | .61 | .74[a] |
| 2 & 6 | .18 | .50 | .14[a] | .66 | .58 | .72[a] |
| 3 & 4 | .62 | .59 | .59 | .72 | .80 | .78 |
| 3 & 5 | .47 | .44 | .43[a] | .76 | .71 | .71[a] |
| 3 & 6 | .41 | .55 | .36[a] | .57 | .72 | .70[a] |
| 4 & 5 | .53 | .47 | .56[a] | .80 | .82 | .74[a] |
| 4 & 6 | .51 | .50 | .36[a] | .59 | .75 | .76[a] |
| 5 & 6 | .38 | .66 | .57[a] | .74 | .77 | .93[a] |

NOTE: Table covers six years of repeated testing.
[a] WAIS Vocabulary was used in place of WISC Vocabulary in years 5 and 6 for Group III.

Table 5-19
WISC Block Design Test-Retest Correlations

| Years Correlated | Mexico | | | United States | | |
|---|---|---|---|---|---|---|
| | I | II | III | I | II | III |
| 1 & 2 | .61 | .59 | .60 | .66 | .66 | .67 |
| 1 & 3 | .59 | .63 | .50 | .58 | .64 | .75 |
| 1 & 4 | .56 | .55 | .56 | .48 | .60 | .58 |
| 1 & 5 | .49 | .52 | .54[a] | .52 | .49 | .69[a] |
| 1 & 6 | .46 | .44 | .55[a] | .50 | .49 | .60[a] |
| 2 & 3 | .65 | .76 | .71 | .71 | .79 | .77 |
| 2 & 4 | .56 | .69 | .72 | .64 | .83 | .72 |
| 2 & 5 | .57 | .66 | .63[a] | .72 | .70 | .68[a] |
| 2 & 6 | .42 | .49 | .59[a] | .64 | .69 | .70[a] |
| 3 & 4 | .78 | .80 | .70 | .75 | .87 | .72 |
| 3 & 5 | .73 | .76 | .56[a] | .72 | .79 | .73[a] |
| 3 & 6 | .48 | .58 | .48[a] | .76 | .83 | .71[a] |
| 4 & 5 | .75 | .79 | .61[a] | .82 | .83 | .70[a] |
| 4 & 6 | .67 | .51 | .55[a] | .80 | .83 | .74[a] |
| 5 & 6 | .60 | .55 | .57[a] | .79 | .80 | .75[a] |

NOTE: Table covers six years of repeated testing.
[a] WAIS Block Design was used in place of WISC Block Design in years 5 and 6 for Group III.

to be seen whether the marked changes in the relative rank order on Vocabulary of the Mexican school children over time can be attributed to any measurable factors in the home environment, in the school, or in the children themselves as revealed by other measures.

## WISC Arithmetic and Picture Completion

The Arithmetic and Picture Completion tests from the Wechsler scales were given in all six years to the three Mexican samples because of special interest in the standardization of the WISC upon Mexican children, with whom the Spanish adaptation had not previously been employed to any extensive degree. In the American samples, these two tests were given only in the first, fourth, fifth, and six years, there not being sufficient time in the testing sessions for the second and third year to include them. Consequently, the average test-retest stability computed for varying intervals between testing, as presented in Table 5-24, is based on partial data from the American samples and complete data from the Mexican samples.

The results for Arithmetic in Table 5-20 are generally comparable across the two cultures for all three groups. While individual stability coefficients vary somewhat, there is no general significant difference in degree of stability across the cultures. The average test-retest stability for Arithmetic, as given in Table 5-24, is significantly lower than that for either Block Design or Vocabulary, the two subtests that were given repeatedly in all samples for the entire six years. At the same time it is sufficiently high, ranging from .36 to .51, depending upon the length of interval between testing, to justify its extensive use in other analyses.

Table 5-21 contains similar results for Picture Completion. The test-retest stability of the Picture Completion scale is essentially the same as that of Arithmetic. There are no apparent cross-cultural differences. The average stability for varying intervals between tests, as given in Table 5-24, is essentially the same as for Arithmetic.

## Human Figure Drawing

Although the Draw-a-Person procedure, calling for two drawings without specifying sex, was used for all six years in Mexico,

Table 5-20
WISC Arithmetic Test-Retest Correlations

| Years Correlated | Mexico | | | United States | | |
|:---:|:---:|:---:|:---:|:---:|:---:|:---:|
| | I | II | III | I | II | III |
| 1 & 2 | .43 | .53 | .51 | — | — | — |
| 1 & 3 | .34 | .49 | .45 | — | — | — |
| 1 & 4 | .46 | .60 | .45 | .27 | .41 | .65 |
| 1 & 5 | .36 | .56 | .53[a] | .42 | .42 | .58[a] |
| 1 & 6 | .26 | .33 | .36[a] | .46 | .33 | .58[a] |
| 2 & 3 | .52 | .48 | .50 | — | — | — |
| 2 & 4 | .50 | .45 | .51 | — | — | — |
| 2 & 5 | .41 | .51 | .44[a] | — | — | — |
| 2 & 6 | .35 | .43 | .58[a] | — | — | — |
| 3 & 4 | .66 | .48 | .57 | — | — | — |
| 3 & 5 | .48 | .52 | .34[a] | — | — | — |
| 3 & 6 | .33 | .46 | .40[a] | — | — | — |
| 4 & 5 | .57 | .49 | .50[a] | .52 | .52 | .69[a] |
| 4 & 6 | .48 | .51 | .52[a] | .58 | .36 | .59[a] |
| 5 & 6 | .39 | .39 | .47[a] | .71 | .40 | .71[a] |

NOTE: Table covers six years of repeated testing.
[a] WAIS Arithmetic was used in place of WISC Arithmetic in years 5 and 6 for Group III.

Table 5-21
WISC Picture Completion Test-Retest Correlations

| Years Correlated | Mexico | | | United States | | |
|---|---|---|---|---|---|---|
| | I | II | III | I | II | III |
| 1 & 2 | .37 | .38 | .60 | — | — | — |
| 1 & 3 | .25 | .37 | .51 | — | — | — |
| 1 & 4 | .37 | .38 | .53 | .19 | .44 | .49 |
| 1 & 5 | .24 | .23 | .38 | .14 | .55 | .26[a] |
| 1 & 6 | —.10 | .36 | .37 | .41 | .47 | .26[a] |
| 2 & 3 | .31 | .53 | .63 | — | — | — |
| 2 & 4 | .40 | .49 | .65 | — | — | — |
| 2 & 5 | .21 | .34 | .48 | — | — | — |
| 2 & 6 | .10 | .38 | .44 | — | — | — |
| 3 & 4 | .49 | .55 | .68 | — | — | — |
| 3 & 5 | .43 | .50 | .32 | — | — | — |
| 3 & 6 | .21 | .34 | .44 | — | — | — |
| 4 & 5 | .51 | .50 | .39 | .38 | .62 | .50[a] |
| 4 & 6 | .44 | .56 | .55 | .38 | .47 | .50[a] |
| 5 & 6 | .54 | .52 | .68 | .68 | .70 | .71[a] |

NOTE: Table covers six years of repeated testing.
[a] WAIS Picture Completion was used in place of WISC Picture Completion in years 5 and 6 for Group III.

it was employed only in the last four years for the American samples. Consequently, only the Harris-Goodenough developmental score can be appropriately applied for the entire six years in all samples. Test-retest stability coefficients for the Harris-Goodenough score on the first figure drawn are presented in Table 5-22.

Stability of the Harris-Goodenough score is consistently high throughout all age groups in both cultures and regardless of the interval between testing. As can be seen in Table 5-24, the Harris-Goodenough score shows the same high degree of stability over time as Location from the Holtzman Inkblot Technique and Vocabulary and Block Design from the Wechsler scales.

The Masculinity-Femininity ratings of the male and female figures drawn represent quite a different score on the Human Figure Drawing Test. As indicated in Chapter 2, the ratings were made on a five-point scale from very masculine to very feminine. Large batches of protocols from children of the same age were rated by experienced judges at a given time to avoid any bias in scoring. Only the last four years are considered comparable cross-culturally, since only one drawing was requested of each child in years 1 and 2 for the American samples.

Test-retest stability coefficients for the Masculinity-Femininity ratings are significantly lower for the Mexican children than for the American children. Most of the test-retest correlations for the three Mexican age groups hovered near zero. Exceptions were the correlations ranging from .32 to .49 for the male figure and .22 to .62 for the female figure when years 5 and 6 are compared. In the American samples, the comparable correlations for years 5 and 6 are .52 to .66 for the male figure and .49 to .69 for the female figure. Unlike the generally low stability for the Mexican data, the average stability coefficients for test-retest intervals of one, two, and three years in Austin are .44, .38, and .45 for the male figure and .49, .45, and .50 for the female figure respectively.

*Time Estimation Test*

Several scores were obtained from the Time Estimation Test, the most important of which is the Delay score obtained by averaging the three independent estimates of the duration of one minute made by the child. Although this test was dropped for first-graders in Austin after it was discovered that many of them

Table 5-22
Harris-Goodenough Score (First Figure) Test-Retest Correlations

| Years Correlated | Mexico | | | United States | | |
|---|---|---|---|---|---|---|
| | I | II | III | I | II | III |
| 1 & 2 | .64 | .65 | .57 | .62 | .62 | .60 |
| 1 & 3 | .47 | .67 | .64 | .50 | .63 | .47 |
| 1 & 4 | .49 | .54 | .56 | .45 | .59 | .48 |
| 1 & 5 | .42 | .49 | .55 | .38 | .46 | .49 |
| 1 & 6 | .49 | .59 | .38 | .43 | .49 | .52 |
| 2 & 3 | .69 | .72 | .64 | .60 | .69 | .68 |
| 2 & 4 | .57 | .60 | .58 | .61 | .68 | .64 |
| 2 & 5 | .68 | .53 | .56 | .50 | .61 | .66 |
| 2 & 6 | .58 | .47 | .54 | .53 | .63 | .63 |
| 3 & 4 | .66 | .68 | .60 | .68 | .74 | .74 |
| 3 & 5 | .67 | .52 | .54 | .51 | .61 | .67 |
| 3 & 6 | .62 | .44 | .61 | .43 | .68 | .69 |
| 4 & 5 | .69 | .57 | .69 | .60 | .69 | .70 |
| 4 & 6 | .63 | .37 | .54 | .58 | .63 | .74 |
| 5 & 6 | .65 | .52 | .59 | .40 | .71 | .62 |

NOTE: Table covers six years of repeated testing.

did not know what a minute was, it was employed for first-graders in Mexico City. The stability coefficients for the Delay score are given in Table 5-23. The youngest children showed very low stability from one year to the next, particularly in the early stages of the longitudinal study. Year 1 scores for Group I in Mexico failed to correlate significantly with any of the subsequent scores obtained in repeated testing, suggesting that the first-graders in Mexico City had the same trouble understanding the nature of the task as did those in Austin, where the test was abandoned in the first year for Group I. The stability of scores does not reach an acceptable level of at least .30 until the third or fourth grade. Even among the older children in Groups II and III, stability frequently drops below .30, suggesting that the ability to estimate the duration of a minute may be in large part a function of other factors in the situation of a more transitory nature, at least for children in a preadolescent stage of development. More stable results are apparent for the older children in both cultures during the last four years of the longitudinal study. The obtained coefficients in the .40's and .50's suggest that the ability to estimate the duration of a minute stabilizes in adolescence.

Table 5-23
TET Delay Score Test-Retest Correlations

| Years Correlated | Mexico I | II | III | United States I | II | III |
|---|---|---|---|---|---|---|
| 1 & 2 | .12 | .23 | .45 | — | .30 | .43 |
| 1 & 3 | .22 | .21 | .37 | — | .38 | .28 |
| 1 & 4 | .15 | .26 | .53 | — | .17 | .27 |
| 1 & 5 | .14 | .11 | .42 | — | .05 | .16 |
| 1 & 6 | .19 | .12 | .42 | — | .29 | .27 |
| 2 & 3 | .22 | .38 | .57 | .41 | .54 | .39 |
| 2 & 4 | .07 | .31 | .52 | .25 | .32 | .28 |
| 2 & 5 | .21 | .19 | .37 | .23 | .14 | .34 |
| 2 & 6 | .15 | .28 | .24 | .26 | .30 | .15 |
| 3 & 4 | .10 | .43 | .56 | .39 | .50 | .41 |
| 3 & 5 | .20 | .39 | .46 | .36 | .29 | .48 |
| 3 & 6 | .28 | .22 | .42 | .30 | .39 | .31 |
| 4 & 5 | .46 | .52 | .51 | .38 | .48 | .50 |
| 4 & 6 | .22 | .25 | .50 | .36 | .46 | .54 |
| 5 & 6 | .41 | .36 | .59 | .28 | .48 | .41 |

NOTE: Table covers six years of repeated testing.

The average test-retest stability with varying interval between testing for the Delay score over the six years of the study is given in Table 5-24. A similar outcome was obtained for the Inaccuracy score derived by summing the absolute deviation in seconds of each estimate from sixty seconds. Inconsistency, the third score for Time Estimation, which was obtained by computing the variance of the three independent estimates, showed no stability through time for any of the age-groups in either culture.

## Embedded Figures Test

Stability coefficients were computed for four scores from the Embedded Figures Test—mean reaction time to correct solution

Table 5-24
Average Test-Retest Stability

| Score | Interval between Tests (in Years) | | | | |
| | 1 | 2 | 3 | 4 | 5 |
|---|---|---|---|---|---|
| Reaction Time | .60 | .55 | .41 | .30 | .29 |
| Rejection | .36 | .35 | .24 | .22 | .21 |
| Location | .75 | .68 | .60 | .51 | .51 |
| Form Definiteness | .56 | .55 | .44 | .40 | .35 |
| Form Appropriateness | .38 | .37 | .30 | .25 | .20 |
| Color | .48 | .38 | .31 | .29 | .25 |
| Shading | .39 | .32 | .21 | .20 | .11 |
| Movement | .60 | .56 | .50 | .44 | .36 |
| Pathognomic Verbalization | .37 | .35 | .22 | .08 | .07 |
| Integration | .43 | .31 | .31 | .33 | .35 |
| Human | .55 | .51 | .41 | .35 | .30 |
| Animal | .54 | .47 | .33 | .34 | .17 |
| Anatomy | .54 | .50 | .36 | .33 | .21 |
| Anxiety | .43 | .40 | .37 | .34 | .21 |
| Hostility | .48 | .46 | .39 | .37 | .26 |
| Barrier | .32 | .31 | .31 | .32 | .35 |
| Penetration | .37 | .31 | .31 | .20 | .10 |
| Vocabulary | .64 | .58 | .56 | .52 | .44 |
| Block Design | .74 | .69 | .63 | .57 | .47 |
| Arithmetic | .51 | .46 | .43 | .43 | .36 |
| Picture Completion | .50 | .46 | .37 | .28 | .35 |
| Harris-Goodenough score | .66 | .59 | .57 | .51 | .49 |
| Time Estimation Test: Delay | .41 | .35 | .26 | .20 | .28 |

NOTE: Scores were obtained during six years of repeated testing.

(Table 5-25), number of items correct (Table 5-26), number of errors (Table 5-27), and number of re-examinations (Table 5-28). Since the Embedded Figures Test was not given to the youngest children in Group I until they reached the fourth year of the study, data for Groups II and III only were employed for computing test-retest correlations.

Mean reaction time to correct solution consistently yields high test-retest correlations, regardless of the interval between testing periods. Of course, the highest stability coefficients are obtained for the oldest children and with a shorter interval of time between tests. The average stability with an interval of only one year between tests is .79, the highest for any test in the present study. The average stability coefficients for two and three years are .72 and .62 respectively. Mean reaction time to correct solution on the Embedded Figures Test is generally higher in stability than that for any other test in the study, regardless of the interval between testing periods. While there is a slight tendency for this score to be more stable among the American children, particularly in Group III, than among the Mexican children, the difference is not large.

The number of items correct on the Embedded Figures Test also proved to be highly stable, especially among the older American children. The average stability ranged from .73 with only a

Table 5-25
Test-Retest Correlations for Mean Reaction Time to Correct Solution on the
Embedded Figures Test

| Years Correlated | Mexico II | Mexico III | United States II | United States III |
|---|---|---|---|---|
| 1 & 2 | .57 | .72 | .69 | .83 |
| 1 & 3 | .59 | .68 | .66 | .74 |
| 1 & 4 | .56 | .56 | .52 | .75 |
| 1 & 5 | .32 | .57 | .53 | .73 |
| 2 & 3 | .78 | .84 | .80 | .82 |
| 2 & 4 | .70 | .63 | .71 | .87 |
| 2 & 5 | .60 | .61 | .70 | .84 |
| 3 & 4 | .84 | .74 | .75 | .85 |
| 3 & 5 | .73 | .72 | .82 | .85 |
| 4 & 5 | .83 | .74 | .76 | .90 |

NOTE: Table covers five years of repeated testing.

Table 5-26
Test-Retest Correlations for Number of Items Correct on the Embedded Figures Test

| Years Correlated | Mexico II | Mexico III | United States II | United States III |
|---|---|---|---|---|
| 1 & 2 | .50 | .64 | .67 | .75 |
| 1 & 3 | .45 | .54 | .67 | .63 |
| 1 & 4 | .41 | .33 | .56 | .67 |
| 1 & 5 | .20 | .30 | .50 | .58 |
| 2 & 3 | .72 | .84 | .77 | .76 |
| 2 & 4 | .63 | .39 | .67 | .83 |
| 2 & 5 | .56 | .49 | .63 | .79 |
| 3 & 4 | .74 | .38 | .72 | .88 |
| 3 & 5 | .67 | .57 | .74 | .80 |
| 4 & 5 | .74 | .34 | .76 | .88 |

NOTE: Table covers five years of repeated testing.

one-year interval between testing periods through .65 for two years and .55 for three years to .40 for a maximum interval of four years. While these values are consistently lower than the stability coefficient for mean reaction time, they are nevertheless sufficiently high to justify use of the score in a variety of situations. Since the number of items correct and the mean reaction to solution time correlate quite highly, for most purposes the more stable mean-reaction-time score should be slightly preferred.

The actual number of errors made in searching for the correct answer on each item of the Embedded Figures Test constitutes still a third score for which stability coefficients across time were computed. The number of errors is less stable than either of the two preceding scores, dropping near zero in several instances. The average stability coefficient drops from .53 for an interval of one year to only .17 for an interval of four years between testing periods.

The fourth score from the Embedded Figures Test, number of re-examinations, is more of a stylistic variable than any of the previous scores. For this reason, it has some interest in its own right in spite of the lack of generally high stability. While individual test-retest correlations ranged from near zero to as high as .76, indicating a great deal of variability across samples and intervals between testing periods, the average stability coefficients are still sufficiently high to justify further systematic analysis of

Table 5-27
Test-Retest Correlations for Number of Errors on the Embedded Figures Test

| Years Correlated | Mexico II | Mexico III | United States II | United States III |
|---|---|---|---|---|
| 1 & 2 | .40 | .41 | .45 | .44 |
| 1 & 3 | .28 | .46 | .48 | .45 |
| 1 & 4 | .21 | .29 | .25 | .41 |
| 1 & 5 | .27 | .15 | .20 | .04 |
| 2 & 3 | .55 | .67 | .56 | .42 |
| 2 & 4 | .44 | .58 | .40 | .17 |
| 2 & 5 | .55 | .49 | .49 | .06 |
| 3 & 4 | .57 | .64 | .54 | .47 |
| 3 & 5 | .50 | .42 | .49 | .14 |
| 4 & 5 | .54 | .51 | .67 | .65 |

NOTE: Table covers five years of repeated testing.

Table 5-28
Test-Retest Correlations for Number of Re-examinations on the Embedded Figures Test

| Years Correlated | Mexico II | Mexico III | United States II | United States III |
|---|---|---|---|---|
| 1 & 2 | .19 | .42 | .66 | .51 |
| 1 & 3 | .13 | .22 | .30 | .41 |
| 1 & 4 | .35 | .15 | .12 | .32 |
| 1 & 5 | .32 | .16 | .14 | .14 |
| 2 & 3 | .19 | .31 | .47 | .48 |
| 2 & 4 | .07 | .39 | .31 | .22 |
| 2 & 5 | .13 | .42 | .21 | .14 |
| 3 & 4 | .26 | .48 | .54 | .64 |
| 3 & 5 | .25 | .40 | .41 | .62 |
| 4 & 5 | .47 | .29 | .57 | .76 |

NOTE: Table covers five years of repeated testing.

the number of re-examinations as an important score on the Embedded Figures Test. The average stabilities for intervals ranging from one to four years are .47, .31, .22, and .15 respectively.

## Test Anxiety Scale for Children

The Test Anxiety Scale for Children was given to all children in both cultures for five consecutive years beginning in year 2. Because the collection of data in Mexico City lagged two years behind that in Austin, it was possible to include the Defensiveness and Lie scales for all five years in Mexico, while only the last four years of the Austin data included these two scales. The Test Anxiety score is the main scale, comprised of thirty items originally developed by Sarason and his colleagues. The Defensiveness Scale, with twenty-seven items, and the Lie Scale, with eleven items, were added later to refine the validity of the Test Anxiety Scale.

Stability coefficients for the Test Anxiety score are presented in Table 5-29. No cross-cultural differences are apparent for any of the three age groups. In general, the stability is sufficiently high to justify extensive study of the Test Anxiety score across time. The average stability coefficients for intervals between testing ranging from one to four years are .68, .50, .46, and .33.

The Defensiveness score, presented in Table 5-30, also reveals no differences between Mexico City and Austin in the degree of stability across time. The level of stability for the Defensiveness score is somewhat below that of the Test Anxiety score. Average coefficients across the four years of repeated testing are .51, .41, .36, and .28.

Unlike the Anxiety and Defensiveness scores, the Lie score does show some significant differences cross-culturally between the children in Mexico City and those in Austin. The differences were particularly pronounced in the early stages of the study, where the stability coefficients for Austin were appreciably higher than those

Table 5-29
TASC Test Anxiety Score Test-Retest Correlations

| Years Correlated | Mexico | | | United States | | |
|---|---|---|---|---|---|---|
| | I | II | III | I | II | III |
| 2 & 3 | .50 | .60 | .64 | .44 | .50 | .63 |
| 2 & 4 | .33 | .42 | .53 | .40 | .39 | .57 |
| 2 & 5 | .26 | .49 | .41 | .30 | .38 | .52 |
| 2 & 6 | .28 | .38 | .39 | .27 | .18 | .45 |
| 3 & 4 | .61 | .59 | .70 | .50 | .59 | .60 |
| 3 & 5 | .52 | .58 | .70 | .46 | .48 | .63 |
| 3 & 6 | .51 | .54 | .62 | .34 | .44 | .58 |
| 4 & 5 | .76 | .71 | .74 | .60 | .60 | .72 |
| 4 & 6 | .34 | .58 | .72 | .50 | .48 | .68 |
| 5 & 6 | .50 | .72 | .79 | .76 | .76 | .76 |

NOTE: Table covers five years of repeated testing.

Table 5-30
TASC Defensiveness Score Test-Retest Correlations

| Years Correlated | Mexico | | | United States | | |
|---|---|---|---|---|---|---|
| | I | II | III | I | II | III |
| 2 & 3 | .25 | .47 | .37 | — | — | — |
| 2 & 4 | .23 | .44 | .34 | — | — | — |
| 2 & 5 | .36 | .37 | .24 | — | — | — |
| 2 & 6 | .28 | .27 | .28 | — | — | — |
| 3 & 4 | .20 | .33 | .44 | .38 | .50 | .59 |
| 3 & 5 | .16 | .38 | .56 | .19 | .51 | .51 |
| 3 & 6 | .07 | .37 | .58 | .09 | .37 | .48 |
| 4 & 5 | .67 | .62 | .66 | .53 | .61 | .64 |
| 4 & 6 | .30 | .47 | .63 | .41 | .42 | .55 |
| 5 & 6 | .35 | .68 | .76 | .52 | .64 | .67 |

NOTE: Table covers five years of repeated testing.

Table 5-31
TASC Lie Score Test-Retest Correlations

| Years Correlated | Mexico | | | United States | | |
|---|---|---|---|---|---|---|
| | I | II | III | I | II | III |
| 2 & 3 | .20 | .27 | .33 | — | — | — |
| 2 & 4 | .11 | .41 | .43 | — | — | — |
| 2 & 5 | .20 | .30 | .36 | — | — | — |
| 2 & 6 | .18 | .18 | .57 | — | — | — |
| 3 & 4 | .32 | .33 | .19 | .40 | .55 | .72 |
| 3 & 5 | .27 | .22 | .26 | .25 | .36 | .51 |
| 3 & 6 | .23 | .04 | .21 | .34 | .28 | .62 |
| 4 & 5 | .64 | .54 | .67 | .55 | .56 | .62 |
| 4 & 6 | .20 | .30 | .70 | .41 | .39 | .61 |
| 5 & 6 | .34 | .48 | .78 | .48 | .70 | .61 |

NOTE: Table covers five years of repeated testing.

for Mexico City. However, as the longitudinal study progressed toward the end of the six-year period, the stability coefficients for Mexico City rose to a level comparable to those in Austin. Average coefficients for the one- to four-year intervals between tests were .44, .36, .28, and .28. While the Lie score is apparently stable enough for short-range predictions over one or two years, the stability of the score falls to a low level for intervals of three or more years except among the older Austin children.

## Object Sorting Test

Test-retest correlation coefficients were computed systematically for eleven scores derived from the Object Sorting Test. Two of these scores—Mean Number of Items per Group and Number of Single Items Not Used—yielded such low levels of stability co-efficients, rarely rising much above .30, that they were dropped from further consideration. Four others—Percent Closed-Public, Percent Closed-Private, Percent Open-Public, and Percent Open-Private—are really part scores on which little additional analysis is contemplated. The remaining four scores—Percent Closed (Total), Percent Open (Total), Percent Public (Total), and Percent Private (Total)—really reflect only two dimensions, the Open-Closed and the Public-Private. For this reason, only Percent Open (Total) and Percent Public (Total) are reported here, the other two being essentially mirror images of them. The third of the three scores for which a detailed analysis is presented here is Number of Groups. Table 5-32 contains the test-retest correlations for these three scores across the three years of repeated testing.

The Austin children generally showed greater stability across

Table 5-32
Test-Retest Correlations for Three Scores on the Object Sorting Test

| Years Correlated | Mexico | | | United States | | |
|---|---|---|---|---|---|---|
| | I | II | III | I | II | III |
| *Number of Groups* | | | | | | |
| 1 & 2 | .09 | .37 | .48 | .29 | .36 | .66 |
| 1 & 3 | .10 | .26 | .27 | .22 | .28 | .67 |
| 2 & 3 | .33 | .45 | .58 | .35 | .62 | .73 |
| *Percent of Open (Total)* | | | | | | |
| 1 & 2 | .25 | .22 | .41 | .30 | .33 | .46 |
| 1 & 3 | .20 | .31 | .32 | .33 | .29 | .37 |
| 2 & 3 | .30 | .32 | .54 | .41 | .43 | .40 |
| *Percent of Public (Total)* | | | | | | |
| 1 & 2 | .30 | .18 | .42 | .13 | .31 | .42 |
| 1 & 3 | .25 | .17 | .26 | .41 | .12 | .50 |
| 2 & 3 | .11 | .35 | .34 | .03 | .09 | .56 |

NOTE: Table covers three years of repeated testing.

time for Number of Groups, the most stable of the three scores
from the Object Sorting Test. Percent Open (Total) and Percent
Public (Total) do not reveal any significant cross-cultural differences.

As in most of the other stability studies, the older children
tended to be more stable through time in their test performance
than the younger ones. All three of the variables from the Object
Sorting Test are sufficiently stable, on the average, to justify further study, although the correlations are not high.

*Other Tests*

Both the Perceptual Maturity Scale and the Word Association
Test were given to all children in the last three years of the longitudinal study. Test-retest correlations for the Perceptual Maturity
Scale are presented in Table 5-33. A marked cross-cultural difference is apparent for all three of the age groups. The score on the
Perceptual Maturity Scale shows a fairly high degree of stability
for the United States, ranging from .42 to .83. For the Mexican
children, however, the test-retest correlations tend to be close to
zero. The only exceptions are the correlations between years 5 and
6 for Groups I and III. Since the means and standard deviations
for the Perceptual Maturity Scale score do not vary markedly
across the two cultures in any of the age groups or years correlated, it can only be concluded that this particular test is highly
unstable for most of the Mexican children, though highly stable
for most of the American children.

For the Word Association Test, three new scores more appropriate for cross-cultural comparison were developed and analyzed
(see Chapter 7) across the last three years. As shown in Table

Table 5-33
Test-Retest Correlations for Perceptual Maturity Scale

| Years Correlated | Mexico | | | United States | | |
|---|---|---|---|---|---|---|
| | I | II | III | I | II | III |
| 4 & 5 | .19 | .22 | .05 | .63 | .56 | .65 |
| 4 & 6 | .06 | .02 | −.06 | .58 | .42 | .65 |
| 5 & 6 | .38 | .16 | .48 | .83 | .46 | .75 |

NOTE: Table covers three years of repeated testing.

5-34, the two paradigmatic and the syntagmatic scores showed satisfactory stability through time for nearly all of the groups.

In Austin the Conceptual Styles Test was given only to Group I and for only two consecutive years, beginning in the second year of the longitudinal study. In Mexico City, however, this test was given to all three groups for the first three years of the study. Consequently, the only comparable cross-cultural data to report are the stability coefficients in Group I for years 2 and 3. Nevertheless, test-retest coefficients were computed for all of the Mexican data even though no comparable American data existed.

Four scores from the Conceptual Styles Test were analyzed for test-retest stability—Time, Number of Analytical Responses, Number of Relational Responses, and Number of Inferential-Categorical Responses. The test-retest coefficients for CST Time varied from .06 to .31 among the three Mexican groups, with an average coefficient of only .24. Test-retest stability for Group I of the American sample was only .16. These results suggest that CST Time is highly unstable over an interval of one or two years.

The part scores derived for analytical, relational, and inferential-categorical responses fared somewhat better on the Conceptual Styles Test. Among the Mexican children, the average stability

Table 5-34
Test-Retest Correlations for Three Scores on the Word Association Test

| Years Correlated | Mexico | | | United States | | |
|---|---|---|---|---|---|---|
| | I | II | III | I | II | III |
| | Proportion Noun-Noun Paradigmatic | | | | | |
| 4 & 5 | .71 | .72 | .50 | .43 | .05 | .63 |
| 4 & 6 | .69 | .65 | .66 | .57 | .19 | .59 |
| 5 & 6 | .62 | .71 | .67 | .60 | .13 | .64 |
| | Proportion Verb-Verb Plus Adjective-Adjective Paradigmatic | | | | | |
| 4 & 5 | .51 | .44 | .63 | .21 | .24 | .74 |
| 4 & 6 | .41 | .50 | .55 | .14 | .39 | .62 |
| 5 & 6 | .19 | .72 | .79 | .24 | .26 | .70 |
| | Proportion Syntagmatic | | | | | |
| 4 & 5 | .65 | .67 | .62 | .41 | .09 | .77 |
| 4 & 6 | .58 | .65 | .61 | .52 | .27 | .68 |
| 5 & 6 | .40 | .76 | .71 | .50 | .53 | .73 |

NOTE: Table covers three years of repeated testing.

coefficients for the analytical, relational, and inferential-categorical scores were .55, .53, and .40 respectively. For the American children in Group I only, the test-retest reliability over a one-year interval was .34 for analytical, .49 for relational, and .29 for inferential-categorical scores. These results suggest that the three different kinds of conceptual styles postulated by Kagan in the Conceptual Styles Test as analytical, relational, and inferential-categorical have sufficient test-retest stability to justify further study. Reaction time, on the other hand, is too unstable for most measurement purposes, particularly where any passage of time is involved.

The second of Kagan's tests employed in the present study, the Visual Fractionation Test, was also given to all three groups of Mexican children in the first three years of the longitudinal study. While all three groups of children in Austin were given the Visual Fractionation Test, it was limited to two successive years, beginning in the second year of the project. Five scores were analyzed systematically for test-retest stability across two years for Austin and three years for Mexico City—number of trials to complete the learning task, mean reaction time for all twenty-four items in the test, and mean reaction time for the eight items involving elements, the eight items involving figures, and the eight items involving grounds. In general, the stability coefficients for all five variables were rather low. Ranging from .10 to .46, the stability coefficients for number of trials to complete the learning task averaged only .27. Mean reaction time for all twenty-four items showed the greatest range of stability, from .11 across the first two years in Mexican Group II to .65 across years 2 and 3 for American Group II. The average stability coefficient for mean reaction time was .30. The stability coefficients for the part reaction time scores on elements, figures, and grounds were essentially the same as the values for mean reaction time on the total test. While slightly more stable than scores for the Conceptual Styles Test, the Visual Fractionation Test yields relatively unstable scores that are likely to be of little value in predictive studies across time.

The test-retest stability over time of the various measures employed, especially over the first several years of the study, played an important role in determining which ones should be retained for the next year of testing and which ones should be discarded. While it was recognized that high test-retest stability is desirable, it was also recognized that such stability could be too high over periods of rapid growth and development in childhood. Unduly high stability coefficients in such a case would mean that the score is not sensitive enough to measure expected normal fluctuations in a developing individual. The more dynamic a personality variable, for example, the more likely it is to change through time.

In Chapter 6, the final chapter in Part Two, are reported the relationships of those test measures that were deemed suitably reliable for systematic correlation with other variables within each of the two cultures, using the complete samples in the United States and Mexico.

# 6. Correlations across Variables within Each Culture

The number of quantitative scores available for each child in each year runs into the hundreds. The sheer magnitude of the task involved in analyzing all possible correlations among such variables requires the development of a selective strategy for concentrating upon the most significant findings, both positive and negative. Preliminary studies of the intercorrelations among test variables were carried out routinely, year by year, as the data were collected in the two cultures. Decisions concerning whether or not a given test should be included in a subsequent year's test battery were based, in part, upon these early studies, as well as upon the degree of test-retest stability over the first several years, the amount of time taken for administration of the tests, and the extent to which new tests were judged to be of greater significance for inclusion in the test battery. As indicated earlier, only the Holtzman Inkblot Technique, the Human Figure Drawing Test, and the Vocabulary and Block Design subtests from the WISC or WAIS were given to every child in all six years of repeated testing. Most other test scores are available for two or more years, although not necessarily in all three groups within both cultures. A few scores, such as those taken from the interview with the mother, from the Parent-Attitude Survey, and from the Personality Research Form, are available in one year only. A small number of variables—the sociometric peer ratings, the grade-point average in high school, and the teacher ratings—are available only for certain of the age groups within the Austin sample. Likewise, such variables as the attitude scales from the inventory dealing with views of life and sociocultural premises and the reading and arithmetic achievement test scores from Manuel's Interamerican Tests are available only for selected subsamples of the Mexico City children. While none of these supplementary data are of value in cross-cultural comparisons, they are mentioned here because of their special value in shedding further light upon the meaning of the data obtained more systematically upon all children in both cultures.

Dimensional studies of the relationship among variables within a single test were carried out routinely for the intercorrelations among test scores obtained in the first year that a given test was administered. Because extensive studies of the dimensions underlying inkblot perception in the HIT had been done previously, factor-analytic studies of the primary dimensions in the HIT are of special interest. Similar methodological studies with subscores from other tests where a number of scores are derived, such as the Personality Research Form and the Object Sorting Test, were also carried out as a means of reducing the variables worthy of concentrated study to a more manageable number. The emphasis upon cross-cultural comparisons dictated still further reductions in certain variables that were available in only the Austin or the Mexico City sample. A total of sixty-two measures survived these earlier studies. Cross-cultural comparisons of similarities and differences in the correlations across variables presented in this chapter are limited to this reduced set of measures.

The complexities, as well as the power, of the cross-cultural longitudinal design employed in the present study are worthy of note before discussing the results of the correlational studies. Unlike the usual situation, where only one or two samples are studied in a correlational analysis of many variables, a total of thirty-six replications of each correlation are available for the variables in the core test battery. For example, the correlation between Movement on the Holtzman Inkblot Technique and Vocabulary from the WISC is replicated thirty-six times—six years of repeated testing in each of the six groups. Since the number of cases in each bivariate correlation is fairly large, ranging as high as 150 in some instances, the results contain far more stability than is the usual case. In one sense, the thirty-six correlations for a given bivariate relationship can be thought of as an empirical distribution of obtained correlations, the mean and standard deviation of which accurately describe the nature of the relationship. Such a sampling distribution permits strong inferences concerning the "true" relationship that ordinarily are not possible.

For many of the test scores not available in all six groups and six years, the amount of replication of bivariate correlations is still impressive, ranging from eighteen for the Object Sorting Test to thirty for the Test Anxiety Scale for Children. Of course, one can also argue that the relationship between two variables ought to change across age groups and cultures, reducing the number of genuine replications. Indeed, in the strict sense of the word, not even the repeated measures can be thought of as "replications," since there are practice and adaptation effects and the child in each case is a year older when tested a second time. Nevertheless, from any scientific point of view, where generalizations are desirable, it should be clear that the correlation between two variables, such as Movement and Vocabulary, ought to show at least some consistency across age groups and repeated measures, if not across cultures. In any event, the present data provide an opportunity that is rarely, if ever, available for examining such stability of findings concerning relationships among variables that typically are reported in the literature as based upon only one or two samples.

The research design also permits examination of the relationships between selected variables in the early years of the study with other variables collected toward the end of the study. Because the total number of possible "lagged" correlations is staggeringly high, only a few highly selected relationships of this kind will be reported. Some of the data in the early stages of the longitudinal study can be thought of as potential "predictors" or precursors of later personality and mental development. Likewise, certain of the variables toward the end of the six years can be considered "outcome" or criterion variables for such prediction studies. For example, one can ask whether or not selected measures from the first two years of the study proved to be significantly related to the personality scales in the Personality Research Form that was administered in the sixth year of the study. In most cases the search for such precursors of later personality characteristics is a way of generating interesting hypotheses about personality development rather than rigorously testing them. The study of correlations between different types of variables as a means of generating new information about personality requires considerable caution, since many factors, some unknown and some of a chance nature, can actually influence the obtained coefficients.

For clarity of presentation, the findings of intercorrelational studies are organized by data domains similar to those outlined in Chapters 3 and 5, as well as in the subsequent chapters of the book. Results for the dimensional studies of the Holtzman Inkblot Technique are presented first, followed by dimensional studies of the measures of mental ability and analyses of the interrelationships among the cognitive-perceptual style variables. Then dimensional studies of the personality-attitudinal measures are summarized. After achieving a better understanding of the variables within each data domain, the correlations across domains and across time are interpreted.

### DIMENSIONS WITHIN THE HOLTZMAN INKBLOT TECHNIQUE

Intercorrelation matrices for inkblot scores were computed routinely for each of the thirty-six sets of data—two cultures by three age groups replicated six times. A casual analysis of these matrices quickly suggests that the magnitude of correlation between any two inkblot variables is likely to vary from one sample to the next. For example, the correlation between Animal and Color in the six matrices for year 1 alone ranges from $-.09$ to $-.38$. In general the amount of variation is relatively small, and in no case is there a marked shift in direction of the relationship between any two variables across different correlation matrices. One could go through each of the pairs of inkblot variables noting the average correlation and range of coefficients. While many such zero-order correlations may be of interest in their own right, it is obvious that a much more systematic method is needed to summarize the patterns of relationships. Factor analysis is a mathematical technique ideally suited for reducing the observed correlations in a matrix to a smaller number of factors that remain relatively invariant in meaning, by allowing the pattern of scores contributing to each factor to shift as needed to accommodate sample differences. The resulting distribution of factor loadings for each inkblot score can then be studied across the different samples to gain further insight into the probable meaning of the score.

Three major technical problems in the application of factor analysis are (*a*) determining how many factors to extract; (*b*) deciding whether to use orthogonal factors or permit them to be correlated; and (*c*) determining how best to rotate the factors in order to get the clearest solution. Use of a high-speed computer makes it possible to employ the principal-components method of factor extraction, with enough iterations of the analysis to stabilize the communality estimates in the principal diagonal. Earlier factor-analytic studies of the HIT repeatedly yielded six factors as the minimum number necessary to explain most of the common variance in the correlation matrix (Holtzman et al. 1961). Since four inkblot scores—Space, Sex, Abstract, and Balance—were omitted from the correlational studies because of their rare occurrence, it was thought that in some samples only five factors might emerge rather than six. Therefore, the following rule was developed for deciding when to stop extracting factors. Six factors were to be extracted except when the eigenvalue for a principal component fell below 1.00, in which case the associated factor was dropped.

An orthogonal rather than an oblique solution was obtained in spite of the fact that in several instances correlated factors might have yielded a clearer picture. Factor analyses in the earlier standardization program for the HIT were all orthogonal. In addition, computational procedures are simpler and more objective for dealing with the orthogonal solution.

The normalized varimax method for rotating the principal axis solution into an approximate simple structure was employed as a first step in achieving a final solution to the rotation problem. Further rotations using graphic methods were necessary in most cases to achieve a final solution consistent with the solutions obtained in the earlier standardization studies.

The six factors repeatedly found in the earlier standardization studies across all ages of normal individuals, as well as mental patients, are as follows:

Factor 1: defined by Integration, Movement, Human, Popular, and Form Definiteness.

Factor 2: defined by Color, Shading, and Form Definiteness (reversed).

Factor 3: defined by Pathognomic Verbalization, Anxiety, Hostility, and Movement.

Factor 4: defined by Location and Form Appropriateness.

Factor 5: defined by Reaction Time, Rejection, and Animal (reversed).

Factor 6 (when present): usually defined by Anatomy, Sex, or Abstract.

It was hypothesized that these same factors would emerge in the present study, although there might be important differences across the different age groups and cultures that would shed light on the meaning of inkblot variables. These inkblot scores defining each factor can be thought of as marker variables to identify factors in the current analyses. From the earlier work one would also expect some additional inkblot scores occasionally to show significant loadings on particular factors. Location (reversed), Anxiety, Hostility, and Barrier often showed moderately high loadings on Factor 1 in the standardization studies. Location (reversed) occasionally appears on Factor 2, while Anatomy and Penetration sometimes show up on Factor 3. In addition to these marker variables and "follower" variables, in any given factor analytic solution, there are likely to be several unexpectedly high loadings of particular inkblot scores on a given factor. These vary from sample to sample and often provide information on a probable shift in meaning of the inkblot score in question.

Results for the factor analyses of HIT intercorrelations for year 1 are presented separately for each age group and culture in Tables 6-1 to 6-6. Loadings of .40 or greater are set in bold type. The marker variables in each matrix are indicated. The proportion of total variance for each inkblot score that can be considered as shared or common variance with the other inkblot variables is known as the *communality*, or $h^2$. Subtracting the communality

Table 6-1
HIT Factor Analysis: United States, Group I, Year I

| Inkblot Score | Factor Loading | | | | | | $h^2$ | $u^2$ |
|---|---|---|---|---|---|---|---|---|
| | 1 | 2 | 3 | 4 | 5 | 6 | | |
| Reaction Time | −12 | 02 | −19 | 09 | 90ᵃ | 02 | 87 | 05 |
| Rejection | −12 | −01 | −01 | 17 | 92ᵃ | 02 | 91 | — |
| Location | −29 | −08 | −43 | 52ᵃ | −33 | 18 | 67 | 28 |
| Form Definiteness | 44ᵃ | −77ᵃ | −12 | −11 | 04 | 03 | 84 | 06 |
| Form Appropriateness | 02 | 37 | −22 | 76ᵃ | −01 | −14 | 79 | 07 |
| Color | 06 | 70ᵃ | −28 | 16 | −25 | 04 | 67 | 26 |
| Shading | 11 | 72ᵃ | −03 | −27 | −19 | −30 | 73 | 01 |
| Movement | 71ᵃ | 00 | 50ᵃ | 21 | −07 | −01 | 82 | 04 |
| Pathognomic Verbalization | 00 | 07 | 66ᵃ | −42 | −03 | −03 | 62 | 28 |
| Integration | 80ᵃ | 10 | −18 | −10 | 04 | −19 | 77 | — |
| Human | 71ᵃ | −37 | −14 | −02 | −15 | 20 | 74 | 08 |
| Animal | 21 | −62 | 10 | −28 | −22ᵃ | −43 | 73 | 07 |
| Anatomy | −21 | 11 | 08 | −59 | −08 | 64ᵃ | 85 | 06 |
| Anxiety | 38 | −02 | 72ᵃ | −12 | −16 | 14 | 72 | 06 |
| Hostility | 45 | −12 | 76ᵃ | 04 | −22 | 07 | 85 | 03 |
| Barrier | 40 | −28 | −17 | −10 | −14 | −58 | 61 | 14 |
| Penetration | 23 | 12 | 25 | −51 | −14 | 36 | 56 | 25 |
| Popular | 73ᵃ | −11 | −21 | 31 | −06 | 11 | 71 | — |

NOTE: Decimals are omitted. N (number of students in sample) = 133.
ᵃ Marker variable from earlier studies.
$h^2$: communality
$u^2$: unique

for a given score from its internal consistency reliability estimate yields an estimate of the proportion of the total variance within the score that can be considered as *unique*, or $u^2$. When $u^2$ is close to zero, it means that essentially all of the reliable variance due to individual differences within the inkblot score is shared in common with one or more of the other inkblot scores. When $u^2$ is substantial, it means that a large part of the reliable variance in the inkblot score is unique.

Inspection of the values for $u^2$ in Tables 6-1 through 6-6 reveals that Reaction Time, Rejection, Location, and Pathognomic Verbalization usually have a substantial proportion of reliable variance that is unique. By contrast, nearly all of the reliable variance is shared in common with other inkblot scores for Form Definiteness, Shading, Movement, Integration, Anxiety, Hostility, Barrier, and Penetration. With only an occasional exception in a specific group, the use of factor scores to represent the common variance present in these latter inkblot scores would capture nearly all of the reliable variance that is present.

Analysis of the pattern of loadings for each factor across the six samples yields both similarities and differences worthy of note. The highlights of this analysis are presented below, one factor at a time.

*Factor 1*

Movement, Integration, and Human invariably have high loadings on Factor 1. The other two marker variables, Form Definiteness and Popular, vary somewhat from one sample to the next. While Popular shows high loadings for the three samples of Austin children, it is only moderately loaded on Factor 1 in the three Mexican samples. In Groups I and III for Mexico, Popular has a higher loading on one of the other factors, indicating that it is measuring something different in Mexico than in the United

Table 6-2
HIT Factor Analysis: Mexico, Group I, Year I

| Inkblot Score | Factor Loading | | | | | | $h^2$ | $u^2$ |
|---|---|---|---|---|---|---|---|---|
| | 1 | 2 | 3 | 4 | 5 | 6 | | |
| Reaction Time | −13 | −30 | −11 | 10 | 65[a] | −15 | 57 | 37 |
| Rejection | −16 | −27 | −07 | −17 | 75[a] | 11 | 72 | 22 |
| Location | −03 | −13 | −17 | 76[a] | −22 | −11 | 69 | 25 |
| Form Definiteness | 55[a] | −59[a] | −22 | −14 | −30 | −11 | 83 | 08 |
| Form Appropriateness | −11 | 35 | 23 | 68[a] | 27 | −01 | 73 | 17 |
| Color | −32 | 69[a] | 18 | 00 | 00 | −15 | 65 | 29 |
| Shading | 36 | 58[a] | −32 | −05 | −17 | 02 | 60 | 01 |
| Movement | 66[a] | 29 | 40[a] | 16 | 08 | 03 | 72 | 12 |
| Pathognomic Verbalization | 38 | 10 | 61[a] | −23 | −03 | 19 | 63 | 21 |
| Integration | 72[a] | 21 | 14 | 18 | 03 | −06 | 62 | — |
| Human | 57[a] | −18 | −14 | 24 | −35 | 23 | 62 | 22 |
| Animal | 20 | −47 | 02 | −24 | −33[a] | −55 | 74 | 18 |
| Anatomy | −06 | −08 | 08 | −13 | −15 | 82[a] | 73 | 10 |
| Anxiety | 12 | 11 | 79[a] | −12 | −11 | −01 | 68 | 24 |
| Hostility | 29 | 14 | 82[a] | −07 | −09 | −05 | 79 | 16 |
| Barrier | 49 | 11 | −36 | 02 | −05 | −30 | 49 | 21 |
| Penetration | 58 | 36 | 07 | −17 | 16 | 03 | 56 | — |
| Popular | 32[a] | −37 | −30 | 18 | −28 | −36 | 59 | — |

NOTE: Decimals are omitted. N = 150.
[a] Marker variable from earlier studies.
$h^2$: communality
$u^2$: unique

Table 6-3
HIT Factor Analysis: United States, Group II, Year 1

| Inkblot Score | Factor Loading | | | | | h² | u² |
|---|---|---|---|---|---|---|---|
| | 1 | 2 | 3 | 4 | 5 | | |
| Reaction Time | −25 | −04 | −26 | 01 | 80ᵃ | 78 | 19 |
| Rejection | −19 | −06 | −03 | 21 | 87ᵃ | 84 | 09 |
| Location | −54 | −21 | −39 | 48ᵃ | −15 | 71 | 26 |
| Form Definiteness | 23ᵃ | −74ᵃ | −29 | 22 | 00 | 73 | 07 |
| Form Appropriateness | −07 | 31 | −09 | 66ᵃ | 46 | 76 | 05 |
| Color | 29 | 74ᵃ | 29 | −19 | −11 | 78 | 05 |
| Shading | 37 | 64ᵃ | 02 | −07 | −21 | 59 | — |
| Movement | 71ᵃ | −08 | 48ᵃ | −15 | −17 | 80 | 07 |
| Pathognomic Verbalization | 55 | −08 | 48ᵃ | 05 | −20 | 59 | 18 |
| Integration | 77ᵃ | −21 | 08 | 16 | 07 | 70 | 15 |
| Human | 60ᵃ | −46 | 04 | 02 | −18 | 59 | 22 |
| Animal | 24 | −43 | 11 | 07 | −51ᵃ | 56 | 17 |
| Anatomy | −41 | 28 | 52 | −34 | −08 | 63 | 17 |
| Anxiety | 35 | −05 | 73ᵃ | −26 | −20 | 79 | — |
| Hostility | 32 | −12 | 73ᵃ | −23 | −25 | 80 | — |
| Barrier | 50 | −04 | −29 | −58 | −07 | 68 | — |
| Penetration | −05 | 21 | 51 | −66 | −07 | 73 | 02 |
| Popular | 67ᵃ | −06 | 05 | −11 | −02 | 48 | — |

NOTE: Decimals are omitted. N = 142.
ᵃ Marker variable from earlier studies.
h²: communality
u²: unique

States. Since Popular was rescaled in Mexico rather than consisting of the same concepts as in the United States, it is not
possible to make a precise comparison for Popular across the two
cultures. It is partly for this reason that Popular was dropped
from further analysis in cross-cultural comparisons. Form Definiteness is shared as a marker variable with Factor 2. For this
reason its loadings tend to be somewhat smaller on Factor 1 than
is the case for Integration and Human, which are two of the primary marker variables for Factor 1 alone.

Location, Anxiety, Hostility, and Barrier are characteristically
follower variables for Factor 1, sometimes showing high loadings
on this factor and at other times showing low loadings. Location
appears to be more important as a variable identified with Factor
1 in the United States than in Mexico. Anxiety and Hostility, two
marker variables for Factor 3, are closely associated with Factor 1

in the oldest age group (seventh-graders), regardless of culture. It is also interesting to note that Pathognomic Verbalization and Penetration have unusually high loadings on Factor 1 for the seventh-graders in both cultures and to some extent for the American fourth-graders and Mexican first-graders. Only two of the six groups, American first-graders and Mexican fourth-graders, show completely consistent patterns for Factor 1.

On the basis of the defining variables and other independent studies of their validity, a high amount of Factor 1 is generally interpreted as indicative of well-organized ideational activity, good imaginative capacity, well-differentiated ego boundaries, and awareness of conventional concepts. The shifting pattern of loadings across the two cultures and the three age groups suggests that this interpretation should be qualified, depending upon the group in question. In particular, for the seventh-graders in both cultures,

Table 6-4
HIT Factor Analysis: Mexico, Group II, Year I

| Inkblot Score | Factor Loading | | | | | | $h^2$ | $u^2$ |
|---|---|---|---|---|---|---|---|---|
| | 1 | 2 | 3 | 4 | 5 | 6 | | |
| Reaction Time | —04 | —02 | —17 | 28 | 72[a] | —18 | 66 | 28 |
| Rejection | —19 | —10 | —29 | —34 | 67[a] | 21 | 72 | 15 |
| Location | —19 | —42 | —06 | 76[a] | —19 | —03 | 83 | 12 |
| Form Definiteness | 37[a] | —73[a] | —01 | —07 | 15 | —20 | 78 | 08 |
| Form Appropriateness | 03 | 21 | —01 | 78[a] | 04 | 08 | 66 | 16 |
| Color | —04 | 81[a] | 17 | 04 | 05 | —06 | 70 | 14 |
| Shading | —15 | 13[a] | 51 | 25 | 17 | 35 | 52 | 03 |
| Movement | 78[a] | 16 | 35[a] | 15 | 06 | 11 | 81 | 02 |
| Pathognomic Verbalization | 37 | 06 | 51[a] | —17 | 15 | —11 | 49 | 03 |
| Integration | 82[a] | 01 | 28 | —06 | 07 | 11 | 79 | — |
| Human | 73[a] | —26 | —27 | 07 | —12 | 29 | 80 | 01 |
| Animal | 37 | —10 | 08 | 13 | —01[a] | —80 | 81 | 02 |
| Anatomy | —34 | 03 | 21 | —69 | —16 | 15[a] | 69 | 17 |
| Anxiety | 17 | 02 | 62[a] | —23 | —25 | —09 | 54 | 09 |
| Hostility | 48 | —12 | 62[a] | 07 | —09 | —22 | 69 | — |
| Barrier | 25 | —43 | 44 | 34 | 11 | —09 | 58 | — |
| Penetration | 35 | —03 | 46 | 02 | 31 | 13 | 46 | 23 |
| Popular | 44[a] | —09 | —31 | 28 | —28 | —25 | 59 | — |

NOTE: Decimals are omitted. N = 143.
[a] Marker variable from earlier studies.
$h^2$: communality
$u^2$: unique

Table 6-5
HIT Factor Analysis: United States, Group III, Year I

| Inkblot Score | Factor Loading | | | | | h² | u² |
|---|---|---|---|---|---|---|---|
| | 1 | 2 | 3 | 4 | 5 | | |
| Reaction Time | −14 | −24 | −16 | 29 | 71[a] | 69 | 18 |
| Rejection | −35 | 13 | −50 | 19 | 08[a] | 44 | 44 |
| Location | −50 | −33 | 02 | 58[a] | 23 | 76 | 19 |
| Form Definiteness | 48[a] | −72[a] | 13 | 17 | 18 | 83 | 03 |
| Form Appropriateness | 13 | 03 | −05 | 89[a] | −05 | 82 | — |
| Color | 27 | 74[a] | 23 | −32 | −05 | 79 | 06 |
| Shading | 36 | 69[a] | 39 | −04 | 22 | 81 | — |
| Movement | 84[a] | 16 | 20[a] | −13 | 04 | 80 | 08 |
| Pathognomic Verbalization | 65 | 07 | 19[a] | −12 | −15 | 50 | 29 |
| Integration | 87[a] | −01 | 01 | −10 | −07 | 78 | 04 |
| Human | 78[a] | −34 | −33 | 05 | 04 | 86 | — |
| Animal | −04 | −64 | 63 | 01 | −01[a] | 81 | — |
| Anatomy | −11 | 19 | −11 | 16 | −82 | 76 | — |
| Anxiety | 72 | 31 | 29[a] | −13 | −14 | 75 | 05 |
| Hostility | 76 | 17 | 36[a] | 00 | −11 | 75 | 03 |
| Barrier | 59 | 15 | 33 | 13 | 18 | 53 | — |
| Penetration | 51 | 37 | 32 | 06 | −39 | 67 | — |
| Popular | 66[a] | 22 | 17 | 16 | 21 | 60 | 12 |

NOTE: Decimals are omitted. N = 142.
[a] Marker variable from earlier studies.
h²: communality
u²: unique

Factor 1 and Factor 3 are closely intertwined. Since a high amount of Factor 3 is generally interpreted as indicative of disordered thought processes coupled with an active though disturbed fantasy life, interpretation of Factor 1 for the seventh-graders in both cultures must be altered. A moderately high amount of Pathognomic Verbalization, Anxiety, and Hostility in these essentially normal young adolescents may not be indicative of psychopathology at all. Or still another way of viewing these results is to consider that seventh-graders are just beginning to enter the turmoils of early adolescence, with a welling up of primary affective processes that break loose from ego control in an active fantasy life. An individual who is low on all of the variables defining Factor 1 for the seventh-graders in Austin and Mexico City is a person who yields a somewhat sparsely worded test protocol devoid of human content or evidence of imaginative fantasy productions.

## Factor 2

Color, Shading, and Form Definiteness (reversed) generally have high loadings on Factor 2 in every group. The only exception is the absence of a loading for Shading on Factor 2 among the Mexican fourth-graders. In this particular case, Shading is loaded on Factor 3, along with Pathognomic Verbalization, Anxiety, and Hostility, rather than on Factor 2. The occasional negative loadings for Location on Factor 2 are consistent with the findings that high use of Color and Shading is associated with use of the whole inkblot rather than small areas. Unlike the samples of children in the earlier standardization studies of the HIT, five of the six samples in the current study reveal significant negative loadings on Factor 2 for Animal. The only exception is the Mexican fourth-graders. These results suggest that children use color and shading

Table 6-6
HIT Factor Analysis: Mexico, Group III, Year I

| Inkblot Score | Factor Loading | | | | | | $h^2$ | $u^2$ |
| --- | --- | --- | --- | --- | --- | --- | --- | --- |
| | 1 | 2 | 3 | 4 | 5 | 6 | | |
| Reaction Time | −12 | −12 | −03 | 32 | 73[a] | −19 | 72 | 24 |
| Rejection | −13 | −01 | −29 | −35 | 72[a] | −09 | 75 | 16 |
| Location | −22 | −33 | −43 | 60[a] | −10 | 06 | 73 | 22 |
| Form Definiteness | 33[a] | −75[a] | 09 | 06 | −16 | −04 | 71 | 18 |
| Form Appropriateness | 24 | 23 | −41 | 53[a] | 30 | 19 | 69 | 08 |
| Color | 15 | 83[a] | 03 | 08 | 13 | −12 | 75 | 03 |
| Shading | 13 | 74[a] | −04 | −26 | 06 | 17 | 67 | — |
| Movement | 71[a] | 10 | 48[a] | −03 | 04 | −19 | 81 | 04 |
| Pathognomic Verbalization | 51 | −05 | 56[a] | −21 | −03 | 15 | 67 | 20 |
| Integration | 76[a] | 16 | 30 | −03 | −03 | −17 | 73 | 04 |
| Human | 70[a] | −23 | −08 | 10 | −14 | −29 | 67 | 12 |
| Animal | 08 | −59 | 10 | −12 | −45[a] | −23 | 64 | 07 |
| Anatomy | −02 | 10 | 11 | −12 | −05 | 88[a] | 82 | — |
| Anxiety | 55 | −13 | 55[a] | −23 | −01 | 08 | 68 | 02 |
| Hostility | 54 | −25 | 52[a] | −13 | −02 | 08 | 68 | — |
| Barrier | 06 | −01 | 44 | 65 | −22 | −14 | 70 | — |
| Penetration | 40 | 29 | 57 | 17 | 02 | 20 | 63 | — |
| Popular | 48[a] | −16 | −66 | 07 | −09 | −10 | 72 | — |

NOTE: Decimals are omitted. N = 150.
[a] Marker variable from earlier studies.
$h^2$: communality
$u^2$: unique

as stimulus determinants only when they cannot find a familiar animal form. This bipolar factor involves sensitivity to the stimulus qualities of the inkblots. The positive pole of this factor would indicate overreactivity to the color or shading, while the negative pole would indicate primary concern for form alone as a determinant.

*Factor 3*

This factor is generally defined by Pathognomic Verbalization, Movement, Anxiety, and Hostility. The earlier studies with adults and psychiatric patients showed a clear separation of Factor 3 and Factor 1 as two independent dimensions. For most of the samples in the present study, however, Factor 3 tends to be correlated with Factor 1, making it difficult to separate the two factors in an orthogonal solution. This interdependence of the two factors is particularly evident among the seventh-graders, as noted earlier. Among the American seventh-graders, Factor 3 shows little resemblance to the typical pattern evident in the other five samples, largely because of the close identification of Pathognomic Verbalization, Anxiety, and Hostility with the marker variables in Factor 1. As in earlier studies, Penetration and Anatomy tend to be follower variables often associated with the three marker variables.

Among normal children, moderately high scores on Factor 3 are indicative of affective expressivity and loose imagination in fantasy productions. While very high scores would be evidence of psychopathology and uncontrolled bizarreness, the amount of Pathognomic Verbalization present in both American and Mexican samples is relatively low when compared with that produced by children diagnosed as emotionally disturbed (Conners 1965) or by adult schizophrenics (Holtzman et al. 1961). These differential results concerning the pattern of relationships for Pathognomic Verbalization, Anxiety, and Hostility suggest that the external correlates of these variables with other data on the same children may likewise show up differently across the three age groups in the two cultures.

*Factor 4*

Location and Form Appropriateness serve consistently as defining variables for this factor in every case. The more an individual

delves into small detail while responding to inkblots, the more
likely he will find a percept for which the form of the blot is highly
appropriate. Of greater interest than this consistency in marker
variables is the presence of other inkblot scores with high loadings
in certain samples. Only the Mexican first-graders and the American seventh-graders failed to show any scores other than Location
and Form Appropriateness with high loadings on Factor 4. Anatomy, Barrier, and Penetration tend to have negative loadings on
Factor 4, except in the case of Barrier for the Mexican seventh-
graders, where the loading is positive. For the first-graders in Austin and the fourth-graders in both cultures, high scores on Anatomy
or Penetration tend to be associated with whole responses having
poor form. Unlike the earlier standardization studies, in the
present samples Barrier tends to be split across several factors, including 4, rather than being concentrated primarily in Factor 1.
This shift is difficult to explain, and caution should be exercised in
the interpretation of its meaning. A further qualification concerning Barrier is its relatively low reliability (see Table 4-1). In
general, Factor 4 is bipolar in nature, the positive pole tending to
indicate perceptual differentiation coupled with a critical sense
of good form, while the negative pole appears more indicative of
immaturity, diffuse bodily preoccupation, and possible psychopathology.

*Factor 5*

Reaction Time and Rejection tend to be closely associated for
obvious reasons. The longer a person takes to look at an inkblot
before he gives a response, the more likely he is to reject the card
without being able to see anything in it. Of greater interest is the
fact that Factor 5 emerges as a significant dimension orthogonal
to the first four factors, indicating that an individual's performance on the other inkblot scores is generally independent of his
reaction time or the number of cards that he rejects. The variable
most commonly associated with Factor 5 other than Reaction Time
and Rejection is Animal. In only two of the six samples is the
loading for Animal significantly high—the American fourth-
graders and the Mexican seventh-graders. In the case of the American seventh-graders, Animal is replaced by Anatomy as a defining
variable in Factor 5, thus eliminating the need for a sixth factor in

this group. Both Animal and Anatomy responses tend to be fairly easy to produce when responding to inkblots. Thus it is not surprising that long reaction times tend to go with low Anatomy or low Animal scores. It is interesting to note that the third content score, Human, has consistently low loadings on Factor 5 in the present samples, as well as in those from the earlier standardization work; Animal and Anatomy allow for a much greater variety of form.

*Factor 6*

Usually defined by Anatomy, Sex, and Abstract, this residual factor is limited to Anatomy in the present study because Sex and Abstract were not included in the correlational analysis. The factor is present in only four of the six samples, being unnecessary in the fourth- and seventh-graders from Austin. In three of the four samples containing Factor 6, Anatomy clearly sticks out as the primary marker variable. In three of these four, Animal is also present with significant loadings but in the reverse direction to Anatomy. Factor 6 can be interpreted simply as an independent dimension dealing with those content scores than are inanimate and unrelated to the other five factors.

*In summary*, it can be concluded that most of the same factor patterns are present in the current samples, regardless of age group or culture, as were found in earlier studies with the Holtz-man Inkblot Technique. In spite of the general consistency of patterns across most of the factors, important exceptions were noted. In particular, the independence of Factor 1 (well-controlled ideational activity and ego differentiation) and Factor 3 (disturbed thought processes and active fantasy life) was impossible to achieve in several of the samples, especially the seventh-graders in both cultures and to some extent the fourth-grade Americans. Whether the convergence of these two factors means that the usual psychopathological interpretations of Factor 3 are unwarranted for these populations or whether among young adolescents this type of intermingling of well-developed inner resources and irrational af-fective processes is to be expected cannot be determined from the present data alone. A closer examination of relationships between the inkblot scores and other data independently gathered on the personality development of these children may shed further light on this question.

A sufficient amount of unique variance is present for most of the inkblot scores in at least one of the samples to justify using all of the inkblot scores in further correlational studies with other variables, rather than combining inkblot variables to yield a smaller number of factor scores for more economical comparison with other data. Consequently, all seventeen of the major inkblot scores have been carried forward for systematic comparison with other perceptual, cognitive, and personality variables, as well as with data from the family and home environment.

## INTERCORRELATIONS AMONG COGNITIVE/MENTAL ABILITIES MEASURES

The primary test representing the domain of mental abilities in the present study is the Wechsler Intelligence Scale for Children. Although the entire WISC was given to all the Mexican children in the first year, in the American study it was administered only to the first-graders. Vocabulary and Block Design were given repeatedly to all children in all six years. Arithmetic and Picture Completion were added to the core battery for the American children in years 1, 4, 5, and 6. In the three Mexican samples, the entire WISC was given repeatedly for the first five years to children in Groups I and II and for the first four years to children in Group III, because of special interest in developing normative data for this test in Spanish on representative samples of Mexican children. In year 6, for all three groups of Mexican children, only the Vocabulary, Arithmetic, Block Design, and Picture Completion subtests were administered, and then only to the subsample comprising the matched cases for the cross-cultural study. During years 5 and 6, for the oldest children in both cultures, the appropriate subtests from the Wechsler Adult Intelligence Scale were substituted for the WISC.

The subtests used in the full battery of the WISC during the first year of the project consisted of Information, Comprehension, Arithmetic, Similarities, Vocabulary, Picture Completion, Picture Arrangement, Block Design, Object Assembly, and Coding. For the Mexican children only, Digit Span and Mazes were also added to the battery.

Several other tests can also be considered as primarily dealing with mental abilities. The Harris-Goodenough developmental score is available from Human Figure Drawing for each of the six years in all three age groups and both cultures. The children's version of Witkin's Embedded Figures Test was given in years 1–5 in Groups II and III and in years 4 and 5 in Group I for both cultures. As indicated earlier, the Embedded Figures Test can also be thought of as dealing with cognitive style rather than mental abilities per se.

Complete intercorrelation matrices for the WISC subtests are available in year 1 for all three groups in Mexico and for first-graders only in the United States. To the WISC variables in these four groups can also be added the Harris-Goodenough score on Human Figure Drawing. For Groups II and III in Mexico, the Time score on the Embedded Figures Test was added to the matrix. An inspection of correlations involving these cognitive tests and other tests within the core battery, as well as earlier research evidence from other studies, suggested that Movement from the Holtzman Inkblot Technique should be added to the matrix prior to factor analysis in order to link together the results reported earlier on the HIT and results for the WISC. A final variable added to the matrix because of special interest in sex differences cross-culturally was the sex of the subject coded in binary form, 2 for female and 1 for male. Digit Span and Mazes were omitted in Group I for Mexico but included in Groups II and III for Mexico. Thus the correlation matrices for the first-graders in Mexico and the United States were exactly equivalent in terms of the variables intercorrelated.

The four intercorrelation matrices resulting from this design—three in Mexico and one in the United States—were factor analyzed, using the principal-components method for extracting factors. The factoring was stopped when the eigenvalue for the associated principal components dropped below 1.0. A normalized varimax rotation of the resulting factors in each matrix yielded an approximate simple-structure solution. Because of special interest in a cross-cultural comparison of the first-graders, these two factor matrices were rotated still further by hand to see how closely the factors could be matched on identical variables in the two independent samples. The results for the first-graders are presented in Table 6-7.

The first factor in both cultures is similar to the Verbal Comprehension factor found by other investigators who have analyzed the intercorrelations of WISC subtests (Cohen 1959; Quereshi 1972). For the Mexican children, the separation of the verbal and performance subtests of the WISC confirms Wechsler's original classification perfectly; Information, Comprehension, Arithmetic, Similarities, and Vocabulary are the only tests with high loadings on Factor 1 in Mexico, while Picture Completion, Picture Arrangement, Block Design, Object Assembly, Coding and the Harris-Goodenough score on the Human Figure Drawing are the only tests with appreciable loadings on Factor 2 for the Mexican children. Among the American children, however, Picture Arrangement and HIT Movement also have appreciable loadings on Factor 1. In earlier studies involving seven-year-olds, Jacob Cohen (1959) discovered that Picture Arrangement was the best single measure of general intelligence among the performance scale tests. The association of HIT Movement with Verbal Comprehension is

Table 6-7
Cross-Cultural Comparison of Factor Loadings for Intercorrelations
among Cognitive Scores for Six-Year-Olds

| | Factors | | | | | | |
| Variable | 1 U.S. | Mexico | 2 U.S. | Mexico | 3 U.S. | Mexico | 4 U.S. |
|---|---|---|---|---|---|---|---|
| Information | 75 | 71 | 11 | 36 | 14 | 00 | −01 |
| Comprehension | 47 | 65 | 24 | 01 | −44 | −31 | −01 |
| Arithmetic | 47 | 55 | 12 | 31 | 42 | −19 | 36 |
| Similarities | 60 | 79 | 13 | 08 | 25 | 15 | −19 |
| Vocabulary | 68 | 63 | 27 | 20 | −25 | −21 | 12 |
| Picture Completion | 20 | 09 | 21 | 58 | 03 | −23 | −70 |
| Picture Arrangement | 60 | 27 | 02 | 54 | 35 | −01 | 04 |
| Block Design | 20 | 15 | 73 | 66 | 08 | 00 | 11 |
| Object Assembly | 36 | 08 | 65 | 83 | −09 | −05 | 12 |
| Coding | −21 | 17 | 53 | 38 | 06 | −13 | 47 |
| Human Figure Drawing | 25 | 06 | 43 | 59 | 56 | 49 | −22 |
| HIT Movement | 43 | 24 | −12 | 02 | 09 | −55 | 54 |
| Child's sex | −26 | −04 | 19 | −24 | 66 | 77 | 05 |

NOTE: Decimals are omitted. Boldface type indicates correlations of .40 or above.

not surprising in view of the earlier analysis of Movement as an imaginative verbal expression of fantasy.

Factor 2 is clearly identical to the perceptual-organization factor found earlier by other investigators. Block Design, Object Assembly, Coding, and Human Figure Drawing all show appreciable loadings on this factor in both cultures. The primary difference between the Mexican and American children concerns the meaning of Picture Completion and Picture Arrangement. As indicated earlier, Picture Arrangement among the American children is more closely associated with Verbal Comprehension. As one would expect from an analysis of the nature of the task, performance on Human Figure Drawing is closely associated with perceptual organization.

The third factor is defined primarily by sex differences in performance on the cognitive tests. In both cultures, the high loading on Factor 3 for Human Figure Drawing results from the fact that girls (coded 2 on sex) received a higher mean score on the Harris-Goodenough developmental scale than did boys (coded 1 on sex).[1] Appreciable loadings for Comprehension (reversed) and Arithmetic on Factor 3 for the American children are essentially minor residual components associated with sex differences. The substantial loading for HIT Movement on Factor 3 for the Mexican children results from the fact that boys among the Mexican first-graders tended to give more movement than did girls.

Although three factors were enough to account for most of the common variance among the intercorrelations for the Mexican six-year-olds, a fourth factor was necessary for the American data. Factor 4 among the American children is difficult to interpret, since it arises largely from Picture Completion, Coding, and Movement, three variables that seem to have the least amount in common with the other variables in the matrix. Unless confirmed in subsequent analyses, Factor 4 is best viewed as a residual factor.

Tables 6-8 and 6-9 contain the results of the factor analysis for the fourth-graders (nine-year-olds), and seventh-graders (twelve-year-olds) in Mexico. All twelve subtests of the WISC are in-

---

[1] It is possible that at least part of the higher mean score for girls can be attributed to a greater representation of items external to the body itself, such as clothing and accessories, rather than to greater articulation of body concept.

cluded, in addition to the Harris-Goodenough score on Human Figure Drawing, the Time score on the Embedded Figures Test, and HIT Movement. Child's sex was added by coding male 1 and female 2 in order to see what sex differences existed and how sex might interact with individual differences on the cognitive tests. The test variables in the matrix are identical for both age groups, making it possible to compare the results directly.

Unlike the results for the Mexican six-year-olds in Group I, here there is no simple complete separation of the verbal tests from the performance tests on the WISC. The first three factors in the two analyses are highly similar, although the actual patterns of loadings differ in important respects. Among the nine-year-olds, Factor 1 is a more general factor than among the twelve-year-olds. Among the nine-year-olds, both verbal and performance tasks load highly on Factor 1, while among the twelve-year-olds, only Information, Similarities, Vocabulary, and Digit Span—all verbal subtests—have high loadings. Witkin and his colleagues (Witkin et al. 1962; Goodenough and Karp 1961) have identified an analytical factor in the WISC that is best represented by Block

Table 6-8
Factor Loadings for Intercorrelations among Cognitive Scores for
Mexican Nine-Year-Olds (Group II, Year I)

| Variable | 1 | 2 | 3 | 4 | 5 | $h^2$ |
|---|---|---|---|---|---|---|
| Information | **62** | —02 | **42** | —13 | 15 | 60 |
| Comprehension | —06 | 32 | **62** | —04 | 22 | 54 |
| Arithmetic | **70** | 06 | 03 | —35 | 04 | 62 |
| Similarities | 38 | —22 | **52** | 03 | 31 | 56 |
| Vocabulary | **43** | 12 | **64** | 12 | 06 | 63 |
| Digit Span | 15 | —02 | 05 | —06 | **85** | 75 |
| Picture Completion | **48** | 18 | 36 | —11 | —36 | 54 |
| Picture Arrangement | 34 | **51** | 04 | 05 | —15 | 40 |
| Block Design | **60** | 37 | 14 | 20 | 23 | 61 |
| Object Assembly | **43** | 34 | 32 | 03 | 31 | 50 |
| Coding | 11 | **63** | —11 | —01 | 06 | 43 |
| Mazes | —05 | **70** | 21 | 01 | —05 | 54 |
| Human Figure Drawing | 21 | 12 | 36 | **72** | —03 | 70 |
| EFT Time | **—70** | —22 | 03 | —29 | —06 | 64 |
| HIT Movement | 04 | —02 | **65** | —04 | —17 | 46 |
| Child's sex | —18 | —06 | —29 | **81** | 01 | 78 |

NOTE: Decimals are omitted. Boldface indicates correlations of .40 or above.
$h^2$: communality

Table 6-9
Factor Loadings for Intercorrelations among Cognitive Tests for
Mexican Twelve-Year-Olds (Group III, Year 1)

| Variable | 1 | 2 | 3 | 4 | 5 | h² |
|---|---|---|---|---|---|---|
| Information | 75 | 24 | 11 | −13 | −06 | 65 |
| Comprehension | 22 | 11 | 77 | −03 | −10 | 66 |
| Arithmetic | 32 | 21 | 26 | −21 | 41 | 44 |
| Similarities | 60 | 06 | 37 | 05 | −19 | 53 |
| Vocabulary | 64 | 10 | 48 | −13 | −03 | 67 |
| Digit Span | 72 | 06 | −18 | 17 | 32 | 68 |
| Picture Completion | 21 | 51 | 04 | −21 | 02 | 36 |
| Picture Arrangement | 08 | 51 | 17 | 12 | 06 | 31 |
| Block Design | 09 | 68 | 04 | 01 | 32 | 58 |
| Object Assembly | −12 | 81 | −05 | −09 | 02 | 68 |
| Coding | 04 | 27 | 28 | 75 | 21 | 76 |
| Mazes | −03 | 19 | 05 | 22 | 72 | 61 |
| Human Figure Drawing | 17 | 51 | 06 | 20 | −48 | 57 |
| EFT Time | −24 | −79 | 04 | 01 | 41 | 69 |
| HIT Movement | 01 | 01 | 77 | 09 | 19 | 64 |
| Child's sex | −03 | −27 | 17 | 77 | −06 | 71 |

NOTE: Decimals are omitted. Boldface indicates correlations of .40 or above.
h²: communality

Design, Picture Completion, and Object Assembly. This factor generally correlates highly with the Embedded Figures Test as well. All four of these measures involve an ability to analyze a complex perceptual field and deal with the figure independently of the ground. While they clearly deal with perceptual organization, they also involve analytical ability, cognitive differentiation, and perceptual field independence. When coupled with Information, Arithmetic, and Vocabulary, this analytical cluster suggests an interpretation for Factor 1 among the nine-year-olds as fairly close to general intelligence.

The second factor in both samples is defined largely by the more important nonverbal or performance tests left over from Factor 1. In the case of the nine-year-olds, Factor 2 is fairly narrow, consisting primarily of Picture Arrangement, Coding, and Mazes. A high score on Mazes has often been interpreted as indicative of planning ability (Porteus 1950). Among the twelve-year-olds, this factor is even closer to the analytical or perceptual field independence proposed by Witkin. The addition of the Human Figure Drawings and the high loadings on Block Design and Object Assembly create a sharper focus upon the field-dependence interpretation. H. F. Faterson and Herman Witkin (1970) have demonstrated convincingly that their Articulation of Body Concept (ABC) score on human figure drawings is a major indicator of the type of psychological differentiation represented by perceptual field independence and analytical ability in perceptual tasks.[2]

Factor 3 is another factor dealing with an important aspect of verbal ability. Among the nine-year-olds, with the exception of Arithmetic, the factor is quite similar to the primary verbal-comprehension factor found among Mexican six-year-olds. For the twelve-year-olds, this verbal factor is defined chiefly by the Comprehension and Vocabulary subtests from the WISC, as well as the Movement score from the Holtzman Inkblot Technique. Since Movement is highly loaded on Factor 3 in both samples, it suggests an interpretation of Factor 3 as dealing with that component of verbal ability characterized by a lively, active imagination and the ability to project outward from one's fantasies. In this sense, it deals particularly with the expressive, imaginative aspects of

[2] Following consultation with Herman Witkin, the Human Figure Drawings for year 1 in Austin Groups II and III were rescored for his Articulation of Body Concept score to determine the extent to which the ABC score, the Goodenough score, and the Harris-Goodenough score were all measures of the same trait. Intercorrelations between the several scores from Human Figure Drawing and selected subtests of the WISC were also computed. The correlation of the ABC score and the Goodenough score was in the .70's, essentially the same as found by Witkin (personal communication). The pattern of correlations between the ABC score and the WISC subtests, on the one hand, and the Goodenough score and the WISC subtests, on the other, were essentially identical, indicating that the two scores are measuring essentially the same thing. Since the correlation between the Harris-Goodenough score and the Goodenough score is in the .90's, it can be concluded that the Harris-Goodenough score reported herein is a good measure of the same cognitive differentiation or field-independent perceptual ability as the ABC score most recently advocated by Faterson and Witkin as a measure of psychological differentiation in children. The correlation of the ABC score with EFT Time is −.42 and −.34 in Groups II and III respectively, while the same correlations for the Harris-Goodenough score are −.37 and −.36 respectively. Comparable correlations between ABC and Block Design are .24 and .21, as compared to correlations of .12 and .32 for the Harris-Goodenough score. If one considers EFT Time as a relatively pure measure of field dependency and Block Design as a fairly pure measure of analytical ability, it is clear that the Harris-Goodenough score is identical to the ABC score in its relative loading on these two dimensions.

verbal ability rather than with factual information, word meanings, and analytical problem solving. The Comprehension subtest of the WISC, which loads highly on Factor 3, involves an ability to project oneself into a variety of complex situations and anticipate various outcomes, a cognitive-perceptual ability similar in many ways to HIT Movement.

Factors 4 and 5 are specific factors in both samples. Factor 4 is defined primarily by sex differences. Among the nine-year-olds, only Human Figure Drawing is highly loaded on this factor, an association due to the fact that nine-year-old Mexican girls received significantly higher scores on the Harris-Goodenough scale than did nine-year-old Mexican boys. Among the twelve-year-olds, the primary sex differences occur on Coding, where girls did significantly better than boys among the Mexican children. Factor 5 is defined entirely by Digit Span for the Mexican nine-year-olds, yielding a rather specific factor that in other studies has been called freedom from distractability (Cohen 1959). Among the older Mexican children, this factor is defined primarily by Mazes.

In general, the dimensional studies of the cognitive tasks in both cultures reveal results consistent with past findings. Repeated significant loadings for HIT Movement on factors dealing with the use of imagination provide a strong link between the cognitive domain and the Holtzman Inkblot Technique. Likewise, the Embedded Figures Test and Human Figure Drawing have several important close linkages with the mental-abilities tests in the WISC. The high magnitude of this relationship involving the Embedded Figures Test suggests that it yields measures that are more properly considered cognitive ability than cognitive-perceptual style.

Although the nine- and twelve-year-olds in the United States were not given the complete WISC, four subtests are available from the WISC that can be used as marker variables for extending the factor analyses into an interpretation of the intercorrelations among the cognitive variables for the older children in the United States. The bivariate correlations for Groups II and III in year 1 are presented in Tables 6-11 and 6-12, together with a more complete picture of the intercorrelations across a number of other variables in the study.

Results of the present factor analyses, as well as past studies, indicate that Vocabulary is the most consistently dependable sub-test to reflect verbal comprehension, while Block Design is the most consistent for perceptual-analytical ability. In addition to these two subtests, Arithmetic, Picture Completion, Human Figure Drawing, and the Embedded Figures Test can be considered tests of cognitive-perceptual ability. For the American nine-year-olds in the upper triangular matrix within Table 6-11, it can be seen that Vocabulary correlates significantly with HIT Movement, HIT Pathognomic Verbalization, HIT Anatomy (reversed), HIT Anxiety, HIT Barrier, and OST Percent Open, as well as Block Design and Arithmetic. Human Figure Drawing and the Embedded Figures Test do not correlate significantly with Vocabulary. These results suggest a pattern similar to Factor 3 for the Mexican nine-year-olds (Table 6-8).

Unlike Vocabulary, Block Design is highly correlated with EFT Time ($-.59$) and with Human Figure Drawing (.29). In Table 6-11, a strong cluster appears involving Human Figure Drawing, Block Design, and Embedded Figures, the cognitive-perceptual differentiation factor proposed by Witkin. While this cluster among the Mexican nine-year-olds proved to be closely linked with verbal comprehension, among the Mexican twelve-year-olds (Table 6-9) it emerged as Factor 2, independent of verbal comprehension. The dimension present among the American nine-year-olds concerning cognitive differentiation looks more like that of the Mexican twelve-year-olds than that of the Mexican nine-year-olds. The significant correlation of HIT Integration with Human Figure Drawing (.29) suggests that Integration may well be related to this cognitive-differentiation factor among the American children. Integration also has significant correlations with Vocabulary and Block Design among the Mexican nine-year-olds, a relationship shared with Human, Movement, and Form Definiteness from the HIT. These results support the interpretation of Factor 1 from the Holtzman Inkblot Technique as a cognitive-perceptual dimension related to the development of well-organized ideational and imaginative capacity.

The intercorrelations of these same variables for both cultures in Group III, year 1, are given in Table 6-12. The most outstanding cluster again involves Block Design, Embedded Figures, and Human Figure Drawing. Arithmetic should also be added. Even

Vocabulary and Picture Completion are significantly related to this cluster, suggesting a pattern more like that found for Factor 1 among the Mexican nine-year-olds than that of the Mexican twelve-year-olds in Group III. A number of inkblot variables are related to this general cognitive-perceptual ability cluster, as evidenced by the large number of significant correlations involving Human Figure Drawing and Vocabulary with inkblot variables. In each case the direction of this relationship suggests that, among American twelve-year-olds, the use of whole responses that have good form definiteness and are well integrated, the use of movement and affective expressivity as measured by HIT Factor 3, and the presence of human content, high Barrier, and Penetration, are indications of well-developed cognitive-perceptual abilities. The pattern of correlations among the Mexican twelve-year-olds in Group III is also consistent with this interpretation.

The present dimensional studies of the cognitive-perceptual abilities are limited to the first year of psychological testing in both cultures. Considering the cross-cultural, linguistic, and age differences encompassed by the dimensional studies on test scores from the first year, it is remarkable that the general patterns of relationships appear so consistently. To be sure, there are important differences that have been noted across both age and culture, but the main dimensions are clearly present in all groups and across more tasks than those traditionally encompassed within the area of intelligence testing.

### INTERCORRELATIONS AMONG COGNITIVE-PERCEPTUAL STYLE VARIABLES

In addition to some of the inkblot variables and the Embedded Figures Test, which have already been discussed above, the Object Sorting Test, Kagan's Conceptual Styles Test, the Visual Fractionation Test, the Time Estimation Test, and Moran's Word Association Test yield scores that are primarily perceptual and cognitive style variables. In most cases these tests were not given in the first year of the project and were only given for two or three years of repeated measures. Consequently, analyses of relationships among these stylistic variables require an examination of intercorrelations in years 1, 2, and 4 rather than in the initial year alone. Although all of the intercorrelations were examined in large matrices, only a few of these are sufficiently significant to justify detailed analysis here.

For the Object Sorting Test, three scores appear to capture most of the important variance for purposes of intercorrelation with other variables—the number of groups used in sorting objects into categories (Gardner's measure of "equivalence range" or category width), the percentage of total sorts scored as "open" (rather than "closed"), and the percentage of total sorts scored as "public" (rather than "private"). These particular scores were chosen for further study after preliminary analysis of the intercorrelations of all eleven scores on the Object Sorting Test, as well as selected correlations of these eleven with variables from other tests. The other scores in the Object Sorting Test were found to be either too unreliable for further analysis or too closely correlated with these three scores to justify their further study.

Although three scores were computed for the Time Estimation Test, only one of these, the Delay score, proved to be worthy of systematic correlation with other variables. The Inaccuracy score, derived by summing the absolute deviation in seconds of each estimate from sixty seconds, was typically so highly correlated with the Delay score that it was dropped in favor of the Delay score. Inconsistency, the third score for Time Estimation, showed so little reliability that it was not judged worthy of further correlational analysis with other variables.

Four scores from the Embedded Figures Test (EFT) were studied systematically in relation to other variables in the study— number of re-examinations of the complex figures, number of errors (incorrect tracings), total number of items correct, and reaction time to correct solution averaged over the twelve items. EFT Re-exams and EFT Errors showed the same pattern of correlations with other cognitive tests, most notably the Harris-Goodenough score on Human Figure Drawing and the Vocabulary and Block Design subtests of the WISC, as did EFT Correct and EFT Time. However, the magnitude of the relationships involving EFT Re-exams and EFT Errors was considerably lower than the magnitude of comparable correlations involving EFT Correct and EFT Time. The intercorrelations of the four scores from the EFT among themselves indicate that EFT Correct and EFT Time are measuring essentially the same thing, the relationship between these two variables ranging from −.86 to −.97. While both EFT Time and EFT Correct have high test-retest stability, EFT Time was chosen for more careful study, since its general distribution characteristics were slightly superior. EFT Errors and EFT Re-exams correlate moderately highly (.48 to .80) with EFT Time. Since neither EFT Errors nor EFT Re-exams show any consistent or highly significant correlations with any of the other cognitive style variables or with any of the personality variables, they were dropped from further consideration at this time.

Four scores from the Conceptual Styles Test were analyzed for intercorrelations with other variables—Total Reaction Time, Number of Analytical Responses, Number of Relational Responses, and Number of Inferential-Categorical Responses. Since the sum of all three part-scores is equal to nineteen, the number of items in the Conceptual Styles Test, the intercorrelations of these part-scores with each other are spuriously high. In general, CST Analytical and CST Relational correlate in the range −.70 to −.85, while the correlation of CST Inferential-Categorical tends to be low with both variables. This result is not surprising in view of the fact that most responses to the CST are scored either analytical or relational by young children. While the correlations between all four scores of the CST and other variables were examined, only CST Analytical and CST Total Reaction Time were worthy of further consideration.

For the Visual Fractionation Test, six scores were examined systematically for intercorrelations with other variables—number of correct answers (VFT Number Correct), number of trials to complete the learning task (VFT Trials), mean reaction time for all twenty-four items in the test (VFT Time), and mean reaction time for the eight items involving elements (VFT Elements), the eight items involving figures (VFT Figures), and the eight items involving grounds (VFT Grounds). VFT Trials is not a cognitive style variable, since it simply involves the number of trials taken to learn the initial task. The three stylistic scores—Elements, Figures, and Grounds—are the scores of greatest interest in the Visual Fractionation Test. In every case, regardless of age group or culture, the intercorrelations among these three part-scores are positive and moderately high, indicating a common factor running through the three of them. Inspection of the correlations between these part-scores and other variables reveals identical patterns for all three scores, suggesting that they are really not measuring different aspects of the child's performance. As in the case of the Conceptual Styles Test, where the part-scores were also unreliable, Elements, Figures, and Grounds in the VFT have generally low reliability, decreasing the likelihood of finding any differentially significant correlations with other variables.

The remaining three cognitive-perceptual style tests employed in the study were the Stroop Color-Word Test, the Word Association Test, and the Perceptual Maturity Scale. The Color-Word Test was given only to the American fourth-graders and seventh-graders during the first and second year of the study. Since no significant correlations were found between the Color-Word Test and any other variables, it was dropped from the project. Within the Word Association Test, only one score was chosen for systematic study, the proportion of associations classified as syntagmatic. Both the Word Association Test and the Perceptual Maturity Scale were given to all three age groups in years 4, 5, and 6.

Extremely few correlations across the various measures of cognitive-perceptual style proved to be significantly different from zero. Occasionally an isolated correlation out of thousands examined would appear to be significant beyond the .01 level, or indeed even beyond the .001 level, but one would expect some such correlations by chance alone. Where a correlation appears significant repeatedly across several years, or where it is consistently significant across two or more age groups or across the two cultures, the relationship is strong enough to merit special attention. In no case, however, were any correlations consistently significant across the cognitive-style-test variables, regardless of age group or culture. Consequently, it can be concluded that the dimensions underlying the cognitive style variables employed in the present study are weak and tenuous at best. Of the measures in this category, only the Embedded Figures Test has high reliability and high stability across repeated testing in both cultures; and, as indicated earlier, it appears more closely related to cognitive-perceptual ability than to cognitive-perceptual style.

Tables 6-10–6-18 contain intercorrelation matrices, as well as means and standard deviations, among selected variables in each of three age groups and both cultures for years 1, 2, and 4. Within

## Table 6-10
### Intercorrelations, Means, and Standard Deviations for Six-Year-Olds (Group I, Year I)

| | SSEX | RT | R | L | FD | FA | C | SH | M | V | I | H | A | AT | AX |
|---|---|---|---|---|---|---|---|---|---|---|---|---|---|---|---|
| Means | 1.5 | 15.5 | 2.6 | 33.7 | 63.5 | 33.5 | 19.3 | 4.2 | 18.8 | 7.9 | 1.8 | 14.6 | 18.9 | 5.7 | 7 |
| Sigma | .5 | 9.2 | 5.2 | 19.8 | 20.2 | 8.5 | 18.0 | 3.9 | 15.8 | 8.5 | 1.8 | 8.9 | 9.6 | 8.2 | 7 |
| SSEX | | 08 | 07 | 09 | 03 | 21 | —01 | —08 | —01 | —07 | 04 | 07 | —08 | —17 | —2 |
| RT | 04 | | 81 | —02 | 09 | 07 | —28 | —15 | —20 | —19 | —03 | —16 | —17 | —11 | —2 |
| R | 24 | 33 | | —16 | —06 | 15 | —12 | —20 | —18 | —06 | —12 | —23 | —27 | —10 | —1 |
| L | 08 | 06 | —24 | | 30 | 26 | —31 | —17 | —26 | —39 | —04 | 13 | 15 | —21 | —3 |
| FD | 06 | —05 | —06 | 10 | | —33 | —60 | —38 | 23 | —09 | 33 | 56 | 64 | —14 | 1 |
| FA | 00 | 13 | 06 | 29 | —47 | | 22 | 15 | 03 | —35 | 01 | —16 | —37 | —45 | —2 |
| C | —06 | —06 | —10 | —16 | —50 | 27 | | 35 | 00 | 14 | —14 | —32 | —38 | 08 | 0 |
| SH | —15 | —16 | —23 | 07 | 01 | 08 | 13 | | 01 | 15 | 17 | —19 | —15 | 07 | 1 |
| M | —20 | —20 | —19 | —09 | 05 | 00 | 04 | 24 | | 20 | 47 | 43 | 19 | —23 | 5 |
| V | —16 | —19 | —13 | —25 | —02 | —22 | 01 | 01 | 43 | | —04 | 01 | 10 | 32 | 4 |
| I | —11 | —18 | —17 | 00 | 23 | —03 | 02 | 24 | 62 | 17 | | 47 | 24 | —25 | |
| H | —18 | —23 | —24 | 11 | 49 | —10 | —18 | 13 | 27 | 15 | 34 | | 30 | —09 | 2 |
| A | 07 | 01 | —23 | 04 | 54 | —35 | —35 | —07 | —06 | 04 | 05 | 08 | | —20 | |
| AT | —09 | —03 | —05 | —14 | 00 | —07 | —09 | —01 | —08 | 14 | —09 | 02 | —23 | | |
| AX | —04 | —14 | —10 | —16 | —05 | —20 | 17 | 00 | 32 | 43 | 16 | —06 | 00 | 14 | |
| HS | —15 | —21 | —15 | —21 | —02 | —11 | 14 | 02 | 46 | 58 | 30 | 00 | 04 | 06 | |
| BR | —05 | 00 | —20 | 11 | 32 | 00 | —12 | 26 | 15 | —05 | 23 | 17 | 12 | —16 | —● |
| PN | —11 | —07 | —14 | —09 | 02 | —03 | 02 | 31 | 38 | 43 | 37 | 09 | 02 | 01 | |
| HFDH | 09 | 19 | 14 | 15 | 00 | 17 | —06 | 11 | —08 | —10 | 00 | 04 | 00 | —03 | — |
| VOC | —21 | 08 | —17 | —15 | 00 | —01 | 04 | 10 | 16 | 08 | 12 | 06 | —02 | 04 | |
| BD | —08 | 05 | 01 | —03 | 09 | —04 | 03 | 07 | 10 | 01 | 13 | 17 | 00 | 01 | — |
| ARIT | —20 | —02 | —08 | —03 | 05 | 06 | —06 | —09 | 17 | —02 | 16 | 10 | —01 | 09 | — |
| PC | —17 | 04 | —09 | —05 | 00 | 00 | 05 | 08 | 08 | —05 | 15 | 11 | —03 | 08 | — |
| INFO | —21 | —05 | —17 | 01 | 04 | 10 | —03 | 10 | 15 | 00 | 13 | 15 | —02 | 04 | — |
| COMP | —22 | —13 | —18 | —06 | —13 | 05 | 05 | 05 | 21 | —02 | 13 | 00 | —11 | 16 | — |
| SIM | 00 | —06 | —07 | 00 | 10 | 04 | —07 | 14 | 16 | —02 | 22 | 05 | 01 | 10 | |
| PA | —11 | 10 | —06 | 16 | —09 | 12 | —04 | 10 | 11 | —05 | 17 | —05 | —05 | —09 | — |
| OA | —22 | 01 | —04 | 03 | 05 | 06 | 03 | 08 | 06 | —05 | 09 | 14 | 03 | 01 | — |
| CODE | —09 | 00 | —13 | —02 | —01 | 05 | 09 | 06 | 10 | 15 | —01 | —01 | 05 | 01 | |
| OSTG | 00 | 01 | —07 | —05 | —01 | 06 | 01 | 22 | —05 | —09 | —02 | 11 | 03 | 03 | |
| OSTO | 00 | 03 | —20 | 13 | 15 | 07 | —14 | 09 | —01 | —05 | 02 | 07 | 10 | 06 | |
| OSTP | —02 | 29 | 05 | —12 | 01 | 02 | 04 | —03 | —06 | —12 | —06 | —08 | 07 | —06 | — |
| | SSEX | RT | R | L | FD | FA | C | SH | M | V | I | H | A | AT | |
| Means | 1.5 | 16.3 | 3.4 | 40.3 | 62.9 | 36.5 | 14.9 | 1.8 | 7.8 | 4.9 | .7 | 13.2 | 23.5 | 4.0 | |
| Sigma | .5 | 10.5 | 6.6 | 19.9 | 19.1 | 7.0 | 18.9 | 2.2 | 10.2 | 7.4 | 1.3 | 9.2 | 14.5 | 6.1 | |

## MEXICO

NOTES:

Table includes selected variables for 133 U.S. subjects (upper matrix) and 150 Mexican subjects (lower matrix).

Decimals are omitted from correlations.

Boldface correlations are significantly different from zero beyond the .01 level.

Actual number of cases for any given correlation may be slightly reduced because of missing data.

| BR | PN | HFDH | VOC | BD | ARIT | PC | INFO | COMP | SIM | PA | OA | CODE | OSTG | OSTO | OSTP |
|---|---|---|---|---|---|---|---|---|---|---|---|---|---|---|---|
| 5.1 | 3.3 | 22.4 | 23.1 | 8.9 | 5.2 | 8.7 | 8.5 | 8.4 | 5.8 | 17.2 | 17.0 | 31.6 | 15.7 | 62.0 | 61.4 |
| 3.6 | 3.4 | 6.9 | 5.3 | 5.8 | 1.1 | 1.9 | 1.9 | 2.3 | 2.4 | 7.7 | 4.9 | 9.4 | 5.9 | 20.3 | 22.5 |

| BR | PN | HFDH | VOC | BD | ARIT | PC | INFO | COMP | SIM | PA | OA | CODE | OSTG | OSTO | OSTP |
|---|---|---|---|---|---|---|---|---|---|---|---|---|---|---|---|
| 20 | −31 | 28 | −06 | 03 | 06 | −05 | −05 | −17 | 06 | −01 | 00 | 12 | −08 | −03 | −04 |
| −05 | −20 | 04 | −06 | 05 | −01 | −03 | 12 | −20 | 04 | 00 | −01 | −07 | 00 | −03 | 29 |
| −24 | −21 | −14 | −10 | −02 | −13 | −20 | 00 | −24 | −03 | −08 | −05 | 06 | −17 | −08 | 14 |
| 14 | −28 | 14 | −02 | 23 | 02 | 18 | 07 | 04 | 00 | 11 | 04 | −08 | 03 | 13 | 03 |
| 43 | −02 | 17 | 11 | 23 | 18 | 23 | 17 | 00 | 13 | 25 | 05 | 12 | 18 | 13 | 06 |
| 00 | −31 | 28 | 19 | 12 | 08 | 00 | 17 | 10 | 12 | 08 | 23 | −03 | −21 | −08 | 21 |
| −28 | 02 | −12 | −05 | −06 | 03 | −12 | −08 | 12 | −06 | −18 | −01 | 01 | −06 | −04 | −15 |
| −07 | 15 | −02 | 03 | 00 | −07 | 11 | 06 | 23 | 06 | 08 | −02 | 01 | −07 | 09 | −09 |
| 18 | 21 | 06 | 28 | 04 | 27 | 00 | 22 | 09 | 13 | 19 | 13 | 15 | −01 | −03 | 10 |
| −05 | 28 | −24 | −05 | −14 | −07 | −12 | −15 | 00 | −14 | −02 | −15 | 15 | 06 | −16 | −35 |
| 35 | 06 | 08 | 21 | 06 | 16 | 12 | 28 | −03 | 32 | 22 | 03 | 12 | 12 | 13 | −03 |
| 33 | 08 | 03 | 05 | 04 | 11 | 03 | 04 | −10 | 00 | 15 | −04 | 12 | 08 | 07 | 02 |
| 35 | 07 | 08 | 03 | 09 | −04 | 24 | 00 | 00 | 10 | 15 | 04 | 15 | 23 | 16 | −09 |
| −35 | 43 | −19 | −20 | −17 | −08 | −06 | −09 | −06 | −18 | −03 | −22 | 02 | 03 | −06 | −20 |
| 00 | 34 | −03 | 09 | 01 | −06 | −01 | 05 | 05 | −08 | 18 | −03 | 12 | 10 | −03 | −16 |
| 09 | 40 | 04 | 15 | 05 | 08 | −02 | 05 | 11 | −03 | 18 | 08 | 16 | 08 | −13 | −09 |
|  | −02 | 24 | 19 | 16 | 08 | 15 | 15 | 05 | 20 | 23 | 19 | −01 | 12 | −03 | 14 |
| 23 |  | 00 | 04 | −05 | 00 | 07 | −01 | 11 | −02 | 12 | 10 | 09 | 07 | −02 | 00 |
| −06 | 07 |  | 10 | 31 | 35 | 22 | 25 | 12 | 33 | 32 | 32 | 03 | 07 | −06 | 15 |
| 10 | 01 | 05 |  | 28 | 15 | 06 | 48 | 40 | 38 | 30 | 39 | 03 | −01 | 08 | 13 |
| 06 | 11 | 28 | 23 |  | 29 | 09 | 31 | 10 | 13 | 23 | 41 | 22 | −01 | 13 | 17 |
| 01 | 04 | 15 | 34 | 28 |  | −06 | 32 | 20 | 27 | 33 | 23 | 08 | 04 | 04 | 22 |
| 08 | 12 | 17 | 24 | 31 | 20 |  | 15 | 08 | 20 | 12 | 02 | −03 | 07 | 07 | 10 |
| 08 | 09 | 27 | 45 | 31 | 52 | 18 |  | 17 | 45 | 43 | 30 | −01 | 01 | 12 | 28 |
| 05 | 04 | −03 | 32 | 14 | 35 | 22 | 34 |  | 17 | 11 | 29 | −02 | −04 | 05 | 01 |
| 06 | 11 | 09 | 37 | 16 | 25 | 16 | 48 | 39 |  | 27 | 25 | 02 | 01 | 00 | 13 |
| 00 | −04 | 22 | 27 | 21 | 15 | 36 | 30 | 17 | 30 |  | 18 | 02 | 07 | −05 | 16 |
| −10 | 05 | 37 | 17 | 49 | 27 | 35 | 34 | 11 | 20 | 40 |  | 11 | −02 | 00 | 15 |
| 01 | 16 | 11 | 23 | 12 | 26 | 13 | 22 | 07 | 13 | 18 | 32 |  | −05 | 02 | −15 |
| 00 | −12 | 11 | 00 | −11 | −04 | −04 | −04 | −09 | −05 | 00 | 00 | 10 |  | 00 | −12 |
| 19 | −09 | 01 | 16 | −12 | 04 | −02 | 16 | 05 | 07 | 06 | −03 | 02 | 16 |  | −12 |
| 19 | 03 | 02 | 21 | 05 | 24 | 06 | 10 | 12 | 07 | 04 | 04 | 22 | 01 | 06 |  |

| BR | PN | HFDH | VOC | BD | ARIT | PC | INFO | COMP | SIM | PA | OA | CODE | OSTG | OSTO | OSTP |
|---|---|---|---|---|---|---|---|---|---|---|---|---|---|---|---|
| 3.4 | 1.2 | 16.2 | 16.3 | 7.4 | 5.4 | 7.8 | 5.8 | 5.6 | 5.1 | 10.0 | 11.3 | 32.7 | 15.0 | 56.8 | 46.5 |
| 2.8 | 1.5 | 6.0 | 4.9 | 4.2 | 1.5 | 2.2 | 1.9 | 2.4 | 2.5 | 6.5 | 5.5 | 9.5 | 6.7 | 24.2 | 24.8 |

es of variables are abbreviated as follows:

X: Subject's Sex
T: HIT Reaction Time
R: HIT Rejection
L: HIT Location
: HIT Form Definiteness
\: HIT Form Appropriateness
C: HIT Color
H: HIT Shading
M: HIT Movement
V: HIT Pathognomic Verbalization
I: HIT Integration

H: HIT Human
A: HIT Animal
AT: HIT Anatomy
AX: HIT Anxiety
HS: HIT Hostility
BR: HIT Barrier
PN: HIT Penetration
HFDH: Human Figure Drawing
—Harris-Goodenough
VOC: WISC Vocabulary
BD: WISC Block Design

ARIT: WISC Arithmetic
PC: WISC Picture Completion
INFO: WISC Information
COMP: WISC Comprehension
SIM: WISC Similarities
PA: WISC Picture Arrangement
OA: WISC Object Assembly
CODE: WISC Coding
OSTG: Object Sorting Test—
Number of Groups
OSTO: Object Sorting Test—Percent Open
OSTP: Object Sorting Test—Percent Public

## Table 6-11
### Intercorrelations, Means, and Standard Deviations for Nine-Year-Olds (Group II, Year 1)

| | SSEX | RT | R | L | FD | FA | C | SH | M | V | I | H | A | AT |
|---|---|---|---|---|---|---|---|---|---|---|---|---|---|---|
| Means | 1.6 | 20.6 | 2.0 | 31.1 | 80.1 | 34.3 | 13.5 | 5.5 | 27.0 | 6.1 | 3.8 | 17.5 | 28.2 | 3.0 |
| Sigma | .5 | 12.8 | 4.5 | 22.9 | 13.9 | 8.8 | 9.3 | 3.5 | 16.5 | 5.5 | 3.7 | 8.6 | 9.0 | 4.5 |
| SSEX | | —03 | 00 | 06 | 07 | 12 | 05 | 14 | —10 | —03 | —02 | 08 | —18 | —09 |
| RT | 06 | | 66 | 16 | 13 | 35 | —34 | —28 | —38 | —34 | —13 | —20 | —27 | —21 |
| R | 18 | 23 | | 05 | 16 | 44 | —26 | —22 | —28 | —24 | —09 | —18 | —36 | —17 |
| L | 04 | 13 | —26 | | 26 | 36 | —53 | —30 | —53 | —41 | —37 | —14 | —12 | —14 |
| FD | —09 | 13 | 04 | 18 | | —03 | —54 | —29 | 02 | 03 | 07 | 42 | 31 | —39 |
| FA | 10 | 18 | —11 | 46 | —19 | | —08 | 02 | —26 | —16 | 19 | —24 | —34 | —10 |
| C | —02 | 01 | —15 | —25 | —43 | 07 | | 52 | 36 | 26 | 32 | —13 | —13 | 26 |
| SH | —01 | 05 | —06 | 00 | —13 | 09 | 22 | | 27 | 21 | 29 | 00 | 01 | 04 |
| M | —21 | —03 | —25 | —12 | 17 | 17 | 13 | 16 | | 57 | 51 | 49 | 29 | —03 |
| V | —13 | —04 | —08 | —26 | 10 | —10 | 10 | 19 | 35 | | 37 | 41 | 32 | 01 |
| I | —20 | —09 | —14 | —22 | 28 | 04 | —03 | 08 | 77 | 40 | | 37 | 15 | —14 |
| H | —18 | 01 | —13 | 09 | 42 | 00 | —22 | —11 | 42 | 12 | 46 | | 25 | —19 |
| A | —04 | 04 | —28 | 08 | 41 | 06 | —09 | —17 | 22 | 15 | 25 | 06 | | —17 |
| AT | —01 | —20 | 06 | —40 | —09 | —43 | 09 | 02 | —25 | 00 | —13 | —28 | —31 | |
| AX | —10 | —17 | —20 | —21 | 01 | —05 | 03 | 09 | 27 | 35 | 27 | 01 | 08 | 21 |
| HS | —29 | —10 | —27 | 01 | 27 | 05 | —01 | 08 | 56 | 41 | 51 | 18 | 37 | —13 |
| BR | —01 | 06 | —23 | 20 | 37 | 07 | —13 | 13 | 29 | 29 | 28 | 14 | 18 | —28 |
| PN | —08 | 05 | —02 | —09 | 13 | 03 | 08 | 11 | 41 | 24 | 42 | 11 | 06 | 00 |
| HFDH | 30 | —04 | —04 | 13 | 25 | 08 | —05 | 04 | 15 | 03 | 14 | 04 | 14 | —04 |
| VOC | —12 | —03 | —11 | 01 | 35 | 00 | —03 | 05 | 34 | 03 | 30 | 24 | 12 | 00 |
| BD | —08 | 07 | 00 | 03 | 27 | 05 | —09 | 01 | 17 | 05 | 21 | 21 | 08 | —09 |
| ARIT | —32 | —03 | —24 | 08 | 07 | —03 | —03 | 09 | 06 | —05 | 06 | 06 | 05 | 02 |
| PC | —21 | —05 | —14 | 17 | 15 | 08 | —09 | 12 | 18 | 06 | 19 | 18 | 02 | 01 |
| OSTG | 08 | 15 | 05 | 15 | 12 | 09 | —14 | —05 | 05 | —11 | 05 | 07 | 01 | —13 |
| OSTO | —17 | —07 | —11 | —02 | —01 | 02 | —10 | —11 | 11 | 08 | 06 | 12 | 03 | —11 |
| OSTP | 04 | 17 | 07 | 09 | 18 | 09 | —05 | 03 | —10 | —15 | —04 | —08 | 08 | —01 |
| TETD | —01 | 22 | 05 | 06 | 18 | 09 | —01 | 20 | 19 | 07 | 08 | 16 | 01 | —04 |
| EFTT | —01 | 06 | 11 | —10 | —16 | —09 | 16 | 05 | —05 | 00 | —12 | —20 | —04 | 07 |
| | SSEX | RT | R | L | FD | FA | C | SH | M | V | I | H | A | AT |
| Means | 1.5 | 21.5 | 3.0 | 44.5 | 75.3 | 39.9 | 6.2 | 2.2 | 15.2 | 2.7 | 2.1 | 15.9 | 27.4 | 5.4 |
| Sigma | .5 | 10.8 | 4.8 | 20.3 | 16.2 | 5.2 | 8.3 | 2.5 | 12.7 | 2.6 | 2.2 | 8.7 | 11.8 | 7.4 |

### MEXICO

NOTES:

Table includes selected variables for 142 U.S. subjects (upper matrix) and 143 Mexican subjects (lower matrix).

Decimals are omitted from correlations.

Boldface correlations are significantly different from zero beyond the .01 level.

Actual number of cases for any given correlation may be slightly reduced because of missing data.

| 10.7 | 6.6 | 3.8 | 35.3 | 38.6 | 21.8 | 10.1 | 11.1 | 13.3 | 79.6 | 49.2 | 127.2 | 123.7 |
|---|---|---|---|---|---|---|---|---|---|---|---|---|
| 6.8 | 3.7 | 3.4 | 9.2 | 5.8 | 10.7 | 1.7 | 2.7 | 3.6 | 14.1 | 20.6 | 69.6 | 33.9 |

| HS | BR | PN | HFDH | VOC | BD | ARIT | PC | OSTG | OSTO | OSTP | TETD | EFTT |
|---|---|---|---|---|---|---|---|---|---|---|---|---|
| −32 | 08 | −09 | 34 | −13 | −17 | −04 | −16 | 04 | −02 | 00 | 10 | 14 |
| −39 | −06 | −22 | 04 | −11 | 12 | −03 | 11 | 18 | −15 | 16 | 29 | −04 |
| −32 | −26 | −24 | −01 | −11 | 05 | −17 | 18 | 26 | −15 | 29 | 07 | 00 |
| −43 | −22 | −40 | −18 | −12 | 00 | −09 | −04 | 02 | −11 | 11 | 13 | 07 |
| −08 | 14 | −37 | 16 | 17 | 08 | −06 | −08 | −02 | 00 | 04 | 14 | −06 |
| −36 | −23 | −32 | 07 | −20 | −11 | −09 | 11 | 25 | −35 | 32 | 11 | 02 |
| 31 | 08 | 36 | 10 | −03 | −12 | 06 | 05 | −03 | 03 | −09 | −21 | 13 |
| 19 | 21 | 23 | 16 | 19 | −03 | 09 | 10 | −06 | 07 | −05 | −11 | 01 |
| 72 | 33 | 26 | 01 | 23 | 00 | 10 | −01 | −13 | 11 | −15 | −18 | −09 |
| 47 | 18 | 21 | 14 | 24 | −08 | 15 | −10 | −13 | 11 | −05 | −03 | −08 |
| 23 | 27 | 01 | 29 | 06 | −04 | 07 | −08 | 04 | −13 | 04 | −08 | −13 |
| 24 | 26 | −02 | 09 | 15 | 06 | 04 | −17 | −13 | 08 | −05 | 02 | −09 |
| 36 | 07 | 00 | 03 | 28 | 04 | 09 | −14 | −14 | 02 | −07 | 02 | −08 |
| 24 | −06 | 59 | 00 | −34 | 00 | 10 | 04 | −10 | 17 | −11 | −01 | 07 |
| 82 | 20 | 50 | −02 | 21 | 10 | 04 | 10 | −18 | 19 | −10 | −22 | −11 |
|  | 17 | 48 | −12 | 15 | 05 | 04 | 12 | −21 | 17 | −12 | −20 | −08 |
| 36 |  | 24 | 10 | 23 | 11 | 21 | 04 | −09 | 19 | −16 | 00 | −10 |
| 35 | 29 |  | −07 | −03 | 06 | 01 | 05 | −12 | 23 | −16 | −15 | 03 |
| 10 | 17 | 20 |  | −02 | 12 | 10 | 01 | 06 | −02 | 01 | 16 | −37 |
| 23 | 21 | 28 | 31 |  | 26 | 25 | 07 | −17 | 28 | −17 | 03 | −14 |
| 18 | 23 | 09 | 29 | 37 |  | 19 | 31 | −20 | 24 | −19 | 09 | −59 |
| 13 | 06 | 03 | 05 | 23 | 22 |  | 17 | −16 | 19 | −33 | 14 | −28 |
| 23 | 18 | 21 | 18 | 36 | 26 | 25 |  | 00 | 06 | 00 | −06 | −25 |
| −06 | 11 | 03 | 25 | 15 | 14 | −01 | 01 |  | −48 | 60 | −02 | 18 |
| 17 | 03 | 07 | 07 | 10 | 09 | 21 | 09 | −13 |  | −38 | 14 | −15 |
| −05 | −02 | 08 | −06 | 04 | 03 | 00 | −05 | 18 | −10 |  | 00 | 16 |
| 05 | 05 | 05 | 04 | 10 | 10 | −12 | 08 | −10 | 00 | 04 |  | −03 |
| −04 | −07 | −02 | −27 | −33 | −55 | −30 | −23 | −14 | −05 | −14 | −05 |  |

| HS | BR | PN | HFDH | VOC | BD | ARIT | PC | OSTG | OSTO | OSTP | TETD | EFTT |
|---|---|---|---|---|---|---|---|---|---|---|---|---|
| 6.1 | 4.8 | 2.0 | 24.5 | 27.6 | 14.8 | 9.2 | 10.0 | 15.1 | 54.3 | 52.0 | 107.5 | 135.7 |
| 4.4 | 3.0 | 2.2 | 6.9 | 7.7 | 8.4 | 1.9 | 2.0 | 3.9 | 18.9 | 17.6 | 54.8 | 31.6 |

Names of variables are abbreviated as follows:

| | | | |
|---|---|---|---|
| SSEX: | Subject's Sex | HS: | HIT Hostility |
| RT: | HIT Reaction Time | BR: | HIT Barrier |
| R: | HIT Rejection | PN: | HIT Penetration |
| L: | HIT Location | HFDH: | Human Figure Drawing— |
| FD: | HIT Form Definiteness | | Harris-Goodenough |
| FA: | HIT Form Appropriateness | VOC: | WISC Vocabulary |
| C: | HIT Color | BD: | WISC Block Design |
| SH: | HIT Shading | ARIT: | WISC Arithmetic |
| M: | HIT Movement | PC: | WISC Picture Completion |
| V: | HIT Pathognomic Verbalization | OSTG: | Object Sorting Test—Number of Groups |
| I: | HIT Integration | OSTO: | Object Sorting Test—Percent Open |
| H: | HIT Human | OSTP: | Object Sorting Test—Percent Public |
| A: | HIT Animal | TETD: | Time Estimation Test—Delay |
| AT: | HIT Anatomy | EFTT: | Embedded Figures Test—Time |
| AX: | HIT Anxiety | | |

Table 6-12
Intercorrelations, Means, and Standard Deviations for Twelve-Year-Olds (Group III, Year I)

| | SSEX | RT | R | L | FD | FA | C | SH | M | V | I | H | A | AT | |
|---|---|---|---|---|---|---|---|---|---|---|---|---|---|---|---|
| Means | 1.5 | 17.9 | 1.2 | 32.9 | 82.4 | 43.9 | 14.9 | 4.7 | 33.2 | 3.2 | 5.5 | 21.1 | 25.2 | 2.7 | |
| Sigma | .5 | 9.7 | 2.8 | 18.3 | 15.6 | 5.4 | 9.9 | 5.1 | 19.5 | 3.6 | 4.4 | 10.5 | 8.7 | 2.8 | |
| | SSEX | RT | R | L | FD | FA | C | SH | M | V | I | H | A | AT | |
| SSEX | | —04 | —03 | —05 | —01 | —07 | 04 | 04 | —11 | 07 | —01 | 05 | —15 | —02 | |
| RT | —04 | | 24 | 25 | —05 | 12 | —12 | 10 | —08 | —23 | —20 | —10 | —20 | —28 | — |
| R | —02 | 30 | | 15 | —23 | 15 | —22 | —22 | —39 | —19 | —31 | —27 | —17 | —02 | — |
| L | 21 | 17 | —15 | | 11 | 33 | —58 | —36 | —56 | —37 | —53 | —17 | 12 | —10 | — |
| FD | —11 | —08 | —04 | 11 | | 15 | —36 | —18 | 27 | 21 | 35 | 59 | 50 | —26 | |
| FA | 11 | 20 | 13 | 31 | —19 | | —14 | 00 | 04 | —06 | 08 | 13 | 00 | 07 | — |
| C | 04 | —16 | —08 | —35 | —50 | 07 | | 69 | 43 | 27 | 28 | —08 | —35 | 04 | |
| SH | —06 | —13 | —16 | —21 | —37 | 14 | 51 | | 50 | 26 | 33 | —01 | —19 | —10 | |
| M | —07 | —05 | —23 | —39 | 16 | —06 | 19 | 17 | | 48 | 78 | 50 | 02 | —11 | |
| V | —13 | —22 | —15 | —43 | 23 | —16 | 07 | 14 | 61 | | 49 | 36 | 04 | —04 | |
| I | —09 | —10 | —20 | —43 | 21 | —01 | 20 | 19 | 70 | 48 | | 61 | 04 | —04 | |
| H | —09 | —08 | —21 | 00 | 41 | 00 | —15 | —16 | 49 | 25 | 53 | | —06 | —11 | |
| A | 00 | —13 | —28 | 01 | 50 | —24 | —32 | —31 | 09 | 16 | 01 | 15 | | —15 | — |
| AT | —12 | —13 | —11 | —17 | —07 | —03 | 05 | 18 | —07 | 15 | —01 | —22 | —20 | | |
| AX | —12 | —15 | —20 | —34 | 21 | —19 | 06 | 03 | 63 | 61 | 49 | 23 | 20 | 08 | |
| HS | —20 | —16 | —19 | —27 | 33 | —14 | —02 | —05 | 59 | 56 | 46 | 29 | 26 | 04 | |
| BR | 09 | —01 | —33 | 06 | 24 | 06 | 05 | 17 | 19 | 13 | 22 | 09 | 06 | —05 | |
| PN | —06 | —09 | —26 | —32 | 00 | 02 | 25 | 39 | 51 | 48 | 42 | 15 | —09 | 17 | |
| HFDH | —07 | 03 | —15 | 00 | 09 | 00 | —06 | 06 | 10 | 08 | 14 | 06 | 07 | —05 | |
| VOC | —13 | 02 | —19 | —11 | 05 | 04 | 19 | 29 | 30 | 19 | 24 | 18 | —04 | 02 | |
| BD | —15 | 00 | —03 | —04 | 23 | 02 | —05 | —05 | 07 | 09 | 12 | 13 | 06 | —10 | |
| ARIT | —19 | —04 | —15 | 02 | 03 | 05 | 06 | 11 | 19 | 07 | 01 | 00 | —02 | 03 | |
| PC | —21 | —02 | —14 | —05 | 04 | 00 | 19 | 17 | 08 | —03 | 10 | 08 | —06 | —05 | |
| OSTG | 00 | 09 | 04 | 06 | 00 | 00 | 04 | —08 | 03 | —04 | —05 | —09 | 00 | —12 | |
| OSTO | 09 | —21 | —18 | —06 | 18 | —06 | —07 | 01 | 16 | 11 | 23 | 21 | 16 | 12 | |
| OSTP | 03 | 19 | 17 | 06 | 03 | 05 | —09 | —12 | —13 | —19 | —07 | 08 | —01 | —12 | — |
| TETD | —28 | —06 | 00 | 00 | 12 | —03 | 04 | 03 | —02 | 01 | 03 | 00 | 03 | 05 | |
| EFTT | 21 | 03 | 15 | 00 | —12 | 00 | —02 | —02 | 00 | —01 | —04 | —09 | —04 | 13 | |
| | SSEX | RT | R | L | FD | FA | C | SH | M | V | I | H | A | AT | |
| Means | 1.5 | 28.2 | 2.3 | 46.7 | 78.3 | 42.3 | 7.0 | 3.6 | 20.9 | 3.0 | 3.2 | 18.1 | 26.7 | 4.0 | |
| Sigma | .5 | 15.5 | 4.4 | 19.5 | 16.6 | 5.1 | 7.6 | 3.3 | 14.0 | 4.2 | 3.0 | 8.2 | 8.9 | 4.4 | |

MEXICO

NOTES:

Table includes selected variables for 142 U.S. subjects (upper matrix) and 150 Mexican subjects (lower matrix).

Decimals are omitted from correlations.

Boldface correlations are significantly different from zero beyond the .01 level.

Actual number of cases for any given correlation may be slightly reduced because of missing data.

## UNITED STATES

| HS | BR | PN | HFDH | VOC | BD | ARIT | PC | OSTG | OSTO | OSTP | TETD | EFTT |
|---|---|---|---|---|---|---|---|---|---|---|---|---|
| 10.2 | 5.7 | 3.5 | 38.4 | 49.3 | 37.9 | 13.1 | 13.9 | 12.4 | 84.7 | 47.9 | 155.2 | 58.3 |
| 7.3 | 3.5 | 3.0 | 9.9 | 7.6 | 11.1 | 1.7 | 3.0 | 4.2 | 14.7 | 19.4 | 54.4 | 37.3 |
| −15 | 09 | 00 | 19 | −08 | 02 | −10 | 07 | 01 | 07 | −07 | −06 | 08 |
| −15 | 07 | −23 | 09 | −13 | −09 | 01 | −04 | −10 | 08 | 03 | −02 | 04 |
| −36 | −34 | −24 | 03 | 10 | 05 | 08 | −09 | 07 | −01 | 11 | 08 | −13 |
| −43 | −24 | −43 | −32 | −15 | −02 | −02 | −16 | 24 | −25 | 19 | 05 | 06 |
| 24 | 30 | 01 | 20 | 26 | 08 | 04 | 22 | 06 | −08 | 05 | 07 | −15 |
| 08 | 12 | 05 | 20 | 08 | 01 | 14 | 00 | 05 | −24 | 09 | 08 | 03 |
| 38 | 34 | 45 | 26 | −10 | 10 | 03 | 14 | −28 | 20 | −12 | 01 | 00 |
| 47 | 35 | 48 | 25 | −07 | 04 | 06 | 29 | −27 | 15 | −01 | −01 | 20 |
| 81 | 49 | 50 | 32 | 14 | 04 | 07 | 21 | −30 | 16 | −13 | 01 | 07 |
| 54 | 49 | 51 | 30 | 05 | −06 | −04 | 14 | −15 | 12 | −12 | 09 | 00 |
| 68 | 44 | 43 | 27 | 12 | −11 | −01 | 14 | −18 | 10 | −20 | −06 | 10 |
| 35 | 31 | 18 | 19 | 24 | 00 | 04 | 13 | 02 | −05 | −06 | 03 | 00 |
| 09 | 00 | −06 | 00 | 15 | 02 | 02 | 07 | 12 | 00 | 02 | 06 | −07 |
| 00 | −13 | 25 | −10 | −09 | 02 | −06 | −17 | 07 | −04 | −01 | −04 | 04 |
| 79 | 50 | 57 | 28 | 09 | 00 | −03 | 13 | −26 | 18 | −21 | 03 | 13 |
|  | 48 | 58 | 23 | 11 | −09 | 01 | 20 | −33 | 20 | −15 | −01 | 20 |
| 12 |  | 40 | 23 | −02 | 03 | 02 | 12 | −24 | 09 | −17 | −03 | 08 |
| 39 | 23 |  | 25 | −03 | 00 | −03 | 17 | −21 | 08 | −03 | 07 | 10 |
| 04 | 02 | 11 |  | 24 | 32 | 26 | 34 | −09 | 00 | 04 | 09 | −36 |
| 18 | 27 | 34 | 11 |  | 29 | 32 | 22 | −04 | 07 | 06 | 06 | −31 |
| 12 | 02 | 04 | 17 | 19 |  | 49 | 38 | 03 | −03 | 13 | 18 | −63 |
| 15 | 10 | 15 | 04 | 26 | 25 |  | 31 | −04 | 02 | 11 | 13 | −39 |
| −06 | 06 | 11 | 15 | 26 | 31 | 10 |  | 01 | 03 | 06 | 14 | −29 |
| 03 | −03 | 02 | 13 | 05 | 14 | 14 | 01 |  | −52 | 55 | −05 | −02 |
| 10 | 17 | −05 | −05 | 08 | −10 | −08 | −03 | −43 |  | −43 | 03 | 10 |
| −21 | −21 | −20 | −04 | −15 | −03 | −10 | 04 | 09 | 01 |  | 04 | −05 |
| 13 | 13 | 07 | 03 | 08 | 15 | 09 | 14 | 11 | −16 | 00 |  | −21 |
| 05 | −11 | 04 | −36 | −26 | −49 | −22 | −36 | −26 | 04 | 04 | −08 |  |
| HS | BR | PN | HFDH | VOC | BD | ARIT | PC | OSTG | OSTO | OSTP | TETD | EFTT |
| 6.7 | 4.9 | 2.9 | 34.0 | 41.9 | 29.7 | 11.4 | 12.5 | 15.3 | 65.3 | 51.2 | 118.8 | 76.5 |
| 4.8 | 3.0 | 2.7 | 8.9 | 7.3 | 9.8 | 1.8 | 2.5 | 3.3 | 16.3 | 15.0 | 46.1 | 36.7 |

Names of variables are abbreviated as follows:

| | | | |
|---|---|---|---|
| SSEX: | Subject's Sex | HS: | HIT Hostility |
| RT: | HIT Reaction Time | BR: | HIT Barrier |
| R: | HIT Rejection | PN: | HIT Penetration |
| L: | HIT Location | HFDH: | Human Figure Drawing— |
| FD: | HIT Form Definiteness | | Harris-Goodenough |
| FA: | HIT Form Appropriateness | VOC: | WISC Vocabulary |
| C: | HIT Color | BD: | WISC Block Design |
| SH: | HIT Shading | ARIT: | WISC Arithmetic |
| M: | HIT Movement | PC: | WISC Picture Completion |
| V: | HIT Pathognomic Verbalization | OSTG: | Object Sorting Test—Number of Groups |
| I: | HIT Integration | OSTO: | Object Sorting Test—Percent Open |
| H: | HIT Human | OSTP: | Object Sorting Test—Percent Public |
| A: | HIT Animal | TETD: | Time Estimation Test—Delay |
| AT: | HIT Anatomy | EFTT: | Embedded Figures Test—Time |
| AX: | HIT Anxiety | | |

Table 6-13
Intercorrelations, Means, and Standard Deviations for Seven-Year-Olds (Group I, Year 2)

| | SSEX | RT | R | L | FD | FA | C | SH | M | V | I | H | A | AT | AX |
|---|---|---|---|---|---|---|---|---|---|---|---|---|---|---|---|
| Means | 1.5 | 16.2 | 2.9 | 36.4 | 69.5 | 37.4 | 18.1 | 4.2 | 15.5 | 4.6 | 1.3 | 13.5 | 22.0 | 4.1 | 8.1 |
| Sigma | .5 | 11.8 | 6.3 | 20.8 | 16.9 | 6.9 | 13.1 | 3.3 | 14.0 | 4.9 | 1.8 | 7.0 | 9.3 | 5.8 | 5.8 |
| SSEX | | —06 | —23 | 18 | 03 | **25** | 13 | —03 | 15 | —03 | 07 | 19 | 10 | —**28** | —11 |
| RT | 00 | | **76** | —08 | **31** | —01 | —**30** | —14 | —11 | —18 | —09 | —19 | —12 | —03 | —07 |
| R | —02 | **55** | | —27 | 11 | —04 | —22 | —20 | —20 | —17 | —14 | —**28** | —**32** | 00 | —13 |
| L | 06 | —05 | —20 | | 21 | **31** | —27 | —10 | —**39** | —**29** | —**39** | —02 | **28** | —05 | —**27** |
| FD | 04 | 06 | —04 | 20 | | —19 | —**59** | —18 | 08 | 12 | 14 | 21 | **60** | —13 | 09 |
| FA | —13 | 11 | 18 | **38** | —**40** | | 21 | —02 | 10 | —23 | 05 | 00 | —11 | —**42** | —05 |
| C | 00 | —15 | —14 | —**25** | —**63** | 21 | | 20 | 14 | 08 | 00 | —09 | —**34** | —12 | 13 |
| SH | —14 | —14 | —22 | —17 | —17 | 13 | 11 | | **27** | 21 | 02 | —02 | —07 | —06 | 20 |
| M | —22 | —10 | —15 | —18 | 12 | 02 | 00 | **28** | | **49** | **65** | **50** | 10 | —**26** | **60** |
| V | —19 | —08 | —08 | —**33** | 03 | —08 | 05 | **34** | **60** | | **29** | **31** | 21 | 02 | **41** |
| I | —18 | —11 | —11 | —11 | 15 | 08 | 03 | **25** | **60** | **44** | | **45** | 13 | —17 | **38** |
| H | —11 | —04 | —16 | 21 | **51** | —11 | —**29** | 05 | **30** | 15 | **35** | | 11 | —09 | **28** |
| A | 03 | —09 | —**28** | 05 | **60** | —**38** | —**42** | —07 | 13 | 05 | 12 | 23 | | —**27** | 05 |
| AT | 03 | —09 | —06 | —22 | —18 | —**24** | 16 | —01 | —10 | 14 | —05 | —13 | —**28** | | 0 |
| AX | —22 | —09 | —02 | —20 | —16 | 05 | 18 | 18 | **42** | **57** | 21 | —09 | —05 | **25** | |
| HS | —**28** | —09 | —12 | —04 | 00 | 09 | 08 | 15 | **59** | **48** | **31** | 06 | 16 | —12 | 6 |
| BR | 11 | —09 | —20 | 03 | **46** | —15 | —21 | 04 | **26** | 11 | 22 | 20 | 19 | —**30** | —0 |
| PN | —18 | —02 | —09 | —15 | —04 | 01 | 02 | 24 | **47** | **39** | 08 | 03 | 05 | 00 | 3 |
| HFDH | **22** | —03 | —15 | 17 | 15 | 00 | —07 | 00 | —03 | —10 | 15 | 19 | 13 | —14 | —0 |
| VOC | —**25** | —08 | —**26** | 07 | **24** | 05 | 05 | 19 | **26** | 13 | **27** | 17 | 14 | —08 | 0 |
| BD | —07 | —01 | —05 | —02 | 01 | 06 | —01 | 16 | —04 | —09 | 06 | 03 | 01 | 05 | 0 |
| OSTG | —04 | 01 | —02 | 11 | 16 | 09 | —06 | —07 | —05 | —10 | 00 | 02 | 11 | —**27** | 0 |
| OSTO | 08 | —08 | 08 | —10 | —09 | —11 | 14 | 03 | 04 | 05 | 06 | 00 | —18 | 12 | —0 |
| OSTP | 08 | 12 | 09 | 20 | 00 | 17 | —02 | 05 | —03 | —15 | 04 | —04 | 00 | —08 | 0 |
| TETD | —11 | 06 | 03 | —10 | 02 | 00 | 03 | 06 | **34** | **36** | 00 | 00 | 02 | —01 | 2 |
| TASC | 08 | 00 | —14 | 03 | 12 | —05 | 00 | 04 | 08 | —12 | 12 | 10 | 15 | —04 | C |
| VFTT | 08 | 15 | —02 | 12 | —06 | 15 | —09 | —03 | 00 | —13 | 02 | —01 | —05 | —17 | — |
| VFTC | —10 | —07 | 02 | 08 | —01 | 15 | —02 | —02 | 09 | 04 | 11 | 05 | —05 | 03 | C |
| CSTT | 08 | **26** | **22** | 08 | —06 | 07 | —14 | —02 | —05 | —07 | —08 | 00 | —06 | —15 | — |
| | SSEX | RT | R | L | FD | FA | C | SH | M | V | I | H | A | AT | A |
| Means | 1.5 | 20.3 | 2.2 | 48.5 | 65.0 | 39.2 | 17.1 | 2.3 | 7.7 | 4.7 | .6 | 12.4 | 24.6 | 4.4 | 6 |
| Sigma | .5 | 20.4 | 5.8 | 22.4 | 19.7 | 5.8 | 23.7 | 2.3 | 11.0 | 8.6 | 1.2 | 8.0 | 13.1 | 6.3 | 7 |

MEXICO

NOTES:

Table includes selected variables for 109 U.S. subjects (upper matrix) and 139 Mexican subjects (lower matrix).

Decimals are omitted from correlations.

Boldface correlations are significantly different from zero beyond the .01 level.

Actual number of cases for any given correlation may be slightly reduced because of missing data.

# UNITED STATES

| HS | BR | PN | HFDH | VOC | BD | OSTG | OSTO | OSTP | TETD | TASC | VFTT | VFTC | CSTT |
|---|---|---|---|---|---|---|---|---|---|---|---|---|---|
| 8.2 | 4.2 | 3.3 | 25.6 | 27.0 | 13.0 | 15.4 | 70.9 | 58.8 | 119.2 | 8.7 | 137.9 | 11.2 | 124.0 |
| 5.5 | 2.8 | 3.0 | 6.6 | 5.6 | 8.2 | 5.0 | 15.7 | 20.8 | 75.3 | 6.1 | 55.5 | 3.8 | 48.4 |
| **HS** | **BR** | **PN** | **HFDH** | **VOC** | **BD** | **OSTG** | **OSTO** | **OSTP** | **TETD** | **TASC** | **VFTT** | **VFTC** | **CSTT** |
| −08 | 17 | −11 | 36 | 11 | 00 | −09 | 06 | 00 | −02 | 02 | 19 | 00 | 21 |
| −14 | −15 | −17 | −09 | −14 | 00 | −17 | 09 | 05 | 17 | −09 | 20 | −02 | 34 |
| −21 | −31 | −19 | −20 | −16 | 00 | −24 | 10 | −07 | 18 | −10 | 02 | 05 | 20 |
| −16 | −06 | −25 | 22 | −01 | 04 | 06 | 04 | 22 | 00 | 17 | 19 | 13 | 03 |
| 18 | 23 | −11 | 22 | 04 | 17 | −09 | 14 | 21 | 04 | 06 | 16 | 05 | 22 |
| 08 | 01 | −06 | 14 | 33 | 05 | −04 | 02 | 00 | 11 | −08 | 12 | 17 | 02 |
| 06 | 03 | 13 | −07 | 06 | −08 | 16 | 02 | −17 | 00 | −07 | −06 | −08 | −21 |
| 16 | 09 | 25 | −06 | 01 | 01 | −04 | 21 | 00 | 12 | −07 | 08 | 00 | 05 |
| 72 | 35 | 50 | 03 | 42 | 12 | −13 | −02 | −16 | 02 | −13 | 00 | 01 | 05 |
| 44 | 30 | 43 | −07 | 19 | 03 | 00 | −08 | −06 | 09 | 05 | −10 | 11 | −05 |
| 43 | 36 | 24 | 10 | 33 | 09 | −04 | −02 | −06 | 03 | −15 | −05 | 12 | 00 |
| 41 | 25 | 24 | 19 | 22 | 10 | −11 | −02 | 05 | 06 | 03 | 10 | 12 | 18 |
| 19 | 23 | −07 | 18 | 10 | 08 | 05 | 11 | 07 | −07 | 05 | 00 | 02 | −02 |
| −20 | −36 | 04 | −19 | −12 | −11 | 12 | −22 | 08 | −08 | 09 | −06 | −02 | 00 |
| 67 | 08 | 42 | −02 | 18 | 10 | 01 | −07 | −09 | −09 | −06 | −08 | 02 | −05 |
|  | 26 | 48 | 07 | 37 | 08 | −04 | −04 | 00 | −03 | 01 | −04 | 14 | −03 |
| 11 |  | 14 | 20 | 30 | 16 | 08 | 13 | 00 | 06 | 06 | 04 | 00 | 04 |
| 47 | 15 |  | −06 | 37 | 09 | −04 | −09 | 01 | 08 | 02 | −04 | 12 | −12 |
| 01 | 13 | −03 |  | 33 | 49 | −01 | 04 | 01 | 10 | 06 | 09 | 08 | 11 |
| 12 | 25 | 09 | 12 |  | 30 | −15 | 12 | −16 | 25 | −11 | 14 | 24 | 02 |
| 04 | −04 | 10 | 36 | 17 |  | −07 | 04 | 02 | 11 | −06 | 03 | 17 | 12 |
| −05 | 15 | 00 | 07 | 06 | −02 |  | −35 | 38 | −14 | 16 | 04 | −10 | −17 |
| 03 | 02 | 15 | 01 | 01 | −10 | −21 |  | −19 | 18 | −13 | 08 | 04 | 00 |
| 00 | −07 | −05 | 03 | 00 | 02 | 26 | −08 |  | −04 | −04 | 17 | 13 | 04 |
| 33 | 07 | 36 | −06 | 03 | 06 | 09 | 11 | −05 |  | −08 | 13 | 13 | 15 |
| −03 | −04 | −14 | 01 | 09 | −09 | 19 | −12 | 02 | 03 |  | −07 | 03 | 00 |
| −07 | −01 | −03 | 12 | −11 | 11 | 13 | −14 | 16 | 08 | 00 |  | 13 | 47 |
| −04 | −01 | −13 | 10 | 21 | 17 | −09 | 12 | 00 | 06 | −11 | 04 |  | 14 |
| −09 | −02 | 00 | 08 | −14 | −06 | −15 | 03 | −10 | 08 | −01 | 39 | −05 |  |
| **HS** | **BR** | **PN** | **HFDH** | **VOC** | **BD** | **OSTG** | **OSTO** | **OSTP** | **TETD** | **TASC** | **VFTT** | **VFTC** | **CSTT** |
| 7.5 | 3.1 | .7 | 18.8 | 19.7 | 10.1 | 17.7 | 62.5 | 50.8 | 110.1 | 16.5 | 98.6 | 9.6 | 138.6 |
| 6.0 | 3.1 | 1.7 | 5.4 | 5.1 | 6.1 | 6.0 | 20.6 | 21.3 | 87.6 | 7.7 | 44.0 | 4.2 | 80.5 |

Names of variables are abbreviated as follows:

| | | | |
|---|---|---|---|
| SSEX: | Subject's Sex | HS: | HIT Hostility |
| RT: | HIT Reaction Time | BR: | HIT Barrier |
| R: | HIT Rejection | PN: | HIT Penetration |
| L: | HIT Location | HFDH: | Human Figure Drawing—Harris-Goodenough |
| FD: | HIT Form Definiteness | | |
| FA: | HIT Form Appropriateness | VOC: | WISC Vocabulary |
| C: | HIT Color | BD: | WISC Block Design |
| SH: | HIT Shading | OSTG: | Object Sorting Test—Number of Groups |
| M: | HIT Movement | OSTO: | Object Sorting Test—Percent Open |
| V: | HIT Pathognomic Verbalization | OSTP: | Object Sorting Test—Percent Public |
| I: | HIT Integration | TETD: | Time Estimation Test—Delay |
| H: | HIT Human | TASC: | Test Anxiety Scale for Children |
| A: | HIT Animal | VFTT: | Visual Fractionation Test—Time |
| AT: | HIT Anatomy | VFTC: | Visual Fractionation Test—Number Correct |
| AX: | HIT Anxiety | CSTT: | Conceptual Styles Test—Time |

| | SSEX | RT | R | L | FD | FA | C | SH | M | V | I | H | A | AT | A |
|---|---|---|---|---|---|---|---|---|---|---|---|---|---|---|---|
| Means | 1.6 | 23.4 | 4.0 | 35.6 | 82.8 | 38.4 | 11.0 | 5.8 | 27.8 | 4.6 | 3.0 | 16.6 | 23.6 | 2.2 | 7 |
| Sigma | .5 | 13.8 | 6.5 | 22.6 | 14.3 | 6.6 | 9.6 | 3.7 | 18.9 | 5.8 | 3.1 | 8.6 | 8.4 | 3.3 | 6 |
| SSEX | | 00 | −05 | 05 | −01 | 01 | 05 | 07 | −15 | −27 | −04 | 00 | −05 | −03 | − |
| RT | 10 | | 77 | 09 | 13 | 26 | −38 | −26 | −41 | −28 | −32 | −31 | −42 | −22 | − |
| R | 06 | 40 | | −12 | 11 | 08 | −34 | −32 | −33 | −19 | −27 | −29 | −44 | −07 | − |
| L | 09 | 09 | −33 | | 30 | 47 | −42 | −13 | −51 | −37 | −48 | −25 | 08 | −21 | − |
| FD | −18 | 04 | −04 | 11 | | −08 | −58 | −54 | 01 | 04 | 06 | 30 | 40 | −21 | − |
| FA | 06 | 15 | 16 | 45 | −35 | | −01 | 16 | −29 | −19 | −19 | −30 | −17 | −12 | |
| C | 02 | −14 | −07 | −26 | −34 | −03 | | 53 | 33 | 20 | 27 | −03 | −10 | 07 | |
| SH | 11 | −24 | −19 | −16 | −38 | 00 | 22 | | 15 | 01 | 14 | −17 | 00 | 00 | |
| M | −18 | −19 | −15 | −32 | 14 | −06 | 17 | 33 | | 60 | 63 | 60 | 29 | 02 | |
| V | 00 | −12 | −18 | −10 | 22 | −24 | 02 | 12 | 23 | | 32 | 31 | 29 | 20 | |
| I | −09 | −07 | −07 | −30 | 28 | −14 | 09 | 20 | 66 | 38 | | 63 | 21 | −02 | |
| H | −03 | 06 | −19 | 23 | 41 | 04 | −17 | −23 | 19 | 20 | 26 | | 22 | −07 | |
| A | 02 | −01 | −21 | 00 | 57 | −43 | −22 | −23 | 05 | 23 | 15 | 23 | | −10 | |
| AT | −08 | −21 | −12 | −24 | −18 | −23 | 02 | 16 | −06 | −04 | −09 | −33 | −29 | | |
| AX | −09 | −20 | −19 | −36 | 07 | −18 | 15 | 37 | 62 | 20 | 31 | −07 | 12 | 11 | |
| HS | −18 | −15 | −24 | −23 | 30 | −25 | 08 | 31 | 68 | 35 | 55 | 09 | 31 | −08 | |
| BR | −08 | −08 | −19 | −14 | 16 | −03 | 13 | 24 | 42 | 16 | 44 | 02 | −03 | −12 | |
| PN | −06 | −09 | −16 | −22 | 16 | −28 | 11 | 31 | 41 | 24 | 46 | 08 | 20 | 03 | |
| HFDH | 29 | 00 | −15 | 17 | 05 | 05 | −01 | 09 | 06 | 22 | 18 | 06 | 11 | −21 | |
| VOC | −26 | −24 | −12 | 04 | 19 | −01 | −01 | 05 | 17 | 21 | 16 | 11 | 03 | −03 | |
| BD | −27 | 03 | −12 | 24 | 22 | 10 | −10 | −03 | 07 | 17 | 11 | 17 | 01 | −22 | − |
| OSTG | 01 | −10 | 02 | 23 | 14 | 21 | 10 | −17 | 00 | −13 | 00 | 01 | 01 | −11 | − |
| OSTO | −04 | 09 | 06 | −10 | −07 | −15 | −01 | 15 | −01 | 10 | −02 | −01 | 03 | 07 | |
| OSTP | −05 | 14 | 15 | 07 | 04 | 08 | −05 | −21 | −01 | −20 | −04 | 02 | −01 | 00 | − |
| TETD | −22 | 19 | 08 | 09 | 27 | 12 | −02 | −06 | 09 | 09 | 09 | 13 | 01 | −05 | |
| TASC | 13 | −04 | −22 | 15 | −09 | 08 | −03 | 10 | 00 | −10 | −09 | 07 | −05 | 02 | |
| VFTT | 13 | 13 | 05 | 09 | −02 | 02 | −01 | −13 | 03 | −09 | −01 | 05 | 05 | 01 | |
| VFTC | 07 | 03 | 01 | 17 | 15 | 15 | −10 | 00 | 00 | 18 | 12 | 00 | 04 | −09 | − |
| EFTT | 19 | 06 | 06 | −19 | −18 | −09 | 09 | 01 | 02 | −12 | −07 | −05 | 03 | 24 | |
| | SSEX | RT | R | L | FD | FA | C | SH | M | V | I | H | A | AT | |
| Means | 1.5 | 22.0 | 2.0 | 58.3 | 73.5 | 41.3 | 6.0 | 2.3 | 11.3 | 2.7 | 1.1 | 15.0 | 27.0 | 3.7 | |
| Sigma | .5 | 17.5 | 4.8 | 21.4 | 15.7 | 4.6 | 8.8 | 2.2 | 12.6 | 2.8 | 1.8 | 7.6 | 11.1 | 5.6 | |

MEXICO

NOTES:

Table includes selected variables for 125 U.S. subjects (upper matrix) and 132 Mexican subjects (lower matrix).

Decimals are omitted from correlations.

Boldface correlations are significantly different from zero beyond the .01 level.

Actual number of cases for any given correlation may be slightly reduced because of missing data.

# UNITED STATES

| HS | BR | PN | HFDH | VOC | BD | OSTG | OSTO | OSTP | TETD | TASC | VFTT | VFTC | EFTT |
|---|---|---|---|---|---|---|---|---|---|---|---|---|---|
| 10.0 | 6.2 | 2.9 | 35.3 | 41.9 | 29.5 | 13.0 | 79.6 | 54.8 | 143.5 | 11.0 | 115.7 | 13.4 | 85.3 |
| 7.5 | 3.4 | 2.8 | 7.2 | 5.5 | 11.2 | 3.3 | 14.6 | 20.8 | 50.1 | 5.4 | 60.7 | 4.2 | 35.8 |
| **HS** | **BR** | **PN** | **HFDH** | **VOC** | **BD** | **OSTG** | **OSTO** | **OSTP** | **TETD** | **TASC** | **VFTT** | **VFTC** | **EFTT** |
| −30 | −03 | −13 | 20 | −24 | −21 | 13 | −06 | 08 | −06 | 11 | 02 | 14 | 17 |
| −42 | −35 | −32 | 00 | −05 | 14 | 12 | −17 | 02 | 13 | 11 | 36 | −04 | 03 |
| −32 | −45 | −25 | −06 | −02 | 13 | 00 | −06 | 02 | 13 | 04 | 11 | −06 | 09 |
| −35 | −12 | −41 | −20 | −05 | −16 | 13 | −09 | 09 | 08 | 01 | 11 | −11 | 19 |
| 08 | 08 | −28 | 16 | 08 | 08 | 06 | −02 | −13 | 09 | 04 | −08 | −03 | −07 |
| −26 | −08 | −12 | −17 | 00 | −10 | 16 | −20 | 13 | 05 | −01 | 23 | −03 | 11 |
| 23 | 22 | 43 | 03 | −04 | −06 | 01 | −01 | 00 | −14 | 09 | 01 | 04 | −04 |
| 06 | 17 | 32 | 00 | 05 | −07 | 09 | 00 | 11 | −12 | 00 | 18 | −04 | −01 |
| 81 | 43 | 54 | 18 | 19 | 09 | −07 | 12 | −03 | −16 | 01 | −23 | 04 | −09 |
| 67 | 14 | 62 | 06 | 18 | 00 | −02 | 03 | 04 | 07 | 01 | −16 | 00 | −02 |
| 48 | 40 | 22 | 27 | 09 | 14 | −02 | 05 | −08 | −11 | 00 | −09 | 04 | −13 |
| 44 | 31 | 04 | 31 | −01 | 11 | −11 | 14 | 02 | −08 | 07 | −19 | 14 | −03 |
| 39 | 16 | 13 | 17 | 05 | 06 | 03 | 05 | −06 | −04 | 00 | −05 | −10 | −13 |
| 14 | −21 | 39 | −06 | −01 | −05 | −29 | 02 | −16 | 05 | −09 | −08 | 01 | 01 |
| 78 | 21 | 57 | 18 | 14 | −01 | −08 | 06 | −01 | −02 | 08 | −13 | −06 | −13 |
|  | 26 | 57 | 09 | 18 | 02 | −09 | 06 | −07 | −04 | 02 | −22 | −13 | −04 |
| 34 |  | 17 | 13 | 13 | −01 | −02 | 16 | −05 | −10 | −08 | −13 | 04 | −14 |
| 56 | 23 |  | −01 | 10 | −12 | 00 | 00 | 00 | −04 | −02 | 00 | −07 | 05 |
| 12 | 05 | 11 |  | 07 | 38 | −02 | 17 | 10 | 02 | 10 | 07 | 27 | −42 |
| 09 | 18 | 12 | 21 |  | 26 | −14 | 20 | −14 | 13 | −23 | −14 | 07 | −27 |
| 15 | 09 | 06 | 26 | 34 |  | −23 | 28 | 01 | 01 | −07 | 01 | 12 | −62 |
| −09 | 05 | 00 | 11 | 11 | 10 |  | −44 | 53 | −06 | 03 | 17 | 03 | 10 |
| 06 | −05 | 09 | −08 | −08 | −04 | −45 |  | −06 | 00 | −09 | −11 | 14 | −15 |
| −04 | −04 | 02 | −12 | 03 | 16 | 35 | −10 |  | −11 | 05 | 11 | 10 | 05 |
| 14 | 06 | 08 | 05 | 10 | 26 | 13 | 09 | 17 |  | 02 | 13 | 02 | −02 |
| 00 | 18 | 03 | −01 | −17 | −10 | −05 | 01 | 08 | −12 |  | 09 | −03 | 10 |
| −01 | −07 | 00 | 00 | −06 | −08 | 09 | 08 | 21 | −01 | 03 |  | −23 | −06 |
| 07 | 15 | 15 | 32 | 27 | 19 | 19 | −05 | 12 | 18 | −09 | −12 |  | −22 |
| −01 | −12 | 00 | −24 | −42 | −60 | −04 | 05 | 00 | −07 | 13 | 11 | −22 |  |
| **HS** | **BR** | **PN** | **HFDH** | **VOC** | **BD** | **OSTG** | **OSTO** | **OSTP** | **TETD** | **TASC** | **VFTT** | **VFTC** | **EFTT** |
| 6.9 | 3.7 | 1.4 | 25.9 | 31.5 | 21.1 | 15.0 | 65.3 | 50.2 | 110.7 | 17.0 | 92.2 | 13.3 | 117.5 |
| 5.2 | 2.9 | 2.2 | 7.1 | 7.2 | 9.3 | 3.8 | 15.9 | 18.0 | 50.9 | 6.1 | 30.4 | 4.6 | 36.1 |

Names of variables are abbreviated as follows:

| | | | |
|---|---|---|---|
| SSEX: | Subject's Sex | HS: | HIT Hostility |
| RT: | HIT Reaction Time | BR: | HIT Barrier |
| R: | HIT Rejection | PN: | HIT Penetration |
| L: | HIT Location | HFDH: | Human Figure Drawing—Harris-Goodenough |
| FD: | HIT Form Definiteness | | |
| FA: | HIT Form Appropriateness | VOC: | WISC Vocabulary |
| C: | HIT Color | BD: | WISC Block Design |
| SH: | HIT Shading | OSTG: | Object Sorting Test—Number of Groups |
| M: | HIT Movement | OSTO: | Object Sorting Test—Percent Open |
| V: | HIT Pathognomic Verbalization | OSTP: | Object Sorting Test—Percent Public |
| I: | HIT Integration | TETD: | Time Estimation Test—Delay |
| H: | HIT Human | TASC: | Test Anxiety Scale for Children |
| A: | HIT Animal | VFTT: | Visual Fractionation Test—Time |
| AT: | HIT Anatomy | VFTC: | Visual Fractionation Test—Number Correct |
| AX: | HIT Anxiety | EFTT: | Embedded Figures Test—Time |

Table 6-15
Intercorrelations, Means, and Standard Deviations for Thirteen-Year-Olds (Group III, Year 2)

| | SSEX | RT | R | L | FD | FA | C | SH | M | V | I | H | A | AT |
|---|---|---|---|---|---|---|---|---|---|---|---|---|---|---|
| Means | 1.5 | 22.6 | 1.5 | 38.2 | 84.1 | 43.6 | 12.3 | 4.0 | 29.3 | 3.6 | 3.4 | 17.1 | 26.7 | 1.9 |
| Sigma | .5 | 10.6 | 3.5 | 21.6 | 16.7 | 6.5 | 10.0 | 4.1 | 20.6 | 5.2 | 3.4 | 9.2 | 8.4 | 2.1 |
| SSEX | | −15 | −10 | −06 | 06 | 00 | 10 | 09 | 00 | 00 | 10 | 12 | −03 | 00 |
| RT | 06 | | 11 | 39 | 00 | 37 | −12 | 04 | −16 | −20 | −33 | −07 | −03 | −16 |
| R | −12 | 55 | | 00 | 08 | 09 | −28 | −28 | −29 | −01 | −24 | −22 | −14 | 01 |
| L | 18 | 06 | −21 | | 22 | 49 | −53 | −32 | −56 | −32 | −56 | −15 | 06 | 00 |
| FD | −07 | 02 | −10 | 25 | | 06 | −41 | −21 | 03 | 22 | 17 | 44 | 51 | −06 |
| FA | 07 | 07 | 08 | 32 | −23 | | −01 | 18 | −03 | −02 | −04 | −03 | −13 | 01 |
| C | 10 | −09 | −08 | −26 | −52 | 07 | | 68 | 56 | 15 | 37 | 04 | −31 | 06 |
| SH | −08 | −20 | −15 | −35 | −32 | 03 | 33 | | 56 | 19 | 39 | 11 | −22 | −02 |
| M | −11 | −16 | −16 | −33 | 21 | −12 | 07 | 40 | | 53 | 78 | 52 | −05 | −02 |
| V | 14 | −05 | −12 | −19 | 10 | −29 | 19 | 16 | 42 | | 49 | 50 | 08 | −06 |
| I | −02 | −18 | −13 | −40 | 11 | −15 | 13 | 26 | 72 | 49 | | 56 | −01 | −05 |
| H | −06 | −11 | −17 | 18 | 52 | −03 | −16 | −11 | 48 | 22 | 35 | | −02 | −10 |
| A | 03 | −17 | −24 | 10 | 57 | −23 | −29 | −21 | 09 | 13 | 17 | 14 | | −08 |
| AT | −11 | −05 | −06 | −23 | −24 | −04 | 02 | 07 | −12 | 05 | −07 | −31 | −25 | |
| AX | −14 | −27 | −13 | −34 | 04 | −29 | 14 | 25 | 51 | 42 | 51 | 11 | 13 | 25 |
| HS | −16 | −30 | −24 | −15 | 20 | −15 | 10 | 27 | 61 | 40 | 63 | 25 | 26 | −09 |
| BR | 07 | 03 | −13 | −21 | 13 | −11 | 02 | 33 | 47 | 20 | 39 | 12 | −10 | −19 |
| PN | 02 | −13 | −07 | −19 | −15 | 03 | 07 | 34 | 40 | 26 | 26 | 11 | −28 | 19 |
| HFDH | 06 | 00 | −07 | −03 | 12 | 03 | −01 | 00 | 10 | 14 | 16 | 05 | −04 | −06 |
| VOC | −24 | −05 | −04 | −08 | 09 | −07 | 09 | 22 | 18 | 01 | 18 | 18 | −03 | −03 |
| BD | −22 | 00 | 04 | −03 | 24 | 03 | −15 | 03 | 11 | −05 | 04 | 17 | 02 | −09 |
| OSTG | −09 | 12 | 11 | 08 | 02 | 05 | −03 | −06 | −06 | 00 | −04 | −03 | −09 | 03 |
| OSTO | 17 | 05 | 01 | −06 | −09 | 00 | 06 | 00 | −15 | 09 | −14 | −10 | 05 | 04 |
| OSTP | −03 | 16 | 13 | 04 | −11 | 07 | 10 | −10 | −21 | 05 | −16 | −11 | −07 | 13 |
| TETD | −13 | −19 | −15 | −07 | 13 | 00 | 00 | 04 | 20 | −14 | 10 | 10 | 02 | 15 |
| TASC | 19 | 05 | 03 | 15 | −07 | −02 | −03 | −23 | −09 | 00 | −05 | −04 | 04 | −11 |
| VFTT | 20 | 24 | 06 | 05 | −10 | 05 | 01 | −02 | −17 | −17 | −15 | −26 | 04 | 03 |
| VFTC | 01 | −08 | −08 | −05 | −01 | 01 | 14 | 17 | 21 | 07 | 14 | 07 | −10 | 04 |
| EFTT | 35 | 10 | 02 | 04 | −08 | −04 | −04 | −10 | −13 | 12 | 00 | −02 | 07 | 01 |
| | SSEX | RT | R | L | FD | FA | C | SH | M | V | I | H | A | AT |
| Means | 1.5 | 28.3 | 1.7 | 59.9 | 75.9 | 42.9 | 6.6 | 2.7 | 13.8 | 2.3 | 1.6 | 14.3 | 27.1 | 3.9 |
| Sigma | .5 | 15.8 | 3.7 | 18.6 | 14.3 | 4.3 | 10.3 | 2.7 | 12.4 | 2.9 | 2.5 | 8.3 | 8.8 | 4.9 |

MEXICO

NOTES:

Table includes selected variables for 131 U.S. subjects (upper matrix) and 138 Mexican subjects (lower matrix).

Decimals are omitted from correlations.

Boldface correlations are significantly different from zero beyond the .01 level.

Actual number of cases for any given correlation may be slightly reduced because of missing data.

# UNITED STATES

| HS | BR | PN | HFDH | VOC | BD | OSTG | OSTO | OSTP | TETD | TASC | VFTT | VFTC | EFTT |
|---|---|---|---|---|---|---|---|---|---|---|---|---|---|
| 10.6 | 6.8 | 3.1 | 39.1 | 53.8 | 42.6 | 13.1 | 82.5 | 54.5 | 168.3 | 10.4 | 108.6 | 14.9 | 36.4 |
| 7.8 | 4.3 | 2.7 | 9.1 | 7.3 | 9.7 | 4.3 | 13.9 | 20.6 | 49.5 | 6.3 | 37.0 | 4.2 | 31.4 |
| −17 | 12 | −07 | 05 | −21 | −09 | −01 | 05 | 05 | −06 | 09 | −02 | −03 | 07 |
| −14 | −07 | −07 | 14 | −09 | −16 | 13 | −10 | 15 | 02 | −06 | 30 | 00 | 13 |
| −21 | −31 | −28 | −03 | 10 | 09 | 19 | −07 | 19 | 05 | −07 | 03 | 09 | −06 |
| −43 | −22 | −34 | −13 | −26 | −15 | 23 | −23 | 23 | 11 | 02 | 27 | −10 | 08 |
| 10 | 32 | −05 | 02 | 05 | 04 | 07 | −05 | −05 | −07 | 13 | −10 | 01 | −05 |
| 04 | 10 | 07 | 06 | −11 | −17 | 14 | −09 | 27 | 02 | 10 | 10 | 04 | 05 |
| 45 | 28 | 47 | 19 | 07 | 12 | −22 | 19 | −09 | 02 | −03 | −10 | 01 | −03 |
| 48 | 40 | 52 | 24 | 04 | −03 | −22 | 17 | −08 | −05 | 04 | −03 | −02 | 07 |
| 86 | 56 | 64 | 20 | 21 | 05 | −27 | 19 | −31 | −13 | 03 | −14 | 04 | 01 |
| 58 | 32 | 25 | −16 | 00 | −20 | −10 | 00 | −27 | −13 | 09 | −03 | −09 | 34 |
| 66 | 56 | 53 | 25 | 27 | 10 | −20 | 19 | −24 | −15 | 04 | −28 | 05 | −03 |
| 44 | 55 | 30 | 13 | 16 | 02 | 13 | −10 | −12 | 00 | 06 | −07 | −07 | 03 |
| 05 | −06 | −08 | −10 | −07 | −10 | −06 | 05 | −10 | −16 | 10 | −11 | −01 | 03 |
| 03 | −06 | 08 | −07 | 02 | −01 | 05 | 05 | −06 | 20 | 05 | 04 | 00 | −04 |
| 82 | 40 | 57 | 00 | 05 | −09 | −35 | 23 | −39 | −06 | 06 | −11 | −07 | 13 |
|  | 45 | 69 | 09 | 14 | −02 | −25 | 20 | −28 | −20 | 11 | −05 | −03 | 09 |
| 21 |  | 36 | 16 | 13 | 08 | −17 | 11 | −20 | −07 | 13 | −12 | −08 | −03 |
| 22 | 31 |  | 23 | 17 | 00 | −19 | 25 | −13 | −12 | 09 | −13 | −03 | −02 |
| 11 | 17 | 19 |  | 40 | 35 | 00 | 14 | 13 | 09 | −07 | −01 | 15 | −40 |
| 12 | 08 | 11 | 11 |  | 33 | −05 | 16 | −10 | 08 | −13 | −10 | 37 | −34 |
| 12 | 10 | 07 | 25 | 29 |  | −05 | 18 | −03 | 19 | −26 | −07 | 28 | −72 |
| −12 | −04 | −08 | −12 | −06 | −17 |  | −67 | 55 | 04 | 05 | 02 | −02 | 06 |
| −05 | −02 | −03 | −01 | 00 | 07 | −42 |  | −31 | 01 | −06 | −06 | 09 | −19 |
| −15 | −25 | −19 | −07 | −08 | −05 | 36 | −08 |  | −01 | 06 | −07 | 10 | −05 |
| 05 | 09 | 03 | 03 | 26 | 13 | −01 | −11 | −05 |  | −19 | 04 | 08 | −28 |
| −07 | 01 | −04 | 17 | −19 | −05 | −04 | 08 | 14 | −23 |  | −07 | −18 | 23 |
| −18 | 08 | −07 | 09 | −14 | −09 | −10 | 07 | −02 | −15 | 11 |  | −26 | 14 |
| 12 | 19 | 06 | 10 | 17 | 14 | 12 | 01 | −01 | 25 | −07 | −31 |  | −35 |
| −11 | −13 | −09 | −31 | −23 | −54 | 07 | 18 | 00 | −26 | 13 | 04 | −20 |  |
| HS | BR | PN | HFDH | VOC | BD | OSTG | OSTO | OSTP | TETD | TASC | VFTT | VFTC | EFTT |
| 6.6 | 4.3 | 1.8 | 35.1 | 43.3 | 35.3 | 14.8 | 69.5 | 50.1 | 131.6 | 14.9 | 89.6 | 15.8 | 50.7 |
| 4.8 | 2.9 | 2.1 | 8.1 | 6.9 | 9.3 | 3.4 | 13.6 | 17.3 | 49.9 | 5.6 | 38.3 | 4.4 | 32.6 |

Names of variables are abbreviated as follows:

| | | | |
|---|---|---|---|
| SSEX: | Subject's Sex | HS: | HIT Hostility |
| RT: | HIT Reaction Time | BR: | HIT Barrier |
| R: | HIT Rejection | PN: | HIT Penetration |
| L: | HIT Location | HFDH: | Human Figure Drawing—Harris-Goodenough |
| FD: | HIT Form Definiteness | | |
| FA: | HIT Form Appropriateness | VOC: | WISC Vocabulary |
| C: | HIT Color | BD: | WISC Block Design |
| SH: | HIT Shading | OSTG: | Object Sorting Test—Number of Groups |
| M: | HIT Movement | OSTO: | Object Sorting Test— Percent Open |
| V: | HIT Pathognomic Verbalization | OSTP: | Object Sorting Test— Percent Public |
| I: | HIT Integration | TETD: | Time Estimation Test— Delay |
| H: | HIT Human | TASC: | Test Anxiety Scale for Children |
| A: | HIT Animal | VFTT: | Visual Fractionation Test—Time |
| AT: | HIT Anatomy | VFTC: | Visual Fractionation Test— Number Correct |
| AX: | HIT Anxiety | EFTT: | Embedded Figures Test— Time |

Table 6-16
Intercorrelations, Means, and Standard Deviations for Nine-Year-Olds (Group I, Year 4)

| | SSEX | RT | R | L | FD | FA | C | SH | M | V | I | H | A | AT |
|---|---|---|---|---|---|---|---|---|---|---|---|---|---|---|
| Means | 1.5 | 13.6 | 1.5 | 40.0 | 73.5 | 36.1 | 12.0 | 2.7 | 19.0 | 6.8 | .9 | 14.6 | 25.0 | 2.9 |
| Sigma | .5 | 8.1 | 3.7 | 21.6 | 15.6 | 6.2 | 10.6 | 2.4 | 14.0 | 7.5 | 1.4 | 6.8 | 9.1 | 4.0 |
| SSEX | | 06 | −05 | 05 | 05 | 11 | 08 | −10 | −06 | 01 | 00 | 06 | 09 | −16 |
| RT | 21 | | 56 | 18 | 15 | 28 | −18 | −08 | −25 | −25 | 03 | −19 | −17 | −03 |
| R | 19 | 54 | | −18 | 00 | 10 | −20 | 02 | −16 | −12 | −06 | −15 | −37 | −03 |
| L | 03 | 18 | −12 | | 16 | 46 | −17 | −15 | −50 | −34 | −37 | −21 | 05 | −08 |
| FD | 02 | 10 | −04 | 10 | | −37 | −57 | −16 | 19 | 22 | 16 | 43 | 62 | −08 |
| FA | 03 | 13 | 05 | 52 | −28 | | 23 | −07 | −30 | −43 | −10 | −37 | −23 | −25 |
| C | 00 | −08 | 00 | −13 | −58 | 19 | | 24 | 06 | −01 | 01 | −23 | −20 | −02 |
| SH | 14 | −15 | 00 | −28 | −39 | 15 | 38 | | 04 | 05 | −02 | −15 | −12 | 08 |
| M | −11 | −11 | −09 | −19 | 18 | 11 | −03 | 16 | | 50 | 54 | 41 | 31 | −12 |
| V | −14 | −14 | −06 | −33 | 10 | −46 | −08 | 01 | 18 | | 33 | 42 | 16 | 17 |
| I | −08 | −05 | 00 | −15 | 25 | 11 | −09 | 09 | 72 | 27 | | 39 | 32 | −02 |
| H | −08 | 06 | −15 | 14 | 43 | −11 | −31 | −23 | 26 | 02 | 25 | | 23 | 16 |
| A | 06 | −04 | −09 | −06 | 56 | −39 | −43 | −36 | −10 | 14 | 00 | 03 | | −32 |
| AT | −04 | −17 | 02 | −34 | −10 | −24 | 12 | 02 | −08 | 06 | −14 | −14 | −09 | |
| AX | −24 | −11 | 04 | −34 | −01 | −29 | 02 | 01 | 33 | 65 | 23 | −15 | 10 | 15 |
| HS | −26 | −01 | 00 | −07 | 10 | −21 | −09 | −10 | 19 | 70 | 20 | 00 | 14 | −06 |
| BR | 15 | −03 | −11 | 03 | 39 | −05 | −18 | −04 | 14 | −02 | 26 | 11 | 00 | −11 |
| PN | 00 | −01 | 09 | −26 | 00 | −27 | 00 | 07 | 21 | 75 | 27 | −11 | 06 | 01 |
| HFDH | 21 | 05 | 03 | −01 | 13 | 04 | −10 | 04 | 05 | 02 | 22 | 10 | −04 | 01 |
| VOC | −17 | −12 | −13 | −06 | −02 | 20 | 12 | 21 | 26 | 02 | 23 | −07 | −07 | 07 |
| BD | −19 | 00 | −04 | 06 | 05 | 17 | 02 | 11 | 16 | −02 | 26 | 11 | −20 | −10 |
| ARIT | −08 | 03 | 07 | 15 | 04 | 25 | −04 | 00 | 13 | −11 | 16 | 00 | −11 | −09 |
| PC | −30 | −07 | 01 | 06 | 13 | 04 | −12 | 03 | 11 | −06 | 07 | 17 | −09 | −01 |
| TASC | 10 | −09 | −10 | −07 | 06 | −10 | −07 | 02 | 00 | −12 | −10 | 08 | 20 | 06 |
| LIE | −02 | 08 | 07 | 00 | −03 | 04 | 06 | −02 | −08 | 02 | 00 | 00 | −05 | 01 |
| DSC | −06 | 18 | 01 | −08 | −04 | 04 | 05 | −01 | 03 | 16 | 09 | −04 | −06 | −02 |
| EFTT | 18 | 13 | 14 | −02 | −06 | −12 | 05 | −07 | −15 | −02 | −27 | −08 | 12 | 12 |
| PMS | −23 | 08 | 00 | 07 | −14 | 03 | 16 | −05 | −04 | 04 | 00 | 01 | −09 | 01 |
| WATS | −32 | −16 | −14 | −25 | −18 | −28 | 25 | 17 | −11 | −08 | −03 | −20 | −01 | 11 |
| SES | −02 | 08 | 02 | −14 | 10 | 05 | −01 | 13 | 38 | 15 | 27 | 11 | 00 | 05 |
| | SSEX | RT | R | L | FD | FA | C | SH | M | V | I | H | A | AT |
| Means | 1.5 | 16.5 | .5 | 59.7 | 71.2 | 41.3 | 14.8 | 2.8 | 8.3 | 2.5 | .8 | 15.4 | 27.1 | 3.4 |
| Sigma | .5 | 10.8 | 1.5 | 20.3 | 16.7 | 5.3 | 17.6 | 3.4 | 11.8 | 4.7 | 1.5 | 8.3 | 10.8 | 3.8 |

MEXICO

NOTES:

Table includes selected variables for 102 U.S. subjects (upper matrix) and 136 Mexican subjects (lower matrix).

Decimals are omitted from correlations.

Boldface correlations are significantly different from zero beyond the .01 level.

Actual number of cases for any given correlation may be slightly reduced because of missing data.

For SES and WATS in Mexico, the N is reduced to 55 and 47 cases respectively.

For SES and WATS in the United States, the N is reduced to 54 cases.

# UNITED STATES

| HS | BR | PN | HFDH | VOC | BD | ARIT | PC | TASC | LIE | DSC | EFTT | PMS | WATS | SES |
|---|---|---|---|---|---|---|---|---|---|---|---|---|---|---|
| 9.6 | 6.3 | 3.4 | 30.2 | 35.7 | 26.5 | 8.9 | 10.8 | 8.9 | 3.4 | 9.7 | 117.2 | 38.5 | 23.3 | 34.0 |
| 6.4 | 3.3 | 2.8 | 8.2 | 6.1 | 11.0 | 1.6 | 2.5 | 5.5 | 2.2 | 3.1 | 42.7 | 12.8 | 11.3 | 7.7 |
| -21 | 17 | -14 | 12 | -09 | 09 | 09 | -22 | 09 | -10 | 05 | -15 | -25 | -04 | 03 |
| -17 | -19 | -26 | 17 | 01 | 00 | 25 | -04 | -09 | -05 | -09 | 03 | 16 | 03 | 14 |
| -19 | -24 | -19 | -03 | -16 | -02 | 08 | 05 | -10 | 06 | -01 | 00 | 10 | -02 | 06 |
| -18 | -11 | -32 | 11 | 15 | 00 | 15 | -04 | 07 | -20 | 01 | 00 | -05 | 18 | 09 |
| 24 | 28 | 04 | 03 | 25 | 10 | 21 | 02 | 08 | -12 | -19 | -07 | -06 | 00 | 40 |
| -19 | -30 | -19 | 10 | 06 | 09 | 14 | 06 | 06 | -14 | -02 | 00 | -01 | 03 | -11 |
| 03 | -14 | 10 | -02 | -24 | -03 | -13 | -02 | 02 | 05 | 06 | 13 | 00 | -08 | -36 |
| 04 | -06 | 10 | -14 | -06 | -07 | -19 | 01 | -06 | 14 | 11 | 04 | 00 | -03 | 06 |
| 70 | 35 | 55 | -11 | 21 | 10 | 09 | 13 | 08 | 02 | -17 | 00 | 00 | -12 | 06 |
| 47 | 29 | 49 | -03 | 08 | -01 | 00 | 04 | 09 | -04 | -07 | -03 | 00 | -36 | 13 |
| 43 | 21 | 33 | -07 | 03 | 00 | 02 | 05 | 04 | 07 | -06 | 08 | 02 | -23 | 20 |
| 26 | 34 | 17 | 05 | 03 | 12 | 04 | 07 | 06 | 04 | 02 | -17 | -16 | -14 | 20 |
| 31 | 10 | 11 | 01 | 09 | 06 | 00 | -02 | 09 | -07 | -14 | 05 | -01 | 07 | 17 |
| -06 | -15 | 00 | -08 | -16 | -20 | -08 | -24 | 07 | -03 | 03 | 04 | -01 | 08 | -08 |
| 75 | 22 | 57 | -07 | 08 | 03 | -10 | 02 | 16 | -03 | -20 | 05 | 05 | -13 | 17 |
|  | 25 | 64 | -07 | 27 | 00 | 09 | 18 | 17 | -13 | -31 | 09 | 00 | -19 | 12 |
|  | 29 | 11 |  | 34 | 14 | 05 | 21 | -12 | 00 | 01 | -06 | -09 | -23 | 23 |
| 60 | -02 |  | -06 | 26 | 09 | 08 | 09 | 17 | -22 | -32 | 02 | 03 | -14 | 09 |
| -01 | 20 | 02 |  | 16 | 46 | 12 | 20 | -08 | -12 | -04 | -37 | 23 | -08 | -04 |
| 05 | 01 | 13 | 26 |  | 40 | 44 | 33 | -07 | -23 | -24 | -32 | 08 | -24 | 24 |
| 09 | 21 | 00 | 26 | 26 |  | 29 | 30 | -23 | 00 | 09 | -71 | 10 | -01 | 27 |
| 00 | 02 | 02 | 24 | 35 | 39 |  | 10 | 02 | -25 | -23 | -22 | -10 | -05 | 16 |
| 06 | 07 | -05 | 27 | 26 | 51 | 30 |  | -25 | 03 | 01 | -19 | 03 | -10 | 20 |
| -08 | -09 | -19 | -09 | -17 | -36 | -20 | -10 |  | -44 | -42 | 21 | -17 | 07 | -12 |
| 01 | 02 | 05 | -07 | -01 | 10 | -01 | -02 | -50 |  | 62 | -08 | -03 | 00 | -02 |
| 10 | 01 | 16 | 00 | 08 | 18 | 02 | 01 | -60 | 71 |  | -09 | 00 | 20 | 09 |
| -07 | -14 | -02 | -45 | -36 | -71 | -44 | -55 | 30 | -03 | -05 |  | -08 | -04 | -35 |
| 13 | -03 | 05 | 12 | 05 | 11 | 03 | 08 | -03 | 07 | 12 | -03 |  | 05 | 00 |
| -09 | -05 | -28 | -15 | -30 | 08 | -23 | 18 | 19 | 06 | -07 | -06 | 25 |  | -04 |
| 30 | -05 | 28 | 13 | 42 | 27 | 19 | 03 | -42 | 11 | 32 | -30 | -03 | -08 |  |
| HS | BR | PN | HFDH | VOC | BD | ARIT | PC | TASC | LIE | DSC | EFTT | PMS | WATS | SES |
| 7.2 | 3.9 | 1.3 | 24.3 | 27.6 | 19.6 | 8.9 | 10.5 | 18.2 | 3.7 | 11.1 | 146.8 | 42.2 | 34.7 | 32.7 |
| 5.8 | 3.0 | 2.7 | 9.2 | 7.2 | 10.2 | 1.8 | 2.3 | 7.8 | 2.7 | 5.2 | 33.0 | 11.2 | 24.7 | 10.6 |

ames of variables are abbreviated as follows:

SSEX: Subject's Sex
RT: HIT Reaction Time
R: HIT Rejection
L: HIT Location
FD: HIT Form Definiteness
FA: HIT Form Appropriateness
C: HIT Color
SH: HIT Shading
M: HIT Movement
V: HIT Pathognomic Verbalization
I: HIT Integration
H: HIT Human
A: HIT Animal
AT: HIT Anatomy
AX: HIT Anxiety
HS: HIT Hostility

BR: HIT Barrier
PN: HIT Penetration
HFDH: Human Figure Drawing— Harris-Goodenough
VOC: WISC Vocabulary
BD: WISC Block Design
ARIT: WISC Arithmetic
PC: WISC Picture Completion
TASC: Test Anxiety Scale for Children
LIE: Lie Scale
DSC: Defensiveness Scale for Children
EFTT: Embedded Figures Test—Time
PMS: Perceptual Maturity Scale
WATS: Word Association Test—Proportion Syntagmatic
SES: Socioeconomic Status

Table 6-17
Intercorrelations, Means, and Standard Deviations for Twelve-Year-Olds (Group II, Year 4)

| | SSEX | RT | R | L | FD | FA | C | SH | M | V | I | H | A | AT |
|---|---|---|---|---|---|---|---|---|---|---|---|---|---|---|
| **Means** | 1.6 | 18.1 | 3.3 | 41.4 | 83.3 | 42.2 | 8.8 | 2.2 | 24.2 | 2.6 | 3.5 | 17.3 | 24.2 | 1.9 |
| **Sigma** | .5 | 9.9 | 5.3 | 19.6 | 14.4 | 4.9 | 7.5 | 2.3 | 14.2 | 2.5 | 3.1 | 8.0 | 7.0 | 2.6 |
| SSEX | | —05 | —10 | —02 | 06 | 00 | 00 | 00 | —13 | 09 | 07 | 12 | 01 | —09 |
| RT | 18 | | **58** | 01 | 23 | 03 | —22 | —10 | **—37** | **—34** | **—28** | **—34** | —05 | —21 |
| R | 10 | **67** | | —18 | 13 | 02 | **—30** | —18 | **—41** | —24 | **—27** | **—36** | **—37** | 00 |
| L | 10 | 04 | —08 | | 18 | **46** | **—27** | 01 | **—40** | —25 | **—51** | 02 | 12 | —11 |
| FD | —15 | 07 | —03 | **24** | | —07 | **—48** | **—27** | 02 | 08 | 11 | **41** | **36** | **—23** |
| FA | 14 | 10 | 15 | **56** | —04 | | 00 | 04 | —14 | —06 | —15 | —03 | —15 | —05 |
| C | 15 | 00 | —08 | —20 | **—31** | 10 | | **29** | **31** | **27** | 18 | —05 | —18 | 10 |
| SH | 00 | —14 | —10 | —14 | **—38** | 09 | **40** | | —02 | 14 | —13 | —18 | 00 | 12 |
| M | —12 | —16 | —17 | **—32** | 13 | 00 | **23** | 18 | | **46** | **73** | **44** | 11 | —02 |
| V | 00 | —09 | —10 | —04 | **23** | 06 | 11 | 04 | **33** | | **50** | **47** | 11 | 08 |
| I | 04 | —13 | —14 | **—28** | 20 | 01 | 20 | 15 | **69** | **51** | | **53** | 16 | 00 |
| H | —07 | —13 | —16 | 13 | **29** | —04 | —18 | —09 | 15 | **25** | 21 | | 18 | —01 |
| A | —02 | 02 | —10 | 00 | **43** | **—32** | —25 | **—30** | —08 | —06 | —09 | 08 | | —21 |
| AT | —21 | —10 | —14 | —17 | —13 | **—26** | 05 | 11 | 06 | —10 | —01 | —21 | **—23** | |
| AX | —08 | —10 | —07 | **—26** | 00 | 02 | **33** | 15 | **57** | 14 | **30** | —11 | —03 | 21 |
| HS | —16 | —12 | —16 | —04 | **23** | 08 | **23** | 08 | **43** | **29** | **34** | —07 | —03 | —07 |
| BR | 13 | —10 | —15 | —09 | **37** | 03 | 08 | 03 | **28** | **26** | **44** | 08 | —03 | —16 |
| PN | —01 | —04 | —10 | —19 | 03 | —06 | 16 | 08 | **31** | 13 | **37** | —10 | 00 | —01 |
| HFDH | **28** | 06 | 08 | 16 | 02 | 14 | **25** | 17 | 03 | 02 | —06 | 00 | —10 | —01 |
| VOC | —20 | —01 | —02 | 11 | **25** | 15 | 06 | 01 | 14 | **24** | 15 | 08 | 01 | —13 |
| BD | —16 | —10 | 00 | 14 | 14 | 21 | —05 | 03 | 07 | 04 | 03 | 00 | —09 | 03 |
| ARIT | **—24** | 04 | 07 | 05 | 19 | —03 | 03 | —08 | 03 | 07 | —02 | 03 | 01 | 01 |
| PC | **—30** | —13 | —19 | 17 | **24** | 12 | 04 | 08 | 15 | 05 | 00 | 20 | 01 | —01 |
| TASC | 12 | —07 | —14 | 02 | —12 | —05 | —05 | —01 | —02 | —07 | —02 | 00 | 11 | 01 |
| LIE | —20 | 15 | **25** | —08 | 03 | 13 | —03 | 00 | —05 | —07 | —06 | —03 | —05 | 05 |
| DSC | —21 | 02 | 10 | —06 | 03 | 01 | —05 | 00 | —09 | —04 | 00 | 11 | —02 | 00 |
| EFTT | 14 | 09 | 02 | —17 | —20 | —19 | 04 | —05 | —12 | —06 | —05 | —02 | 08 | 04 |
| PMS | —22 | 08 | —05 | 01 | —08 | —06 | 11 | 04 | —14 | 08 | —13 | —07 | —04 | 11 |
| WATS | —14 | 11 | 09 | —09 | 11 | **—35** | —15 | —10 | —08 | —07 | —07 | 10 | 12 | 13 |
| SES | —14 | —27 | —08 | —08 | 09 | 04 | 20 | 09 | **26** | 09 | 27 | 04 | —27 | 09 |
| | SSEX | RT | R | L | FD | FA | C | SH | M | V | I | H | A | AT |
| **Means** | 1.5 | 25.2 | .9 | 64.1 | 76.5 | 43.6 | 5.3 | 2.1 | 8.5 | 1.3 | 1.1 | 15.8 | 27.7 | 3.2 |
| **Sigma** | .5 | 17.5 | 2.7 | 18.2 | 16.3 | 4.6 | 8.7 | 3.0 | 9.7 | 1.0 | 2.0 | 8.3 | 10.5 | 3.9 |

MEXICO

NOTES:

Table includes selected variables for 111 U.S. subjects (upper matrix) and 129 Mexican subjects (lower matrix).

Decimals are omitted from correlations.

Boldface correlations are significantly different from zero beyond the .01 level.

Actual number of cases for any given correlation may be slightly reduced because of missing data.

For SES and WATS in Mexico, the N is reduced to 76 and 69 cases respectively.

For SES and WATS in the United States, the N is reduced to 68 cases.

# UNITED STATES

| HS | BR | PN | HFDH | VOC | BD | ARIT | PC | TASC | LIE | DSC | EFTT | PMS | WATS | SES |
|---|---|---|---|---|---|---|---|---|---|---|---|---|---|---|
| 7.6 | 6.2 | 2.5 | 38.9 | 50.8 | 40.9 | 12.6 | 12.9 | 9.9 | 2.3 | 9.0 | 38.8 | 44.6 | 20.0 | 32.9 |
| 4.7 | 3.6 | 2.3 | 10.0 | 8.1 | 10.4 | 1.7 | 2.8 | 5.3 | 2.1 | 2.8 | 31.5 | 14.3 | 9.8 | 7.5 |
| -22 | 18 | 04 | 09 | -12 | -14 | -22 | -31 | 26 | -05 | -19 | 13 | -21 | 01 | -20 |
| -27 | -19 | -22 | 10 | -13 | 09 | -04 | 01 | 28 | -32 | -29 | 01 | 12 | -15 | 00 |
| -35 | -36 | -27 | -06 | -18 | 08 | -02 | 06 | 09 | -16 | -09 | 00 | 02 | -07 | 08 |
| -18 | -13 | -23 | -22 | -11 | -16 | -10 | -19 | 10 | 00 | -14 | 19 | 10 | -14 | -21 |
| -04 | 11 | -12 | 08 | 00 | 14 | -08 | 00 | 18 | -12 | -14 | -09 | 00 | 01 | 01 |
| -08 | -09 | -01 | 05 | -04 | -01 | 13 | 02 | -03 | 04 | -07 | 05 | -01 | 13 | -04 |
| 18 | 20 | 16 | -03 | 08 | -16 | 11 | -02 | -04 | 05 | 13 | 21 | -11 | 14 | 00 |
| 06 | 11 | -01 | -04 | -09 | -07 | 06 | 06 | -05 | 02 | -01 | 18 | 05 | -16 | -13 |
| 73 | 38 | 39 | 24 | 19 | 03 | 13 | 18 | -03 | 12 | 13 | -06 | -01 | 05 | 06 |
| 27 | 19 | 30 | 04 | 10 | -09 | 14 | 03 | -03 | -01 | -02 | -02 | -22 | 19 | 06 |
| 46 | 35 | 47 | 26 | 29 | 09 | 18 | 15 | 00 | 04 | 06 | -16 | -04 | 17 | 13 |
| 16 | 16 | 19 | 04 | 12 | -10 | 00 | -03 | 00 | 11 | 07 | 04 | -13 | 09 | 10 |
| 17 | 02 | 00 | 00 | 00 | 04 | 02 | 01 | -03 | -01 | -07 | -08 | 00 | 03 | -03 |
| -04 | -20 | 23 | -09 | -20 | -03 | 11 | 03 | -07 | 05 | 00 | 09 | -07 | 30 | -09 |
| 73 | 30 | 45 | 10 | 13 | 01 | 03 | 08 | -05 | 13 | 17 | -10 | -08 | 01 | 08 |
|  | 28 | 35 | 05 | 07 | 00 | 09 | 14 | 00 | 11 | 13 | -05 | -06 | -02 | 07 |
| 13 |  | 25 | 20 | 09 | 13 | 02 | 08 | 04 | 10 | 01 | -12 | 02 | -09 | 00 |
| 56 | 22 |  | 13 | 05 | -05 | 04 | -02 | 00 | 03 | -04 | -09 | -12 | 13 | 14 |
| 01 | 23 | 11 |  | 20 | 36 | 12 | 23 | 06 | -06 | -12 | -37 | 03 | 12 | -22 |
| 20 | 24 | 11 | 18 |  | 24 | 26 | 12 | -12 | -04 | 02 | -32 | 06 | 01 | 38 |
| 14 | 12 | 03 | 27 | 34 |  | 39 | 27 | -05 | -09 | -15 | -72 | 25 | -01 | 23 |
| 16 | 09 | 07 | 27 | 35 | 39 |  | 20 | -20 | 05 | -01 | -33 | 00 | -04 | 15 |
| 14 | 00 | 01 | 14 | 36 | 25 | 20 |  | -15 | 02 | 24 | -23 | 07 | 27 | -02 |
| -16 | 04 | 05 | -15 | -10 | -14 | -07 | -12 |  | -51 | -59 | 22 | 20 | -16 | -20 |
| -08 | -09 | -14 | -02 | -01 | 10 | 05 | 03 | -41 |  | 63 | 00 | -10 | 14 | 14 |
| -03 | -05 | -09 | 02 | 02 | 11 | 08 | 17 | -48 | 59 |  | 06 | -12 | 14 | -01 |
| -16 | -09 | -08 | -30 | -35 | -71 | -39 | -36 | 12 | -07 | -10 |  | -09 | -04 | -18 |
| -02 | 00 | 05 | 07 | 11 | -01 | 08 | 10 | 07 | 00 | 01 | -02 |  | -12 | -03 |
| -08 | -01 | -03 | -19 | -35 | -08 | 05 | 09 | 03 | 02 | 13 | 03 | -11 |  | -09 |
| 29 | 13 | 02 | 02 | 12 | 21 | 10 | 14 | -31 | -04 | 01 | -19 | -22 | 02 |  |
| HS | BR | PN | HFDH | VOC | BD | ARIT | PC | TASC | LIE | DSC | EFTT | PMS | WATS | SES |
| 5.2 | 3.9 | 1.2 | 29.9 | 40.4 | 31.6 | 10.9 | 13.1 | 15.4 | 3.5 | 10.6 | 70.6 | 47.8 | 26.6 | 30.5 |
| 3.8 | 3.1 | 2.2 | 8.4 | 7.9 | 9.7 | 1.7 | 2.2 | 6.9 | 2.6 | 4.4 | 40.4 | 14.4 | 22.9 | 10.3 |

ames of variables are abbreviated as follows:

| | | |
|---|---|---|
| SSEX: | Subject's Sex | |
| RT: | HIT Reaction Time | |
| R: | HIT Rejection | |
| L: | HIT Location | |
| FD: | HIT Form Definiteness | |
| FA: | HIT Form Appropriateness | |
| C: | HIT Color | |
| SH: | HIT Shading | |
| M: | HIT Movement | |
| V: | HIT Pathognomic Verbalization | |
| I: | HIT Integration | |
| H: | HIT Human | |
| A: | HIT Animal | |
| AT: | HIT Anatomy | |
| AX: | HIT Anxiety | |
| HS: | HIT Hostility | |
| BR: | HIT Barrier | |
| PN: | HIT Penetration | |
| HFDH: | Human Figure Drawing—Harris-Goodenough | |
| VOC: | WISC Vocabulary | |
| BD: | WISC Block Design | |
| ARIT: | WISC Arithmetic | |
| PC: | WISC Picture Completion | |
| TASC: | Test Anxiety Scale for Children | |
| LIE: | Lie Scale | |
| DSC: | Defensiveness Scale for Children | |
| EFTT: | Embedded Figures Test—Time | |
| PMS: | Perceptual Maturity Scale | |
| WATS: | Word Association Test—Proportion Syntagmatic | |
| SES: | Socioeconomic Status | |

Table 6-18
Intercorrelations, Means, and Standard Deviations for Fifteen-Year-Olds (Group III, Year 4)

| | SSEX | RT | R | L | FD | FA | C | SH | M | V | I | H | A | AT | A |
|---|---|---|---|---|---|---|---|---|---|---|---|---|---|---|---|
| Means | 1.5 | 21.1 | .3 | 43.5 | 83.1 | 40.7 | 12.6 | 4.0 | 25.0 | 4.0 | 2.1 | 15.2 | 27.3 | 1.9 | 8 |
| Sigma | .5 | 11.8 | .8 | 19.8 | 15.8 | 6.1 | 8.6 | 3.4 | 14.9 | 5.5 | 2.6 | 8.2 | 9.2 | 2.3 | 5 |
| SSEX | | —26 | —16 | —09 | 08 | 02 | 06 | 09 | 00 | —03 | 18 | 11 | —02 | —14 | — |
| RT | —02 | | 37 | 22 | —14 | 24 | 07 | 00 | —11 | 06 | —18 | —09 | —16 | 04 | —( |
| R | —07 | 63 | | —12 | —05 | 00 | 00 | —10 | —01 | —07 | 00 | —08 | —03 | —02 | — |
| L | 19 | 10 | —06 | | 23 | 39 | —24 | —04 | —42 | —23 | —47 | 03 | 10 | —02 | — |
| FD | 03 | 06 | 02 | 19 | | —30 | —37 | —22 | 08 | —05 | 14 | 31 | 55 | —19 | — |
| FA | 30 | 15 | 00 | 59 | —06 | | 09 | 19 | 05 | —05 | 04 | 15 | —47 | 06 | |
| C | 01 | —23 | —14 | —26 | —56 | 05 | | 28 | 16 | 34 | 11 | —09 | —41 | 00 | : |
| SH | 00 | —14 | —18 | —35 | —33 | 01 | 45 | | 09 | —01 | 06 | —07 | —25 | —01 | |
| M | 02 | —21 | —26 | —40 | 15 | —17 | 10 | 42 | | 28 | 67 | 37 | —21 | —06 | |
| V | 05 | —13 | —08 | —31 | 01 | —25 | 14 | 08 | 41 | | 26 | 22 | —11 | 00 | |
| I | 14 | —17 | —17 | —35 | 21 | —13 | 00 | 32 | 66 | 35 | | 52 | —16 | —03 | |
| H | —16 | —04 | —08 | 00 | 45 | —17 | —34 | —15 | 34 | 16 | 38 | | —17 | —05 | |
| A | —01 | 04 | 02 | 04 | 58 | —24 | —45 | —25 | —03 | —05 | 02 | 19 | | —17 | — |
| AT | —15 | —24 | —18 | —26 | —22 | —28 | 25 | 15 | 05 | 00 | 04 | —17 | —16 | | |
| AX | 02 | —32 | —29 | —40 | 09 | —27 | 08 | 30 | 66 | 44 | 55 | 15 | 00 | 18 | |
| HS | 10 | —28 | —28 | —11 | 24 | —08 | —03 | 18 | 55 | 35 | 45 | 21 | 12 | —05 | |
| BR | 22 | —07 | —14 | —11 | 17 | 00 | 03 | 19 | 35 | 24 | 35 | —04 | —11 | —10 | |
| PN | 09 | —17 | —15 | —12 | —07 | 01 | 05 | 29 | 46 | 11 | 35 | 09 | —27 | —07 | |
| HFDH | —01 | —03 | —14 | —11 | 05 | —10 | 15 | 11 | 21 | 17 | 23 | 01 | —06 | 03 | |
| VOC | —30 | —09 | —02 | —06 | 04 | —09 | 00 | 04 | 14 | 02 | 03 | 06 | —07 | 01 | |
| BD | —15 | 02 | —01 | 03 | 18 | 06 | —06 | 07 | 11 | —02 | 08 | 06 | —07 | —04 | |
| ARIT | —15 | 10 | 00 | 02 | 07 | 05 | —01 | 13 | 03 | —08 | 02 | —04 | —12 | 00 | |
| PC | —41 | —04 | 02 | —20 | 04 | —06 | 11 | 10 | 10 | —10 | —01 | 06 | —11 | 03 | |
| TASC | 16 | 17 | 09 | 17 | 06 | 22 | —07 | —14 | —10 | —02 | —04 | 02 | 00 | —08 | — |
| LIE | 01 | —02 | 11 | —14 | 05 | —12 | 02 | —07 | 00 | —02 | 04 | 05 | 19 | —08 | |
| DSC | —06 | 01 | 07 | —18 | 01 | —21 | —06 | —05 | —01 | —01 | —05 | 06 | 20 | 05 | |
| EFTT | 30 | 08 | 10 | 05 | —13 | 09 | —06 | —14 | —06 | —03 | —05 | 00 | 08 | —01 | — |
| PMS | —27 | 14 | 15 | 07 | 11 | 03 | —06 | —03 | —07 | —16 | —02 | 01 | 05 | —12 | — |
| WATS | —23 | —12 | —18 | —06 | —13 | 04 | 09 | 13 | 05 | 10 | 08 | 19 | —14 | —07 | |
| SES | 04 | —25 | —18 | 14 | —03 | 20 | 00 | 20 | 04 | 00 | 01 | —01 | 07 | —12 | |
| | SSEX | RT | R | L | FD | FA | C | SH | M | V | I | H | A | AT | |
| Means | 1.5 | 29.5 | .6 | 61.2 | 80.2 | 44.8 | 8.6 | 3.0 | 14.6 | 2.3 | 1.9 | 14.8 | 27.2 | 3.1 | |
| Sigma | .5 | 21.0 | 1.9 | 17.3 | 16.1 | 4.3 | 11.6 | 3.0 | 12.0 | 3.5 | 2.3 | 8.2 | 9.4 | 3.7 | |

MEXICO

NOTES:

Table includes selected variables for 122 U.S. subjects (upper matrix) and 127 Mexican subjects (lower matrix).

Decimals are omitted from correlations.

Boldface correlations are significantly different from zero beyond the .01 level.

Actual number of cases for any given correlation may be slightly reduced because of missing data.

For SES and WATS in Mexico, the N is reduced to 58 cases.

For SES and WATS in the United States, the N is reduced to 63 cases.

# UNITED STATES

| HS | BR | PN | HFDH | VOC | BD | ARIT | PC | TASC | LIE | DSC | EFTT | PMS | WATS | SES |
|---|---|---|---|---|---|---|---|---|---|---|---|---|---|---|
| 9.8 | 7.6 | 3.3 | 44.7 | 58.5 | 48.9 | 14.4 | 16.1 | 8.6 | 1.6 | 8.8 | 19.9 | 52.1 | 26.0 | 32.1 |
| 5.3 | 4.1 | 2.8 | 10.4 | 6.7 | 7.3 | 1.3 | 2.1 | 4.7 | 2.0 | 3.1 | 21.5 | 13.8 | 13.6 | 8.2 |

| HS | BR | PN | HFDH | VOC | BD | ARIT | PC | TASC | LIE | DSC | EFTT | PMS | WATS | SES |
|---|---|---|---|---|---|---|---|---|---|---|---|---|---|---|
| 23 | 16 | −08 | 08 | −27 | −07 | −32 | −03 | 33 | −35 | −37 | 03 | −27 | 09 | 08 |
| 04 | −09 | 02 | 04 | 02 | 02 | −04 | −12 | −02 | 08 | 18 | −09 | 06 | 12 | 04 |
| 05 | −18 | −12 | 00 | 05 | 03 | 01 | 00 | 03 | 06 | 14 | −04 | 06 | 15 | 03 |
| 26 | −10 | −20 | −15 | −10 | −08 | 00 | −33 | −05 | −01 | 04 | 09 | 02 | −05 | −01 |
| 13 | 30 | −21 | 08 | 19 | 05 | 05 | 19 | 15 | −06 | −19 | 02 | −05 | −02 | 16 |
| 03 | 08 | 16 | −04 | −03 | 00 | 00 | −20 | −09 | −02 | −02 | −05 | 01 | 17 | −08 |
| 11 | 03 | 11 | 17 | 08 | 23 | 17 | 12 | 07 | −15 | 09 | −15 | 12 | 03 | 02 |
| 08 | 05 | 25 | 11 | 05 | 21 | 22 | 12 | −09 | −13 | −07 | −16 | 16 | 03 | −17 |
| 72 | 41 | 35 | 16 | 34 | 12 | 11 | 33 | −05 | −05 | −11 | −09 | −09 | 16 | 05 |
| 44 | 14 | 21 | −06 | −04 | −07 | −06 | 02 | 05 | −09 | 01 | 05 | −04 | −02 | 03 |
| 46 | 39 | 29 | 18 | 15 | 06 | 01 | 25 | 02 | −04 | −23 | −04 | −09 | 14 | 09 |
| 21 | 28 | 01 | 04 | 09 | 03 | 07 | 05 | −17 | 05 | −04 | 04 | 02 | 00 | 14 |
| 05 | −21 | −29 | −14 | −01 | −17 | −16 | −04 | 15 | 06 | −04 | 20 | −09 | 02 | 09 |
| 06 | −10 | 17 | 01 | 16 | −02 | 09 | −05 | 02 | 01 | 03 | 05 | 15 | −15 | −04 |
| 57 | −04 | 33 | −10 | 06 | −02 | 05 | −05 | −09 | −14 | −01 | −01 | −10 | 00 | 00 |
|  | 23 | 40 | 14 | 25 | 10 | 14 | 28 | −06 | −03 | −09 | −05 | −07 | 16 | 10 |
| 32 |  | 29 | 24 | 19 | 19 | −03 | 39 | 06 | −14 | −24 | −08 | −08 | −08 | 02 |
| 28 | 30 |  | 08 | 06 | 10 | 10 | 09 | −10 | −05 | −11 | −11 | −05 | 07 | −07 |
| 9 | 21 | 09 |  | 30 | 43 | 23 | 37 | −09 | −10 | −15 | −47 | 04 | 10 | 08 |
| 05 | 01 | 13 | 08 |  | 33 | 43 | 40 | −11 | −01 | 04 | −26 | 04 | −02 | 10 |
| 48 | 21 | 14 | 22 | 34 |  | 38 | 52 | −03 | −11 | 06 | −71 | 15 | 06 | 02 |
| 42 | 10 | 06 | 07 | 33 | 23 |  | 24 | −35 | 08 | 10 | −44 | 23 | −19 | 13 |
| 90 | 03 | 12 | 16 | 45 | 51 | 29 |  | −07 | −10 | −07 | −32 | 11 | 08 | 12 |
| 9 | −01 | 01 | −08 | −13 | 00 | −22 | −11 |  | −41 | −41 | 02 | −14 | 09 | −14 |
| 7 | −03 | −06 | 04 | 04 | −06 | −04 | 00 | −48 |  | 63 | 15 | 20 | 04 | 08 |
| 2 | −19 | −07 | −02 | 03 | −07 | −05 | 02 | −52 | 62 |  | 03 | 25 | −01 | −01 |
| 9 | −18 | −08 | −27 | −27 | −40 | −30 | −40 | 21 | 13 | −01 |  | 01 | −01 | 05 |
| 1 | −11 | 06 | 05 | 27 | 16 | 18 | 12 | −01 | 06 | 13 | −07 |  | 10 | −02 |
| 8 | −04 | 15 | −09 | −07 | −17 | 11 | 17 | −17 | 05 | 03 | −05 | 06 |  | 02 |
| 8 | −03 | −04 | −07 | 13 | 04 | 16 | 14 | −30 | 03 | −06 | −22 | −14 | 29 |  |

| HS | BR | PN | HFDH | VOC | BD | ARIT | PC | TASC | LIE | DSC | EFTT | PMS | WATS | SES |
|---|---|---|---|---|---|---|---|---|---|---|---|---|---|---|
| 7 | 4.5 | 2.1 | 37.3 | 49.8 | 42.6 | 12.2 | 15.4 | 14.3 | 2.2 | 9.2 | 24.5 | 49.6 | 20.7 | 31.6 |
| 2 | 3.0 | 2.3 | 9.8 | 6.6 | 7.2 | 1.8 | 2.2 | 6.8 | 2.1 | 3.9 | 22.1 | 15.2 | 15.4 | 8.7 |

nes of variables are abbreviated as follows:

SEX: Subject's Sex
RT: HIT Reaction Time
R: HIT Rejection
L: HIT Location
FD: HIT Form Definiteness
FA: HIT Form Appropriateness
C: HIT Color
SH: HIT Shading
M: HIT Movement
V: HIT Pathognomic Verbalization
I: HIT Integration
H: HIT Human
A: HIT Animal
AT: HIT Anatomy
AX: HIT Anxiety
HS: HIT Hostility

BR: HIT Barrier
PN: HIT Penetration
HFDH: Human Figure Drawing— Harris-Goodenough
VOC: WISC Vocabulary
BD: WISC Block Design
ARIT: WISC Arithmetic
PC: WISC Picture Completion
TASC: Test Anxiety Scale for Children
LIE: Lie Scale
DSC: Defensiveness Scale for Children
EFTT: Embedded Figures Test—Time
PMS: Perceptual Maturity Scale
WATS: Word Association Test— Proportion Syntagmatic
SES: Socioeconomic Status

these eighteen independent correlation matrices are included the following cognitive-perceptual style variables: Number of Groups, Percent Open, and Percent Public from the Object Sorting Test; the Delay score from the Time Estimation Test; the Time score for the Embedded Figures Test; the Total Reaction Time score for the Conceptual Styles Test; both the Time score and the Number Correct for the Visual Fractionation Test; the Proportion Syntagmatic score from the Word Association Test; and the score from the Perceptual Maturity Scale. While these matrices are more interesting for what they reveal across different domains, they also illustrate the general lack of correlation among the cognitive-perceptual style measures.

INTERCORRELATIONS AMONG THE
PERSONALITY-ATTITUDINAL VARIABLES

The only direct measures of personality traits obtained in both cultures are the scores on the Personality Research Form obtained in all three age groups in both cultures in the last year of the study and the scores on the Test Anxiety Scale for Children that was administered to all individuals from the second year on. The TASC contains only one major score and two minor ones, the latter two being the Lie and Defensiveness scales. Within the PRF, however, there are fifteen major personality scales covering the major dimensions that can be measured by a self-report inventory. Factor-analytic studies by Jackson (1967) have revealed seven underlying dimensions, three of which contain more than one scale. Since all of this earlier work was done with American high-school and college students, it was deemed desirable to repeat the factor analyses separately for the American and Mexican children in the present study.

The Personality Research Form was given only to the reduced sample of Mexican children who were matched with their American counterparts in the final year of the project. Consequently, the factor analyses were carried out on intercorrelations for the combined age groups of Mexican children in order to obtain a sufficient number of cases, 168, to produce stable results. The matched pairs of American children were also combined into one over-all sample of 160 cases so that a precise, cross-cultural comparison of the two factor analyses could be made. In addition to the fifteen scales within the PRF and the three TASC scores, six other measures were added to the two correlation matrices—the Harris-Goodenough score from Human Figure Drawing; the Vocabulary and Block Design subtests from the WISC or WAIS, scaled for age using Wechsler's norms; the Movement score from the HIT; a binary coding of the child's sex (2 for female and 1 for male); and a tertiary coding for the child's age group (1 for sixth-graders, 2 for ninth-graders, and 3 for twelfth-graders). These additional variables in year 6 were included to aid in the interpretation of the results, as well as to shed further light on the meaning of fairly consistent correlations among the variables involved and several of the PRF scales. The upper triangular matrix of Table 6-19 contains the intercorrelations, means, and standard deviations for the American children, while the lower triangular matrix contains the identical statistics for the Mexican children.

A principal-component factor analysis was undertaken separately on the two samples, stopping the factoring when the eigenvalue dropped below 1.0. A normalized varimax rotation was followed by a factor-matching program developed by Veldman (1967) to see how closely the factor patterns in the two cultures could be matched. This objective procedure yielded seven factors in both cultures. Considering that the analysis was done independently on both samples, the obtained dimensions are surprisingly similar across the Spanish version in Mexico and the English version in the United States. Three of the factors matched perfectly with no exceptions; two more were an excellent match with only trivial exceptions; the remaining two factors were clearly good matches cross-culturally, although there were notable variations in the loadings of individual variables. The results will be presented one factor at a time, beginning with those factors arising primarily from the Personality Research Form in both cultures.

### Factor 1: Persistent Achievement Drive

One of the clearest factors appearing consistently in both cultures in the analysis of the Personality Research Form and other variables is defined largely by Achievement, Endurance, Order, and Understanding. A person with a high score on this factor would be one who aspires to accomplish difficult tasks, who is willing to work long hours, who is concerned with neatness and

| | | | | | | | | | | | |
|---|---|---|---|---|---|---|---|---|---|---|---|
| Mean | 2.1 | 1.5 | 23.4 | 13.3 | 13.5 | 44.8 | 9.6 | 1.7 | 8.3 | 11.6 | 16.1 |
| Standard deviation | 0.8 | 0.5 | 16.3 | 2.8 | 2.9 | 9.8 | 5.7 | 2.0 | 3.5 | 3.4 | 2.7 |
| Variable | AGE | SEX | M | VOC | BD | HFD | TASC | LIE | DSC | AC | AF |
| Age | | —06 | 15 | **25** | 15 | **41** | —07 | **—28** | —09 | —12 | 06 |
| Sex | —08 | | —17 | —09 | —18 | 05 | 16 | —12 | —14 | —13 | **39** |
| HIT: Movement | 17 | —14 | | 17 | 13 | 08 | —08 | —01 | —10 | 08 | —03 |
| Vocabulary | 13 | —10 | 13 | | **44** | 31 | —19 | —18 | —08 | 11 | 09 |
| Block Design | 17 | —21 | 13 | 16 | | **34** | **—27** | —05 | 01 | 19 | 06 |
| Human Figure Drawing | 30 | 04 | —09 | 14 | **24** | | —14 | —16 | —04 | —01 | 14 |
| TASC: Test Anxiety | —17 | 16 | —12 | —19 | —17 | 01 | | **—37** | **—48** | —12 | —09 |
| TASC: Lie | —04 | —17 | —09 | 06 | 05 | —12 | **—38** | | **58** | **26** | —10 |
| TASC: Defensiveness | 04 | —14 | 01 | 09 | 04 | —18 | **—51** | **45** | | 12 | —05 |
| Achievement | 12 | —06 | 08 | 19 | 18 | 10 | —05 | 13 | 06 | | 15 |
| Affiliation | 09 | 03 | 02 | —10 | 02 | 13 | —18 | —02 | —02 | —02 | |
| Aggression | —04 | 05 | —14 | 05 | —06 | —06 | 12 | —02 | —20 | 03 | —11 |
| Autonomy | —14 | 00 | —06 | 13 | 00 | —06 | **—28** | **25** | 18 | —03 | 00 |
| Dominance | —06 | —13 | 03 | 02 | 06 | 07 | 04 | —09 | —16 | **35** | 14 |
| Endurance | 05 | —08 | 02 | 13 | 15 | —03 | —16 | 04 | 21 | **45** | —09 |
| Exhibition | 03 | 01 | —05 | 00 | 12 | —02 | —02 | 01 | —11 | **22** | **24** |
| Harmavoidance | —11 | 18 | —17 | —18 | —14 | —09 | **23** | **—22** | **—24** | **—23** | —16 |
| Impulsivity | 03 | 12 | 00 | 13 | —01 | 01 | —08 | —02 | —07 | **—24** | 05 |
| Nurturance | 01 | **22** | —02 | —12 | —01 | 07 | 11 | —09 | —06 | 15 | **27** |
| Order | 02 | —06 | 07 | —04 | 03 | —05 | 05 | —06 | 00 | **37** | —01 |
| Play | 11 | —08 | 15 | —04 | 10 | 11 | —04 | —01 | —11 | **—21** | **33** |
| Social Recognition | —13 | 08 | —11 | —08 | —08 | 01 | 18 | —10 | **—25** | 06 | 16 |
| Understanding | 18 | 09 | 03 | 15 | 10 | 15 | 01 | —01 | 00 | **41** | 15 |
| Infrequency | —19 | 18 | —11 | —06 | **—27** | —03 | —01 | 06 | 12 | —08 | —16 |
| Mean | 2.1 | 1.5 | 9.1 | 9.7 | 12.3 | 38.8 | 14.6 | 2.9 | 9.4 | 11.6 | 12.5 |
| Standard deviation | 0.8 | 0.5 | 8.9 | 3.2 | 2.7 | 10.7 | 6.9 | 2.6 | 3.9 | 2.7 | 2.9 |

MEXICO

NOTES:

Decimals omitted from correlations.

Boldface correlations are significantly different from zero beyond the .01 level.

N = 160 American and 168 Mexican children, matched cross-culturally for socioeconomic status, age, and sex.

# UNITED STATES

| | AG | AU | DO | EN | EX | HA | IM | NU | OR | PL | SR | UN | IN | |
|---|---|---|---|---|---|---|---|---|---|---|---|---|---|---|
| | 8.0 | 6.9 | 9.2 | 10.2 | 10.3 | 9.3 | 10.6 | 13.9 | 9.9 | 14.0 | 12.5 | 11.7 | 1.1 | |
| | 3.6 | 2.9 | 4.3 | 3.9 | 3.9 | 4.1 | 3.3 | 3.6 | 3.8 | 2.8 | 3.5 | 3.1 | 1.9 | |
| | −05 | −06 | −01 | −22 | −01 | −15 | 30 | 02 | −21 | 07 | −04 | −09 | −19 | AGE |
| | −31 | −18 | −26 | −12 | −02 | 32 | 09 | 49 | −10 | 03 | 14 | 05 | −11 | SEX |
| | 07 | 06 | 06 | −08 | 06 | −07 | 24 | −09 | −07 | −06 | −10 | 07 | 00 | M |
| | 09 | −07 | 18 | −04 | 18 | −33 | 26 | 00 | −18 | 15 | 10 | 31 | −16 | VOC |
| | 02 | −06 | 08 | 09 | −03 | −20 | 14 | −08 | −10 | 00 | −05 | 09 | −09 | BD |
| | −11 | −03 | −08 | −03 | −04 | −14 | 13 | 15 | −18 | 14 | 06 | 09 | −26 | HFD |
| | 13 | −02 | −29 | −05 | −09 | 03 | 08 | 06 | 02 | 01 | 09 | 00 | 18 | TASC |
| | −09 | 32 | 18 | 30 | −11 | 05 | −32 | −15 | 23 | −22 | −23 | −06 | 12 | LIE |
| | −09 | 32 | 10 | 18 | −10 | 01 | −16 | −13 | 08 | −14 | −29 | 00 | 07 | DSC |
| | −23 | −04 | 22 | 69 | −01 | −02 | −34 | 11 | 42 | −28 | −05 | 41 | −10 | AC |
| | −20 | −47 | 08 | 00 | 29 | 17 | 07 | 58 | 04 | 17 | 36 | 12 | −38 | AF |
| | | 17 | 40 | −27 | 33 | −31 | 31 | −34 | −21 | 39 | 22 | −20 | 18 | AG |
| | 06 | | 10 | 14 | −04 | −34 | 13 | −32 | −11 | −04 | −36 | 03 | 34 | AU |
| | 32 | −06 | | 12 | 57 | −24 | 18 | −03 | −03 | 20 | 26 | 05 | 06 | DO |
| | −11 | 07 | 27 | | −13 | −09 | −42 | 14 | 45 | −34 | −17 | 36 | −04 | EN |
| | 30 | 00 | 40 | 11 | | −13 | 26 | 12 | 02 | 35 | 38 | 01 | 03 | EX |
| | −13 | −21 | −27 | −01 | −23 | | −34 | 07 | 22 | −28 | 12 | −07 | −05 | HA |
| | 38 | 15 | 02 | −18 | 29 | −13 | | −05 | −61 | 41 | 01 | −24 | 05 | IM |
| | −21 | −27 | 11 | 15 | 05 | 06 | −18 | | 10 | −01 | 24 | 17 | −28 | NU |
| | −16 | −31 | 16 | 33 | 05 | 03 | −45 | 23 | | −26 | 11 | 25 | 01 | OR |
| | 02 | −04 | 00 | −32 | 19 | −23 | 23 | −02 | −12 | | 29 | −26 | −07 | PL |
| | 17 | −27 | 23 | −16 | 29 | 01 | 00 | 14 | 21 | 03 | | −02 | −15 | SR |
| | −04 | −04 | 19 | 25 | 06 | −06 | −19 | 29 | 30 | −13 | 07 | | −15 | UN |
| | 18 | 17 | 02 | −03 | −06 | 04 | 17 | −17 | −23 | −17 | 06 | −18 | | IN |
| | 8.4 | 8.6 | 9.6 | 10.2 | 10.1 | 9.5 | 9.0 | 12.8 | 12.0 | 10.7 | 10.7 | 12.1 | 3.5 | |
| | 2.5 | 2.9 | 3.5 | 3.0 | 3.1 | 3.2 | 2.6 | 3.0 | 3.5 | 2.6 | 3.0 | 2.7 | 2.8 | |

organization, and who wants to understand many areas of knowledge. Factor 1 in the present study includes two additional variables—Order and Understanding—besides those found by Jackson. The factor is a clear one, easy to interpret.

### Factor 2: Extroversion

Inspection of Table 6-21 reveals that Factor 2 contains identical defining variables in both cultures. While Jackson does not report an introversion-extroversion factor, this broad dimension is evident in most personality inventories. The particular configuration of defining variables for Factor 2 clearly indicates that extroversion would be an appropriate label for the factor. Individuals scoring high on this factor would be persons who want to be the center of attention, who want to be influential leaders, who may be argumentative, who want to be held in high esteem by acquaintances, and who enjoy social activities of a playful nature.

### Factor 3: Affiliative Nurturance

Nurturance, affiliation, and being female are the variables that load highest on Factor 3. In the earlier work by Jackson, Affilia-

Table 6-20
Factor 1: Persistent Achievement Drive

| Defining Variables | Factor Loadings | |
| --- | --- | --- |
| | United States | Mexico |
| Achievement | .81 | .75 |
| Endurance | .83 | .71 |
| Order | .66 | .62 |
| Understanding | .65 | .56 |
| Play | —.44 | —.53 |

Table 6-21
Factor 2: Extroversion

| Defining Variables | Factor Loadings | |
| --- | --- | --- |
| | United States | Mexico |
| Exhibition | .82 | .75 |
| Dominance | .79 | .67 |
| Aggression | .59 | .51 |
| Social Recognition | .55 | .48 |
| Play | .52 | .34 |

tion, Nurturance, and Aggression (reversed) were joined by Exhibition and Social Recognition to produce a factor dealing with the degree and quality of personal orientation. A person with a high score on this factor would be one who enjoys being with friends and helping other people when in need.

### Factor 4: Nonconformity

Autonomy, Infrequency, and Impulsivity are the variables from the Personality Research Form that consistently load highly on Factor 4, suggesting the label Nonconformity for this factor. Inspection of Table 6-23 reveals that Harmavoidance, Order, and Social Recognition (all reversed) also have significant loadings in one or the other culture on this factor. When taken together, these six variables indicate that a high scorer on this factor is a person who tends to be individualistic, who expresses his feelings freely, who tends to be disorganized, and who is not particularly concerned about what others think of him (at least outwardly). Within the American culture (but not in Mexico), he may also be an adventurous, risk-taking individual. This factor has some

Table 6-22
Factor 3: Affiliative Nurturance

| Defining Variables | Factor Loadings | |
| | United States | Mexico |
| --- | --- | --- |
| Nurturance | .80 | .66 |
| Child's sex (femaleness) | .80 | .62 |
| Affiliation | .69 | .60 |
| Aggression | —.45 | —.27 |

Table 6-23
Factor 4: Nonconformity

| Defining Variables | Factor Loadings | |
| | United States | Mexico |
| --- | --- | --- |
| Autonomy | .78 | .58 |
| Infrequency | .41 | .53 |
| Impulsivity | .40 | .47 |
| Harmavoidance | —.63 | —.17 |
| Order | —.35 | —.47 |
| Social Recognition | —.48 | —.27 |

similarity to a factor dealing with impulse expression and control found by Jackson.

## Factor 5: Intellectual Ability

Defined largely by the cognitive-perceptual abilities in the WISC and Human Figure Drawing, Factor 5 clearly reflects actual intellectual ability rather than desire for achievement or understanding. Scores scaled for age using Wechsler's norms were employed in this correlational analysis for Block Design and Vocabulary but not for the Human Figure Drawing. The relatively high loadings for age, as defined by the three groups, are not at all surprising, considering the nature of this factor. The negative loadings for Infrequency in both cultures are consistent with Jackson's interpretation of Infrequency, high scorers being those who are careless or who poorly comprehend the task.

## Factor 6: Test Anxiety

The three scales from Sarason's Test Anxiety Scale for Children all have high loadings on Factor 6, as evident in Table 6-25. Of greater interest, however, is the fact that no other scales show

Table 6-24
Factor 5: Intellectual Ability

| Defining Variables | Factor Loadings | |
| --- | --- | --- |
| | United States | Mexico |
| HFD Developmental Scale | .71 | .67 |
| WISC Block Design | .66 | .64 |
| WISC Vocabulary | .68 | .43 |
| Age-Grade | .57 | .63 |
| Infrequency | —.45 | —.44 |
| Harmavoidance | —.40 | —.30 |

Table 6-25
Factor 6: Test Anxiety

| Defining Variables | Factor Loadings | |
| --- | --- | --- |
| | United States | Mexico |
| TASC Defensiveness | —.83 | —.75 |
| TASC Test Anxiety | .79 | .69 |
| TASC Lie | —.74 | —.68 |

appreciable loadings on this particular factor. The highest loading among the American children is only .26 for Social Recognition. For the Mexican children, several of the PRF variables (Harmavoidance, Aggression, and Autonomy reversed) have loadings ranging from .33 to .37, while Sex has a loading of .33. Inspection of the actual correlations among these variables in Table 6-19 suggests that there are indeed significant relationships between the TASC and the PRF. Most likely these were completely swamped by the rotational procedures because of the very strong correlations among the three scales within the TASC.

*Factor 7: HIT Movement*

Factor 7 is a residual factor consisting almost entirely of HIT Movement. The loadings for Movement in the United States and Mexico are .86 and .83, respectively. The only loadings approaching significance on Factor 7 from the PRF are Play ($-.33$) and Social Recognition ($-.29$) in the United States and Mexico respectively. For the Mexican children, the developmental score on Human Figure Drawing also approaches significance on Factor 7 with a loading of $-.37$. Inspection of the zero-order correlations between Movement and the other variables in Table 6-19 indicates, at least for the combined samples, that Movement is simply unrelated to personality traits measured by self-report inventories.

### INTERCORRELATIONS ACROSS DOMAINS OF VARIABLES

Of greatest interest are the correlations between variables in one domain, such as the cognitive–mental-abilities measures, and those in another, such as the personality-attitudinal measures. Some of these relationships are presented in the nine intercorrelation matrices in Tables 6-10–6-18. The number of variables in these matrices is sharply reduced from the total number that have been studied. In addition, the matrices only include data from years 1, 2, and 4, the most critical of the six years in the longitudinal study. A more intensive examination of the correlation between specified pairs of variables for all six years in all six groups will be presented later.

For convenience of analysis, the variables from each child's test performance have been divided into three major domains—variables primarily dealing with cognitive-perceptual abilities, those concerned with cognitive-perceptual style, and personality or attitude scales from self-report inventories. In addition, the variables in the Holtzman Inkblot Technique can be thought of as cutting across several of these domains. Correlations between inkblot scores and variables from the other domains will be examined first.

Inspection of Tables 6-10–6-18 reveals a number of individual correlations between inklot scores and other test variables that are significantly different from zero beyond the .01 level when considered alone. It must be remembered in reviewing such correlations that, if chance alone were operating, one in a hundred correlations would be of sufficient magnitude to be classified as significantly different from zero at the .01 level or beyond. With many hundreds of correlations between inkblot scores and the other variables, some correlations should prove to be significant at the .01 level even if only chance factors were operating. Consequently, one must exert considerable caution in the interpretation of isolated correlations. As a general rule of thumb, only when a single correlation is significant beyond the .001 level (where chance would be accountable for the magnitude of the correlation only one in a thousand times) is the correlation worth mentioning. Where a correlation is significant at the .01 level and inspection of the comparable correlation in the remaining tables reveals a strong trend in the same direction, the relationship may be a real one.

Applying these conservative rules to the correlations in Tables 6-10–6-18 yields only a few relationships worthy of note. A number of inkblot scores repeatedly correlate with the cognitive-ability tests, such as Human Figure Drawing, Vocabulary, and Block Design. Such variables as Movement, Integration, Human, and Barrier, which all cluster together in Factor 1 on the HIT, show the most consistent relationships with the measures of mental ability. It is important to note that these correlations appear in both cultures, although they seem to be a bit stronger in the American samples than in the Mexican. Clearly, the variables comprising Factor 1 in the HIT have a small but significant cognitive component.

Such variables as Pathognomic Verbalization, Anxiety, Hostility, and Penetration, defining variables for Factor 3 on the HIT, also occasionally show significant correlations with one or more of the cognitive tests. To ascertain the extent to which such correlations are consistent throughout the data, special tables were organized, taking all of the correlations for only two variables at a time—thirty-six correlations where data are available in all three groups, both cultures, and all six years.

The correlation for Movement and Vocabulary is presented in Table 6-26. All thirty-six of the correlations are positive, and most of them are significantly different from zero at a high level of confidence. There appear to be no systematic differences between the two cultures or across the three age groups. Nor are there any noticeable trends associated with age itself. Whatever fluctuations occur are undoubtedly due to a combination of many trivial (chance) factors. It is safe to conclude that the correlation between Movement and Vocabulary is rather likely to range between .15 and .35.

Although in the same direction, the correlation between Movement and Block Design is substantially lower than that between Movement and Vocabulary. Inspection of Table 6-27 reveals a range of correlations from −.07 to .29, with only seven of the thirty-six correlations significant beyond the .05 or .01 level.

The correlation between Movement and the Harris-Goodenough

Table 6-26
Correlation of Movement and Vocabulary

| Age | United States I | United States II | United States III | Mexico I | Mexico II | Mexico III |
|-----|------|------|------|------|------|------|
| 17 | | | .25[b] | | | .21 |
| 16 | | | .25[b] | | | .31[b] |
| 15 | | | .34[a] | | | .14 |
| 14 | | .09 | .31[a] | | .26[c] | .27[b] |
| 13 | | .31[b] | .21[c] | | .27[b] | .18[c] |
| 12 | | .19[c] | .14 | | .14 | .30[a] |
| 11 | .13 | .07 | | .19 | .25[b] | |
| 10 | .20[c] | .19[c] | | .11 | .17 | |
| 9 | .21[c] | .23[b] | | .26[b] | .34[a] | |
| 8 | .18 | | | .32[a] | | |
| 7 | .42[a] | | | .26[b] | | |
| 6 | .28[b] | | | .16[c] | | |

[a] Correlation significant beyond the .001 level.
[b] Correlation significant at the .01 level.
[c] Correlation significant at the .05 level.

Table 6-27
Correlation of Movement and Block Design

| Age | United States | | | Mexico | | |
|---|---|---|---|---|---|---|
| | I | II | III | I | II | III |
| 17 | | | .04 | | | .06 |
| 16 | | | —.07 | | | .01 |
| 15 | | | .12 | | | .11 |
| 14 | | .29[b] | .19[c] | | .18 | .08 |
| 13 | | .20[c] | .05 | | .03 | .11 |
| 12 | | .03 | .04 | | .07 | .07 |
| 11 | .14 | .06 | | .17 | .06 | |
| 10 | .10 | .09 | | .20[c] | .07 | |
| 9 | .10 | —.01 | | .16 | .17[c] | |
| 8 | .24[c] | | | .19[c] | | |
| 7 | .12 | | | —.05 | | |
| 6 | .04 | | | .10 | | |

References as in Table 6-26.

score from Human Figure Drawing reveals still another pattern of relationship between the Holtzman Inkblot Technique and the cognitive-perceptual ability variables. The correlations in Table 6-28 range all the way from —.29, significant in the wrong direction at the .05 level, to .33, significant beyond the .001 level in the expected direction. The erratic fluctuation of these correlations suggests an unstable relationship, even though individual correlations might appear impressively large. Similar results, though at a slightly lower level, were obtained for Integration, Human, and Barrier concerning their relationships with Vocabulary, Block Design, and Human Figure Drawing. In each case the inkblot score was more closely related to Vocabulary than to either of the other two cognitive variables.

Factor 3 in the Holtzman Inkblot Technique is the factor concerned with affective expressivity and loose imagination in fantasy productions. Since a certain amount of verbal ability may facilitate high scores on these variables, it is of some interest to examine their relationship to Vocabulary, Block Design, and Human Figure Drawing as well. The correlation between Pathognomic Verbalization and Vocabulary is generally close to zero, ranging from —.15 to .24. Six of the thirty-six correlations are significantly different from zero beyond the .05 level. When compared with Block Design, however, Pathognomic Verbalization shows no correlation of any significance. A similar situation holds for the other variables defining Factor 3 (with the exception, of course, of Movement). These results confirm the hypothesis that Factor 1 from the Holtzman Inkblot Technique (and not Factor 3) has a significant cognitive component related to verbal ability. It is especially noteworthy that these results are consistent in both cultures regardless of age.

Some correlations between inkblot variables and the cognitive-perceptual style variables are also evident in Tables 6-10–6-18. Given the rationale underlying the Percent Public score from the Object Sorting Test and Pathognomic Verbalization from the HIT, one would expect a negative relationship to emerge. The correlations for OST Percent Public and Pathognomic Verbalization are given in Table 6-29. Six of the eighteen correlations are significantly negative, while the remainder are negative or zero. Although the relationship is not a strong one, it is clearly evident in the hypothesized direction. Individuals with high scores on Pathognomic Verbalization tend to have fewer of their sorts in the Object Sorting Test classified as public than do those who have little or no pathognomic verbalization in their inkblot responses. This finding, present in both cultures, confirms the results obtained by Holtzman, Donald R. Gorham, and Moran (1964) in a study of chronic paranoid schizophrenic men who were given a

Table 6-28
Correlation of Movement and Human Figure Drawing

| Age | United States | | | Mexico | | |
|---|---|---|---|---|---|---|
| | I | II | III | I | II | III |
| 17 | | | .14 | | | —.29c |
| 16 | | | .17 | | | .14 |
| 15 | | | .16 | | | .21c |
| 14 | | .16 | .22c | | —.16 | .20c |
| 13 | | .33a | .20c | | —.01 | .10 |
| 12 | | .24b | .32a | | .03 | .10 |
| 11 | —.09 | .21c | | .03 | .00 | |
| 10 | —.05 | .18c | | .14 | .06 | |
| 9 | —.12 | .01 | | .05 | .15 | |
| 8 | .08 | | | —.01 | | |
| 7 | .03 | | | —.04 | | |
| 6 | .06 | | | —.09 | | |

References as in Table 6-26.

Table 6-29
Correlation of OST Public and HIT Pathognomic Verbalization

| Age | United States I | United States II | United States III | Mexico I | Mexico II | Mexico III |
|-----|-----|-----|-----|-----|-----|-----|
| 17 | | | | | | |
| 16 | | | | | | |
| 15 | | | | | | |
| 14 | | | —.28[b] | | | .00 |
| 13 | | | —.27[b] | | | .05 |
| 12 | | | —.12 | | | —.19 |
| 11 | | —.24[b] | | | —.11 | |
| 10 | | .04 | | | —.20[c] | |
| 9 | | —.05 | | | —.15[c] | |
| 8 | .16 | | | .02 | | |
| 7 | —.06 | | | —.15 | | |
| 6 | —.35[a] | | | —.12 | | |

References as in Table 6-26.

number of cognitive-perceptual tests as well as the Holtzman Ink-blot Technique.

Among the American children, but not the Mexican, the number of groups used in the Object Sorting Test tends to correlate negatively with such inkblot variables as Color, Shading, Movement, Anxiety, and Hostility among the older children, especially those in Group III. An inkblot protocol with very low Color, Shading, and Movement scores is generally interpreted as indicative of a flat affect and rigid personality. A high number of groups in the Object Sorting Test means that the individual does not see the diverse abstract ways in which the objects can be categorized. Both a high score on OST Number of Groups and a low score on the inkblot determinants reveal an individual with a constricted perceptual field.

No consistent correlations were found between the part scores for either the Visual Fractionation Test or the Conceptual Styles Test and any other variables in the study. To be sure, an occasional isolated correlation might appear significant, but it always disappeared upon replication. When the part scores for Figures, Elements, and Grounds in the VFT and for Analytical, Relational, and Inferential-Categorical in the CST are ignored and only the total time scores are considered, some relationships across the several domains do appear. Five of the variables in the study involve time in one way or another—HIT Reaction Time, the Delay score for Time Estimation, EFT Time, VFT Time, and CST Time. The intercorrelations of these five variables in each group and year where the variables are present were studied carefully to see if there was any common factor running through them. HIT Reaction Time proved to be correlated positively with TET Delay, VFT Time, and CST Time, but not with EFT Time. The highest correlations were between HIT Reaction Time and the Time scores on the Visual Fractionation Test and the Conceptual Styles Test, where the correlations were consistently significant, ranging from .20 to .62. The highest correlation of .62 occurred for CST Time in Group II, year 2, for the Mexican children. The correlations for TET Delay and EFT Time were generally negative, ranging from zero to −.29 in both cultures. A high score on TET Delay indicates accurate perception of one minute, while a low score on EFT Time indicates rapid performance on the perceptual task imposed by the hidden figures. This finding is the only consistent one involving EFT Time and the other variables concerned with a temporal factor. VFT Time and CST Time correlated consistently with each other in both cultures for Group I in both year 2 and year 3; the correlations generally ranged from .28 to .47, indicating that a person who was rather slow in one task was likely to be somewhat slow in the other. From these results it can be concluded that there is a low-order but consistent temporal factor running through several tasks in the battery.

The relationships between inkblot scores and scales from the Personality Research Form or the Test Anxiety Scale for Children are generally very low. As noted earlier, HIT Movement has no relationship to such scales as Understanding or Achievement from the PRF. On an a priori basis, one might expect some relationship between Anxiety on the HIT and Test Anxiety on the TASC. Since both measures are available in all three groups in both cultures for all years except the first, there are a total of thirty replications of the correlation between HIT Anxiety and the TASC total score. In no case does the correlation reach significance at or beyond the .01 level. The obtained correlations range from −.20 to .16. From the results, it is safe to conclude that there is no relationship between anxious content in inkblot responses, as reflected in the HIT Anxiety score, and specific anxiety about taking tests, as measured by the TASC. When Anxiety was compared with the Lie and Defensiveness scales from the TASC, similar results were obtained. Several interesting correlations were found, however, between such variables as Color, Pathognomic Verbalization, and Integration from the Holtzman Inkblot Technique and Exhibition, Impulsivity, Nurturance, Harmavoidance, Play, and Understanding from the Personality Research Form. Since these relationships generally involve scores on the two tests at two different points in time, they are discussed later in this chapter in a special study on the early precursors of later personality development.

Four of the tests dealing with cognitive-perceptual ability merit special consideration because of their high stability through time, their consistent pattern of relationships with other variables, and the fact that scores on them are available for many replications across cultures, groups, and years. The intercorrelations among Vocabulary and Block Design from the WISC (or WAIS), the Harris-Goodenough score from Human Figure Drawing, and the Time score from the Embedded Figures Test are presented in Tables 6-30–6-35. In all cases a number of significant correlations appear, regardless of age or culture. For Vocabulary and Block Design in Table 6-30, there appears to be a slightly stronger correlation among the American children in Groups I and III than among those in Group II. This difference is particularly evident for age eleven. The Group I American children show a correlation of .51 between Vocabulary and Block Design when they are eleven years old, while the comparable Group II children show a correlation of only .17. Without a strong a priori hypothesis for explaining this difference, the most likely explanation is that it is merely a chance occurrence.

Vocabulary and Human Figure Drawing are less consistently correlated than Vocabulary and Block Design, as can be seen in Table 6-31. Only the Group III American children show a highly consistent pattern in all six years. This somewhat more erratic pattern for the correlation of Vocabulary and Human Figure Drawing, as contrasted with several of the other cognitive variables, is consistent with the results obtained in the earlier factor analysis of the cognitive-perceptual ability variables. Human

Figure Drawing is a more complex test than Vocabulary, and the precise factorial content of performance on the drawing task shifts somewhat across age and culture.

Vocabulary and the Embedded Figures Test show the same high degree of consistency found for Vocabulary and Block Design. Although data are not available for the youngest children in both

Table 6-30
Correlation of Vocabulary and Block Design

| Age | United States | | | Mexico | | |
|---|---|---|---|---|---|---|
| | I | II | III | I | II | III |
| 17 | | | .40[a] | | | .23 |
| 16 | | | .25[b] | | | .13 |
| 15 | | | .33[a] | | | .34[a] |
| 14 | | .31[b] | .31[a] | | .21 | .21[c] |
| 13 | | .19 | .33[a] | | .35[a] | .29[b] |
| 12 | | .24[b] | .29[a] | | .34[a] | .19[c] |
| 11 | .51[a] | .17 | | .29[c] | .37[a] | |
| 10 | .37[a] | .26[b] | | .30[a] | .34[a] | |
| 9 | .40[a] | .26[b] | | .26[b] | .37[a] | |
| 8 | .34[a] | | | .31[a] | | |
| 7 | .30[b] | | | .17[c] | | |
| 6 | .28[b] | | | .23[b] | | |

References as in Table 6-26.

Table 6-31
Correlation of Vocabulary and Human Figure Drawing

| Age | United States | | | Mexico | | |
|---|---|---|---|---|---|---|
| | I | II | III | I | II | III |
| 17 | | | .36[a] | | | .28[c] |
| 16 | | | .35[a] | | | .27[b] |
| 15 | | | .30[b] | | | .08 |
| 14 | | .16 | .27[b] | | .10 | .03 |
| 13 | | .16 | .40[a] | | .06 | .11 |
| 12 | | .20[c] | .24[b] | | .18[c] | .11 |
| 11 | .29[b] | .12 | | .37[b] | .34[a] | |
| 10 | .26[b] | .07 | | .16 | .21[c] | |
| 9 | .16 | —.03 | | .26[b] | .31[b] | |
| 8 | .15 | | | .24[b] | | |
| 7 | .33[a] | | | .12 | | |
| 6 | .10 | | | .05 | | |

References as in Table 6-26.

Table 6-32
Correlation of Vocabulary and EFT Time

| Age | United States | | | Mexico | | |
|-----|---|---|---|---|---|---|
|     | I | II | III | I | II | III |
| 17 | | | | | | |
| 16 | | | —.33[a] | | | —.21[c] |
| 15 | | | —.27[b] | | | —.28[b] |
| 14 | | | —.32[a] | | | —.31[a] |
| 13 | | —.33[a] | —.35[a] | | —.27[b] | —.24[b] |
| 12 | | —.33[a] | —.32[a] | | —.36[a] | —.27[b] |
| 11 | | | —.29[b] | | | —.39[a] |
| 10 | | —.43[a] | —.28[b] | | —.34[a] | —.43[a] |
| 9 | | —.33[b] | —.15 | | —.37[a] | —.34[a] |
| 8 | | | | | | |
| 7 | | | | | | |
| 6 | | | | | | |

References as in Table 6-26.

Table 6-33
Correlation of Block Design and Human Figure Drawing

| Age | United States | | | Mexico | | |
|-----|---|---|---|---|---|---|
|     | I | II | III | I | II | III |
| 17 | | | .35[a] | | | .15 |
| 16 | | | .37[a] | | | .30[b] |
| 15 | | | .43[a] | | | .22[c] |
| 14 | | .28[b] | .37[a] | | .26[c] | .17[c] |
| 13 | | .37[a] | .35[a] | | .29[b] | .25[b] |
| 12 | | .36[a] | .32[a] | | .27[b] | .17 |
| 11 | .45[a] | .35[a] | | .27[c] | .43[a] | |
| 10 | .34[b] | .38[a] | | .36[a] | .26[b] | |
| 9 | .46[a] | .12 | | .26[b] | .29[b] | |
| 8 | .45[a] | | | .45[a] | | |
| 7 | .49[a] | | | .36[a] | | |
| 6 | .31[a] | | | .28[b] | | |

References as in Table 6-26.

cultures, nor for year 6, the twenty-four correlations in Table 6-32 are all highly consistent, ranging from —.15 to —.43.

When Block Design and Human Figure Drawing are correlated, the results are highly consistent throughout the thirty-six replications. As given in Table 6-33, the correlations range from .12 to .49. Clearly, Block Design and Human Figure Drawing have much more in common than Vocabulary and Human Figure Drawing.

The correlations between Block Design and the Time score for the Embedded Figures Test are among the highest of any bivariate relationships in the longitudinal study. The coefficients in Table 6-34 range from $-.41$ to $-.78$, indicating that the Embedded Figures Test and Block Design have a great deal in common. These results are highly consistent with the earlier factor analysis showing that EFT Time should be considered a cognitive-abilities measure rather than a measure of cognitive style.

The correlation between Human Figure Drawing and the Embedded Figures Test is likewise highly consistent throughout all replications. The coefficients in Table 6-35 range from $-.20$ to $-.48$. No differences are noted across age or culture, the relationship being highly consistent.

From the above detailed analysis of six bivariate relationships among four cognitive variables, it is evident that all four of these cognitive tasks show a high degree of consistency across ages and cultures. The results clearly confirm Witkin's contention that the Embedded Figures Test, Block Design, and Human Figure Drawing constitute a cluster that measures the degree of cognitive-perceptual differentiation among children. When these results are taken together with the other earlier results from the factor analysis, it is also evident that Vocabulary and Block Design measure somewhat different cognitive abilities, while also reflect-

Table 6-34
Correlation of Block Design and EFT Time

| Age | United States | | | Mexico | | |
|---|---|---|---|---|---|---|
| | I | II | III | I | II | III |
| 17 | | | | | | |
| 16 | | $-.68$[a] | | | $-.42$[a] | |
| 15 | | $-.72$[a] | | | $-.41$[a] | |
| 14 | | $-.59$[a] | | | $-.47$[a] | |
| 13 | | $-.69$[a] | $-.73$[a] | | $-.62$[a] | $-.55$[a] |
| 12 | | $-.73$[a] | $-.64$[a] | | $-.72$[a] | $-.50$[a] |
| 11 | | $-.78$[a] | | | $-.71$[a] | |
| 10 | $-.76$[a] | $-.63$[a] | | $-.75$[a] | $-.61$[a] | |
| 9 | $-.72$[a] | $-.60$[a] | | $-.72$[a] | $-.56$[a] | |
| 8 | | | | | | |
| 7 | | | | | | |
| 6 | | | | | | |

References as in Table 6-26.

Table 6-35
Correlation of Human Figure Drawing and EFT Time

| Age | United States | | | Mexico | | |
|---|---|---|---|---|---|---|
| | I | II | III | I | II | III |
| 17 | | | | | | |
| 16 | | | —.47[a] | | | —.20[c] |
| 15 | | | —.48[a] | | | —.28[b] |
| 14 | | | —.40[a] | | | —.35[a] |
| 13 | | —.30[b] | —.41[a] | | —.30[b] | —.32[a] |
| 12 | | —.38[a] | —.37[a] | | —.31[a] | —.37[a] |
| 11 | | | —.43[a] | | | —.41[a] |
| 10 | —.38[a] | —.43[a] | | —.45[a] | —.25[b] | |
| 9 | —.38[a] | —.38[a] | | —.46[a] | —.28[b] | |
| 8 | | | | | | |
| 7 | | | | | | |
| 6 | | | | | | |

References as in Table 6-26.

ing a general factor of mental ability in both cultures and at all ages.

Like the variables within the Holtzman Inkblot Technique, the cognitive variables show some significant correlations with the personality-attitudinal variables represented by the Personality Research Form and the Test Anxiety Scale for Children. For the PRF, these are better represented in the special study of precursors of later personality development. In the case of the TASC, however, data are available for both sets of variables for all three groups in both cultures across five years. Table 6-36 contains the repeated correlations of Vocabulary and the TASC total score. While the relationship is not a highly consistent one, it is clear that poor performance on Vocabulary is more likely to be associated with high test anxiety as measured by the TASC in both cultures and at all ages. Similar results were obtained in an analysis of the correlation between Block Design and the TASC total score.

## PRECURSORS OF LATER PERSONALITY TRAITS

Only rarely is an opportunity presented for examining home, family, peer group, and other environmental factors, as well as early perceptual and cognitive abilities, as they relate to later personality development in a large number of children. Because strictly comparable data from the home and family are available cross-culturally for only a limited number of variables out of the parental interview, the correlations between the family and home environment, on the one hand, and the child's personality and mental development, on the other, are less rich than would be desired. Six variables concerning the mother and the home environment are sufficiently comparable cross-culturally to justify systematic analysis in the present study. These variables are the Socio-Economic Status Index, the level of the mother's education, the number of special interests of the child, the number of recreational activities engaged in by the family, the mother's satisfaction with the child's progress in school, and the minimum educational level aspired to by the mother for the child. In addition, the four factor-analytic dimensions from the Parent-Attitude Survey completed by the mother can be considered in the context of the family environment, making a total of ten variables gathered from the interview with the parents midstream through the six-year longitudinal study.

Since the Personality Research Form was given in the last year of the longitudinal study, it provides a number of personality measures that can be considered criterion variables against which to compare the cognitive, perceptual, and personality data from the earlier years, especially the first year of the six-year study.

Table 6-36
Correlation of Vocabulary and TASC Test Anxiety

| Age | United States | | | Mexico | | |
|---|---|---|---|---|---|---|
| | I | II | III | I | II | III |
| 17 | | | —.22[c] | | | —.10 |
| 16 | | | —.37[a] | | | —.25[b] |
| 15 | | | —.12 | | | —.14 |
| 14 | | —.15 | —.16 | | —.11 | —.14 |
| 13 | | —.15 | —.14 | | —.25[b] | —.20[c] |
| 12 | | —.13 | | | —.11 | —.13 |
| 11 | —.31[b] | —.22[c] | | —.10 | —.20[c] | |
| 10 | —.27[b] | —.24[b] | | —.16 | —.18[c] | |
| 9 | —.08 | | | —.18[c] | —.29 | |
| 8 | —.27[b] | | | .01 | | |
| 7 | —.12 | | | .09 | | |
| 6 | | | | .36 | | |

References as in Table 6-26.

The data obtained from mothers halfway through the study can also be thought of as measures of potential influences upon the child's later development. In addition, test data collected in the first several years of the study can be compared with the variables from the parental interview, as well as with the Personality Research Form. At a given point in time, Groups I, II, and III are three years apart, making it necessary to consider the correlations separately for each age group. Since the number of cases in the Mexican sample for which there are parental-interview data and scores on the Personality Research Form is appreciably lower than the comparable number of cases for the American children, because of the fact that only part of the Mexican sample was included in the matched subsample, the resulting correlations are less stable than those presented earlier dealing with the data from the first several years of the project. Consequently, one must exercise caution in the interpretation of isolated correlations that are not substantiated elsewhere.

Before turning to the relationships between test data in the early years of the study and personality traits as measured by the PRF, there are several relationships between the test data and the variables from the parental interview that merit special attention. Both Vocabulary and Arithmetic from the WISC show some significant correlations with the minimum educational level aspired to by the mother for her child; the higher the performance on the Vocabulary or Arithmetic subtest, the higher the educational level sought for the child. These correlations range from as high as .45 for the American children in Group II, year 2, to a negligible relationship among the children in both cultures in Group III. When the same parental variable was examined for possible correlations with Block Design and Picture Completion, no significant correlations could be found. From the results, it can be concluded that in both cultures the verbal-abilities tests are more likely to be closely associated with parental aspiration for the child's educational level than are the performance tests dealing with nonverbal aspects of mental ability.

The number of recreational activities engaged in by the family is also related to Vocabulary, but only among the youngest children in both cultures. For the Mexicans in Group I, the correlations between Vocabulary and number of recreational activities range from .16 to .43, depending upon the year in which the Vocabulary score was obtained. For the American children, the comparable correlations are barely significant, ranging from .06 to .27. It is interesting to note that this relationship between Vocabulary and the number of recreational activities engaged in by the family exists only for the youngest children in both cultures. Since the number of recreational activities is also positively correlated at a low level with the Socio-Economic Status Index, as is the Vocabulary score of the child, one cannot conclude that engaging in a number of recreational activities as a family will necessarily stimulate greater vocabulary development on the part of the child.

The degree of satisfaction expressed by the mother concerning the child's progress in school tends to be uncorrelated with the child's actual performance on tests of cognitive-perceptual ability. Exceptions to this generalization are the significant correlations in Mexico on Arithmetic for Groups I and III, .35 and .30 respectively, in the third year of testing, the same year in which the interview data were collected from the mother. For the American samples only, additional data are available for Group III concerning actual grades made in school and ratings by the teachers during the fourth year of the study. Mother's satisfaction with the child's progress in school correlated .36 with grade-point average and .40 with teacher's ratings of the child for the tenth-graders in Group III. Among the American children in Groups I and II, sociometric data were also obtained in the first year of the study. Children who were rejected by their peers in the first grade had mothers who were less satisfied with their progress in school three years later (r of −.27). No such relationship was found for the fourth-graders in Group II, however.

The four scales for the Parent-Attitude Survey that were derived from the earlier factor analysis also show some significant correlations with earlier test data. A number of low but positive correlations were found between Factor 1 and the cognitive tests in Mexico but not in the United States. At the same time, it should be pointed out that the Socio-Economic Status (SES) Index correlated substantially with Factor 1 from the Parent-Attitude Survey in Mexico—correlations of .46, .52, and .31 for Groups I, II and III respectively—while the SES Index showed no correlation with Factor 1 for the American families. Since the cognitive tests also correlate significantly with the Socio-Economic Status Index, one cannot conclude that Mexican mothers who show a high degree of "active optimism" are thereby directly stimulating their children to perform better on tests of mental abilities. A more likely explanation of the relationships discovered is that mothers in well-educated families in which the father has a high-status occupation have good reason to be more active and optimistic in orientation, while at the same time their children are more likely to have a better home and school environment for the stimulation of intellectual development.

Factor 2 in the Parent-Attitude Survey deals more directly with attitudes about child rearing. An individual who obtains a high score on this scale is likely to be one who is permissive and somewhat liberated in the acceptance of the child's behavior, as opposed to a parent who believes in strict authoritarian control. No significant and consistent relationships were found between any of the earlier test scores and the mother's attitudes concerning child rearing. Only the Socio-Economic Status Index shows a significant correlation with the Factor 2 attitude scale, and then only for the American sample—.44, .40, and .31 for Groups I, II, and III respectively.

The third factorially based dimension in the Parent-Attitude Survey also deals with the mother's attitude about child rearing. A high score would suggest self-assured calmness, while a low score would indicate some parental anxiety. Among the Mexican families in Groups I and III, but not for any of the Americans, significant correlations were found between the Percent Open score on the Object Sorting Test and this third scale in the Parent-Attitude Survey—.43 and .31 for Groups I and III respectively, in year 2. It is interesting to note that, for these same groups, a negative correlation was found between the parental attitude score and Aggression on the Personality Research Form several years later: $-.14$ and $-.42$ for Groups I and III respectively. When taken together, these results suggest that, among the Mexican families, a high degree of self-assured calmness on the part of the mother is related to greater openness and lower aggression. Among the American families in Group I, but not in Groups II or III, a high score on this third parental attitude scale was positively correlated with Aggression (.33), just the opposite of what was found for the Mexican families. When taken together with the additional finding that the mother's score on this third attitude scale correlates positively with the child's score on PRF Play (.34), one can tentatively conclude that "self-assured calmness" within the social context of the American family and neighborhood may actually stimulate social aggressiveness of an extroverted type, while the same general attitude in Mexico would have the reverse effect because of the different sociocultural premises concerning competitiveness within the Mexican and American societies.

The Socio-Economic Status Index, based upon the father's education and occupation, is a primary variable for classifying the family and home environment. As one would expect, children who come from upper-class families do much better than others on most of the tests dealing with cognitive-perceptual abilities. A more rigorous analysis of variance with socioeconomic status as one of the independent variables is reported in subsequent chapters, where the cross-culturally matched sample is analyzed. Because the level of the mother's education is more closely correlated with the SES Index in the United States than in Mexico, it is of some interest to examine the correlation between mother's educational level and the child's performance on cognitive tests. Table 6-37 shows the correlations of the mother's educational level and Vocabulary by culture, group, and age of the child when tested. Although the relationship between these two variables is consistent and positive for the younger children in the United States, the relationship is erratic at best for the Mexican families. Apparently, the level of the mother's education is not as important a factor in the child's performance on tests of mental ability for Mexican families as it is for American families, particularly in the early years of the child's development.

Several variables from the Holtzman Inkblot Technique, when administered in the early years of the longitudinal study, correlate significantly with personality traits as measured by the Personality Research Form in the last year of study. High scores on Color tend to be associated with high scores on Exhibition, Impulsivity, and Nurturance in two or more of the six samples. Color for the first three years of test data for the Mexican children in

Table 6-37
Correlation of Vocabulary and Mother's Education

| Age | United States | | | Mexico | | |
|---|---|---|---|---|---|---|
| | I | II | III | I | II | III |
| 17 | | | .26 | | | −.10 |
| 16 | | | .24[b] | | | .29[c] |
| 15 | | | .22[c] | | | .19 |
| 14 | | .29[a] | .05 | | −.01 | .17 |
| 13 | | .31[a] | .10 | | .15 | .09 |
| 12 | | .30[a] | .00 | | .15 | .23[c] |
| 11 | .12 | .33[a] | | .00 | .14 | |
| 10 | .31[b] | .45[a] | | .31[c] | .23 | |
| 9 | .26[b] | .44[a] | | .21 | .08 | |
| 8 | .33[a] | | | .35[b] | | |
| 7 | .23[c] | | | .11 | | |
| 6 | .36[a] | | | .39[b] | | |

References as in Table 6-26.

Group I correlates significantly with Exhibition—.28, .30, and .29. The comparable correlations for Group II in Mexico are .30, .22, and .31. Although these results are not substantiated in the oldest group of Mexican children or in any of the American groups, the results suggest that a high amount of Color in young children may be related to later development of "show-off" tendencies or extroversion. Such a correlation is entirely consistent with many of the clinical studies concerning the meaning of color in inkblot perception (Hill 1972). Color correlates significantly with Impulsivity only for the first two years of Group I in Mexico, .31 and .29, and for the first year in Group II in Mexico, .28. Again, the relationship discovered is consistent with earlier experimental research and clinical studies involving the meaning of color. The positive correlation between Color and Nurturance appears in Group II in both cultures—at ages ten and eleven for the American children (.25 and .22 respectively) and at age twelve for the Mexican children (.22). The traditional interpretation of Color as indicative of affective response to one's interpersonal environment and sensitivity to the emotions of others is consistent with these findings, even though they are of low order and only occasionally appear.

Integration proves to be related to Harmavoidance, Play, and Understanding in several of the samples. For Harmavoidance, among the Mexican children, four significant correlations are for eight-year-olds in Group I (−.28), nine- and ten-year-olds in Group II (−.28 and −.27), and sixteen-year-olds in Group III (−.26). A high score on Integration for these children tends to be associated with a low score on Harmavoidance. The significant correlations between Integration and Play show a similar pattern among the Mexican children—.32 and .34 for seven- and eleven-year-olds in Group I and .28 for thirteen-year-olds in Group III. Among the American children, this relationship is reversed. In all three groups, negative correlations prevail, although only in the case of sixteen- and seventeen-year-olds in Group III are the correlations at all significant, −.22 and −.29 respectively. The very tentative nature of these low-order findings makes it very hazardous to speculate upon the meaning of any possible cross-cultural difference. In the case of the correlation between Integration and Understanding, the situation is somewhat stronger. Among the American children in all three groups, significant positive correlations are obtained, ranging from .20 for Group I ten-year-olds to .34 for Group III thirteen-year-olds. Among the Mexican children, the relationship is unclear. While two correlations do appear significant at the .05 level, one is reversed in direction, −.25 for Group II ten-year-olds. The other is .28 for Group III seventeen-year-olds.

Still another correlation involving the earlier scores on the Holtzman Inkblot Technique and later personality traits as measured by the Personality Research Form is the relationship between Pathognomic Verbalization and Impulsivity and Play. The only correlations for Pathognomic Verbalization and Impulsivity that reach statistical significance are in a positive direction—.22 for American Group II eleven-year-olds, .22 for fifteen-year-old Americans in Group III, and .32 for ten-year-old Mexicans in Group I. For these children, the higher the earlier scores on Pathognomic Verbalization, the higher the score on Impulsivity from the Personality Research Form in the last year of study. The correlation between Pathognomic Verbalization and Play tends to be negative, barely reaching significance in three instances: −.20 for ten-year-old Americans in Group II, −.21 for fourteen-year-old Americans in Group III, and −.31 for fifteen-year-old Mexicans in Group III. The higher the score on Pathognomic Verbalization for these children, the lower the score on Play. In both of these instances the obtained results are significant in the expected direction, although the relationship is of low order and only occasionally appears significant.

By considering only the American children, the number of cases can be increased somewhat for the study of potential precursors of later personality development. In addition, other information about the child is often available to shed further light on the meaning of any relationship. An analysis of such precursors of later personality traits for the American children has been summarized elsewhere (Holtzman 1969). Only the highlights can be presented here.

The most significant precursors of PRF Achievement for the younger children in Groups I and II were variables from the interview reflecting family opportunities for intellectual stimulation. For the older groups, the home-environmental variables proved to be unimportant, being replaced by evidence of actual performance in school.

Sociometric rejection by one's peers in the first grade led to low Affiliation six years later (r of −.32), as well as high scores on Aggression and Impulsivity (.28 and .32). Sociometric attraction in both the first and fourth grades for Group I led to low Aggression (−.33), low Autonomy (−.41), and high Nurturance (.25) by the time the child was in the sixth grade.

The more the mother shared activities with the child in his early school years, the higher his Nurturance (.29) and the lower his Dominance (−.25) when in the sixth grade. This relationship failed to hold for the older children in Groups II and III. High parental aspirations for the child's education proved to be negatively related to Nurturance in Groups II and III (−.35 and −.31 respectively).

A number of the individual interview items with the mother proved to be positively correlated with PRF Understanding. For the youngest children, the global rating on opportunity for intellectual stimulation was the most significant (r of .27). For the American children in Group II, the following interview items were correlated with Understanding: number of special lessons (.27), reading of unassigned books (.38), use of books in the home (.41), and extent to which mother shares activities with the child

(.27). For Group III, the oldest group of Americans, the items correlated with PRF Understanding were reading of unassigned books (.29), use of books in the home (.25), extent to which mother and father both discussed the child's progress (−.28), and high-school rank in senior class (−.27). All of these correlations are in the direction one would expect from the nature of the interview items and the rationale behind the Understanding scale in the Personality Research Form. Although a comparable analysis cannot be made of the Mexican data, since a number of these items proved to be different in meaning in the interview with the Mexican mothers, there is no reason to believe that the results would be any different if adequate data were at hand. While the relationships between the family and home-environmental variables and the child's performance, as well as his later personality development, are of a much lower order than one would expect from the earlier studies by Dave (1964) and Wolf (1964), they are nevertheless somewhat encouraging concerning the positive impact of the family upon the child's development. A more complete presentation of the relationships between the interview data and children's scores on the psychological tests for the Americans is presented elsewhere (Stitt 1970).

In a separate study by S. F. Currie, Holtzman, and Swartz (1974), additional data on forty-six children within the youngest group of Americans were obtained four years after completion of the longitudinal study. These forty-six children, equally divided between boys and girls, constituted more than half of the group that completed the six-year period of testing and were all children from families that have continued to live in Austin, Texas, over a ten-year span, thus representing a particularly stable sample in relation to current population mobility. Ratings of personal adjustment were obtained for these children from their school counselors and teachers on a four-point scale, ranging from "well-adjusted" to "serious problems of adjustment." School achievement per se was unimportant in the ratings, while a child's concept of himself and his relationship with others was central. The ratings were based primarily upon actual behavior and events surrounding the lives of the children involved.

Seven early indicators proved to be significant precursors of personal adjustment nine years later. The number of Elizabeth M.

Koppitz's Emotional Indicators in the Human Figure Drawing
(Koppitz 1968) correlated −.44 with the Adjustment Index.
Sociometric rejection by peers in the first grade was correlated
−.33 with the Adjustment Index nine years later. No significant
sex differences were found. Four of the inkblot scores proved significantly related to later personal adjustment—Pathognomic
Verbalization (r of −.38), Anxiety (−.37), Hostility (−.39),
and Form Appropriateness (.28). With the exception of Form Appropriateness, all of these inkblot variables are marker variables
for Factor 3, dealing with psychopathology in inkblot responses.
In the case of Form Appropriateness, the direction of the relationship indicates that children with poor form level are more likely
to be maladjusted in later life. The last of the seven indicators is
the level of the father's occupation; the higher the occupational
level, the better the adjustment (r of .27). These results strengthen
substantially some of the earlier interpretations of the meaning
of variables in the Holtzman Inkblot Technique.

---

The dimensional studies of the major cognitive, perceptual, and
personality measures employed, and the cross-domain relationships
among variables revealed clearly the main factor patterns and
several of the significant individual correlations that had been
found previously. Despite these findings, however, there were
important differences involving culture as well as age. Those variables suitably stable and relevant to cross-cultural comparisons
were carried forward in the matched cross-cultural design, constructed to control systematically for major subcultural variation.

The five chapters in Part Three contain the major cross-cultural
results from the study. In Chapter 7 the findings on the several
cognitive-perceptual measures are reported.

# PART THREE

## Cross-Cultural Comparisons:
## Methodology and Results

---

Could it be that a North American village school was better
than the annex of an Institute that boasted of having produced
Ignacio Ramírez and Ignacio Altamirano?

José Vasconcelos

*A Mexican Ulysses*
trans. W. Rex Crawford

---

# 7. Components of Performance on
# Cognitive-Perceptual Measures

In most cross-cultural studies of personality development, it is not possible to control systematically major subcultural variation that often accounts for a great deal of the obtained variance in results. Where two cultures are markedly different, there is even a question as to whether enough overlap in such factors as socioeconomic status and life style exists between the two cultures to permit systematic control. One of the major objectives of the present study was to control precisely for such subcultural variation in order to eliminate the possibility of serious confounding of culture and subcultural factors that influence a child's performance on psychological tests.

Chapters 7–11 deal with this problem by the use of matched cross-cultural samples in which the socioeconomic status of the family is precisely controlled, as well as the sex and age of the child. The many measures obtained from the child, as well as selected data from the parental interview and attitude questionnaire, are divided for convenience of presentation into cognitive-perceptual (Chapter 7), inkblot scores from the Holtzman Inkblot Technique (Chapter 8), personality-attitudinal measures (Chapter 9), parental and home variables (Chapter 10), and the attitudes and values of the mother (Chapter 11).

## Design for Analysis of Variance

Matched cross-cultural samples were developed using the Socio-Economic Status (SES) Index, an over-all socioeconomic index based upon education and occupation in a modified version of R. J. Havighurst's procedure (Havighurst et al. 1955, pp. 9–10). Father's occupation and education were each scaled in ten levels, with cross-cultural education equivalents as outlined in Table 7-1. Father's education was weighted by three, father's occupation by two, and the two variables were combined to obtain an over-all socioeconomic index, whose range was from 5 to 45. Matching was accomplished on the three groups, the two sexes, two levels of the SES Index, and the year of testing, to control age, so that the only major difference remaining was the primary cultural difference between children in Mexico City and those in Austin, Texas. A four-way analysis of variance design was formulated (two cultures by two SES levels by three groups by two sexes). The two SES levels were obtained by classifying cases with SES Index less

Table 7-1
Education Equivalents in Mexico and the United States

**Mexico**

No formal schooling .................................................. 0
Six years or less ..................................................... 1
Some **secundaria** .................................................. 2
Finished **secundaria** (ninth grade) ........................... 3
Some **preparatoria** ................................................ 4
Finished **preparatoria** (twelfth grade) ....................... 5
Some university, polytech, or **escuela normal superior** ...... 6
Professional title (**licenciado**, four years)................... 7
**Licenciado** (more than four years) ........................... 8
Advanced or professional degree (M.D., Ph.D.) .......... 9

**United States**

No formal schooling .................................................. 0
Six years or less ..................................................... 1
Some junior high school ............................................ 2
Finished junior high school (ninth grade) ..................... 3
Some high school .................................................... 4
Finished high school (twelfth grade) ........................... 5
Some college or post high school ............................... 6
College graduate (B.A., B.S., etc.) ............................. 7
Some post college (M.A., M.S., etc.) .......................... 8
Advanced or professional degree (M.D., LL.D., Ph.D.) ..... 9

than 28 as "low" and those equal to or higher than 28 as "high." This cutting score was chosen after inspection of the data revealed that only rarely would a father with less than a high-school education be classified as high SES, and then he would have to be at least a small business owner or manager. In turn, this cut-off point assures that a father with post–high-school education could not be classified as low SES unless his occupational level was no higher than manual worker. While this procedure yields a much larger number of high SES cases than of low, it is clearly a more rational approach to the definition of SES types than an arbitrary median cutting score.

A total of 203 matched pairs, one member of each pair being an American and the other a Mexican, were used in the design. Only the first time that a test was administered in each culture was employed in the analysis, leaving to a different analysis of variance the question of repeated measures on the same tests. While most variables employed in the analysis were obtained in the first year of testing, a number were not introduced until the subsequent years in the six years of the study. All of the data growing out of the parent interview and the Parent-Attitude Survey were collected in the fourth year of the study. Occasionally missing data occurred because of an invalid test performance or inability to obtain test data within the time frame demanded by the design. In such cases, degrees of freedom have been adjusted for the within-cell-mean-square estimate to take the missing cases into account.

Table 7-2 illustrates the number of cases in each cell of the matched cross-cultural design. While this design could be applied repeatedly to each of the six years for many of the test variables in the study, for purposes of systematic cross-cultural comparison, the analysis has been largely limited to data obtained from the first time a given test was administered. Only the results of this analysis for the cognitive-perceptual measures are presented in this chapter.

## MENTAL ABILITIES
### Four Subtests from the WISC

The most direct measures of mental abilities come from the WISC. Results for the Arithmetic subtest are presented in Table

7-3 in full to illustrate the nature of the analysis-of-variance design.[1]

All four of the main effects in the analysis of variance are significant beyond the .01 level, especially age group and culture. Most of the variance is accounted for by the age differences in the three groups, the older children having done better on arithmetic than the younger. Children from families of relatively high SES level tended to score higher than those from lower-class families. The American children obtained higher scores on Arithmetic than the Mexicans; and boys tended to do better than girls. Of greater interest, however, are the interactions involving age group, SES level, culture, and sex. Only those interactions dealing specifically with culture are presented here. The highly significant interaction

Table 7-2
Number of Cases in Each Cell of Matched Cross-Cultural Samples

| | Low SES Boys | Low SES Girls | High SES Boys | High SES Girls | Total |
|---|---|---|---|---|---|
| | | Mexico | | | |
| Group I | 5 | 10 | 16 | 26 | 57 |
| Group II | 11 | 14 | 28 | 25 | 78 |
| Group III | 8 | 12 | 23 | 25 | 68 |
| | | United States | | | |
| Group I | 5 | 10 | 16 | 26 | 57 |
| Group II | 11 | 14 | 28 | 25 | 78 |
| Group III | 8 | 12 | 23 | 25 | 68 |
| Total | 48 | 72 | 134 | 152 | 406 |

[1] The residual mean square consists of the residual variance between the matched pairs combined with the residual within pairs. Each of these independent residual components contains 191 degrees of freedom. The combined residual will tend to be slightly conservative for testing the significance of culture and any interactions of culture with socioeconomic status, sex, and age group. A series of analyses of variance were run on selected performance variables to determine the extent to which the between-pair residual was significant over and above the within-pair residual. In no case did the F-ratio for testing these two components approach significance at the .05 level. Therefore, it is safe to conclude that the combined residual with 382 degrees of freedom is an appropriate error-variance estimate for F-ratios involving the four primary factors of sex, socioeconomic status, age group, and culture, as well as their higher-order interactions.

Table 7-3
Analysis of Variance for First Year of WISC Arithmetic

| Source of Variation | Mean Square | Degrees of Freedom | F-Ratio | P-Value |
|---|---|---|---|---|
| Age Group (A) | 2,497 | 2 | 1,038.0 | .0000 |
| SES Level (B) | 21 | 1 | 8.7 | .0040 |
| Culture (C) | 40 | 1 | 16.7 | .0002 |
| Sex (D) | 19 | 1 | 7.9 | .0054 |
| AB | 2 | 2 | 0.8 | .7051 |
| AC | 55 | 2 | 22.9 | .0001 |
| AD | 2 | 2 | 0.8 | .6339 |
| BC | 10 | 1 | 4.2 | .0414 |
| BD | 0 | 1 | 0.0 | .9114 |
| CD | 7 | 1 | 2.9 | .0855 |
| ABC | 3 | 2 | 1.2 | .5672 |
| ABD | 5 | 2 | 2.1 | .3312 |
| ACD | 8 | 2 | 3.3 | .1708 |
| BCD | 2 | 1 | 0.8 | .6490 |
| ABCD | 5 | 2 | 2.1 | .3258 |
| Residual | 2.404 | 382 | | |
| Total | | 405 | | |

Table 7-4
Mean Raw Scores on WISC Arithmetic by Age Group and Culture

| Age Group (Years) | United States | Mexico |
|---|---|---|
| I (6.7) | 4.95 | 5.36 |
| II (9.7) | 9.95 | 8.99 |
| III (12.7) | 12.85 | 11.23 |

Within-cell mean square: 2.404

between age group and culture is presented in Table 7-4. While the Mexican children in the first grade scored higher on Arithmetic than the Americans, this advantage was soon lost. The advantage of the American children in the fourth grade had widened still further by the seventh grade, suggesting that something was happening in the American schools to bring about a more rapid development of arithmetic ability than was taking place in the Mexican schools.

The interaction between culture and social class is also of interest. While no significant difference existed between the upper- and lower-class families of American children, a marked difference was apparent in the Mexican families. Children from working-class families did less well (mean raw score of 8.09) than did their upper-middle-class counterparts (mean raw score of 8.97). The absence of any higher-order interactions between culture, SES level, and age of the child when first tested strongly suggests that culture and age are additive effects influencing performance on Arithmetic. Because of the nature of arithmetic mental ability, it is most likely that the school environment, teaching style, and curriculum of the elementary grades in the United States account for the lack of social class differences as well as the more rapid development of arithmetic ability, as compared to the situation in Mexico.

The other WISC subtest that contributes heavily to verbal IQ is Vocabulary. As in the case of Arithmetic, all four main effects are highly significant, with most of the variance accounted for by age differences. Only the four-way interaction of all four variables proved significant beyond the .05 level. The means for each of the basic cells in the design are presented in Table 7-5.

Among the Americans, the differences between boys and girls and between working-class and upper-middle-class families are negligible. The only primary variable of any importance is the age

Table 7-5
Mean Raw Scores on WISC Vocabulary by Age Group, Culture, SES Level, and Sex

|  | Age Group (Years) | | |
|  | I (6.7) | II (9.7) | III (12.7) |
|---|---|---|---|
| Lower-Class Boys | | | |
| United States | 25.0 | 36.6 | 48.0 |
| Mexico | 15.4 | 31.0 | 41.1 |
| Upper-Class Boys | | | |
| United States | 22.2 | 40.8 | 51.2 |
| Mexico | 17.2 | 30.4 | 45.3 |
| Lower-Class Girls | | | |
| United States | 18.2 | 38.1 | 45.6 |
| Mexico | 14.4 | 23.6 | 36.8 |
| Upper-Class Girls | | | |
| United States | 23.7 | 37.2 | 49.0 |
| Mexico | 17.3 | 29.1 | 44.3 |

Within-cell mean square: 43.47

of the child. Essentially the same picture is evident for upper- and lower-class Mexican boys. No striking pattern exists other than the very steady increase in Vocabulary raw score with increasing age. At the same time, there is a consistently lower mean level of performance for the Mexican boys than for those in the Austin sample. In a similar manner there appear to be no appreciable differences with age among the lower- and upper-class girls in the American sample. For the Mexican girls, however, the pattern is distinctly different. The upper-class Mexican girls started out only slightly ahead of the lower-class girls but the gulf between them widened appreciably with increasing age so that, by the age of twelve years and eight months, the upper-class Mexican girls were considerably more advanced than girls from working-class families. These differential results suggest a sex-linked difference between the environment of boys and girls in Mexico and the environment in the United States. The lower-class Mexican girl is placed at an increasingly noticeable disadvantage as contrasted to Mexican boys of either social class and upper-class Mexican girls.

Although not as striking as in the case of Vocabulary and Arithmetic, main-effect differences for age group, culture, and sex are significant at or beyond the .01 level for the Picture Completion subtest, as well. The difference in upper and lower social class does not quite reach significance when considered alone. The four-way interaction, however, is significant beyond the .01 level, as in the case of Vocabulary. The mean raw scores for each cell in the analysis are presented in Table 7-6. In this case, however, the lower-class Mexican boy performed more poorly than any other group among the youngest children. By the age of nine, this difference disappeared and boys of either social class from either culture performed at about the same level.

Among the girls, the lower-class Mexican took longer to catch up with the upper-class child, not narrowing the gap until toward the end of the elementary grades. These results suggest that whatever mental ability is measured by Picture Completion represents a skill that is developed largely in the broader cultural milieu rather than within the deliberately planned school curriculum per se. With a variety of stimuli on television, in the mass media, on the street, within the family, and, of course, even in the poorest of schools, children of both cultures and social classes have nearly equal opportunities to develop ability in recognizing missing parts of a larger, familiar whole, as in a picture of a well-known object.

The WISC Block Design subtest yields only two main effects that are highly significant—age group and culture. In addition, the interaction between these two factors is significant beyond the .01 level. The resulting means for age and culture are presented in Table 7-7. Both Mexican and American school children started out at the same level in the first grade. The Mexican child fell behind rather noticeably during the next several years. This gap of about seven raw-score points persisted unaltered through at least age twelve.

The lack of any interactions approaching significance other than the one between age and culture, as well as the absence of

Table 7-6
Mean Raw Scores on WISC Picture Completion by Age Group, Culture, SES Level, and Sex

|  | Age Group (Years) | | |
|---|---|---|---|
|  | I (6.7) | II (9.7) | III (12.7) |
| Lower-Class Boys | | | |
| United States | 9.0 | 11.2 | 13.3 |
| Mexico | 5.8 | 11.7 | 12.6 |
| Upper-Class Boys | | | |
| United States | 8.8 | 12.0 | 13.8 |
| Mexico | 8.8 | 10.4 | 13.3 |
| Lower-Class Girls | | | |
| United States | 7.9 | 11.9 | 12.9 |
| Mexico | 6.7 | 8.9 | 11.4 |
| Upper-Class Girls | | | |
| United States | 8.7 | 10.0 | 14.2 |
| Mexico | 7.8 | 10.0 | 11.8 |

Within-cell mean square: 6.028

Table 7-7
Mean Raw Scores on WISC Block Design by Age Group and Culture

| Age Group (Years) | United States | Mexico |
|---|---|---|
| I (6.7) | 7.7 | 8.0 |
| II (9.7) | 22.2 | 14.9 |
| III (12.7) | 35.9 | 29.6 |

Within-cell mean square: 83.43

any significant main effects for sex or social class, suggest that there are no sex or social-class differences in Block Design within either culture.[2]

## Human Figure Drawings

Shortly after the first year of the cross-cultural testing, Harris published his adaptation of the Goodenough scoring system for the Draw-a-Man Test which made it possible to score either male or female figures on a standardized basis. While data are available from the first two years of testing on the Harris-Goodenough score, the third year of testing is the first in which a strictly uniform basis for comparison of the two cultures is possible.[3] A separate analysis of the Human Figure Drawings for four years of repeated testing, beginning with the third year, has been presented by Luis M. Laosa, Swartz, and Díaz-Guerrero in a study of the Human Figure Drawings (1974). The present analysis deals only with the third year in which the Human Figure Drawings were collected, the first year in which uniform data in both cultures were obtained, permitting use of the Harris-Goodenough score on drawings of both male and female figures.

Three of the four main effects for the Harris-Goodenough score of mental development were significant at or beyond the .01 level. Regardless of age group, socioeconomic status, or culture, girls tended to achieve slightly higher scores than boys; the over-all mean for girls was 34.9, while that for boys was 32.4.

Barely significant at the .05 level, an interaction between age

[2] It must be remembered that interpretive statements such as this one refer only to results in the matched cross-cultural sample, which has a restricted range on social class. When the full range of social class is taken into account, significant social-class main effects and interactions with age or sex may appear. In separate studies of the complete Mexican sample, for example, both sex and socioeconomic class do yield significant effects for Block Design as well as for other measures.

[3] As indicated in Chapter 5, the Draw-a-Person procedure (one figure only) was employed for the Austin sample in year 1 and the Draw-a-Man procedure (one figure only) was employed for the Austin sample in year 2. Because the Mexican data were collected two years later than the Austin data, the standard Harris-Goodenough procedure was employed from the beginning in Mexico. While both male and female drawings can be scored for the Harris-Goodenough, the difference in total possible score is just enough to make a slight but significant difference in any large-sample cross-cultural comparison.

group and culture is probably largely due to minor ceiling effects for the fifteen-year-old Austin children. The means for each of the three age groups for the Harris-Goodenough score on the first figure drawn are presented separately for the two cultures in Table 7-8. For the Americans, most of the growth occurs between the ages of nine and twelve. For the Mexican children, the growth is almost linear throughout the six-year age span.

The sex of the first figure drawn did not differ across the two cultures. Only the sex of the child proved related to the sex of the first figure drawn. Ninety-two percent of the boys drew a male figure first, while 80 percent of the girls drew a female figure first. Since culture was clearly insignificant as a factor influencing the sex of the first figure drawn, application of the Harris-Goodenough scoring system to the first figure without regard for the figure's sex is fully justified. The sex of the first figure drawn is clearly not confounded with culture, socioeconomic status, age group, or interactions among these primary variables and the sex of the child.

Analysis of the Harris-Goodenough score for the second figure drawn yielded similar results with one exception: a highly significant interaction between culture and sex was obtained. Among the boys in both cultures no significant difference appeared between the Americans and Mexicans, who received mean scores of 31.8 and 29.7 respectively. For the girls, however, the cultural difference was quite marked; the mean score for the American girls was 36.3, as contrasted to only 27.7 for the Mexican girls. In all cases the means for the Harris-Goodenough score on the second figure drawn tended to be lower than the mean scores for the first figure drawn, suggesting that some children were tired or bored and consequently filled in less detail when drawing a human

Table 7-8
Mean Scores in Year 3 on the Harris-Goodenough Score (First Figure)
by Age Group and Culture

| Age Group (Years) | United States | Mexico |
|---|---|---|
| I (8.7) | 27.7 | 23.5 |
| II (11.7) | 40.2 | 30.4 |
| III (14.7) | 43.0 | 37.2 |

figure a second time. A comparison of the means for the first and second figures drawn for the boys and girls in each culture suggests that this drop in score was relatively greater for American boys and Mexican girls than it was for American girls and Mexican boys, thus producing the obtained interaction between sex and culture. A slight but significant drop in standard deviation from 8.7 on the first drawing to 7.8 on the second is consistent with the above interpretation.

## PERCEPTUAL COGNITIVE STYLE

While sometimes difficult to separate from the more purely cognitive abilities, stylistic dimensions in perceptual and cognitive tasks continue to generate considerable interest. Three main streams of activity, though starting out independently with different constructs, have moved much closer together in recent years: (*a*) the program of research by Gardner (1959) on cognitive control principles, such as equivalence range, or category width, in the Object Sorting Test; (*b*) Witkin's work on field independence or psychological differentiation as measured by the Embedded Figures Test; and (*c*) the work of J. Kagan, H. A. Moss, and I. E. Siegel (1963) on styles of conceptualization as represented in the Conceptual Styles Test. Of these particular instruments only the Object Sorting Test was given initially to all three groups in both cultures.

### Object Sorting Test

Two different kinds of scores were obtained in the Object Sorting Test—those reflecting Gardner's concept of equivalence range and those growing out of the work of McGaughran and Moran (1956) involving a scoring system for two dichotomized dimensions of conceptualization, the open-closed dimension and the public-private dimension.

The total number of groups or categories of objects employed by the subject in the Object Sorting Test is used as a measure of equivalence range. A study by Samuel Messick and Nathan Kogan (1963), however, suggests that the number of categories containing two or more designated objects and the number of residual categories for single items needed to account for miscellaneous objects left ungrouped are two relatively independent components of the total equivalence-range score. Consequently, both the number of groups and the number of single items omitted were used as independent scores bearing upon the concept of equivalence range.

Main effects for age group and culture proved to be highly significant for the number of categories employed in the Object Sorting Test. The number dropped slightly but consistently with increasing age, suggesting that older children include more objects within a given category and therefore use fewer categories than is true of young children. This tendency holds true regardless of social class, sex, or culture.

A significant triple interaction between age group, SES level, and culture, as well as a significant four-way interaction, can be accounted for largely by the unusually high number of categories typically employed by lower-class Mexican boys. While most of the cells in the analysis-of-variance design have mean scores ranging from 12 to 15, the youngest lower-class Mexican boys obtained a mean score of 22.6.

The number of single items not used in the Object Sorting Test showed a striking developmental trend for the American children, the mean number of residual items dropping from 14.2 in Group I to only 2.7 in Group III. Among the Mexican children, the drop was much less pronounced and occurred several years later in the developmental continuum, as indicated by the significant interaction between age group and culture in Table 7-9.

Taken together these results indicate that the developmental shift with increasing age among American children moves more rapidly toward wide equivalence range (inclusion of more items in each category) than is the case with the Mexican child.

The open-closed dimension is roughly similar to the concept of

Table 7-9
Mean Score on Number of Single Items Not Used on the Object Sorting Test
by Age Group and Culture

| Age Group (Years) | United States | Mexico |
|---|---|---|
| I   (6.7) | 14.2 | 9.9 |
| II  (9.7) | 6.1 | 10.4 |
| III (12.7) | 2.7 | 5.5 |

Within-cell mean square: 77.86

abstract versus concrete. More precisely, closed concepts tend toward restrictiveness while open-ended concepts tend toward infinite freedom in the variety of objects that would be included within their limits. The public-private dimension concerns the degree of conceptual extensionality, or the extent to which the principle underlying the individual concept is shared and freely communicated by the majority of persons within the same culture. The "public" end of this dimension tends to be more conventional, while the "private" end tends to be more autistic or idiosyncratic. Taking these two dimensions together in dichotomized form produces four conceptual areas that can be scored for each group of objects formed by the subject in the Object Sorting Test—closed-public, closed-private, open-public, and open-private. By taking the percentage of each conceptual area with respect to the total number of groups or categories of objects formed by the subject, one can obtain a standard score showing the tendency of the individual toward one or another of the conceptual styles.

Percent Closed-Public proved highly significant for age group and culture as well as for the interaction of age with SES level and with culture. Among lower-class children in both cultures, no increase or decrease across age groups is apparent. Among upper-class children, however, there is a marked and consistent drop, from 22.7 in Group I, to 17.7 for Group II, down to 11.5 for Group III. Results for the culture-by-age-group interaction are presented in Table 7-10. A consistent drop in the percentage of categories classified as closed-public is present with increasing age among the American children but only tenuous at best among the Mexican.

The percentage of closed-private categories drops consistently and significantly in both cultures with increasing age. Children

Table 7-10
Mean Score on OST Percent Closed-Public by Age Group and Culture

| Age Group (Years) | United States | Mexico |
|---|---|---|
| I (6.7) | 18.6 | 18.0 |
| II (9.7) | 11.7 | 21.2 |
| III (12.7) | 8.1 | 17.1 |

Within-cell mean square: 183.5

from working-class families tend to use closed-private reasoning as a basis for sorting objects more often than is the case with upper-middle-class children in both cultures. American children generally use significantly fewer closed-private categorizations than their Mexican counterparts. The mean percent of closed-private for American children is 9.2, as contrasted to 18.7 for the Mexican children.

Percent Open-Public also shows a significant rise with increasing age, especially in Group III where the mean score for Percent Open-Public is 38.8. American children, in general, give a significantly higher percentage of open-public responses (37.8) than do the Mexican children (31.9), although the difference in absolute terms is rather small.

Percent Open-Private shows the greatest amount of cross-cultural difference, especially in the interaction between culture and age. As indicated in Table 7-11, the American children show a steady rise from the six-year-olds through the twelve-year-olds, while the Mexicans drop slightly but consistently over the same developmental period.

Clearly, there are age-linked cross-cultural differences in the cognitive style represented by the several scores employed for the Object Sorting Test. The most striking results occur for Percent Open-Private. Figure 7-1 summarizes the interactions between age group and culture for all of the scores taken together. While the majority of categorizations are open for all groups in both cultures, there is a more marked tendency for the older American children to use open concepts almost exclusively. Only slight differences among the age groups in Percent Closed is apparent, while Percent Private rises from 43.3 for first-graders to 52.5 for both fourth- and seventh-graders for the American children. By

Table 7-11
Mean Score on OST Percent Open-Private by Age Group and Culture

| Age Group (Years) | United States | Mexico |
|---|---|---|
| I   (6.7) | 29.1 | 34.3 |
| II  (9.7) | 43.1 | 27.5 |
| III (12.7) | 47.8 | 26.0 |

Within-cell mean square: 413.7

contrast, among the Mexican children Percent Private steadily diminishes with increasing age, dropping from 54.6 to 45.9 and 43.5 across the three age groups.

*Embedded Figures Test*

Witkin's Embedded Figures Test was given initially only to children in Groups II and III, because it proved too difficult for first-

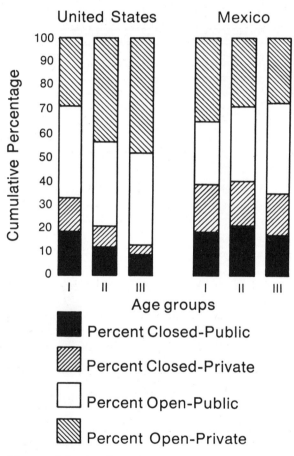

Figure 7-1. Age-by-culture interaction for the Open-Closed and Public-Private dimensions in the Object Sorting Test.

graders. Later, however, it was possible to obtain test data from the children in Group I, in years 4 and 5 of the study, when they were sufficiently mature to cope effectively with the task. Scores for Groups II and III in the first year were analyzed separately from scores for all three groups in the fourth and fifth years. In each analysis, four summary scores were analyzed systematically. The number-of-errors score (EFT Errors) consisted of the total number of errors across the twelve figures, an error occurring when the child offered as a solution a completed but incorrect tracing. The number of items correct out of the twelve figures (EFT Correct) constituted a second score. The third score consisted of the average time taken per figure (EFT Time). The number of times during the test that the child re-examined the simple figure (the simple and complex figures were never shown simultaneously) in order to refresh his memory of what it was he was searching for in the complex figure constituted the number–of–re-exams score (EFT Re-exams). Because data on time taken per figure were recorded for each of the twelve figures as a first step in data analysis, it was also possible to examine time per figure, taking one figure at a time in the analysis-of-variance design. The results for total scores are presented first, giving particular attention to cross-cultural comparisons in the first year. This analysis is followed by a more fine-grained item-analysis of results for the time scores on the twelve individual figures.

Highly significant differences were obtained for all four of the summary scores on the EFT in the cross-cultural comparison of children in Mexico and the United States. The American children made fewer errors than did the Mexican children (means of 8.7 and 11.8 respectively), regardless of age, socioeconomic status, or sex of the child. Consistent with this result are the findings that the American children obtained higher scores on EFT Correct (8.1 compared to 7.1), lower scores on EFT Time (91 seconds compared to 106 seconds), and lower scores on EFT Re-exams (8.7 compared to 13.9). In the case of EFT Re-exams, a significant interaction ($p < .01$) occurred between culture and age group. For the American children, the nine-year-olds obtained a mean of 10.5, as compared to one of 6.9 for the twelve-year-olds. The same means for the Mexican children were 18.6 and 9.2 respectively. The nine-year-old Mexican children showed an unusual tendency to re-examine the simple figures frequently in order to refresh their memories as they searched for the complex figures.

Analyses of similar data for the second and third years of repeated testing for the two older age groups revealed essentially the same outcome. The American children tended to make fewer errors, got more figures correct, took less time to complete the task, and needed fewer re-examinations of the simple figures than did their Mexican counterparts. In years 4 and 5, a slightly different analysis was undertaken, since by that time the children in the youngest group were old enough to take the Embedded Figures Test. Comparisons across all three age groups then were possible. It should be noted, however, that the children in the two older age groups had taken the test repeatedly, while those in the youngest group were taking it for the first time in year 4 and the second time in year 5. For this reason, year 5 probably constitutes the most appropriate one in which to make a comparison across all three age groups; it represents the first year in which any possible practice and adaptation effects were present for all three groups. Unlike the results from the earlier analysis of only the two older groups, by year 5 the differences between the Mexican and American children had diminished to the point where they were no longer significant, regardless of the score analyzed. The mean number of errors for all children had dropped to 5.8, while the number of items correct had risen to 9.6 (out of 12 figures). The average reaction time per item for all children had dropped to fifty-nine seconds, and the number of re-examinations had fallen to 3.0. Apparently, the task had become so easy for the older children, particularly in Group III, that the significant differences evident in Group I were overshadowed completely. Convergence of EFT Time scores for the two cultures and both sexes in years 4 and 5 for Group III is clearly present in Figure 7-2. The task was so easy for the sixteen-year-olds that the average solution time per figure was only eighteen seconds.

Mean EFT Time scores for the five years of repeated testing for Groups II and III in Figure 7-2 show the improvement in performance with increasing age that one would expect from a developmental function. While Mexican girls, regardless of age, were generally the slowest in finding the hidden figures, the Mexican boys caught up with the Americans by the age of thirteen

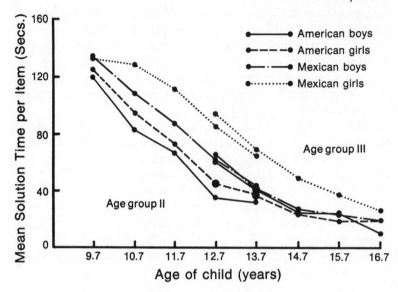

Figure 7-2. Time score on the Embedded Figures Test as a function
of age, age group, sex, and culture.

and thereafter were indistinguishable from them. Few, if any,
practice effects due to repeated testing are evident. For the two
ages where Groups II and III overlap (12.7 and 13.7), the mean
scores for identical ages are strikingly similar, except for the
twelve-year-old Americans; and even this difference disappears
one year later. If practice effects due to repeated testing were a
major factor to consider, the twelve- and thirteen-year-olds in
Group II would have obtained mean Time scores significantly
lower than their age counterparts in Group III.

Item analysis of Time scores for each of the twelve individual
figures provides further insight into the meaning of cross-cultural
differences on the Embedded Figures Test. The mean scores in the
initial year of testing are presented in Table 7-12, separately for
the two cultures and for each of the twelve items. For five of the
items (3, 5, 7, 9, and 12) no differences are apparent in the over-
all mean scores between the two cultures. In the case of item 5,
however, a significant interaction (p <.05) exists for sex and
culture, as well as age group and culture. In the case of sex, the

Mexican girls took the longest time (147 seconds), while the Mexican boys took the shortest (122 seconds). The American means were 130 for girls and 137 for boys, an insignificant sex difference. In the case of age, the American nine-year-olds took longer than their Mexican counterparts (means of 171 and 155 respectively), while for the twelve-year-olds, opposite results occurred (96 and 114 respectively).

Of the five items showing no over-all mean score differences, all are "conceptual items" that must be figured out by the subject. All of these items involve simple figures that are masked in the complex designs and therefore defy direct perception and are difficult to locate. And all contain, or seem to the subject to contain, alternative correct solutions. Of course, an equally plausible and alternative explanation for these particular five items' showing no over-all mean score differences—since the organization of each complex figure is such that it more strongly embeds the simple figure sought—is that children find them too difficult and that, in effect, a ceiling was reached in both cultures.

Of the seven items showing significant differences in the over-all mean scores between the two cultures, five of them (1, 2, 4, 6,

Table 7-12
Mean Time Scores on Individual Items for Embedded Figures Test in Year 1

| Item Order | Item Code[a] | Culture United States | | Mexico |
|---|---|---|---|---|
| 1 | F1 | 94 | c | 118 |
| 2 | G1 | 40 | d | 62 |
| 3 | C2 | 99 | b | 97 |
| 4 | D2 | 50 | c | 73 |
| 5 | E5 | 133 | b | 135 |
| 6 | A3 | 78 | e | 116 |
| 7 | C3 | 107 | b | 109 |
| 8 | D1 | 94 | c | 117 |
| 9 | E1 | 118 | b | 112 |
| 10 | G2 | 72 | e | 106 |
| 11 | C1 | 77 | d | 110 |
| 12 | E3 | 128 | b | 131 |

[a] See Witkin (1950) for descriptions of figures.
[b] No difference between cultures.
[c] Culture difference significant at .01 level.
[d] Culture difference significant at .001 level.
[e] Culture difference significant at .0001 level.

and 11) involve simple figures that are "perceptual items." Each of these simple figures is capable of being perceived as a whole in the complex figure by the subject, who needs only to remember the configuration of the simple figure in order to locate it.

It is apparent from these results that the Mexican and American children differ on this cognitive measure of field dependence-independence. It should be pointed out, however, that the cultural differences obtained seem to be occurring mainly on those individual items measuring cognitive-perceptual style rather than cognitive ability.

## Conceptual Styles Test

The abbreviated form of the Conceptual Styles Test (CST) used in the present study contains nineteen sets of three pictures each, the best nineteen from the original thirty-set version of the CST developed by Kagan (Kagan, Moss, and Siegel 1963). Each picture is a black-and-white line drawing of a familiar object. The items are constructed so that an analytic concept competes with a relational or inferential-categorical concept as a basis for grouping the familiar objects. Usually the analytic concept is a much less obvious association to the stimuli than the relational or inferential-categorical. The child is asked to pick out two of the pictures in each set that go together in some way. Reaction time is recorded for each item. The nineteen items are scored for the number of analytical responses represented by the child's choices, the number of relational responses, and the number of inferential-categorical responses. From these data seven scores have been derived for analysis: (*a*) number of analytical responses; (*b*) number of relational responses; (*c*) number of inferential-categorical responses; (*d*) mean reaction time for those responses classified as analytical; (*e*) mean reaction time for those responses classified as relational; (*f*) mean reaction time for those classified as inferential-categorical; and (*g*) mean reaction time for all nineteen items combined. Since the number of analytical, relational, and inferential-categorical responses must add up to nineteen, obviously the above scores do not represent truly independent ones, a feature that should be kept in mind when interpreting the results. Since the Conceptual Styles Test was given only to the youngest group of children, the analysis of variance does not include age group as a factor. A total of 111 children are included in the analysis, involving the matched samples across the two cultures. The test was given in the second year of the study, when the youngest children were in the second grade.

The Mexican children proved to be more analytical in their categorizations than the American children. The mean number of items out of the total of 19 that were classified as analytical for the Mexican children was 10.04, as contrasted to 6.28 for the American children. The Americans, on the other hand, tended to choose objects from the sets of pictures on a relational basis more often than did the Mexican children. The mean number of items classified as relational responses for the American children was 6.46, as compared to only 3.84 for the Mexican children. No differences were apparent between the two cultures in the number of responses classified as inferential-categorical. Only one other source of variance proved significant with regard to the conceptual style of the child; boys in both cultures chose objects on a relational basis significantly more often than did girls (means of 6.14 and 4.15 respectively).

The mean reaction time for the responses classified as analytical, relational, or inferential-categorical failed to reveal any differences due to culture, sex, socioeconomic status, or the interaction of these factors. Nor did total reaction time yield any significant differences attributable to these sources.

## Time Estimation Test

The second year of the longitudinal study was the first year in which the Time Estimation Test was given to all children in both samples. At three different times during the testing sessions, the child was simply requested to estimate the duration of one minute. Three scores were obtained: (*a*) Delay, the sum of the three time estimates in seconds; (*b*) Inaccuracy, the sum of the absolute difference of each estimate from sixty seconds; and (*c*) Inconsistency, obtained by computing the standard deviation of the three estimates; the higher the score, the greater the inconsistency among the three estimates.

The Delay score proved to be significant for all four main effects, especially for culture and age group. No interactions were significant. The older the child, the closer his Delay score to the veridical response of 180 seconds. Groups I, II, and III achieved mean Delay scores of 110.6, 124.9, and 144.6 respectively. The length of a minute appeared to be shorter for lower-class children than for those from upper-class families (mean delay scores of 116.5 and 136.9 respectively). Time perception of one minute for Mexican children was shorter than that for American children (means of 110.4 and 143.0 respectively). And boys tended to be closer to the veridical response than girls (mean Delay scores of 133.2 and 120.2 respectively). It is interesting to note that in all cases the mean scores fell short of the veridical response of 180 seconds for the sum of the three one-minute estimates.

Similar results were obtained for the Inaccuracy score—older children, children from upper-class families, American children, and boys tended to give more accurate estimates of a minute than did their opposites. These results must be qualified, however, by the presence of significant higher-order interactions involving the four main effects. In general, boys tended to become more accurate with increasing age at a faster rate than did girls. While there was not much difference among the children of either sex in the second grade, boys in the fifth and eighth grades were considerably more accurate than girls. For the oldest children the sex difference was large, boys and girls obtaining mean Inaccuracy scores of 40.2 and 68.4 respectively. Table 7-13 contains the mean Inaccuracy scores separately for the two sexes, cultures, and social classes. A significant interaction among these three factors was obtained (p = .02). It is interesting to note that upper-class American boys and girls and upper-class Mexican boys achieved virtually identi-

Table 7-13
Mean Inaccuracy Score on the Time Estimation Test as a Function of Sex, Culture, and Social Class in Year 2

|  | Boys | Girls |
|---|---|---|
| Lower SES: |  |  |
| United States | 54.7 | 86.2 |
| Mexico | 87.2 | 92.6 |
| Upper SES: |  |  |
| United States | 61.2 | 60.6 |
| Mexico | 60.4 | 76.0 |

Within-cell mean square: 1547.1

cal mean scores. Lower-class American boys were the most accurate in their estimate of a minute, while lower-class Mexican girls were the least accurate, followed closely in inaccurate estimates by lower-class Mexican boys and lower-class American girls.

The degree of consistency in estimating a minute is reflected by the standard deviation of the three time estimates as measured by the Inconsistency score. While none of the main effects were significant, an interaction of culture by sex occurred, largely because of the significantly higher consistency of Mexican girls (5.9) as contrasted to Mexican boys (9.3) and American girls and boys (8.4 and 8.0 respectively). Even this interaction, however, must be qualified by a significant quadruple interaction of all four main effects. The lower-class Mexican girls tended to be the most consistent of all, regardless of age (mean Inconsistency score of 3.9). No particular pattern, however, was discernible among the other groups of children, who had means varying from 5.1 to 13.6.

## *Visual Fractionation Test*

The Visual Fractionation Test (VFT), as developed by Kagan (Kagan, Moss, and Siegel 1963), assesses the degree to which the child attaches a new label to component parts of a complex visual stimulus, while associating the new label to the entire stimulus. The stimuli are four designs, each containing three sets of components: element, figure, and ground. The ground component for each of the four designs is a repetitive background pattern. The figural component for each design refers to the shape or pattern into which the discrete elements fall. The elements are discrete geometric forms that trace out the figural form.

For the learning task of the VFT, twelve figures—four designs each repeated three times in a random order—are arranged in a booklet form for presentation to the subject. Each figure is printed on the front side of a page, and a card labeled with a corresponding three-letter nonsense syllable is attached face down to the back of the previous page. The child's task is to learn the correct association of nonsense syllable and design. The entire set of twelve figures is repeated until all associations are correctly given, stopping in any event after five trials.

For the transfer trial, two illustrations of each of the three component parts—ground, figure, element—for each of the four designs (twenty-four items in all) are arranged in booklet form in a random order. The four nonsense syllables (WOM, FAM, SEP, and PUF) are printed on separate cards for use during the transfer trial.

Three kinds of scores were obtained on the VFT: (*a*) number of trials to complete the learning task; (*b*) mean reaction time on the transfer trial for the eight items involving elements, the eight items involving figures, and the eight items involving grounds, as well as the over-all reaction time for all twenty-four items; and (*c*) number of items on the transfer trial that are correct for all twenty-four items combined.

As would be expected in an associative learning task of this type, striking differences were obtained across the three age groups for all of the scores on the Visual Fractionation Test. Number of trials in learning the association of the nonsense syllables with the appropriate designs dropped from a mean of 3.45 for the second-graders to a mean of 2.65 for the fifth-graders and a mean of 2.03 for the eighth-graders for all samples combined. A highly significant difference was found across the two cultures, the American children generally taking more trials (3.04) than the Mexican children (2.38). A significant interaction involving age group, sex, and culture is plotted in Figure 7-3. Among the second-graders in Group I, little difference is apparent between boys and girls of either culture, although the Mexican children tend to take slightly fewer trials on the average than the American children. Among the older children, however, a rather striking interaction is apparent between sex and culture. While no significant difference exists between Mexico and the United States for the girls, the Mexican boys in Groups II and III learn the association of nonsense syllables to the appropriate designs much more rapidly than the American boys.

The generally superior ability of the Mexicans on the Visual Fractionation Test is also demonstrated in the analysis of reaction time when analyzed either for elements, figures, and grounds or for all twenty-four items combined. The average Mexican child took only 3.80 seconds to respond with an association of a nonsense syllable to each of the eight designs stressing elements. The mean reaction time for the American children was 4.89 seconds. The mean reaction times for the eight items involving figures were 4.15

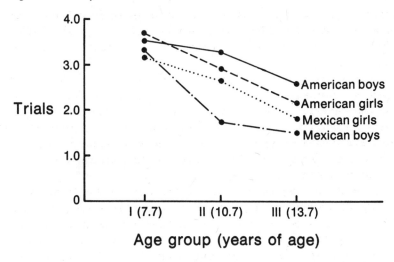

Figure 7-3. Number of trials in learning the task on the Visual Fractionation Test as a function of age group, culture, and sex.

seconds for the Mexicans and 4.91 seconds for the Americans. In dealing with the eight designs that stressed association of nonsense syllables with grounds, the cross-cultural difference was even more dramatic; the Mexican children obtaining a mean reaction time of only 3.70 seconds, as contrasted to a mean of 5.63 seconds for the Americans. When all twenty-four items are combined to yield one mean reaction time for each child, the average Mexican responded in 3.89 seconds, compared to 5.14 seconds for the average American. The only other source of variance that proved consistently significant was the age of the child; the older the child, the more rapid the reaction time.

The number of associations correct out of the twenty-four items in the transfer task yielded no significant differences on any factor other than age of the child. As would be expected, the older the child, the larger the number of items correct out of twenty-four in the transfer task. Means for second-, fifth-, and eighth-graders were 10.6, 12.8, and 15.0 respectively. In spite of the fact that the Mexican children generally responded much more quickly in the transfer task and took fewer trials in the initial learning task, they did neither better nor worse, on the average, than did the American children, with respect to the number correct in the transfer task.

*Perceptual Maturity Scale*

Van de Castle's Perceptual Maturity Scale (1965), a seventy-two item test constructed by pairing selected figures indicative of high and low perceptual maturity from Welsh's Figure Preference Test, was administered to children in both Austin and Mexico City for three years, beginning in the fourth year of the longitudinal study. An analysis of variance for data obtained in the initial testing period of the fourth year indicated highly significant differences for two main effects—age group and sex. As one would expect from the initial standardization data by Van de Castle, scores on the Perceptual Maturity Scale increased with age group from a mean of 39.2 among fourth-graders (Group I) to 47.2 among seventh-graders (Group II) and then still again to 49.8 among tenth-graders (Group III). Boys tended to receive higher scores (48.6) than did girls (42.2) in both cultures. One interaction proved to be significant beyond the .05 level, the interaction of culture and age group. While both cultures showed an increase with age, the slope of increase was considerably flatter for the Mexican children than it was for those in the American sample. Among children in Groups I and II, the Mexicans received higher scores than did the Americans, while in Group III the reverse proved to be the case.

The Perceptual Maturity Scale of Van de Castle reflects perceptual style in the sense that the respondent is asked to choose among seventy-two matched pairs of items drawn from the much larger pool of artistic and geometric figures studied by Welsh. In general, Van de Castle found that the simpler geometric forms were developmentally lower on the age scale than were the more complicated asymmetrical and free-flowing figures.

*M-F Ratings on the Male and Female Figures of the Human Figure Drawings*

Masculinity-Femininity (M-F) ratings were scored on a five-point scale for each of the figures on each protocol of the Human Figure Drawings. A score of 5 indicated a most feminine drawing, while a score of 1 indicated a masculine-appearing drawing. Using actual drawings as anchor points for the rating scale, a high degree of consistency (reliability .95) was obtained across independent scorers. Analysis of variance for the M-F ratings of male figures yielded four effects significant beyond the .01 level—culture, sex, sex-by-age-group interaction, and culture-by-sex interaction. The Mexicans drew more masculine men than did the Americans. Boys generally drew more masculine men than did girls. This sex difference is more pronounced among the seventh- and tenth-graders than among children in the fourth grade. A highly significant interaction between culture and sex is due almost entirely to the unusually high mean score (3.63) for the American girls, indicating that they generally drew more feminine males, as contrasted to boys in both cultures or Mexican girls.

Sex differences on the M-F ratings of the female figures are even more pronounced than the ratings for male figures, with boys drawing more masculine female figures than girls (means of 2.63 and 3.66 respectively). Again, a highly significant interaction between culture and sex arises, largely because the American boys tended to draw masculine female figures (mean of 2.40, compared to 2.87 for Mexican boys, 3.78 for American girls, and 3.54 for Mexican girls).

The meaning of the above interactions between sex and culture is apparent in Table 7-14. In general, female figures should be more feminine than male figures if there is a strong differentiation between masculinity and femininity among boys and girls respectively. This statement is tempered somewhat by drawing ability. In Table 7-14 it can be seen that the greatest amount of sex differentiation is present among the Mexican girls, followed closely by Mexican boys. The American boys show the poorest degree of differentiation with American girls not far behind. These

Table 7-14
Mean Masculinity-Femininity Ratings for Male and Female Human Figure Drawings

| Sex | Culture | Sex of Figure | | Male-Female Difference |
| | | Male | Female | |
|---|---|---|---|---|
| Boys | Mexico | 2.32 | 2.87 | .55 |
| | United States | 2.60 | 2.40 | —.20 |
| Girls | Mexico | 2.55 | 3.54 | .99 |
| | United States | 3.65 | 3.78 | .15 |

marked cultural differences, linked with the sex of the child, probably arise in part from the greater stress in Mexican culture upon
differentiating the two sexes.

## Word Association Test

A Spanish or English version of the eighty-word list provided
in the appendix of Moran's paper (1966) was administered individually during the last three years of the study with instructions
to "tell me the first word that comes to mind when you hear this
word." An examiner read the word to the child and recorded each
response and its reaction time. Both the Spanish and English
versions of the list are provided in Appendix D.

There were certain difficulties inherent in the adaptation and
translation into Spanish of Moran's word list. As the current investigators gained experience in cross-cultural research methodology and increased their sensitivity to cultural and linguistic issues,
it became apparent that certain of the words in the Spanish list
were inadequate. Weaknesses of these particular words included
psychometric inadequacies and cultural and linguistic incompati-
bilities vis à vis the English version. In translating words, for
example, the complex problems of differential frequency of occurrence, the subtle connotations of some words, and the differences in grammatical form-class membership of otherwise similar
words across languages were encountered.

Some specific examples of inadequate translations, aside from
the problem of differential frequency of occurrence across languages, included the following. The stimulus word *high* was translated as *alto*. For purposes of everyday communication, such a
translation would be adequate most of the time. The Spanish word
*alto*, however, in addition to meaning "high," also can mean "stop"
and "tall." Thus, there are semantic differences; and, in terms of
form class, *high* and *alto* are not completely comparable. Differences such as these potentially could confound cross-cultural comparisons of grammatical associative tendencies.

Despite such problems, many individual words in the Spanish
list were judged to be adequate for certain cross-cultural analyses.
The English and Spanish lists were submitted to a thorough cultural-linguistic contrastive analysis. This contrastive analysis revealed that thirty-three stimulus words are in fact highly satis-

factory for cross-cultural analyses of grammatical associative tendencies among Mexican and U.S. schoolchildren. Only these stimulus words were used in the analyses involving grammatical associative tendencies presented here. These stimulus words, as shown in Table 7-15, in both English and Spanish, consist of twenty-two nouns, nine adjectives, and two verbs.

Stimulus-response associative pairs were "scored" for grammatical relationships, that is, paradigmatic responses (noun-noun, verb-verb, adjective-adjective) and syntagmatic responses (noun-verb, noun-adjective, verb-noun, verb-adjective, adjective-noun, adjective-verb). In cases in which the form-class membership of a word potentially could be ambiguous, the first form class assigned to it in *Webster's New Collegiate Dictionary* (1970) was used. In order to adjust for unscorable responses (e.g., multiword responses, blanks, neologisms), each category was converted from a raw score to a proportion of total scored.

Since the Word Association Test was administered only during the last three years of the longitudinal study in both cultures, separate analyses were carried out for each score using the subsample of children in the larger matched bicultural sample who completed the test. There were a total of 283 children, nearly equally divided by culture, age group, and trial (or year of testing). A culture by age-group by year analysis of variance was computed for each dependent variable.

Very few unscorable responses were given in general by children in either culture, an average of less than one per protocol. There was a tendency for the number of unscorable responses to drop slightly with repetition of the task; means for years 4, 5, and 6 were .76, .42, and .38 respectively. The youngest children gave slightly more unscorable responses than the two older groups (mean of .70 for Group I as compared with means of .36 and .50 for Groups II and III). And American children gave relatively more unscorable responses (.63) than did Mexican children (.41).

Any potential biases in results due to minor differences in the number of scorable responses and to differential frequency of occurrence of stimulus words classified as nouns, verbs, and adjectives were eliminated by converting raw scores into proportions. The three scores computed in this manner were the proportions of stimulus-response associations classified as Noun Paradigmatic

Table 7-15
Cross-Culturally Comparable Word Lists

| Stimulus: Grammatical Category | English | Spanish |
|:---:|---|---|
| 1 | milk | leche |
| 1 | joy | alegría |
| 1 | bread | pan |
| 1 | sickness | enfermedad |
| 3 | beautiful | hermosa |
| 3 | green | verde |
| 1 | pain | dolor |
| 1 | boy | muchacho |
| 1 | lamp | lámpara |
| 1 | shack | cabaña |
| 1 | scissors | tijeras |
| 1 | eagle | aguila |
| 3 | sour | agrio |
| 2 | tug | remolcar |
| 1 | tobacco | tabaco |
| 2 | strangle | estrangular |
| 1 | knife | cuchillo |
| 1 | whiskey | wisky |
| 1 | butterfly | mariposa |
| 1 | stool | banquito |
| 1 | justice | justicia |
| 1 | tablet | tableta |
| 1 | foot | pie |
| 1 | radio | radio |
| 3 | yellow | amarillo |
| 3 | bitter | amargo |
| 3 | soft | suave |
| 3 | black | negro |
| 3 | thirsty | sediento |
| 1 | woman | mujer |
| 1 | cottage | casucha |
| 3 | sweet | dulce |
| 1 | needle | aguja |

1: Noun
2: Verb
3: Adjective

(i.e., noun-noun stimulus-response pairs), Verb/Adjective Paradigmatic (verb-verb plus adjective-adjective stimulus-response pairs), and Syntagmatic (all stimulus-response pairs of different grammatical form, i.e., noun-verb, noun-adjective, adjective-verb, etc.). Whereas previous studies generally have employed a single paradigmatic category encompassing noun-noun, verb-verb, and adjective-adjective pairs, more recent evidence (Laosa 1971; Laosa, Swartz, and Moran 1971) indicates that the development of paradigmatic associative tendencies to verbs and adjectives is independent of such tendencies to nouns. Therefore, paradigmatic responses were divided into two separate categories in the present study, Noun Paradigmatic and Verb/Adjective Paradigmatic.

Age group yielded a significant difference for Noun Paradigmatic (p < .05) because of a slight increase in noun-noun associations for the oldest group of children in both cultures. The mean proportions were .50, .51, and .54 for Groups I, II, and III respectively. Neither culture nor year nor any interaction was significant for Noun Paradigmatic.

The culture by age-group interaction for Verb/Adjective Paradigmatic proved to be highly significant (p < .001). The mean proportions were .27, .27, and .21 for American children and .22, .22, and .23 for Mexican children in Groups I, II, and III respectively. While the two younger groups of American children produced more verb-verb or adjective-adjective associations than did the Mexican children, the older groups did not differ across the two cultures.

The culture by age-group interaction was significant for Syntagmatic (p < .05). Mean proportions were .23, .21, and .26 for American children and .29, .26, and .21 for Mexican children in Groups I, II, and III respectively. Whereas syntagmatic responses decreased strikingly with age for the Mexicans, in the United States they decreased only slightly between Groups I and II and then increased notably for the oldest Americans. Mexicans gave relatively more syntagmatic responses than Americans in the two youngest age groups; however, the opposite was true among the oldest children in Group III.

It is difficult to interpret the present data without looking at even longer developmental curves than the ones employed in the present study, including younger as well as older age levels. The observed differences may reflect differential developmental progressions in the two cultural-linguistic groups. D. R. Entwistle (1966), for instance, found a falling off of paradigmatic responses to nouns and high frequency verbs between the fifth grade and college among Anglo-Americans. The two studies, however, are difficult to compare, since Entwistle employed a different word list and did not include any age groups between fifth grade and college.

To what extent may the present findings reflect artifacts of translation? Entwistle's (1966) data suggest that the timing of the syntagmatic-paradigmatic shift may be a partial function of the particular stimulus words employed. Also, the potential for producing syntagmatic responses seems to vary greatly from one specific word to another, even within the same form class, and this phenomenon may be partly a function of the number of different usages and meanings a word has. Despite the care taken to produce highly comparable word lists across languages, and despite the seemingly straightforward nature of scoring these grammatical categories, it is possible that the observed differences still may reflect to some extent artifacts of translation.

The present word-association findings suggest a number of important questions that await empirical as well as theoretical analyses. One area of research that appears to hold promise is the investigation of associative tendencies among bilinguals who are asked at different times to respond to English and Spanish versions of the Word Association Test. Data of such kind from young children should shed further light on important issues in language development. Systematic investigations of relevant linguistic variables that may account for the obtained results, such as the contrastive linguistic structures of English and Spanish, the relative clarity with which class membership is marked in the two languages, and the rate of semantic and syntactic evolution for individual words across languages, also warrant further research efforts.

---

The description of the development of the matched cross-cultural design has been reported in the present chapter, along with the results from the several cognitive-perceptual measures employed in the investigation. Several of the "structural" variables in the Holtzman Inkblot Technique also can be thought of as perceptual or cognitive style measures. In Chapter 8 the cross-cultural results for these structural inkblot variables are presented, together with the other more content-oriented scores.

# 8. Components of Performance on the Holtzman Inkblot Technique

As an approach to personality through inkblot perception, the Holtzman Inkblot Technique yields twenty-two standardized scores, many of which can be properly thought of as perceptual style variables, since they measure reliable individual differences in perception. Others are more directly related to personality. It is very difficult to make meaningful distinctions between perceptual-cognitive style variables in inkblot perception, which are often employed as indirect measures of personality, and the more content-oriented inkblot variables, where the personality inference is more easily recognized. Inkblot scores generally referred to as "structural," such as the determinants, are classified here as perceptual style variables. Those dealing with content are classified as personality variables. Within these major headings, the variables are organized into still smaller clusters in accordance with earlier factor analysis studies and clinical analysis of the meaning of the inkblot variables. Only seventeen of the twenty-two inkblot variables are discussed in detail here. Space, Sex, Abstract, and Balance occur too rarely in young children for systematic analysis, and Popular was not scored for Mexico.

*HIT: Reaction Time and Rejection.* The younger children in both cultures reacted more quickly to inkblots, on the average, than did children in Groups II and III, a finding consistent with the hypothesis that short reaction time indicates more impulsive behavior, the type of impulsive reaction more typical of young children than of older children or adults. This developmental trend was more sharply accentuated for lower-class children than for upper-class children in both cultures, as evidenced by a significant interaction between age group and social class. The youngest lower-class children reacted more quickly to inkblots (mean Reaction Time of 11.8) than did their upper-class counterparts (mean of 18.9), while no social-class differences were found for the older children. American children reacted more quickly to the inkblots than Mexican children. Mean Reaction Time for the American child was 17.9 seconds, as compared to 21.7 seconds for the Mexican.

The Mexican child rejected on the average 3.2 inkblots, while the American child rejected on the average 2.2 inkblots, a slight difference that failed to reach significance.

*HIT: Location, Form Definiteness, and Form Appropriateness.* Three variables in the Holtzman Inkblot Technique—Location, Form Definiteness, and Form Appropriateness—frequently show a complicated interrelationship related to perceptual-cognitive style. If an individual strives for whole responses and has high standards of form definiteness, it is very difficult for him to achieve high scores on Form Appropriateness. On the other hand, if an individual insists that the inkblot must "really look like" the reported percept and form definiteness must also be specific, good response may be obtained by ignoring the whole inkblot and concentrating on smaller detailed areas. Still another perceptual style involves the use of vague, nonspecific percepts, where the form appropriateness cannot be challenged even when the whole inkblot is employed for the response.

The only significant factor influencing Location in the present analysis is culture. The American children tended to use more whole responses, as evidenced by a mean score of 33.0, compared to the mean score of 43.3 obtained by the Mexican children. For

Form Definiteness, however, no differences between the two cultures were obtained—both groups achieved an average FD score of about 73. Highly significant differences were obtained, however, for age group and social class. Form Definiteness increased with increasing age, and upper-class children obtained higher mean scores than lower-class children in both cultures.

Form Appropriateness proved to be significant for age group, culture, and interaction of age group and culture. As one would expect from the nature of the variable, the older the child, the higher the mean score on Form Appropriateness in both cultures. For the two younger groups of children, the Mexicans scored higher on Form Appropriateness than the Americans. This difference disappeared for Group III, as shown in Figure 8-1, where the interaction of culture and age group is illustrated.

The most dominant factor within the Holtzman Inkblot Technique for describing correlations among the twenty-two variables in terms of a smaller set of abstract dimensions is the developmentally relevant Factor 1, which previous studies have indicated is a measure of well-organized ideational activity, good imagina-

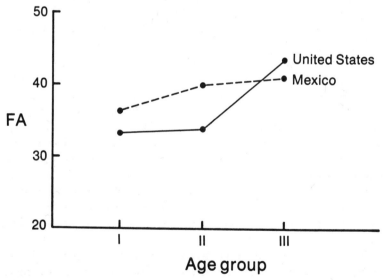

Figure 8-1. Form Appropriateness: interaction of culture and age group.

tive capacity, well-differentiated ego boundaries, and awareness of conventional concepts. The primary variables defining Factor 1 are Movement, Integration, Human, Barrier, and Popular. Factor 2, defined primarily by Color and Shading, and to a lesser extent by Form Definiteness, involves sensitivity or responsiveness to the stimulus qualities of the inkblots. The positive pole of this factor indicates overreactivity to the color or shading, while the negative pole indicates primary concern for form alone as a determinant. Factor 3 is best defined by Pathognomic Verbalization, although loadings on Anxiety and Hostility are often high also. A high amount of this factor would be indicative of disordered thought processes coupled with an active though disturbed fantasy life. Results for each of these clusters of inkblot variables will be presented one at a time, followed by results for the last three variables analyzed—Animal, Anatomy, and Penetration.

*HIT Factor 1: Movement, Integration, Human, and Barrier.* Striking differences were obtained for three of the four main effects—age group, culture, and sex—on Movement. Mean scores for Movement increased consistently with increasing age. American children received a mean score on Movement nearly twice as high (25.7) as did Mexican children (14.1). This difference occurred consistently for all age groups, both sexes, and both socioeconomic levels. Boys in both cultures tended to give more Movement (21.9) than girls (17.8).

Integration shows essentially the same pattern as Movement. With the exception of lower-class fourth-graders, the American children always received higher mean Integration scores (3.35) than did their Mexican counterparts (1.98). Age group also proved to be a highly significant factor, with Integration increasing from 1.19 in the first grade to 2.56 in the fourth grade and to 4.25 in the seventh grade.

On Human, no differences between Mexicans and Americans were apparent. Strong developmental trends were present in both cultures; the mean scores on Human rose from 12.8 for the first-graders through 15.9 for the fourth-graders to 18.3 for the seventh-graders. Upper-class children in both cultures gave more human responses (17.1) than their lower-class counterparts (14.2). And boys tended to score higher on Human (16.7) than girls (14.6). Earlier research with the human-content score in inkblots suggests that a high degree of human is indicative of a high level of inter-personal socialization.

The results for Barrier are also consistent with those obtained for Integration and Movement. With the exception of the youngest group of upper-class children, differences between the American and Mexican samples were consistently obtained, with the Americans having the higher mean scores. In general the mean score for all American children was 5.25, while that for Mexican children was 4.18, a difference significant beyond the .01 level.

The results for the above four variables—Movement, Human, Integration, and Barrier—are fairly consistent with respect to cultural differences and differences attributable to sex, age group and social class. It is possible that the amount of verbosity in the individual inkblot protocol is partly responsible for some of the obtained results. As E. I. Megargee has pointed out (1966), length of response in terms of the number of words used is correlated about .40 with inkblot scores that cluster in Factor 1. In the case of the youngest lower-class Mexican children, the testing situation may have been sufficiently novel, and possibly even threatening, to create a high degree of reticence on the part of some children.

*HIT Factor 2: Color and Shading.* The extent to which Color entered in as a determinant of the percept differs markedly in the two cultures. The Mexican children obtained an average score of 8.70 while the American children obtained a mean score nearly twice as high, a score of 16.07. In only one comparison did the mean for the Mexican children reach or surpass the mean score on Color for the Americans. In Group I among upper-class children, the mean for Mexican children was 16.9, while that for American children was 16.0. A significant interaction between culture, age group, and social class was obtained for Color. Mean scores for this interaction are presented graphically for each age group in Figure 8-2. Most of this interaction can be accounted for by the particularly high degree of color response evident among the lower-class Americans in Group I. A mean score on Color of 27.9 indicates an unusually high degree of responsiveness to the color in the inkblot.

Further insight into the meaning of the above significant differences could probably be obtained by breaking down the over-all Color score into its three components, C1, C2, and C3, indicating

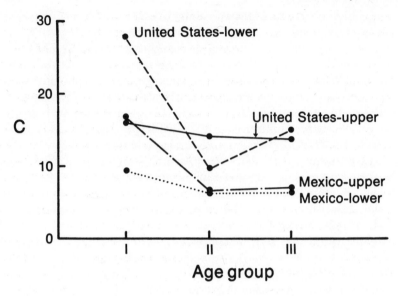

Figure 8-2. Color: interaction of culture, age group, and social class.

the extent to which color dominates over form as a determinant. It is quite probable that among the youngest, lower-class American children, a large number of color-dominated responses were given, accounting for the unusually high Color score. An earlier study by J. L. Sanders, Holtzman, and Swartz (1968), using only the American samples, showed a relatively high amount of pure color and color-dominated responses in Group I which was not apparent in Groups II and III. Apparently, the emphasis on color is not present in the Mexican sample at any age, indicating again the more impulsive, reactive behavior typical of the young American child, as contrasted to the Mexican or to the older American.

The mean score on Shading also proved to be considerably higher for the American children in general (4.39) than for the Mexicans (2.53). As shown in Figure 8-3, this cultural difference was accentuated among the youngest children, diminishing somewhat in Group II and disappearing in Group III. Although Shading stays fairly constant across the three age groups for the American children, it shows a significant rise with increasing age for the Mexicans. In this respect, Shading behaves more like a Factor 1 variable, such as Movement or Human, for the Mexican children. It should be pointed out that Shading frequently shows significant loadings on Factor 1, as well as Factor 2, especially among children.

*HIT Factor 3: Pathognomic Verbalization, Anxiety, and Hostility.* This cluster of inkblot variables tends to be associated with disordered thought processes and, in a severe form, is often indicative of psychopathology. While few of the cases in either the Mexican or the American sample received scores on Pathognomic Verbalization so high as to indicate serious psychopathology, the presence of pathognomic verbalization in fairly high amounts among the youngest children is not surprising. In general, the American children received higher scores on Pathognomic Verbalization than did the Mexican children. The mean score for Americans of 6.40 is more than twice that for Mexicans of 3.09. This generalization must be qualified, however, by the highly significant interaction involving age group, culture, and socioeconomic level, as presented in Figure 8-4. The greatest differences in age trends appear between the Mexican and American lower

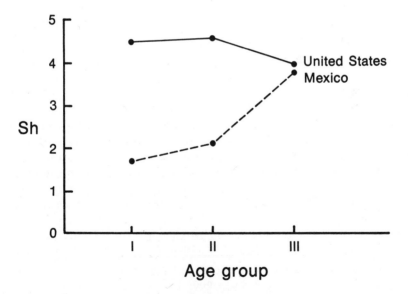

Figure 8-3. Shading: interaction of culture and age group.

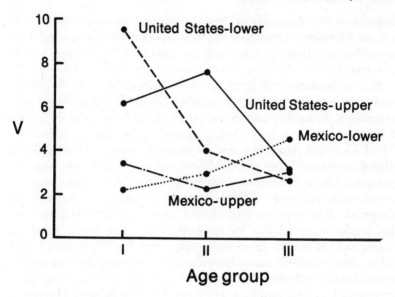

Figure 8-4. Pathognomic Verbalization: interaction of culture, age group, and social class.

classes. In general, there is a convergence of the two social classes and the two cultures with increasing age, especially in Group III, where no significant differences are apparent across the two cultures or social classes. The unusually high score on Pathognomic Verbalization for the youngest lower-class Austin children, a mean of 9.5, is indeed outstanding. The specific qualitative nature of the disordered thinking that resulted in high Pathognomic Verbalization for the youngest lower-class Austin children might well reveal that they attempted to combine percepts unsuccessfully, thereby creating a number of fabulized combinations and invalid integrations.

American children also tended to give more responses scored high on Anxiety than Mexican children, regardless of age, social class, or sex. The mean score on Anxiety for Americans was 9.1, compared to a score of only 5.6 for the Mexican children. Similar results were obtained for Hostility, although sex also proved to be a significant determinant. Boys generally gave significantly more responses containing hostile symbolism (9.97) than was the case for girls (6.40). A significant interaction between culture and sex is of considerable interest. American girls did not differ appreciably from Mexican boys in their mean scores on Hostility, 7.44 and 7.23 respectively. Mexican girls received the lowest mean score (5.35), while American boys received the highest (12.71). These results suggest that American culture encourages the expression of hostility in various symbolic forms, particularly on the part of boys.

*HIT: Animal, Anatomy, and Penetration.* The remaining three inkblot scores analyzed systematically in the analysis-of-variance design tend to be somewhat independent of the other variables. No cross-cultural differences were obtained for Animal. Mexican and American children alike, regardless of sex, socioeconomic level, or age, tended to give about the same number of animal responses. Significant differences were obtained, however, for sex and age group. Boys tended to give more animal responses than girls in both cultures, and the mean score for Animal increased from 22.3 for Group I to 28.2 and 27.1 for Groups II and III.

The use of skeletal and visceral anatomy as content in inkblot responses is reflected in the Anatomy score. While no main effects proved significant, the interaction between culture and age group was significant at the .01 level and is presented in Figure 8-5. The American children show a steady decline in the amount of anatomy across the three age groups, while the Mexicans show a sharp increase in Groups II and III.

Penetration represents yet another inkblot score related to pathology when present to a high degree. It also tends to be influenced by the amount of rich verbal response given by the subject, a tendency that is similar to the relationship between response length and most of the variables in Factor 1. American children obtained a higher mean score (3.43) on Penetration than did Mexican children (2.05). Age group also proved to be a significant source of variance for Penetration, particularly when culture is also taken into account. While the American children showed no significant difference across the three age groups, the Mexicans increased from .79 for Group I to 2.22 for Group II and 3.14 for Group III. These results are probably due in large part to the lower degree of verbosity among the young Mexican children, as contrasted to their American counterparts. For the seventh-

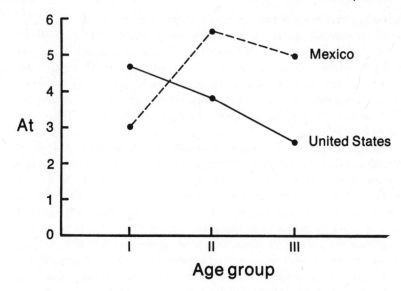

Figure 8-5. Anatomy: interaction of culture and age group.

graders in Group III, the difference between the Mexican and American children has narrowed to the point where it is no longer significant.

*Longitudinal Analysis of Inkblot Perception through Time*

Repeated administration of the Holtzman Inkblot Technique to all children in both cultures for the six years of the longitudinal study makes it possible to employ a repeated-measures analysis-of-variance design to determine the components of variation arising from changes in an individual's perception through time. Such a trend analysis is a powerful method of studying growth and development within an individual, provided that practice and adaptation effects are minimal. The use of an overlapping design where Groups I, II, and III overlap three years permits some correction for such practice or adaptation effects. In addition, Form A was given to some subjects in the first year, while Form B was given to others, alternating forms in subsequent years to yield a counterbalanced design. The striking similarities of Forms A and B, assuring their interchangeability as parallel forms for repeated testing, constitute another advantage of the Holtzman Inkblot Technique for longitudinal research involving repeated measures.

As in the case of the design where only the first year's data were employed, matched pairs of children, equated on socioeconomic status, sex, and age group, were employed. The actual number of such matched pairs was 196, slightly fewer than the 203 used when only the first year's data were employed. The analysis-of-variance design consisted of five main factors: (*a*) socioeconomic status, high or low; (*b*) sex, male or female; (*c*) age group, I, II, or III; (*d*) culture, Mexican or American; and (*e*) year of repeated testing or trial, 1–6. With six years of repeated test data for both Mexican and American children matched in 196 pairs, a total of 2,352 scores were available for each of the seventeen inkblot variables studied.[1] Only the results that involved culture and the interaction of culture with change over the six-year period of repeated testing are reported here.

*Location.* Mexican children tended to use smaller areas of the inkblot than did American children, to an even greater degree in the analysis of repeated testing than in the earlier analysis of the initial tests only. The results are plotted in Figure 8-6. While American children also tended to use smaller detail areas of the blots with each year of repeated testing, the gap between the two cultures widened from ten points initially to seventeen points after six years.

Adaptation to repeated testing is also apparent in Figure 8-6. Children of all ages in both cultures tended to use smaller detail areas more often than whole inkblots as the test was repeated. In spite of the noticeable adaptation of Location to repeated testing, the stability of individual differences through time was high. Estimates of test-retest reliability over the six-year period are given

---

[1] Occasionally one or more scores were missing for an individual. In this analysis-of-variance design, a missing observation for any one subject on one variable for one testing period would result in the loss of eleven valid observations. Five observations would be lost for the subject's other five trials, and six observations from the matched subject would be eliminated. To avoid the loss of a considerable number of valid scores when missing data occurred, a linear regression model (Witzke 1973) was employed to estimate the value of that missing score, based on all other valid scores on that variable for that subject. Within-cell-mean-square degrees of freedom were reduced to account for the number of scores estimated.

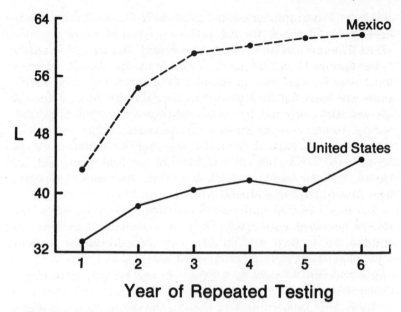

Figure 8-6. Location as a function of culture and year of testing.

by the intraclass correlation coefficient obtained from the between- and within-subjects residual variances. The obtained value of .80 for Location is higher than the test-retest coefficient for any of the other inkblot variables, most of which were in the .70's and .60's. These values are highly comparable to the computed correlation coefficients for test-retest stability when only two years are taken at a time and when the entire samples are used (see Chapter 5).

*Form Definiteness.* As indicated in Figure 8-7, when tested initially, boys reported more specific percepts than did girls in both cultures. While this difference favoring higher Form Definiteness for boys continued to hold up fairly well throughout the six years of repeated testing for American children, the sex difference gradually narrowed and then reversed for the Mexicans. In the last two years, the Mexican girls received higher scores on Form Definiteness than did the Mexican boys.

Six of the inkblot variables showed significant interactions among culture, age group, and year of testing, revealing important differences in developmental trends in Mexican and American children. The graphs presented in Figures 8-8–8-12 illustrate the developmental trends for the entire age span of six to seventeen years. The three years of overlap between Groups I and II and between Groups II and III provided double the number of age-linked test scores for ages nine to fourteen. The means for these overlap years are based on both groups to simplify the presentation and are partially corrected for minor practice effects due to repeated testing. In all cases the mean scores are fairly stable for each age in each culture, since they are based on large numbers of cases— 56 for ages six, seven, and eight; 131 for ages nine, ten, and eleven; 140 for ages twelve, thirteen, and fourteen; and 65 for ages fifteen, sixteen, and seventeen.

*Reaction Time.* As indicated in Figure 8-8, mean Reaction Time slowly increased with age, more so for Mexican than American children (F = 3.20, 10/798 d.f., p < .001). Mexicans generally took longer before giving a response to an inkblot, except for the oldest children, as seen by the two growth curves converging at age seventeen.

*Form Appropriateness.* Figure 8-9 shows that, among the young

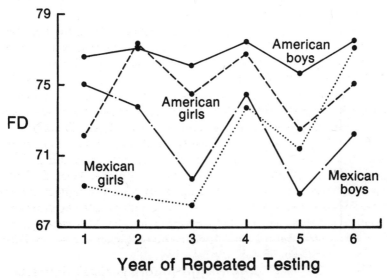

Figure 8-7. Form Definiteness as a function of culture, sex, and year of testing.

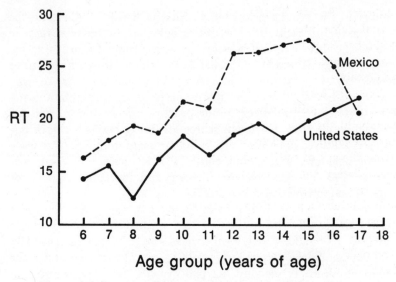

Figure 8-8. Reaction Time as a function of culture and age.

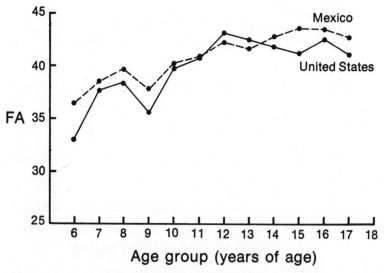

Figure 8-9. Form Appropriateness as a function of culture and age.

children, the Mexicans tended to report percepts that fitted the actual form of the inkblot more often than did the Americans (F = 4.90, 10/798 d.f., p < .001). This difference favoring the Mexicans disappeared by the age of twelve, reappearing again in later adolescence.

*Shading.* As shown in Figure 8-10, the youngest American children gave significantly more responses with shading as a determinant than did their Mexican counterparts. With increasing age this gap narrowed gradually until it disappeared in adolescence. From the age of twelve on, no differences in mean Shading scores were discernible between the two cultures.

A significant interaction of culture by socioeconomic status was also obtained for Shading (F = 9.44, 1/184 d.f., p < .01). The American lower-class children gave the greatest amount of Shading, while the Mexican lower-class children gave the least. The over-all difference between upper-class Mexicans and Americans was not significant.

*Pathognomic Verbalization.* Figure 8-11 shows that the American children generally gave more inkblot responses containing

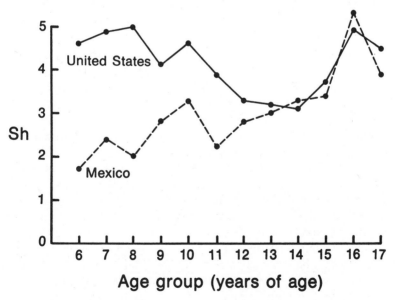

Figure 8-10. Shading as a function of culture and age.

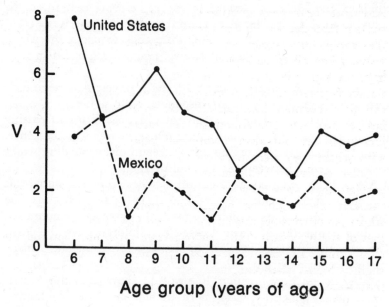

Figure 8-11. Pathognomic Verbalization as a function of culture and age.

Pathognomic Verbalization than did the Mexican children. This difference was particularly striking among the younger children where, except for seven-year-olds, V scores for the Americans averaged two to three times the amount of V for the Mexicans ($F = 3.83$, 10/798 d.f., $p < .001$).

*Human and Animal.* The two major content scores, Human and Animal, are presented together in Figure 8-12, where their complementary nature easily can be seen. Among the younger children, the Mexicans tended to give more Animal responses to inkblots and fewer Human responses than did the Americans. From the age of nine on, the mean scores on Human are almost identical in both cultures. Mean scores on Animal tend to converge by age thirteen.

*Hostility.* The cross-cultural developmental trends for Hostility are complex, as evidenced by a significant four-way interaction involving sex as well as age group, year of repeated testing, and culture ($F = 4.43$, 10/540 d.f., $p < .001$). The very youngest

American boys gave considerably more responses with hostile content than did the Mexican boys, nearly four times as much on the average for six-year-olds. This gap narrowed somewhat in later years, when all three groups are considered, although American boys got higher Hostility scores at nearly every age. For the girls, the six-year-olds in both cultures were low in Hostility. The Mexican girls remained low, not differing appreciably from Mexican boys at any age. The American girls increased in Hostility with increasing age but always remained below the American boys with whom they were matched.

*Color.* American children were more responsive to color in the inkblots than were Mexican children. This difference was particularly marked among the children from working-class families, where Americans obtained a mean score (14.9) more than twice that of the Mexicans (6.8). Among children from upper-middle-class families the mean Color score for Americans (12.5) was only slightly higher than the mean for Mexicans (10.1), yielding a significant interaction between socioeconomic level and culture (F = 9.52, 1/184 d.f., p < .01).

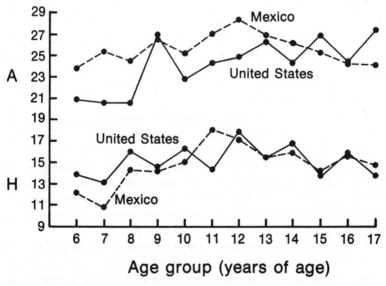

Figure 8-12. Human and Animal as functions of culture and age.

*Rejection.* The last of the variables having a highly significant interaction involving culture was Rejection, the number of inkblots that the subject turned back to the examiner without reporting a percept. In the first year only, Mexican girls rejected more ink-blots (4.5) than did American girls (2.5). There were no differences between Mexican and American boys, both of whom rejected fewer inkblots initially (1.9) than did girls of either culture. In subsequent years of repeated testing, no differences due to sex or culture were apparent, although a gradual drop in the number of rejected inkblots did occur, until in the last year the over-all mean was only 1.0.

The striking over-all mean differences attributable to culture on most of the inkblot scores are similar to the results reported earlier for the first-year data. In general, the American child produced faster reaction times, used larger portions of the inkblots in giving his responses, gave more definite form to his responses, and was still able to integrate more parts of the inkblot while doing so. He used more color and ascribed more movement to his percepts than did the Mexican child. At the same time his active fantasy life and attempts to deal with all aspects of the inkblots in an active manner produced a higher amount of deviant thinking and anxious and hostile content.

These results are easier to interpret when viewed in the light of the different pattern of values and beliefs implicit in the two cultures. As Díaz-Guerrero (1965) has pointed out, Americans tend to be more active than Mexicans in coping with the stresses of life. Most Mexicans, particularly women, believe that life is to be endured rather than enjoyed, that it is better to be safe than sorry, and that it is better to proceed slowly than fast. In general, when faced with a testing situation, the Mexican child is willing to cooperate, although he seldom takes the initiative. He will try to please the adult examiner and will tend to be cautious. By contrast, the American child will see the testing situation as a challenge to be mastered, an opportunity to show how much he can do.

Of greatest interest, however, are the interactions of culture with age, repeated testing, sex, and socioeconomic level. Only by examining the entire set of inkblot data with carefully matched cross-cultural samples can developmental trends and more complex interactions be rigorously tested. Within the present study several major conclusions are evident.

*First,* on certain variables, like Shading and Human, the American and Mexican children become more alike with increasing age. Earlier studies indicated that in children these variables are related to perceptual maturity and ego differentiation.

*Second,* cross-cultural differences for Color and Shading, the two inkblot variables most closely related to expression of affect and impulse control, are exaggerated for working-class children and diminished for children from upper-middle-class families. The traditional values of each culture are more likely to be characteristic of working-class families, while the worldly values more common among highly educated families are likely to transcend the two cultures.

*Third,* repeated testing for six years produces marked adaptation effects for some inkblot variables and none for others, indicating that overlapping longitudinal designs to correct for such effects are essential. It is quite possible that, the first time a person takes it, the Holtzman Inkblot Technique yields more sensitive results in some respects than later repetitions of the task, even though alternate forms are used a year apart.

---

Cross-cultural results for both the perceptual-style and the personality variables scored on the Holtzman Inkblot Technique have been presented in this chapter. The significant differences between the two cultures were interpreted in light of the different cultural patterns of values and beliefs. In the next chapter, the cross-cultural results from the several personality-attitudinal measures are given.

# 9. Components of Performance on Personality-Attitudinal Measures

*Personality Research Form*

The Personality Research Form (PRF) is one of the most comprehensive paper-and-pencil questionnaires developed for measuring broadly relevant personality traits among normal individuals in such settings as schools and colleges. Consisting of three hundred items divided into fifteen twenty-item scales, Form A of the PRF has sufficiently high reliability and validity when used with North American high school and college students to justify its translation into Spanish for use in the present cross-cultural longitudinal study. Because the test requires a reading level above the fourth grade and some exposure to the typical life experiences of a teenager, the PRF was not administered until the last year of the study, when the children in Groups I, II, and III were in the sixth, ninth, and twelfth grades respectively. Completed PRF questionnaires were obtained from all but 78 of the 406 cases in the matched sample. Since these cases were spread rather uniformly across all twenty-four cells of the research design, it is unlikely that the results of the analysis of variance are adversely affected. The results of the factor analysis of intercorrelations among the fifteen scales, as reported in Tables 6-20–6-23, indicate that most of the common variance across the fifteen scales can be accounted for by four major factors, tentatively labeled as follows: Persistent Achievement Drive, Extroversion, Affiliative Nurturance, and Nonconformity. The presentation of results from the analyses of variance for the scales in the PRF is organized in clusters according to these four factors.

*Persistent Achievement Drive.* Five scales—Achievement, Endurance, Order, and Understanding on the one hand and Play on the other—are clustered together as defining variables for Factor 1 on the PRF (see Table 6-20). Of the five scales, only Play and Order revealed a significant main effect. On Play, the American children obtained a markedly higher mean (14.1) than did the Mexican (10.6), suggesting that they spent more time in social activities and doing things "just for fun." A slight but significant age difference was also noted for Play, the two older groups being essentially identical in mean score, while the youngest group in the sixth grade had a lower mean score. For Order, Mexican children, regardless of age, socioeconomic class, or sex, received higher scores (12.2) than did the American (10.3). A high scorer on Order is one who is concerned with keeping personal effects and surroundings neat and organized, as contrasted to the low scorer, who tends to be disorganized and untidy.

A high scorer on Understanding is a person who is curious and wants to understand many areas of knowledge. No main effects proved to be significant in the analysis of scores for Understanding, although the interaction between age and culture was significant at the .05 level. Among sixth-graders, the American children tended to have slightly higher scores (12.3) than did the Mexican children (11.4). For the two older groups, this difference was reversed, the Mexican teen-agers obtaining higher scores than the Americans.

For Endurance, a significant interaction was obtained between socioeconomic status and sex. Among the boys, the upper class obtained higher Endurance scores (11.1) than the lower class (9.6); while among the girls, this difference was reversed—the upper class obtaining lower scores (9.6) than the lower class (10.4).

No differences were obtained for any of the sources of variance on Achievement, the fifth of the variables in this cluster.

*Extroversion.* Exhibition, Dominance, Social Recognition, and, to some extent, Play and Aggression are defining scales for Factor

2 in the PRF (see Table 6-21). High scorers on Dominance are those who attempt to control their environments and to influence and direct other people. They generally enjoy the role of leader and may assume it spontaneously. Of the main effects, only sex proved to be significant in the analysis of Dominance, boys receiving a higher mean score (10.1) than girls (8.7). The interaction involving culture and socioeconomic status proved to be significant at the .01 level. Among upper-class children, no significant differences between American and Mexican children were apparent. However, among lower-class children, the Mexicans received a higher mean score (10.3) than did the Americans (8.3).

Only culture proved to be significant for Social Recognition, the Americans achieving higher scores (12.5) than the Mexicans (10.8) on the average. Apparently, American teen-agers tend to be more concerned about what other people think of them than the Mexican teen-agers, although the difference is not large.

Exhibition revealed no significant main effects or higher-order interactions. Apparently, teen-agers in both cultures, regardless of sex, age, or socioeconomic status, show the same degree of exhibitionism or modesty.

Some interesting significant differences are present for Aggression, the fifth scale in this cluster. Both social class and sex proved to be highly significant main effects. Children from lower-class families received higher scores (9.1) than did those from upper-class families (7.9), regardless of age, sex, or culture, a finding consistent with the common observation that children of working-class families tend to be more openly aggressive than upper-class children. A highly significant interaction between culture and sex results from the lack of any sex differences among the Mexicans (means for boys and girls of 8.5 and 8.7), as contrasted to the marked difference obtained for the American teen-agers (means for boys and girls of 9.9 and 7.0).

*Affiliative Nurturance.* The two scales most closely identified with Factor 3 are Affiliation and Nurturance (see Table 6-22). Low scores on Aggression are also related to this cluster, which, in the factor analyses, was closely identified with being female rather than male. The highly significant main effects for sex on Aggression were reported above. In the analysis of Affiliation, highly significant differences were also obtained for culture and sex, as well as the interaction between these two variables. While, in general, the Americans were higher on Affiliation than the Mexicans, this difference was much more pronounced among the girls than among the boys, as can be seen in Table 9-1. No sex differences were obtained for the Mexican children on Affiliation, as contrasted to the major difference found for the American children.

Similar results were obtained for Nurturance. In this case, however, the significant interaction between sex and culture was due to the lack of any difference between the Mexican and American boys (11.8 and 12.0 respectively), while the girls differed considerably across culture (13.1 for the Mexicans and 15.4 for the Americans). While girls in both cultures tended to be more sympathetic, maternal, and comforting to others in need of help than boys, this trait was particularly characteristic of the American teen-age girl.

*Nonconformity.* In the factor analysis for the American children, Autonomy, Harmavoidance reversed, and Social Recognition reversed are the variables with highest loadings, followed closely by Infrequency, Impulsivity, and Order reversed (see Table 6-23). The factor is less sharply defined among the Mexican children, although Autonomy still has the highest loading, followed closely by Infrequency, Impulsivity, and Order reversed. A high scorer on Autonomy is one who enjoys being unattached and who tries to break away from confinement or restrictions of any kind, as contrasted to the low scorer, who tends to be conforming and dependent upon others. Culture, age group, and sex all prove to be significant factors with respect to scores on Autonomy. In general, sixth-graders showed a greater need for autonomy than ninth- or twelfth-graders, although the differences were not large. Boys tended to seek autonomy more than girls, although again the difference was small (8.3 for boys and 7.5 for girls). The most sig-

Table 9-1
Means for the Affiliation Scale of the Personality Research Form by Culture and Sex

|  | Boys | Girls |
|---|---|---|
| United States | 14.8 | 17.1 |
| Mexico | 12.2 | 12.5 |

nificant difference is attributable to culture. Mexican teen-agers had a stronger need for autonomy (8.7), in general, than American teen-agers (7.1).

On Impulsivity, age group and culture proved to be highly significant main effects. Ninth- and twelfth-graders obtained higher mean scores on Impulsivity (10.1 and 10.4 respectively) than did children of either culture in the sixth grade (8.6). In general the American children obtained higher scores than did the Mexicans (10.5 and 8.9 respectively).

Though not as striking, similar results across the three age groups were obtained for Harmavoidance and Order, two scales reflecting control rather than impulse expression and therefore opposite in meaning to Impulsivity. A striking sex difference, as well as a sex-by-culture interaction, also appeared for Harmavoidance. In general, as would be expected from the nature of the scale, girls tended to receive higher mean scores (10.2) than did boys (8.4). This sex difference was much more marked among the American children than among the Mexican. An inspection of triple interactions involving culture, sex, and age, as well as culture, sex, and social class (both with $p < .05$), indicates that the older American boys tended to be the least fearful, while American girls tended to be the most fearful and cautious where danger might be involved.

*Infrequency.* The results from analyses of variance for the PRF scales are tempered somewhat by significant cross-cultural differences in scores on the Infrequency scale, a measure of tendency to endorse improbable statements; the Mexicans obtained a mean score of 3.5, as compared to a mean of 1.1 for the Americans. This difference is probably due to minor irregularities in the translation from English to Spanish. It is unlikely that the results obtained for the substantive personality scales would have been altered appreciably by elimination of the difference on Infrequency scales.

## Test Anxiety Questionnaire

The Test Anxiety Scale for Children (TASC), as developed by Sarason and his associates (1960), is a thirty-item paper-and-pencil questionnaire designed to measure children's test anxiety as a convenient way of studying some of the properties of anxiety in general. Subsequent to the initial development of TASC, additional items constituting a Lie Scale (eleven items) and a Defensiveness Scale for Children (twenty-seven items) were added to the items for the TASC, making a total of sixty-eight items given to each child in questionnaire form. The Lie and Defensiveness scales were not added to the TASC until the third year of testing in Austin, although they were included in the Mexican questionnaire for most of the children in the second year of testing as well as in every subsequent year. Consequently, the first year in which uniform data were collected on all three scales in both cultures was the third year of the study.

The Test Anxiety Scale proved to be highly significant for socioeconomic status, culture, and sex, although none of the higher-order interactions approached significance. Lower-class children received a higher mean score (14.7) on the TASC than did children from upper-class families (12.0), indicating that children from less well educated families tend to be more anxious about taking tests in school than children from highly educated families who also have higher occupational status in society. About the same difference, significant beyond the .001 level, was obtained between boys and girls, boys receiving a mean of 12.1, as compared to a mean of 14.5 for girls. The most striking difference appeared in the comparison of Mexican and American children. The mean for all of the Mexican children was 16.8, as contrasted to only 9.8 for the Americans. While subtle irregularities in translation from English to Spanish could account for a slight dissimilarity in responses, a difference of this magnitude points to a rather fundamental divergence in the conscious way in which school experiences are viewed in the two cultures. Further insight into the nature of this cross-cultural difference can be obtained by examining the Lie Scale and the Defensiveness Scale for the same children.

Small but statistically significant differences were also obtained for the Lie Scale for both culture and sex but not for socioeconomic status. As can be seen in Table 9-2, the Mexicans received a mean of 4.0 (out of a possible maximum score of 11), while the American children received a mean of 2.8, a difference of only slightly over one point. Boys tended to receive a higher score than girls, although the difference is only significant at the .05 level. Unlike

Table 9-2
Means for the TASC Scales by Culture and Sex

| Scale | $s^2_w$ | United States Boys | Girls | Mexico Boys | Girls |
|---|---|---|---|---|---|
| TASC | 36.3 | 9.2 | 10.4 | 15.0 | 18.7 |
| L | 8.0 | 3.0 | 2.6 | 4.5 | 3.5 |
| DSC | 16.7 | 9.8 | 9.2 | 11.4 | 9.9 |

$s^2_w$: within-cell mean square
TASC: Test Anxiety Scale for Children
L: Lie Scale
DSC: Defensiveness Scale for Children

the comparison for the Test Anxiety Scale, the Lie Scale shows a significant downward trend in mean score with increasing age. The third-graders obtained a mean of 4.5, compared to means of 3.0 and 2.7 for sixth- and ninth-graders respectively. Differences for the Defensiveness Scale are even smaller (though significant at the .05 level) for culture and sex as well as age. These trends are identical with those obtained for the Lie Scale.

When taken together, results on these three scales strongly suggest that children in Mexico are considerably more anxious about taking tests in school than are their counterparts in the United States. Slightly higher scores on the Lie Scale and Defensiveness Scale are not at all sufficient to explain the much higher score of the Mexican children on the Test Anxiety Scale. Since all three of the main effects that proved significant are additive, there being no significant interactions in the analysis of any of the scales, the most anxious of all are the lower-class younger Mexican girls, and the least anxious of all are the upper-class older American boys. The actual mean for the youngest lower-class Mexican girls on the Test Anxiety Scale was 24.4 out of a possible 30 points. This mean contrasts sharply with that of the older upper-class American boys, who received a mean of only 7.6 on the TASC.

*Occupational Values Inventory*

The Occupational Values Inventory was developed specifically for the cross-national study of school children (Díaz-Guerrero 1972a). Originally, the instrument involved 105 items, consisting of all possible pairs of fifteen different career values, such as altruism, esthetics, and independence. The number of times a particular phrase, such as "work in which you can help other people," was chosen by the child constituted his score for that particular career value. In the present study, the paired comparison method was modified by simply using a rank-order method for placing the fifteen career-value phrases in order from the most valued to the least valued. The rank-order position of each career value constituted the score for analysis.

Since the Occupational Values Inventory was given in the same testing session as the Personality Research Form, essentially the same missing cases, seventy-seven, appear in the analysis of variance, scattered evenly across the twenty-four cells of the design. Results of the analysis are presented, one variable at a time, beginning with the career value generally judged most important. Rank scores have been converted into normalized scores varying from one to nine and having an arbitrary mean and standard deviation of five and two respectively. The higher the score on this normalized scale, the higher the value attached to the item by the respondent.

*Self-Satisfaction.* "Work in which you can feel good about doing the job well" was given a top ranking by both the Mexican and American children. None of the sources of variance proved to be significant at or beyond the .01 level. Regardless of sex, socioeconomic status, culture, or age, feeling good about doing the job well was valued highly.

*Economic Returns.* "Work in which you can make a lot of money" was also valued highly by a large number of children in both cultures. Both sex and socioeconomic status proved to be significant beyond the .01 level, boys valuing financial success more highly than girls and lower-class children valuing money more highly than children from upper-class families, regardless of the culture or the age of the child.

*Altruism.* "Work in which you can help other people" revealed a significant interaction between culture and sex. The mean scores by sex and culture are presented in Table 9-3, together with similar data for the other fourteen items in the Occupational Values Inventory. While no sex differences were obtained for the Mexican children, American girls valued this trait significantly more

Table 9-3
Mean Scores for Each Value Item in the Occupational Values Inventory,
by Culture and Sex

| Phrasing of the Value | $s^2_w$ | United States Boys | Girls | Mexico Boys | Girls | Significant F-Ratios |
|---|---|---|---|---|---|---|
| Feel good about doing job well | 2.31 | 5.92 | 6.38 | 5.81 | 6.17 | |
| Make a lot of money | 4.08 | 6.29 | 5.80 | 6.48 | 5.55 | s |
| Help other people | 4.08 | 4.89 | 6.68 | 5.53 | 5.73 | S, cs |
| Learn about many interesting things | 2.74 | 5.50 | 5.59 | 5.17 | 6.19 | s |
| Get ahead | 2.55 | 5.82 | 4.77 | 5.64 | 5.91 | CS |
| Be with people you like | 2.23 | 5.83 | 6.47 | 4.70 | 5.06 | C, s |
| Have a nice place to work[a] | 1.86 | | | | | |
| Group I | | 4.90 | 5.45 | 6.03 | 4.63 | CS |
| Group II | | 5.64 | 5.46 | 5.44 | 5.22 | |
| Group III | | 5.42 | 5.00 | 4.52 | 5.68 | cs |
| Free to do in your own way | 3.40 | 5.74 | 5.12 | 5.05 | 4.79 | |
| Make or invent new things | 4.05 | 4.46 | 3.96 | 6.00 | 4.90 | C, S |
| One day become famous | 3.92 | 4.61 | 4.16 | 5.29 | 5.25 | C |
| Always sure of having a job | 2.83 | 5.08 | 5.43 | 4.24 | 4.21 | C |
| Be doing many different things | 2.91 | 4.56 | 5.00 | 4.27 | 4.62 | |
| Lead other people | 3.80 | 4.08 | 4.09 | 4.20 | 4.51 | |
| Same kind of work your father does | 3.96 | 4.23 | 2.56 | 4.11 | 3.22 | S |
| Musician or an artist | 5.20 | 2.63 | 3.72 | 3.12 | 3.65 | s |

[a] Since sex by culture by age-group interaction is significant at the .001 level, means for sex and culture are presented separately for the three age groups.
$s^2_w$: within-cell mean square
S: sex difference significant at .001 level
s: sex difference significant at .01 level
C: culture difference significant at .001 level
CS: sex by culture significant at .001 level
cs: sex by culture significant at .01 level

highly than did American boys. No other sources of variance approached significance.

*Intellectual Stimulation.* "Work in which you can learn about many interesting things" was also highly valued by many children in both cultures. The presence of a triple interaction involving age group, socioeconomic status, and culture complicates the interpretation of the results. The meaning of this interaction becomes clear when age trends are plotted separately for the American and Mexican children, using the mean difference between upper- and lower-class children within each of the six cells. Inspection of Figure 9-1 suggests that social-class differences were particularly important among the sixth-graders in Mexico, where a mean difference of 2.2, favoring the upper social class, was obtained. This difference was reversed for the oldest group, where lower-class children actually valued work that was intellectually stimulating more highly than did upper-class children. Among the American children, only a slight difference, regardless of age, is apparent.

*Success.* "Work where you can get ahead" received an over-all ranking of fifth place among the fifteen occupational values that were ranked by the children. An interesting sex-by-culture interaction is apparent in Table 9-3. Valuing this traditional form of occupational success was more characteristic of boys than girls among the American children, while the reverse was true for the Mexicans. In both cultures, the older teen-agers in Groups II and III (means of 5.73 and 5.82) valued success more highly than the sixth-graders (5.05).

*Associates.* "Work in which you can be with people you like" was valued more highly by American children (mean of 6.15) than by Mexican children (mean of 4.88). Regardless of age group, socioeconomic status, or culture, girls valued this type of work situation more highly than did boys.

*Surroundings.* "Work in which you would have a nice place to

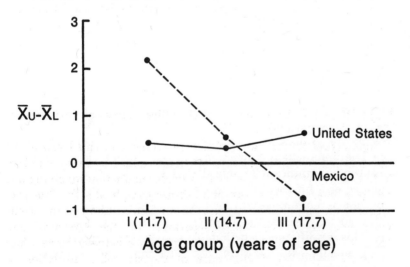

Figure 9-1. Mean social-class difference in the value of intellectually stimulating work as a function of culture and age group.

work" yielded a highly significant triple interaction involving sex, culture, and age group. As shown in Table 9-3, results of the analysis by sex and culture are different for each of the three age groups. Among the sixth-graders, Mexican boys valued this type of work significantly more than did Mexican girls, while just the opposite occurred for the American boys and girls. Among the ninth-graders, no significant difference was apparent for either sex or culture. Among the twelfth-graders, the interaction of sex and culture is a mirror image of that obtained for the sixth-graders, Mexican girls and American boys valuing a nice place to work more highly than American girls or Mexican boys. In other words, Mexican girls and American boys showed an increase in the importance of a nice place to work with increasing age, while Mexican boys and American girls showed the reverse.

*Independence.* "Work which you are free to do in your own way" was valued more highly by the oldest group of children (mean of 5.59) than by ninth-graders (5.26) or sixth-graders (4.68). No other main effects or interactions were sufficiently significant to justify interpretation, age group being the only highly significant factor influencing this occupational value.

*Creativity.* "Work in which you could make or invent new things" was valued more highly by Mexican than by American children and by boys than by girls, as illustrated in Table 9-3. The interaction of age group and culture proved to be significant at the .02 level. The American children dropped slightly in the relative importance of this aspect of work, while the means for Mexican children increased with increasing age.

*Prestige.* "Work in which you can one day become famous" was valued significantly more highly by the Mexican children than by the Americans, regardless of age group, social class, or sex. The interaction between age group, social class, and sex proved to be significant beyond the .01 level. Mean sex difference is plotted as a function of social class and age in Figure 9-2. Prestige is much more important for boys than girls among upper-class sixth-graders, while in the lower-class sixth-graders the reverse is true. This sex difference attributable to social-class differences narrows gradually with increasing age. This interaction is present in both cultures.

*Security.* "Work in which you are always sure of having a job"

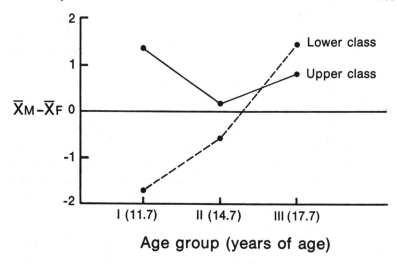

Figure 9-2. Mean sex difference in value assigned to prestige of work as a function of social class and age group.

was valued more highly by American children than by Mexican, regardless of age or sex. A significant interaction between social class and culture, however, requires some qualification of the above interpretation. Among upper-class children, the cross-cultural difference is rather slight (means of 4.92 and 4.48 for Austin and Mexico City respectively). For lower-class children, the cross-cultural difference is quite large (means of 5.59 and 3.98 for American and Mexican children respectively). These results suggest that the importance of always being sure of having a job is much greater for the lower-class American child than for his upper-class counterpart, while the reverse is true for the Mexican.

*Variety.* "Work in which you would be doing many different things" received a relatively low rating when compared with the other occupational values. No differences attributable to age, social class, culture, sex, or their interactions were discovered in the analysis of variance for this value.

*Management.* "Work in which you could lead other people" was generally valued third from the bottom of the list. As in the case of variety, this occupational value produced no significant differences in either main effects or higher-order interactions.

*Follow Father.* "Work in which you would do the same kind of work your father does" was more appealing to younger children than to older teen-agers. Quite understandably, sex proved to be a highly significant factor, with boys preferring to follow in their fathers' footsteps much more than girls. Children from upper-class families also valued this aspect of work more highly than those from lower-class families (means of 3.91 and 3.15 respectively). Of some interest is the presence of a significant interaction involving age group, culture, and sex. With the exception of Mexican sixth-graders and American twelfth-graders, boys invariably valued following in their fathers' footsteps more highly than did girls. For the youngest Mexicans and oldest Americans, this sex difference was not significant.

*Esthetics.* "Work like that of a musician or an artist" was valued least of all by most of the children in the study. Girls in both cultures valued this aspect of work more highly than did boys. Children in the sixth grade valued esthetics more highly than did those in the ninth or twelfth grade. This statement must be qualified, however, by the presence of a significant interaction involving age group, social class, and culture. Lower-class Mexican and upper-class American children showed the age trend of declining interest in being a musician or an artist more markedly than the other two groups. The lower-class American children showed no age difference in valuing this trait.

It is interesting to compare the results for Groups I and II combined from the Mexican sample within the current study with those reported by Díaz-Guerrero (1972) in his analysis of results on the Occupational Values Inventory for ten- and fourteen-year-olds in Mexico. In all but three of the fifteen occupational values, almost identical rank orders were obtained. The Mexican children in the present study ranked security much lower in importance, third from the bottom, than did those in the cross-national study, who ranked security sixth in importance. The top-ranking occupational value in the cross-national study, intellectual stimulation, dropped to sixth place in the present study. The greatest change of all from the cross-national study to the present one involved the occupational value of economic returns. This trait was placed at the top of the list by the sixth- and ninth-grade Mexicans in the present study, although it was ranked only ninth by the ten- and fourteen-year-olds from the cross-national study.

---

The results from the Personality Research Form, the Test Anxiety Scale for Children, and the Occupational Values Inventory revealed important differences between school children in Mexico and the United States with respect to their responses on standardized measures of personality, attitudes, and values. In the next chapter, characteristics and perceptions of the children's mothers are revealed. Responses of mothers in the extensive interviews shed light upon important characteristics of the home environment and family life style.

# 10. Components of Parental and Home Variables

Individual interviews were conducted with the mother of each child in Mexico City and Austin midway through the six-year longitudinal study. Items for the interview were drawn from a number of previous studies dealing with family and social background factors as they influenced developmental processes in children, as well as from careful study of variables within the contemporary Mexican and American family that might be of special cross-cultural interest. A more detailed description of the interview schedule is given in Chapters 2 and 4 and in Appendix A.

The methodological aspects of the interview and the coding and reliability studies of parental responses are presented in Chapter 4. This chapter deals specifically with the cross-cultural similarities and differences in parental responses to interview items. In addition, significant differences involving sex, age of the child, social class, and interactions of these variables with culture are also presented. From this analysis, using the matched cross-cultural samples of 406 cases, descriptive portraits of families and their variations in metropolitan Mexican and American cities emerge. Similarities and differences among these families on major social and environmental factors central to the environment of the developing child in each culture give deeper insight into the meaning of the cross-cultural results obtained for the child's performance on cognitive, perceptual, and personality tests.

The presentation of results is given one item at a time, organized for convenience of interpretation according to the nature of the item and the underlying environmental dimension that is involved. Results for those items of a demographic and factual nature are presented first, followed by ratings of the home environment made by the examiner immediately after the interview, since these items also contribute heavily to a richer definition of family life style and social class in the two cultures. The next section contains results for those items that can be grouped into one or more major subenvironment clusters: (a) degree of intellectual stimulation in the home; (b) parental aspirations for the child; (c) variety and richness of the home environment for social, cultural, artistic, and recreational development (socialization); and (d) degree of parental interest in the academic progress of the child. And, finally, those items dealing specifically with the parent's judgment of the child are presented, indicating the mother's perception of the child at the time of the interview.

## Social Class and Family Life Style

One of the major variables in the four-way analysis-of-variance design employed in this study is the two-level socioeconomic status of the family as measured by a combination of father's occupational level and father's education. The two levels of socioeconomic status can best be described as (a) upper-middle-class, professional, well-educated families, constituting the "upper" class, and (b) working-class, unskilled, semiskilled, or skilled workers, white-collar clerical workers, and blue-collar workers, who are often characterized as lower-middle-class or upper-lower-class families, constituting the "lower" class in the present study. It should be emphasized that this range of social class is a rather restricted one when the entire population is considered, since it contains only stable families who remain in one city with children enrolled in school for a period of six years. Very few unskilled lower-class families are included, and only a very small number of genuinely upper-class wealthy families are included. Nevertheless, this range of social class comprises the great bulk of families in both cultures who establish the dominant values and major themes of the two cultures. Because of the restriction in range of social class, differences that are found attributable to social class are all the more significant. Analyses of items especially pertinent to social class and family life style are presented one at a time.

*Father's Occupation.* Three-way analyses of variance were done separately for the lower-class and upper-class samples for father's occupation, father's education, and mother's education to see the extent to which the use of the combined SES Index as a basis for matching cross-culturally on social class actually eliminated differences on father's occupation, father's education, and mother's education as separate variables. Some residual differences may still exist without creating serious problems for the remainder of the analysis, since education and occupation have subtle but important differences in meaning in the two cultures anyway. The use of the combined SES Index is a more stable approach to determining social class than either variable making up the index would be if treated in isolation from the other. For father's occupation, both culture and age-by-sex interaction proved to be significant beyond the .01 level for the lower-class sample in both cultures. A mean score on the father's occupational scale of 5.6 was obtained by the Mexican lower-class sample, while the Austin lower-class fathers were rated 4.7 on the occupational scale. Both means fall between skilled manual workers (rating of 4) and white-collar workers (6). Among the upper-class samples in both cultures no significant differences were obtained for any of the main effects or their interactions. The mean occupational-level score for both Mexican and American upper-class families was 7.7, slightly closer to the professional level (8) than to the small business owner's level (7). The significant sex-by-age-group interaction was due to the fact that the fathers of girls in Group I, the youngest families, received a mean occupational level score of 5.5, compared to 4.4 for the fathers of boys, while just the reverse occurred for the Group II families. No differences between the fathers of boys and the fathers of girls were found in Group III, the oldest families.

*Father's Education.* Significant differences in education were obtained for fathers classified as lower-class for culture as well as for the interaction of culture and age group. Among the Group I lower-class Mexican fathers, the mean educational level was 1.6, a score equivalent to about the seventh grade (see Table 7-1). For Group II and III lower-class fathers in Mexico, the score increased to 2.0 and 2.7 respectively, scores equivalent to "some junior high school." Among the American lower-class fathers, the mean educational level stayed about the same in the three age groups, hovering around "some high school." This difference is to be expected because of the differences in the nature of the two educational systems. In the United States, the overwhelming majority of young parents have at least entered high school, and most have graduated from it. In Mexico, it is much more unusual for lower-class families to go beyond *secundaria*, a level equivalent to the American ninth grade, and this was especially true twenty years ago, when the fathers in this study were of school age. In the sample of upper-class fathers, no significant differences in educational level were found. Both the Mexican and the American fathers received mean scores of 7.3 on the educational-level scale, a level equivalent to the college graduate.

The significantly higher occupational level of lower-class fathers in the Mexican sample than in the United States sample is purely an artifact of the matching process, where compensatory measures had to be taken to balance the obvious discrepancy in fathers' education. The net result is "equivalency" on the over-all socioeconomic-status-level index, as measured by a combination of father's occupation and father's education. While the lower-class children differed slightly but significantly in both father's occupation and father's education across the two cultures, the difference was relatively small compared to the major difference between the lower-class and upper-class categories employed in all subsequent analyses of variance.

*Mother's Education.* Although the educational level of the mother was not used explicitly in the formula for defining social class, it correlated highly enough with father's education among the American children (and to a much lesser extent among Mexican families) to justify its analysis in the same three-way design as employed for checking father's education and father's occupation, treating the upper- and lower-class samples separately. Among the lower-class families, American mothers achieved a mean score of 5.0, equivalent to the completion of high school. By contrast, the Mexican mothers received a score of only 1.8, equivalent to "some *secundaria*" (about eighth grade). Among the upper-class American families, the average educational level of mothers was 6.2 (some college), while that of the Mexican upper-class mothers was 3.2 (some *preparatoria*, or high school). In general, it can be concluded that mothers are less well educated than fathers among upper-class families in Mexico, especially as compared to the American family, where the two parents tend to have very similar levels of education. Within the lower-class families of both cultures, the two parents have similar levels of education.

*Number of Siblings in the Family.* The Mexican family tends to be considerably larger than the American family of comparable age and socioeconomic status. The average number of siblings in the Mexican family in the study was 3.7, as contrasted to only 2.0 in the American family. The lack of any significant interactions with age or social class suggests that this is purely a cultural phenomenon.

*Father's Age.* As would be expected from the definitions of Groups I, II, and III as initially first-, fourth-, and seventh-graders in the longitudinal study, father's age differed significantly across the three age groups, ranging from a mean of thirty-nine in Group I to forty-two in Group II and forty-six in Group III. This pattern must be qualified slightly by the presence of an interaction significant at the .01 level between age group, culture, and sex. For Mexican girls in all three groups, the mean age for fathers remained nearly constant at approximately forty-three years. For the fathers of American boys, the opposite occurred, with age shifting rapidly from a mean of thirty-six in Group I to forty-eight in Group III. For the Mexican boys and American girls, the slight increase in age of the father from Group I to Group III was essentially the same as that for the over-all means in each of the three groups. Social class also proved significant beyond the .01 level, with lower-class fathers being younger than upper-class fathers for children of comparable age by approximately two and a half years.

*Mother's Age.* Although culture did not prove to be significant for mother's age, mothers in both cultures having identical ages for comparable children, age group showed the same trend; mothers in Group I had a mean age of thirty-five, those in Group II of thirty-nine, and those in Group III of forty-two years. These results are slightly qualified by a significant interaction of age group and sex of the child. For the youngest boys in the sample, the mothers were four years younger in age than was the case for the girls in the sample, regardless of culture. The fact that this shows up in both cultures suggests that it is an important phenomenon worthy of additional study. No differences in age were found between the mothers of boys and girls in Groups II and III.

*How Long in Present Home?* As one would expect, the families in both cultures are relatively stable compared to the general population, since they agreed to a six-year longitudinal study of their children in the first place in order to be included in the sample. No social-class, cultural, or sex differences were discovered with respect to the number of years in the present home. Only the age of the child made any difference. Families in Group I had lived in their present home an average of 5.9 years, those in Group II an average of 7.4 years, and those in Group III an average of 9.2 years.

*Cities of Residence since Marriage.* American parents in the sample had lived in an average of 2.3 different cities since marriage, including Austin. The Mexican families had lived in an average of only 1.3 cities since marriage. The apparent lesser mobility of the Mexican families may well be a result of the tremendous metropolitan area represented by Mexico City, as contrasted to the much smaller metropolitan area of which Austin is the center. A significant interaction between sex and culture was also obtained—the American families with girls in the sample tended to move about more often than those with boys, while the reverse proved to be the case among the Mexican families.

*Adults Living in the Home.* In all but 6 percent of the families in both cultures, father and mother were present and living in the home, another indication of the above-average stability of the families included in the present study. The only major difference between the two cultures involved the extent to which other relatives outside the nuclear family lived in the same home. Within the Mexican families, 18 percent had other relatives present, while only 3 percent of the American families involved other relatives in the same home. This difference favoring the extended family in Mexico proved to be the case regardless of social class or age of the child.

*Schools Attended by the Child.* The finding that the older the child the more schools he has attended is self-evident and of little importance. Of more interest is the significant interaction between culture and age of the child. Among the children in Group I, who were in the fourth grade at the time of the parental interview, children in both the American and Mexican sample had generally attended only the one school in which they were first enrolled. Children in Group II, who were in the seventh grade at the time of the interview, differed appreciably across the two cultures, largely because all children in Austin shift to a new school when they enter junior high school, whereas many in Mexico City continue within the same school. The mean number of schools attended in Austin for Group II was 2.4, as contrasted to 1.4 in Mexico City. By the time the child reached the tenth grade (Group III at the time of the interview), the two cultures showed an identical mean number of schools attended by a child (2.5).

*Religious Affiliation and Frequency of Church Attendance.* As one would expect, the overwhelming preference for Mexican families was the Roman Catholic church. Only one family out of the entire sample proved to be non-Catholic. Among the Americans, only 14 percent were Catholic, the great majority of the remainder being Protestant. Only 2 percent of the families in both cultures never went to church. Among the Mexican families, 85 percent went at least once a week. This dropped to 63 percent for the American families. When frequency of church attendance is divided into only two categories, "no or rarely" and "frequently," an interaction between social class and culture emerges. Among the Americans there is no difference between the lower and upper class; 20 percent of the families rarely if ever attended church. Among the Mexicans, however, all but one family in the lower-class sample attended church frequently. For the upper-class Mexicans, 9 percent of the mothers claimed the family attended church rarely if ever.

*Who Attends Church.* An analysis of which members of the family attended church reveals that the overwhelming majority in both cultures attended as an entire family if they went at all. In 20 percent of the families, only the mother and child attended church. The child went alone to church in 12 percent of the families. In only 2 percent of the families did the father go alone with the child. No culture or social-class differences were apparent.

*Clubs to Which the Parents Belong.* Several items in the interview asked about the number and variety of clubs to which the mother, the father, or both parents belonged. Marked inconsistencies between several of these items in the frequency of the mothers' responses suggest that this set of data should be interpreted with considerable caution. Only in those cases where the specific kind of club was carefully defined by the interviewer can the results be interpreted with any high degree of confidence, particularly where the question concerns the mother's estimate of the father's activities rather than her own clubs. In general, the American mothers belonged to more clubs of various types than did the Mexican mothers. Nineteen percent of the American mothers belonged to religious clubs, compared to only 6 percent for the Mexican mothers. Not a single Mexican mother claimed membership in any business or professional club, although 7 percent of the American mothers belonged to one or more such organizations. Nor did any Mexican mothers belong to any cultural or educational organizations, although 14 percent of the American mothers claimed membership in such clubs.

The greatest number of mothers in both cultures belonged to one or more social organizations of a fraternal, athletic, charitable, or service nature. Three-fourths of the lower-class mothers in both cultures belonged to no social clubs. Among the upper-class mothers, slightly over half of the Mexican and slightly under half of the American mothers belonged to no social clubs. The most significant difference between the two cultures concerned the upper-class mothers who claimed membership in two or more social organizations. While only 5 percent of the upper-class Mexican mothers could name two or more social clubs to which they belonged, one out of four upper-class American mothers claimed membership in at least two such organizations. An even more striking cultural difference is present when the level of activity in clubs is considered. Among the upper-class American women, 40 percent stated that they spent a great amount of time on club activity, while only 13 percent of upper-class women in Mexico made such a statement.

*Special Interests of Mother and Father.* The following question was used as a basis for determining any special interests on the part of either the mother or father: "Do you or your husband have any special sports, interests, or hobbies in which you are presently active?" The kinds of special interests held by the father in each culture according to social class are given in Table 10-1. American fathers tended to have slightly more special interests than their Mexican counterparts, regardless of social class. The most popular interest was sports and related physical activities. This was about the only special interest indicated for lower-class Mexican fathers. Only the upper-class fathers were perceived by their wives as having special interests in intellectual activities. With the exception of one lower-class American father, the same held for special interests in artistic activities.

Table 10-2 contains similar results for the special interests expressed by the mother. In general, the mothers mentioned special interests of their own less frequently than they did the special interests of their husbands. As with the fathers, only the American mothers showed any special interests in intellectual or artistic activities. The American mothers also mentioned special interests in domestic activities, such as sewing and cooking. Among the Mexican mothers only sports were mentioned to any significant degree as a special interest in which they were presently active.

*Watching Television.* The number of hours per week that the mother watched television is significantly different in the two cultures when the age of the child is taken into account. In Table 10-3 it can be seen that no appreciable difference existed between the

Table 10-1
Kinds of Special Interests in Which the Father Was Active, according to the Mother

| Type Interest | Lower Class United States | Mexico | Upper Class United States | Mexico |
|---|---|---|---|---|
| None | 53% | 75% | 49% | 62% |
| Sports | 33% | 23% | 31% | 32% |
| Hobbies (crafts) | 10% | 1% | 8% | 4% |
| Intellectual activities | 0 | 0 | 6% | 0 |
| Artistic activities | 2% | 0 | 5% | 0 |
| Other | 2% | 1% | 1% | 2% |
| Total number responding | 57 | 59 | 134 | 143 |

Table 10-2
Kinds of Special Interests in Which the Mother Was Active

| Type Interest | Lower Class | | Upper Class | |
|---|---|---|---|---|
| | United States | Mexico | United States | Mexico |
| None | 68% | 85% | 54% | 75% |
| Sports | 8% | 11% | 11% | 24% |
| Hobbies (crafts) | 2% | 0 | 5% | 0 |
| Intellectual activities | 2% | 0 | 6% | 0 |
| Artistic activities | 2% | 0 | 5% | a |
| Domestic activities | 18% | 2% | 17% | 1% |
| Other | 0 | 2% | 2% | a |
| Total number responding | 59 | 60 | 142 | 142 |

a Percentage less than 1.

Table 10-3
Average Number of Hours per Week of Television Viewing by Mothers

| Age Group of Child | Mexico | United States |
|---|---|---|
| I | 11.6 | 8.5 |
| II | 9.5 | 7.7 |
| III | 8.1 | 8.7 |

American and Mexican mothers of teen-age children (Group III), both of them averaging about eight hours per week of television viewing. Among the younger children, however, especially those in the fourth grade at the time of the interview (Group I), television watching was more prevalent among the Mexican mothers than the American. Lower-class mothers in both cultures tended to watch television more often than upper-class mothers, a difference of two hours per week of viewing time on the average.

The number of hours per week that father watched television is also highly significant across both social class and culture, although there is no interaction between the age of the child and either culture or social class. According to the mothers' best estimates, the American father watched television an average of 9.7 hours per week, as compared to the Mexican father, who watched television for 7.0 hours per week on the average. As in the case of the mothers, lower-class fathers watched television more often than upper-class ones.

*Working Mothers.* A significant interaction between social class and culture is present when considering whether or not the mother worked outside the home. Among the Mexicans there was no difference between upper and lower social classes; only 9 percent of the mothers in either group worked outside the home to earn extra income for the family. Among the American mothers, 52 percent of the lower-class mothers worked, while only 31 percent of the upper-class mothers held jobs outside the family. In general, the great majority of Mexican mothers served as housewives, which was not generally true of the American mothers. Nearly all the working mothers in either culture were employed in office work or as teachers in the schools.

*Neighborhood and Home Ratings by the Interviewer.* Immediately following the interview with the mother, the interviewer completed a rating schedule, judging in a comparative way the amount of traffic around the house, the compactness of dwelling units in the neighborhood, the amount of play space for children, the general status of the neighborhood, the type of dwelling unit in which the family lived, the condition inside the home, the home furnishings, the amount of living space in the home, the condition of the yard, lawn, and grounds, a comparison of the home with others in the neighborhood, and ratings of the parent's level of grammar and pronunciation, degree of loquacity, amount of cordiality expressed to the interviewer, and personal appearance. While these scales are admittedly subjective and therefore highly difficult to interpret with respect to cross-cultural differences or even, to a large degree, for any differences involving social class, some of the results are nevertheless of interest in defining more specifically the nature of family life style and social class in the two cultures. Upper-class families in both cultures lived on larger lots than did lower-class families. This difference was especially marked in Mexico, as evidenced by a highly significant interaction between social class and culture. Among the Americans, the difference between lower- and upper-class dwelling units, as far as the size of the lot and spaciousness of the area is concerned, was only slight. In a similar manner, no difference was found for lower- and upper-class Americans while a major difference was found in favor of better conditions for upper-class Mexicans in the amount of children's play space.

Lower-class families generally lived in unpretentious but neat homes, while upper-class families lived in larger homes in established status areas. A rather curious finding concerned the highly significant difference in the type of neighborhood in which boys and girls in the study lived. In every case except that of the upper-class Mexican family, the boys in the study came from more deteriorated neighborhoods than did the girls. It may well be that families with daughters make special efforts, where they have the means to do so, to move into a more acceptable neighborhood than is the case when only boys are present in the family.

Conditions inside the home were judged by the interviewers to be generally well kept for the families with tenth-grade children but considerably less so for the younger families, regardless of social class or culture. As one would expect, upper-class families were judged to have neater homes than lower-class families. Furnishings within the home were of better decor in families with girls than in families with boys. The older the family, the better the condition of the furnishings. The same finding held for the condition of the yard and the lawn outside the home.

Regardless of culture, lower-class mothers were judged by the interviewer to use poorer grammar and to be less talkative, less cordial, and less well dressed than upper-class mothers. These findings are entirely consistent with the general definition of upper and lower social class on the basis of father's education and occupation.

## Socialization of the Child

Many of the items in the interview schedule were designed to evaluate the extent to which the family provides a stimulating environment for social and cultural development, as well as the development of certain artistic and recreational skills. Some items deal with important aspects of the child's early socialization within the family, while others are concerned more directly with current activities—special lessons, recreation as a family, and shared activities between the parents and the child. These items that deal specifically with intellectual stimulation will be taken up separately because of their special importance as environmental forces within the home that may influence the child's development of cognitive abilities.

*Number and Variety of Family Recreational Activities.* Only culture proved to be significant as a variable accounting for whether or not the family engaged in any type of family recreation, although there was a strong trend toward an interaction between social class and culture. Fifty-two percent of both the lower- and upper-class families in Mexico claimed to have at least one kind of special family recreation in which the entire family participated. Among the American families, this percentage rose to 63 percent for lower-class families and 71 percent for upper-class families.

In both cultures and for both social classes, sports and physical activities constituted the preferred family recreation for the large majority. Of those mothers who stated a type of recreation in which the entire family participated, 78 percent in both cultures preferred sports or physical activities. The lower-class families in both cultures showed an even higher percentage, 86 percent, as compared to 74 percent for upper-class families.

*Number and Variety of Places Visited as a Family.* The Americans tended to take more trips and visit a larger variety of places each year than the Mexican families. Only 14 percent of the American families claimed they made no trips of any kind during the year, whereas 26 percent of the Mexican mothers made such a statement. A significant interaction was obtained between age group, culture, and social class. Among all upper-class families of both cultures, as well as lower-class Americans, families of all ages traveled frequently. Among lower-class Mexicans, only 53 percent of the youngest families took at least one trip per year; this percentage increased consistently to 85 percent for the oldest families. While lower-class Mexican parents might travel frequently themselves, many did not take the family on major trips until the children were older. The most frequently stated reason for making a trip was recreational; 58 percent of the families in both cultures stated this purpose for family trips. Visiting friends or relatives was the stated purpose for trips made by 8 percent of the families. While no Mexican families gave educational or intellectual enrichment as the primary purpose of a trip, six American families did. The remaining 13 percent in both cultures stated some combination of the above reasons as the primary purpose of any trip participated in by the entire family.

*Special Lessons for the Child.* Information was obtained from each mother concerning the nature of any special lessons or instructions outside of school in which the child was currently engaged. Usually such special lessons were directed toward the attainment by the child of special social, intellectual, or athletic skills, such as dancing, piano playing, or swimming. A significant interaction between social class and culture was found when the presence or absence of special lessons currently in progress for the child was analyzed. Among the Americans, no differences were obtained between the lower and the upper class; in 44 percent of the American families, the child was taking special lessons in at least one area. Among the upper-class Mexican families, 36 percent of the children were taking special lessons, while in the lower class only 13 percent were currently involved in such instruction outside of school. The age of the child is also of some importance in differentiating Mexican from American families with respect to any special instruction outside of school. Among the families in the youngest and oldest groups, there were no significant differences between the American and Mexican children. For Group II, where the children were currently in the seventh grade, 51 percent of the American families were involved in special lessons for the child, while only 21 percent of the Mexicans were so engaged.

*Other Shared Activities with Child.* Several items in the interview asked about any special times when the family was together routinely or any special activities in which the father or mother took part with the child. Neither social class nor culture made any significant difference with respect to the special times that the family was together routinely. Only 8 percent of the families in either social class in both cultures claimed they were unable to get together at any time on a regular basis. The great majority (62 percent) get together at least at mealtimes, if not for other occasions. The remaining 30 percent regularly congregated at times other than meals.

When asked about any special activities that the father shared with the child, the range of responses obtained proved to be significantly different across several of the main factors studied. An interaction between social class and culture resulted from the rather high number of lower-class American fathers who shared activities with their children (72 percent), compared to the relatively small number of lower-class Mexican fathers who did so (42 percent). In the upper class in both cultures, the difference proved to be insignificant—65 percent of the American fathers and 53 percent of the Mexican fathers shared activities to some extent with the children. A significant interaction between the age and sex of the child was also obtained. Among the younger children (fourth-graders) fathers shared activities considerably more with sons than with daughters. This difference decreased consistently with age, although at all ages fathers shared more with sons than with daughters. The differential treatment of sons and daughters by the father was significantly greater among lower-class families than upper-class ones in both cultures.

Analysis of activities that the mother shared with the child also shows significant but complex interactions among age group, culture, social class, and the sex of the child. As one would expect, in general the mother shared activities more with the daughter than with the son. The only exception to this general rule was the lower-class family in both cultures for the youngest children, where the mother tended to favor the boy rather than the girl. A significant interaction between social class and culture arises because only 48 percent of the lower-class Mexican mothers shared any activities with the child, as contrasted to the majority of mothers (60 percent) among the Americans and among the upper-class Mexicans.

*Television Watching by the Child.* About 10 percent of the children in both cultures watched television as much as twenty hours a week. There were no cultural differences in television watching by the child, nor were there any interactions between culture and any of the other variables with respect to this activity. Boys tended to watch television more often than girls—about twelve hours per week on the average for boys, as compared to ten per week for girls. Children in lower-class families tended to watch television more often than those in upper-class families—twelve and ten hours per week on the average respectively. Television watching was a pervasive activity in both cultures and social classes. Only 6 percent of the children in both cultures failed to watch television at least three hours per week.

*Child's Use of Free Time.* The mother was asked to estimate how the child used his free time. The results are presented in

Table 10-4. In only 1 percent of the cases in both cultures did the mother feel the child had no free time. Over twice as many American mothers said that their child usually spent his free time with a friend: 12 percent, as compared to only 5 percent for Mexican mothers. Slightly more Mexican mothers (55 percent) stated that their child spent most of his free time in group activities than was the case for the American mothers (46 percent). American children tended to spend more free time alone (38 percent) than Mexican children (27 percent).

*Parental Help in Choosing Child's Friends.* Mexican mothers helped to choose their children's friends significantly more often (56 percent) than did the American mothers (32 percent). Although slightly more mothers (47 percent) helped choose their daughters' friends than was the case for sons (40 percent), the trend is not statistically significant. No systematic differences were observed between the two social classes or across the three age groups, nor were there any significant interactions involving any of the main factors in the design.

*Child's Duties in the Home.* The extent to which the child is given a useful role in helping with the family chores can also be a form of socialization that helps to instill a sense of discipline and responsibility. When considering children who had no duties whatsoever in the home as compared to those who had at least one hour a week of regular chores, several significant results emerged. Only 12 percent of the American children had no duties in the home, as compared with three times as many (36 percent) in the Mexican homes. Regardless of social class, all but four American children in the two youngest groups had regularly assigned duties in the home. Only among the oldest group of upper-class American

Table 10-4
Child's Use of Free Time, according to the Mother

| Response | United States | Mexico |
| --- | --- | --- |
| No free time | 1% | 1% |
| Mostly alone | 38% | 27% |
| Usually with a friend | 12% | 5% |
| Mostly group activities | 46% | 55% |
| Other | 3% | 12% |
| Total number responding | 199 | 173 |

teen-agers did the percentage of children without any chores in the home (21 percent) rise to anywhere near the level characteristic of the Mexican families. A sex-by-culture interaction indicated that boys were not given duties in the home nearly as often in Mexico as were the girls, whereas among the American children there was no sex difference. This trend was particularly characteristic of the upper-class Mexican family, where slightly less than half of the boys had any chores in the home. The number of hours spent at such activities by the child tended to be rather low on the average. In both cultures only 10 percent of the children spent more than five hours a week on duties in the home. The great majority of these children were girls rather than boys.

## Intellectual Stimulation of the Child

*Newspapers and Magazines in the Home.* The great majority of the American families received at least one newspaper regularly in the home. Only 18 out of 203 families subscribed to no newspapers. A significant age-group by social-class by culture interaction emerged, due to the fact that in Mexico only the upper-class families characteristically received newspapers regularly in the home (about 80 percent). Among the lower-class Mexican families, the number receiving newspapers in the home rose steadily with the age of the child, from 47 percent among the youngest families to 56 percent in Group II and 75 percent among the oldest families.

News magazines and magazines of general interest constitute another sign of an intellectually stimulating home environment. Upper-class families generally tended to take more magazines than did lower-class families, regardless of culture. A major cultural difference was also discovered; only 20 percent of American families failed to take at least one general-interest magazine, while 45 percent of the Mexican families had no general-interest magazine in the homes. The same proved to be the case for women's magazines dealing with fashions, clothes, and home furnishings; only 18 percent of the Mexican families had such magazines in their homes, as compared to 38 percent of the Americans. Intellectual, scientific, and technical magazines were relatively rare in the Mexican home, although they were not unusual in the American home. Not a single lower-class Mexican family had any intellectual magazines in the home. Only the youngest lower-class families in Austin failed to have any intellectual magazines in the home. While only 31 percent of the upper-class Americans in Group I subscribed to intellectual, scientific, or technical magazines, this percentage rose steadily with the age of the family, reaching 44 percent in Group II and 52 percent in Group III. The lower-class Americans in Groups II and III also showed significant gains in the percentage of families subscribing to intellectual magazines, 24 and 40 percent respectively. Regardless of age, only one in five Mexican families of upper-class status subscribed to intellectual, scientific, or technical magazines.

The mother was also asked by the interviewer to report on the extent to which the child read newspapers or magazines that might be in the home. Readership of news magazines increased markedly with the age of the child in both cultures, especially for boys. The reading of intellectual, technical, and scientific magazines by the child was relatively rare among the younger children in both cultures but not uncommon among the older American children. Fashion magazines were read primarily by the older girls in the family.

*Dictionary and Encyclopedia in the Home.* Possession of either a dictionary or encyclopedia or both in the home was almost universal among American families. Only one out of the entire Austin sample failed to have either a dictionary or an encyclopedia. In Mexico, all but 9 percent of the families had at least one or the other study aid. Among American families, no social-class differences were observed in the possession of dictionaries or encyclopedias. The great majority (79 percent) had both a dictionary and an encyclopedia for the child to use in his studies. Among Mexican families, a significant difference existed between the lower and upper social classes: for the upper class, 36 percent had only an encyclopedia, and 38 percent had both an encyclopedia and a dictionary for the child to use. The figures for lower-class Mexican families are 22 percent and 23 percent respectively.

Use of the dictionary or encyclopedia by the child for his studies is perhaps more important than mere possession of such study aids. According to the mother's estimate, half of the American children, regardless of social class, used the dictionary or encyclopedia a great deal. Only 13 percent of the lower-class Mexican children and 20 percent of the upper-class Mexican children apparently made much use of either the dictionary or the encyclopedia.

*Mother's Recollection of Preschool Reading, Counting, or Writing.* "Before the child could read, did the mother or father read to the child?" This question was answered negatively by 23 percent of the Mexican families but by less than 1 percent of the American. The majority of American parents, regardless of social class, claimed that they read to the child very regularly (60 percent), as contrasted to only 13 percent of the Mexican parents. One explanation of this cultural difference may be the fact that many Mexican parents frequently tell stories to their children but do not read to them. Story-telling by American parents has been largely replaced by reading from children's books.

"Could the child read, count, or write before school?" No significant differences were uncovered between upper and lower classes in either culture in answer to this question. In general, 59 percent of the Mexican mothers said that their child could not do any of these three tasks before entering school. Only 22 percent of American mothers replied in a similar manner; half of them stated that their child could do at least two of these three tasks before entering school.

*Active Encouragement of Child's Reading.* Several questions concerned the extent to which the mother actively encouraged the child to read and the manner in which she carried out this encouragement. The majority of mothers in both cultures and both social classes did not make any special efforts to encourage their child to read. Where such encouragement was given, it more often appeared among upper-class Mexican mothers (40 percent) than among upper-class American mothers (19 percent). The same trend was apparent to a lesser degree among the lower-class mothers in the two cultures: one out of four lower-class Mexican mothers actively encouraged her child to read, while only one out of nine lower-class American mothers gave an unqualified "yes" to this question. The Mexican mothers tended to be more insistent in keeping after the child to read than the American mothers. Indeed, seven of the American mothers even stated that they actively discouraged reading by the child, a response nonexistent among the Mexican mothers.

*Languages Spoken in the Home.* Among the upper-class Mexican families, the majority (63 percent) had members who spoke a foreign language. This figure dropped to 35 percent for lower-class Mexican families. Among the American families there was no difference between lower and upper classes; only one out of four families had a member who spoke a foreign language.

*Parents in School Themselves.* With increased commitment to adult education in both cultures, it is of some interest to see the extent to which parents in the Austin and Mexico City samples were themselves taking academic or vocational courses that would set examples for their children. While the majority of fathers of all age groups and both cultures and social classes were not currently taking any courses of an academic or vocational nature at the time of the interview, enough were actively involved to make some interesting comparisons. Among the upper-class Mexican fathers, 17 percent were taking one or more courses, as compared to only 10 percent for the upper-class American fathers. The great majority of American fathers who were taking any courses came from the youngest families in Group I, whereas the Mexican fathers were scattered more equally across all three age groups. Less than 10 percent of the lower-class fathers in either culture were taking any courses at the time of the interview.

An even smaller number of the mothers were taking any academic or vocational courses. While upper-class mothers in both cultures tended to take slightly more courses than lower-class ones, the difference was not great enough to be significant. No trends were discernible across the different age groups. In general, about one out of every eleven mothers was taking some kind of academic or vocational course at the time of the interview.

*Teaching Experience of Father and Mother.* Since teachers make up a significant portion of the general population, it is not surprising that a number of parents had had professional experience as teachers, at least among the upper-class families in both cultures. Only three fathers and six mothers among all the lower-class families in both Austin and Mexico City had ever had any teaching experience of an academic or vocational nature. Among the upper class, however, one-third of the American fathers and one out of six Mexican fathers had had teaching experience. Of the upper-class mothers, one out of five Americans and one out of seven

Mexicans had had teaching experience of either an academic or a vocational nature. In twenty-one of the upper-class families, both mother and father were teachers. Among both the Mexican and American fathers who had had teaching experience, the great majority (83 percent) were college teachers. Only four of the mothers in the entire combined sample were college teachers, the majority being teachers in the elementary or high schools.

## Parental Aspirations for the Child

While only a few items deal specifically with the parents' hopes and expectations for the child's development, this area is of sufficient importance in the study of the home environment as it affects child development to justify examining in detail what information is available.

*Degree of Mother's Satisfaction with the Child's Progress in School.* A four-point scale ranging from "very dissatisfied" to "very satisfied" was employed for measuring the degree of the mother's satisfaction with the child's progress in school. Among upper-class children, the degree of satisfaction of the Mexican mothers rose with increasing age, while the satisfaction of the American mothers dropped. Among lower-class families, the satisfaction of the Mexican mothers first rose and then fell with increasing age, while the satisfaction of the American mothers remained uniformly high at all ages. It must be remembered that the Mexican mothers, even in the upper-class families, tended to be relatively uneducated as compared to the American mothers. It is quite possible that the Mexican mother is proud of her children doing better than she did, while the American mother has higher expectations that fail to materialize when the child reaches high school. This significant interaction between culture, age group, and social class is presented in Table 10-5.

*Amount of Education Parent Wants Child to Have.* When asked how much education the mother would like her child to receive, the overwhelming majority in both cultures wanted their children to have a college education. Among the American mothers, aspirations were uniformly high for sons and daughters. Among Mexican mothers, however, aspirations for sons were even higher than in the case of American mothers, while their hopes for daughters fell considerably lower in the amount of education that would be

Table 10-5
Mother's Satisfaction with Child's Progress in School

| Age Group of Child | Percent of Mothers Satisfied | | | |
| | Lower Class | | Upper Class | |
| | United States | Mexico | United States | Mexico |
|---|---|---|---|---|
| I | 73 | 47 | 83 | 76 |
| II | 80 | 80 | 88 | 71 |
| III | 80 | 55 | 65 | 88 |

ideal. Mothers from upper-class families in both cultures had higher aspirations than those in lower-class families.

A more realistic question is the minimum amount of education that the mother feels the child *must* receive. All four main effects in the analysis of variance proved to be highly significant. The older the child, the higher the minimum amount of education that the mother felt the child must receive. Upper-class mothers in both cultures, American mothers of both social classes, and mothers of boys all had significantly higher aspirations than did their opposite counterparts. For the overwhelming majority of families in both cultures, parents strongly believed that their children should have at least as much education as they themselves had had. In most cases, of course, the aspirations were considerably higher.

A closer look at the specific grade level indicated by the parent as a minimum education her child must receive reveals an interesting sex-by-culture interaction. In general, the aspiration level for American parents centered around obtaining a college degree or falling short of it. For Mexican parents, the critical grade level was completing high school or falling short of it. Among the American boys, 71 percent of their mothers felt that completion of a college degree at the bachelor's level was the minimum education they must receive. For American girls, however, the mother's aspiration for completion of a college degree as a minimum fell to only 30 percent, a marked sex difference favoring higher education for the boys. Among the Mexican boys, 71 percent of the mothers believed that completion of high school was the minimum education they must receive. For Mexican girls, this figure fell only slightly to 64 percent, an insignificant difference from the boys. No sex differences are apparent for the Mexicans when considering the critical point of completing high school, although the Americans show a marked sex difference favoring the boys with respect to completing college.

*Type of Work Desired for Child When Grown.* The mother was asked what type of work she would like to see her child do when grown. Separate analyses were made for sons and daughters. Two-thirds of the American mothers (63 percent) expressed no preference, a point of view taken by only one-third of the Mexican mothers (36 percent). The majority of Mexican mothers of all social classes wanted their sons to go into the highest levels of professional work (61 percent) as contrasted to only 32 percent of the American mothers. Only a tiny handful of mothers in either culture expressed a desire for their sons to engage in any kind of work below the professional level.

The type of work desired for daughters was divided more broadly into no preference, general area, and specific occupation. As in the case of the aspirations for boys, no social-class differences were observed, only cultural ones. Specific choices of an occupation were made three times as often by Mexican mothers (62 percent) as by American mothers (21 percent). The majority of American mothers (59 percent) expressed no preference for the kind of work they desired for their daughters, as compared to only 41 percent of Mexican mothers.

*Father's Satisfaction with Work.* Related to aspirations for the child's occupational level when grown is the degree of satisfaction that the father appears to have with his own work. The mothers were asked to rate the degree of satisfaction that their husbands had with their present work conditions on a four-point scale, ranging from very dissatisfied to very satisfied. Pooling together the two levels of dissatisfaction and the two levels of satisfaction yielded the following results: The highest proportion of satisfied fathers occurred in upper-class American families (94 percent). At the opposite extreme were the lower-class American fathers (58 percent), followed closely by the lower-class Mexicans (61 percent). The upper-class Mexicans fell between these two extremes (70 percent) in the proportion of fathers who appear to be satisfied with their present work. Further inquiry revealed that the father had previously wanted to enter another kind of work in one-third of the cases. Regardless of culture or social class, the majority of disappointed fathers (78 percent) had wanted a professional career and had failed to achieve it.

## Parental Interest in Academic Progress of the Child

Several items in the interview schedule deal specifically with the amount of interest and involvement of the parents in the progress of the child in his school work. Some of these concern the extent to which the parents discuss matters between them or with the child, while others deal with the extent of homework the child has and the involvement of the parents in helping with the homework. Still others deal with the kinds of contacts between the parents and teachers, as well as the purpose of the contacts.

*Discussion between Parents concerning the Child's Progress in School.* While the majority of parents in both cultures and social classes discussed among themselves how the child was doing in school, it is interesting to note that 15 percent of the Mexican mothers never discussed with their husbands how the child was getting along in school, while only 6 percent of the American parents failed to discuss this topic. A significant interaction between social class, culture, and the sex of the child emerged from the analysis of variance. When the mother's responses are divided into "never" or "seldom," as compared to "often" or "very often," different results are obtained in the two cultures for upper- and lower-class sons and daughters. Among Mexican lower-class parents, the progress of daughters was discussed more often than the progress of sons, while the reverse was true for the upper-class Mexican families. The majority of American parents with boys often discussed their child's progress among themselves, regardless of social class. The same was not true for girls in the American family; lower-class parents did not often discuss the progress of their daughters, while upper-class parents frequently discussed their daughters' progress. In general, Mexican parents discussed among themselves more frequently how their children were getting along in school than Americans. These results are summarized in Table 10-6.

Topics discussed most often by parents when talking together about how their child was getting along in school are presented in Table 10-7. In general, the American parents were able to specify the topics they discussed more frequently than were the Mexican parents. Only the general progress and efforts made by the child in

Table 10-6
Frequency of Discussion by Parents of Child's Progress in School

|  | Parents Answering "Often" | |
|---|---|---|
|  | United States (%) | Mexico (%) |
| Lower class | | |
| Parents of sons | 60 | 50 |
| Parents of daughters | 27 | 79 |
| Upper class | | |
| Parents of sons | 60 | 82 |
| Parents of daughters | 56 | 70 |

Table 10-7
Topics Discussed by Parents concerning Child's Progress in School
(Expressed in Frequencies)

Homework Assignments

|  |  | United States | Mexico |
|---|---|---|---|
| Age group | I | 15 | 9 |
|  | II | 18 | 2 |
|  | III | 7 | 4 |
| Total |  | 40 | 15 |

General Progress and Effort of the Child

|  |  | United States | Mexico |
|---|---|---|---|
| Age group | I | 36 | 35 |
|  | II | 50 | 43 |
|  | III | 44 | 38 |
| Total |  | 130 | 116 |

Relation of Child to His Peers

|  |  | United States | Mexico |
|---|---|---|---|
| Age group | I | 2 | 2 |
|  | II | 10 | 1 |
|  | III | 0 | 2 |
| Total |  | 12 | 5 |

Relation of Child to Teachers and School Authorities

|  |  | United States | Mexico |
|---|---|---|---|
| Age group | I | 8 | 3 |
|  | II | 5 | 0 |
|  | III | 3 | 2 |
| Total |  | 16 | 5 |

school showed any strong degree of comparability between the Mexican and American parents. Discussing the relation of the child to his peers, a more social topic than the others, was very rare except among the parents of American seventh-graders (Group II).

*Parental Discussion with Child concerning His School Work.* The mother was asked to rate how often she or her husband discussed with their child the child's progress in school. An analysis of variance of these ratings yielded only one highly significant effect. Mexican parents stated that they discussed his progress in school with the child much more often than was the case with American parents.

The mother was also asked by the interviewer to indicate which parents typically talked to the child about progress in school. Table 10-8 summarizes the results of this analysis. In only 4 percent of the cases in both cultures and social classes was there no communication between either parent and the child concerning progress in school. In only 3 percent of the cases did the father alone assume this role. The most common approach, with the exception of the lower-class Mexican family, was for both parents to talk to the child. Among lower-class Mexican families, responsibility for discussing school progress with the child fell generally upon the shoulders of the mother.

The percentages of parents who discussed school assignments with their children are presented in Tables 10-9 and 10-10 for the highly significant interactions obtained between social class, culture, and sex and between age group and culture. For American

Table 10-8
Which Parent Discussed School Progress with Child

|  | Neither (%) | Father (%) | Mother (%) | Both Parents (%) |
|---|---|---|---|---|
| Lower class |  |  |  |  |
| United States | 2 | 3 | 32 | 63 |
| Mexico | 7 | 3 | 61 | 29 |
| Upper class |  |  |  |  |
| United States | 1 | 3 | 26 | 70 |
| Mexico | 7 | 3 | 38 | 52 |
| All groups combined | 4 | 3 | 36 | 57 |

Table 10-9
Parents Who Discussed School Assignments with Their Child, by Social Class,
Culture, and Sex

|  | Lower Class | | Upper Class | |
|  | United States (%) | Mexico (%) | United States (%) | Mexico (%) |
| --- | --- | --- | --- | --- |
| Parents of boys | 34 | 51 | 32 | 12 |
| Parents of girls | 55 | 23 | 28 | 25 |

Table 10-10
Parents Who Discussed School Assignments with Their Child,
by Age Group and Culture

| Age Group | United States (%) | Mexico (%) |
| --- | --- | --- |
| I | 38 | 50 |
| II | 42 | 22 |
| III | 33 | 11 |

boys no differences in social class are apparent; but, in the case of American girls, lower-class parents were more likely to discuss assignments with their daughters than were upper-class parents. The reverse was true for the Mexican families. For Mexican girls, no differences in social class are apparent, while for Mexican boys, more lower-class parents discussed assignments with the child. Only 12 percent of the parents of upper-class boys discussed school assignments with their sons. From Table 10-10 it can be seen that, as the Mexican child grew older, there was less communication between the parents and the child with respect to school assignments, a marked trend that was absent in the American families.

The same interaction between culture and age was found for the percentages of parents who discussed with their child his over-all progress and efforts in school. In Table 10-11, it can be seen that little difference between the two cultures existed for the younger groups. Among the tenth-grade teen-agers, however, 83 percent of the American parents talked to their child about his progress, while only 43 percent of the Mexican parents discussed this matter with their children.

*Amount of Homework.* The mother was asked to estimate the amount of homework that her child had each day. A tabulation of results obtained for each of the three age groups and the two cultures is given in Table 10-12. A striking interaction between the age of the child and the culture is apparent. Among the youngest children in both samples, homework was a rarity in the American family, while it was universally present in the Mexican home. By the seventh grade (Group II), the majority of American children had some homework, while the Mexican children continued universally to have a heavy homework load each day. By the tenth grade (Group III), a small percentage of Mexican children had little or no homework, but the great majority still had a heavier homework load than was characteristic of the American tenth-grader. Much of this difference may be due to the facts that study halls are common in American schools and that many of the courses, especially in the lower grade levels, are designed as self-contained units with provision for most of the learning to take

Table 10-11
Parents Who Discussed with Their Child His General Progress and Effort in School

| Age Group | United States (%) | Mexico (%) |
|---|---|---|
| I | 38 | 31 |
| II | 69 | 65 |
| III | 83 | 43 |

Table 10-12
Mother's Estimate of the Amount of Homework the Child Had

| | None or Only Occasionally (%) | About ½ Hour per Day (%) | 1–2 Hours per Day (%) | More than 2 Hours per Day (%) |
|---|---|---|---|---|
| Age group I | | | | |
| United States | 82 | 9 | 7 | 2 |
| Mexico | 0 | 17 | 67 | 16 |
| Age group II | | | | |
| United States | 36 | 24 | 36 | 4 |
| Mexico | 0 | 22 | 55 | 23 |
| Age group III | | | | |
| United States | 15 | 20 | 53 | 12 |
| Mexico | 8 | 9 | 44 | 39 |
| All ages combined | | | | |
| United States | 42 | 18 | 34 | 6 |
| Mexico | 2 | 17 | 55 | 26 |

place in the classroom. The Mexican school, on the other hand, expects the child right from the beginning to develop strong habits of independent work outside the classroom. Children in the elementary grades are usually graded fairly severely in Mexico, whereas the "social pass" is not uncommon in the American school.

Related to the estimated amount of homework is the mother's opinion concerning whether there is too much, too little, or just the right amount of homework for her child. Inspection of Table 10-13 shows that the great majority of mothers in both cultures and both social classes (73 percent) believed their child received an appropriate amount of homework. A cultural difference is apparent among upper-class families, where the dissatisfied American mother believed her child received too little homework and the unhappy Mexican mother thought her child received too much.

*Type of Homework.* The mother was asked to indicate in which school subjects her child usually had homework; as can be seen in Table 10-14, mathematics and science homework were highest among the Mexican fourth-graders, falling off with increasing age; the reverse appeared to be true for the American children. The areas of English, reading, and language show a similar drop for the Mexican child; for the American, the percentages having at least some homework in these areas remained fairly stable across the three age groups. History, geography, and the social sciences did not account for much homework among the youngest children in either sample. No significant interactions emerged involving age group and culture, the Americans in all groups having more homework in this area than the Mexicans. When interpret-

Table 10-13
Mother's Opinion concerning the Amount of Homework Given Child

|  | Too Little (%) | Appropriate (%) | Too Much (%) |
|---|---|---|---|
| Lower class |  |  |  |
| United States | 8 | 82 | 10 |
| Mexico | 15 | 71 | 14 |
| Upper class |  |  |  |
| United States | 21 | 73 | 6 |
| Mexico | 13 | 69 | 18 |
| All groups combined | 15 | 73 | 12 |

Table 10-14
School Subjects Mentioned by Mother in Which Child Usually Had Homework

|  |  | United States (%) | Mexico (%) |
|---|---|---|---|
| | | *Mathematics and Science* | |
| Age group | I | 66 | 89 |
| | II | 88 | 70 |
| | III | 78 | 50 |
| | | *English, Reading, and Language* | |
| Age group | I | 59 | 68 |
| | II | 43 | 52 |
| | III | 56 | 32 |
| | | *Social Science, History, and Geography* | |
| Age group | I | 18 | 9 |
| | II | 63 | 48 |
| | III | 56 | 25 |

ing these results concerning the type of homework, it must be kept in mind that the figures reported are a result of the mother's awareness of what homework the child was doing. It may be more an index of what the mother felt was important at the moment than of what homework was actually assigned within the schools.

*Helping the Child with Homework.* The mother was asked how often the child was helped with school homework. A tabulation of responses to this question is given in Table 10-15. A significant

Table 10-15
How Often Child Was Helped with Homework

|  | Never (%) | Occasionally (%) | Regularly (%) |
|---|---|---|---|
| Age group I | | | |
| United States | 25 | 61 | 14 |
| Mexico | 32 | 4 | 64 |
| Age group II | | | |
| United States | 27 | 56 | 17 |
| Mexico | 63 | 10 | 27 |
| Age group III | | | |
| United States | 43 | 33 | 24 |
| Mexico | 71 | 17 | 12 |
| All ages combined | 44 | 31 | 25 |

interaction is apparent between culture and age group. Among fourth-graders, the Mexican child was helped regularly with his homework, while the American child was given assistance only occasionally. Among the seventh-grade children, the majority of Mexicans received no help within the family, while the majority of Americans were given help occasionally. Among tenth-graders, the percentage of children receiving no help in the Mexican family rose still further. While the comparable figure for the American tenth-grader also rose, an increased percentage of American teenagers were given regular help with their homework.

*Incentives to Encourage Studying.* The mother was asked what reasons were given the child to encourage him to study. Table 10-16 contains a tabulation of the main reasons cited by the mothers. Among American families, it was more common to give no reason but rather just to expect that the child would do his homework. Immediate material rewards were never given as a reason for encouraging study among the American mothers, although a substantial number of Mexican mothers used this incentive. Being prepared for a future job was the most common reason employed by Mexican mothers, while getting through school (and making good grades) was the most common reason employed by American mothers.

*Parental Contact with Child's Teachers.* The last of the items in the interview schedule dealing with parental interest and involvement in the child's school work concerned the frequency of contact between the parent and the child's teachers during the current year. While a significant difference was obtained between the

Table 10-16
Reasons Given Child by Mother to Encourage Studying

| Reason | Lower Class United States (%) | Mexico (%) | Upper Class United States (%) | Mexico (%) |
|---|---|---|---|---|
| None | 46 | 22 | 46 | 24 |
| Immediate material reward | 0 | 25 | 0 | 13 |
| Job preparation | 14 | 34 | 4 | 33 |
| Becoming cultured | 3 | 5 | 1 | 13 |
| Avoiding trouble in future | 7 | 9 | 12 | 5 |
| Getting through school | 27 | 0 | 32 | 8 |
| Emotional satisfaction | 3 | 5 | 5 | 4 |

Mexican and American lower classes, especially among the tenth-graders (Group III), no other trends were apparent. Among the lower-class Mexican families, 68 percent of the parents had repeated contact with the teachers, as compared to only 42 percent for the lower-class Americans. Similar figures for the upper-class Mexicans and Americans were 57 and 52 percent respectively. In general, slightly over half of all the parents had repeated contact with the child's teachers during the year.

## Mother's Assessment of the Child

Several items in the interview ask the mother to rate the child or to compare the child with other children on a particular trait. Special interests the child may have developed, the child's health, and the extent to which he reads unassigned books are all considered part of the mother's assessment of the child.

*Special Interests of the Child.* The mother was asked to indicate the activities, hobbies, pastimes, sports, and other special interests of the child, as well as to indicate the degree of interest the child had in such activities. More special interests were mentioned for boys than for girls in both cultures and both social classes. Twice as many special interests were mentioned for American children (an average of 2.1 per child) as for Mexican children (an average of 1.1 per child). An interaction between age group and sex proved to be significant, regardless of culture. Among fourth-grade children, special interests were indicated for 95 percent of the boys but only 66 percent of the girls. This gap narrowed somewhat in Group II (85 percent for boys and 70 percent for girls) and Group III (93 percent for boys and 76 percent for girls). Among all the American children, only 10 percent had mothers who could not recall any special activities, hobbies, pastimes, or sports for their children, as contrasted to 31 percent among the Mexican children whose mothers said they had no special interests.

The primary special interests of the children according to the mothers are summarized in Table 10-17, where a significant interaction between sex and culture is evident. The most popular activities for boys in both cultures were sports and various hobbies involving crafts and mechanics. Sports were popular in all groups. None of the Mexican girls showed any interests in hobbies or crafts, although 14 percent of the American girls had this as a

Table 10-17
Primary Special Interest of the Child according to the Mother

| Type of Interest | Boys | | Girls | |
|---|---|---|---|---|
| | United States | Mexico | United States | Mexico |
| None | 3% | 17% | 10% | 43% |
| Sports | 44% | 57% | 31% | 37% |
| Hobbies, crafts | 36% | 12% | 14% | 0 |
| Artistic activities | 9% | 4% | 24% | 14% |
| Intellectual activities | 8% | 1% | 9% | 2% |
| Others | 0 | 9% | 12% | 4% |
| Total number responding | 91 | 90 | 106 | 111 |

primary interest. Artistic interests were also popular among American girls and, to a lesser extent, among Mexican girls. Only the American children showed any strong interests in intellectual activities. In general, Mexican girls had fewer interests than any of the other groups; 43 percent of their mothers could think of no special interest that engaged their attention.

*Mother's Assessment of Child's School Performance.* The mother was asked to compare her child's class rank in school with that of his classmates, placing the child in the lower, middle, or upper third of his class. Half of the mothers placed their children in the upper third, while only 7 percent put their children in the lower third of their classes. An understandable positive halo effect undoubtedly affected the mother's judgment of her child's performance in many cases. Lower-class mothers tended to rate their children lower in academic performance than did upper-class mothers, probably reflecting a reality of the classroom. American mothers tended to rate their children higher in comparison to classmates than did the Mexican mothers. There was also a slight but significant tendency to rate girls higher than boys. No interactions among any of the major variables were significant.

*Child's Reading of Unassigned Books.* One indication of intellectual curiosity on the part of the child is the extent to which he reads books voluntarily (excluding comic magazines). Each mother was asked to estimate how much time on a regular basis the child spent reading unassigned books. The results of this analysis are presented in Table 10-18. Differences in social class were present in both cultures. Among the lower-class Mexican families,

38 percent of the children never read unassigned books, as compared to only 23 percent among the upper-class Mexicans. Upper- and lower-class Mexicans had the same percentage of heavy readers. Among the American families, the overwhelming majority of both upper- and lower-class children read unassigned books. The only difference between upper- and lower-class Americans was the larger percentage of heavy readers among the upper-class children.

*Positive and Negative Comments by Parents about Their Child.* The interviewers were trained to listen carefully for any evaluative comments of a positive or negative nature that the mother might make about the child. Nearly all mothers made some positive comments about the child during the interview. Only three American mothers and twelve Mexican mothers failed to make a single positive statement. Comments by forty-four of the American mothers were highly enthusiastic, whereas only three of the Mexican mothers were observed to make very positive comments about their children. This difference is probably a matter of cultural style in expressing one's feelings rather than any inherent difference in evaluation of the child.

In a similar manner, any negative comments made by the mother about the child were recorded. In only 24 percent of the cases were there no negative comments by the mothers. In general, the Mexican mothers were more hesitant to express any negative comments than were the Americans.

Further insight into the manner of expressing approval or dis-

Table 10-18
Mother's Estimate of Extent to Which Child Read Unassigned Books

|  | Never (%) | 3 Hours or Less per Week (%) | More than 3 Hours per Week (%) |
|---|---|---|---|
| Lower class |  |  |  |
| United States | 6 | 72 | 22 |
| Mexico | 38 | 35 | 27 |
| Upper class |  |  |  |
| United States | 9 | 58 | 33 |
| Mexico | 23 | 50 | 27 |
| All groups combined | 18 | 54 | 28 |

approval of the child can be gained by analysis of the mother's responses to queries concerning how she expressed approval of the child and how her husband expressed such approval or disapproval. Table 10-19 summarizes the results for method of expressing approval by the mother. While most of the parents in both cultures employed verbal means of expressing approval, this technique was more prevalent among the Americans. Unlike the Americans, the Mexicans often used material rewards or physical embraces as a means of expressing approval. Similar results were obtained in an analysis of the means for expressing approval of the child used by the father, according to the mother. It is also interesting to note that a combination of different methods was more likely employed by the upper class in both cultures than by lower-class parents.

The general approaches employed by the mothers for disapproving of the child's behavior are given in Table 10-20. No significant differences are apparent across the two cultures. By far the most

Table 10-19
Method Usually Employed by the Mother for Approving of the Child's Behavior

| Method | Lower Class | | Upper Class | |
|---|---|---|---|---|
| | United States | Mexico | United States | Mexico |
| None | 5% | 4% | 7% | 6% |
| Physical expression | 5% | 16% | 4% | 13% |
| Verbal expression | 64% | 58% | 67% | 48% |
| Material reward | 0 | 16% | 0 | 19% |
| Combination | 26% | 6% | 22% | 14% |
| Total number responding | 58 | 55 | 134 | 138 |

Table 10-20
Method Usually Employed by the Mother for Disapproving of the Child's Behavior

| | Lower Class | | Upper Class | |
|---|---|---|---|---|
| | United States | Mexico | United States | Mexico |
| Method | | | | |
| None | 4% | 5% | 3% | 2% |
| Physical punishment | 0 | 3% | 1% | 2% |
| Verbal reprimand | 75% | 65% | 59% | 59% |
| Both physical and verbal methods | 2% | 5% | 5% | 12% |
| Withholding of privileges | 19% | 22% | 32% | 25% |
| Total number responding | 57 | 60 | 137 | 138 |

common technique was verbal reprimand or scolding rather than physical punishment. Among the upper-class families, withholding of privileges and other more complex forms of disapproval were employed more frequently than among the lower-class families in both cultures.

*Serious Illnesses or Accidents Happening to the Child.* In general, children in both cultures and social classes had apparently enjoyed fairly good health. Since no significant differences were found across either culture or social class, only the over-all figure is reported here. In the entire sample, 50 percent of the mothers could recall no serious illness or accident that the child had ever had. Only 11 percent of the children in the entire sample had ever had a serious accident. Ten percent had been chronically ill at one time, while 22 percent of the mothers could recall a serious acute illness.

---

This chapter has presented some of the findings from the individual interviews conducted with the mothers in Mexico and the United States. Included are results for those items on the interview of a demographic and factual nature; the examiners' ratings of the home environment made immediately after each interview; findings for those items dealing with the amount of intellectual press in the family, divided into four separate subenvironmental clusters; and, finally, parents' judgment of their children at the time of the interview.

In Chapter 11 the cross-cultural results from the Parent-Attitude Survey and the Parent Trait Survey, completed by the mothers during the interview sessions, are presented and discussed.

# 11. Attitudes and Values of the Mother

Following the interview of the mother, she was handed the Parent-Attitude Survey (See Appendix B), containing sixty-eight attitude statements followed by a short section called Parent Trait Survey with fifteen traits to be rated according to their importance for bringing up children. A five-choice response continuum followed each attitude statement so that the mother could indicate her degree of agreement or disagreement with the statement. In the coding of data from the Parent-Attitude Survey, Strongly Agree was scored 1, Strongly Disagree was scored 5, and the gradations in between were scored 2, 3, and 4 respectively.[1] Results for the Parent-Attitude Survey will be given first, followed by findings for the Parent Trait Survey.

Originally, when the sixty-eight items were organized into the Parent-Attitude Survey, it was hoped that the intercorrelations among the items would be sufficiently high to reveal important dimensions through factor analysis. Unfortunately, the intercorrelations among the items are generally so low that only two major and two minor dimensions emerged from the factor analysis of

[1] Direction of coding was reversed for the eleven positively phrased items among the fifty items in the Hereford Parental Attitude Scales.

the combined American and Mexican data (Chapter 4). For this reason, the dependent variables used in the analysis of variance are of three kinds: (*a*) the individual items themselves, treated one by one; (*b*) the original clustering of items into scales in accordance with the original source of the item, such as the five scales drawn from Hereford's studies of parental attitudes in Austin; and (*c*) the four factors that emerged from the factor analysis of the total sample. Availability of a high-speed computer makes it possible to run large numbers of complex analyses of variance simultaneously at reasonably low cost.

The analysis-of-variance design for the items and scales in the Parent-Attitude Survey consisted of a three-way design with culture, social class, and age group. Sex was not included in this design, since the attitude statements are rather general and it is unlikely that the sex of the child would make any difference.

## Hereford's Parental Attitude Scales

Each of the five parental attitude scales taken from Hereford's work consists of about ten items, the best items from his original studies. The theoretical range of scaled scores varies from 0 to 45 for Confidence, from 0 to 55 for Causation, and from 0 to 50 for Acceptance, Understanding, and Trust.

*Confidence.* Both culture and social class proved highly significant as independent variables affecting the scores on the Confidence scale. The American mothers received a higher mean score (32.2) than did the Mexican mothers (28.3). In a similar manner, upper-class mothers in both cultures obtained higher scores on Confidence: 31.1, as compared to 29.4 for the lower-class mothers. Individuals with high scores on the Confidence scale tend to agree with such an item as "Raising children isn't as hard as most parents let on" and to disagree with such items as "I feel I am faced with more problems than most parents." The lack of any interactions indicates that these primary differences for culture and social class are present regardless of variation on the other independent variables.

*Causation.* While both culture and social class again proved to be highly significant, a significant interaction between the two variables is of special interest. Among the American parents, no difference in social class for the Causation score was apparent. For the Mexican mothers, however, upper-class respondents received a considerably higher mean score (42.0) than did the lower-class parents (37.3). The mean for American mothers was 45.9, higher than that for either class of Mexican mothers. A parent who receives a high score on Causation tends to agree with such an item as "Most all children are just the same at birth; it's what happens to them afterwards that is important" and to disagree with such an item as "If a child is born bad, there's not much you can do about it."

*Acceptance.* Results in the analysis of variance for the Acceptance scale are essentially the same as for the Confidence scale. Only two of the three main effects, culture and social class, proved to be significant, and no interactions approached significance. American mothers received higher mean scores (33.3) than did the Mexican mothers (27.9). Mothers in the upper social class in both cultures obtained a higher mean score (31.8) than did mothers in the lower-class groups (29.4). Parents who score very high on the Acceptance scale tend to agree with such statements as "If you put too many restrictions on a child, you will stunt his personality" and to disagree with such a statement as "Children should be toilet-trained at the earliest possible time."

*Understanding.* Only culture proved to be highly significant for the Understanding scale, although a difference significant at the .05 level did occur between upper and lower social classes. American mothers obtained a mean score of 41.0, as compared to a mean of 35.9 for Mexican mothers. A person who scores high on Understanding is likely to agree strongly with such an item as "Family life would be happier if parents made children feel they were free to say what they think about anything" and disagree with such items as "Talking to a child about his fears most often makes the fear look more important than it is."

*Trust.* Results for the Trust scale are identical to those obtained for Confidence and Acceptance. The difference between Mexican and American mothers is even greater for this scale than for the other four. American mothers received a mean score of 35.6, as contrasted to only 28.8 for the Mexican mothers. Upper-class mothers in both cultures obtained a mean of 33.5, compared to a mean of 30.9 for lower-class mothers. No interactions approached significance. A person scoring high on Trust is one who would strongly agree with such an item as "Children have a right to activities which do not include their parents" and to disagree with such an item as "Children who are not watched will get into trouble."

The overwhelming number of items in the five Hereford scales are phrased in a negative form, so that disagreeing with the item would represent a contribution to a high score. Only occasionally are positively phrased items included in the scales. Because of this imbalance, it is quite possible that response-set differences across the two cultures and social classes may account for a significant part of the obtained differences in mean responses on the scales. It may well be that Mexican mothers were more hesitant to disagree with an item statement than were American mothers, regardless of the item's content. An individual item analysis comparing positively phrased with negatively phrased items from the same scale is one way of determining the extent to which such differences in style of responding influenced the outcome. Two items of comparable item-total-score correlation from the original Hereford studies were selected from each of the five scales, one positively phrased item and one negatively phrased item, in order to study more systematically the effect of any "tendency to agree" as a response set making interpretation difficult. Items are presented one pair at a time in Table 11-1, together with mean scores for the upper and lower classes in both Mexico City and Austin.

If lower-class mothers and Mexican mothers had a tendency to agree with the statement regardless of its content, this bias will become evident in a comparison of mean scores for the positively and negatively phrased item pairs in each scale.

Item 60 is a negatively phrased item with which most of the Americans disagreed. By contrast, the lower-class Mexican mothers tended to agree with this statement. The upper-class Mexican mothers fell in between. Presumably, the reverse pattern of mean responses would occur in the positively phrased item if tendency to agree were operating strongly. The reason for this reversal, of course, is the fact that the coding of positively phrased items was reversed, so that a response of Strongly Agree was coded 5, rather than 1 as in the negatively phrased items. This reversal must be kept in mind when interpreting the mean scores in Table 11-1 for those items preceded by (+), indicating positive phrasing. What we actually find when we look at Item 1 is no difference across either social class or culture. All four groups got essentially the same mean score for this item. Only the lower-class Mexican mothers show even a slight tendency toward a possible response

Table 11-1
Mean Differences for Positively and Negatively Phrased Items from the
Hereford Parental Attitude Scales

| Item | | | Lower Class U.S. | Lower Class Mex. | Upper Class U.S. | Upper Class Mex. | |
|---|---|---|---|---|---|---|---|
| | | **Confidence Scale** | | | | | |
| (−) | 60. | Parents sacrifice most of their fun for their children. | 3.80 | 1.89 | 4.22 | 2.95 | (* # † |
| (+) | 1. | Raising children isn't as hard as most parents let on. | 3.25 | 3.21 | 3.21 | 3.24 | |
| | | **Causation Scale** | | | | | |
| (−) | 38. | Psychologists now know that what a child is born with determines the kind of person he becomes. | 4.19 | 3.42 | 4.07 | 3.91 | (* † |
| (+) | 13. | Most all children are just the same at birth; it's what happens to them afterwards that is important. | 3.37 | 3.93 | 2.80 | 3.70 | (* # |
| | | **Acceptance Scale** | | | | | |
| (−) | 14. | There is no reason why a child should not learn to keep his clothes clean very early in life. | 2.12 | 2.08 | 2.80 | 2.26 | (# ) |
| (+) | 9. | If you put too many restrictions on a child, you will stunt his personality. | 3.48 | 4.21 | 3.18 | 4.23 | (* # |
| | | **Understanding Scale** | | | | | |
| (−) | 10. | If you let children talk about their troubles they end up complaining even more. | 4.24 | 3.46 | 4.35 | 3.87 | (* # |
| (+) | 63. | Children should have a share in making family decisions just as grown-ups do. | 3.93 | 4.06 | 3.81 | 3.19 | (# † |
| | | **Trust Scale** | | | | | |
| (−) | 6. | Children have no right to keep anything from their parents. | 3.59 | 2.42 | 3.93 | 2.92 | (* # |
| (+) | 35. | Children have a right to activities which do not include their parents. | 4.43 | 4.07 | 4.50 | 4.13 | (*) |

NOTE: Since the coding of positively phrased items was reversed in the Hereford scales, a respon of Strongly Agree was coded 5, rather than 1 as in the negatively phrased items. This reversal m be kept in mind when interpreting mean scores in this table.
  — : negatively phrased item
  + : positively phrased item
  * : culture difference significant ≤ .01
  # : social-class difference significant ≤ .01
  † : culture-by-social-class interaction significant ≤ .01

set. The mean score of 3.21 indicates slight agreement with the positively phrased item, while a mean score of 1.89 indicates definite agreement with the negatively phrased item from the same scale.

The two items from the Causation scale show significant differences in culture for the lower-class mothers. While there was no significant difference between the two cultures among upper-class women for Item 38, a marked difference was obtained for the positively phrased item in this same scale. A closer look at the results for the lower-class mothers on the two items shows that a tendency to disagree with the negatively phrased version was accompanied by a tendency to agree with the positively phrased version. Whatever response set is present is at least a subtle and probably minor one. Among the upper-class American mothers, if anything, there was a tendency to disagree with the items regardless of content, as evidenced by the sharp drop in mean score in moving from Item 38 to Item 13.

Items 14 and 9 from the Acceptance scale are more nearly logical opposites in their negative and positive phrasing, respectively, thereby providing a somewhat better test of any existing response-set influences than the previous two pairs. Among all of the groups except the upper-class mothers, there is a marked shift, which is particularly evident among the lower-class Mexicans, indicating that the Mexican mothers who agreed with Item 14, the negatively phrased one (mean score of about 2), also tended to agree with the positively phrased item on the same topic (mean score of over 4 for Item 9). The presence of a response set on the part of Mexican mothers to agree with the statement regardless of content could account for this difference.

Items 10 and 63 from the Understanding scale show little difference in means when the content is reversed from negative to positive, except possibly for the upper-class Mexican mothers. No pervasive response set is apparent here.

The last scale for which a pair of items is analyzed shows a significant shift from the negatively phrased to the positively phrased version of the item for Mexican mothers, which raises the question concerning a possible response set to agree regardless of content. The American mothers show much less tendency to agree regardless of content.

The above analysis of ten items drawn specifically as pairs of positively and negatively phrased items from the same scales can only indirectly deal with the question of possible response sets or biases on the part of mothers filling out the Parent-Attitude Survey. Minor variations of wording in items that are reversed in their phrasing can often produce significant semantic deviation from the intended logical opposite, making it impossible to isolate accurately any response-set tendencies by this method. Given the content of these items, it is fairly clear that Mexican mothers, particularly those of the lower class, tended to agree more with negatively phrased items (or at least disagree less) than was the case for American mothers. Whether this tendency represents a genuine feeling of acceptance for the statement as presented or whether it signifies a tendency to be polite and not highly disagreeable cannot be determined from a statistical analysis of these items by themselves.

## Other Scales and Individual Items

Two scales from the Texas Cooperative Youth Study—Orientation to Society and Authoritarian Discipline—were included in the Parent-Attitude Survey. Each contains four items. Agreement with the items in Orientation to Society would indicate a pessimistic or negative outlook. Agreement with the items in Authoritarian Discipline would indicate adherence to authoritarianism and strict discipline in child rearing. Table 11-2 shows the mean scores for lower and upper social classes as well as for Mexican and American mothers on the four items comprising Orientation to Society and the four items making up Authoritarian Discipline. In all cases highly significant cross-cultural differences were obtained. In general, the lower-class Mexican mothers were the most pessimistic in their world outlook, while the upper-class American mothers were the most optimistic. Social-class differences among the Americans tended to be small or even nonexistent when compared to the generally larger differences for the Mexican upper and lower social classes.

Social-class differences tended to be considerably less, only occasionally reaching significance, for comparisons involving the Authoritarian Discipline scale. Belief in strict authoritarian disci-

Table 11-2

Mean Scores for Items Comprising the Orientation to Society and Authoritarian Discipline Scales

| Item | Lower Class U.S. | Lower Class Mex. | Upper Class U.S. | Upper Class Mex. | |
|------|------|------|------|------|------|
| **Orientation to Society** | | | | | |
| 41. These days a person doesn't really know whom he can count on. | 3.79 | 2.46 | 4.23 | 2.93 | (* #) |
| 48. In spite of what most people say, the life for the average person is getting worse, not better. | 4.08 | 3.17 | 4.29 | 3.53 | (* #) |
| 55. It's hardly fair to bring children into the world with the way things look for the future. | 4.42 | 3.17 | 4.48 | 3.69 | (* # †) |
| 62. When you get right down to it no one is going to care much what is going to happen to you. | 4.31 | 3.24 | 4.34 | 3.38 | (*) |
| **Authoritarian Discipline** | | | | | |
| 44. If children are to grow up and get somewhere in life, they must be continuously kept after. | 3.24 | 2.94 | 3.65 | 3.20 | (* #) |
| 51. Children who always obey grow up to be best adults. | 3.64 | 2.66 | 3.81 | 3.24 | (* #) |
| 58. Too much freedom will make a child wild. | 2.61 | 2.24 | 2.82 | 2.40 | (*) |
| 65. Strict discipline develops a fine strong character. | 3.43 | 2.80 | 3.26 | 2.93 | (*) |

NOTE: The lower the score, the greater the agreement with the statement.
*: culture difference significant $\leq$ .01
#: social-class difference significant $\leq$ .01
†: culture-by-social-class interaction significant $\leq$ .01

pline is more characterstic of the Mexican mother than the American, especially the Mexican lower-class mother.

## Other Items in the Parent-Attitude Survey

Ten of the items in the Parent-Attitude Survey did not come originally from the Hereford scales or those in the Texas Cooperative Youth Study. Eight of these ten were taken from cross-cultural studies between Brazil and the United States (Rosen 1964), which revealed considerable differences in life style and attitudes that were related to very important social variables. The last two items were developed specifically for the present study by Díaz-Guerrero in the hope that they would capture some of the particular attitudes often expressed by Mexicans as part of their philosophy of life. Mean scores for these ten items are presented by culture and social class in Table 11-3. In every case, culture proved to be highly significant. In all but two cases, social class was also a significant source of variance. In only three cases was there a significant inter-action between social class and culture—Items 17, 23, and 30. A common pattern running through all these means is the significantly greater amount of disagreement with the item statements expressed by American mothers. The significant interactions are due primarily to the much wider difference between upper- and lower-social-class mothers in Mexico than in the United States.

Table 11-3
Mean Scores for Items from Rosen's Scales and Díaz-Guerrero's Studies

| Item | Lower Class U.S. | Lower Class Mex. | Upper Class U.S. | Upper Class Mex. | |
|---|---|---|---|---|---|
| 3. Nowadays with world conditions the way they are the wise person lives for today and lets tomorrow take care of itself. | 4.21 | 3.23 | 4.46 | 3.99 | (* |
| 8. The secret of happiness is not expecting too much out of life and being content with what comes your way. | 3.43 | 2.49 | 3.56 | 2.74 | (*) |
| 11. A good son would try to live near his parents even if it means giving up a good job in another part of the country. | 4.66 | 3.80 | 4.76 | 4.15 | (* |
| 17. All a man should want out of life in the way of a career is a secure, not-too-difficult job, with enough pay to get by. | 4.47 | 3.22 | 4.67 | 4.24 | (* |
| 23. Nothing is worth the sacrifice of moving away from one's parents. | 4.21 | 3.13 | 4.51 | 3.89 | (* |
| 30. Planning only makes a person unhappy since your plans hardly ever work out anyway. | 4.32 | 2.71 | 4.29 | 3.64 | (* |
| 37. When a man is born the success he is going to have is already in the cards, so he might just as well accept it and not fight against it. | 4.63 | 4.09 | 4.75 | 4.46 | (* |
| 49. Much of what a son does should be done to please his parents. | 3.97 | 2.73 | 4.22 | 3.38 | (* |
| 57. If a person doesn't always get much done but can enjoy life as he goes along, that is the best way. | 2.68 | 2.04 | 3.29 | 2.19 | (* |
| 64. A boss should understand and not penalize a worker who sometimes without warning takes a little time off for fun. | 3.93 | 2.14 | 3.74 | 2.21 | (* |

NOTE: The lower the score, the greater the agreement with the statement.
*: culture difference significant ≤ .01
#: social-class difference significant ≤ .01
†: culture-by-social-class interaction significant ≤ .01

Only occasionally were sources of variation other than culture and social class statistically significant beyond the .01 level. Be-, cause the age differences among the mothers in Groups I, II, and III were only three to six years, it was unlikely that marked differences in attitudes would be expressed by mothers in the three groups. The occasional interaction that proved to be significant typically shows no trend with age worth noting. For this reason, no attempt is made to present or interpret results for any of the major factors other than culture and social class.

## Four Dimensions from Factor Analysis

The factor analysis employing the combined samples yielded two major factors and two minor ones. Factor scores were generated for each subject and employed in the analysis-of-variance design as dependent variables to see the extent to which significant variation in these factor scores could be attributed to culture, socioeconomic status, age of the child, and the interactions among these sources of variation. The results are presented for each factor separately.

*Factor 1: Internal Determinism.* Culture, social class, and the interaction of these two components all proved to be highly significant (p <.001) for Factor 1. As in the analyses of the Hereford scales and the individual items, the Austin mothers appeared much more optimistic and favored environmental interpretation of causation more than was true for the Mexican mothers. The interaction between social class and culture, however, indicates that no simple, broad generalization can be made. Among the Austin mothers, no difference in upper and lower social class was apparent, both social classes receiving essentially the same mean scores on Internal Determinism. For the Mexican mothers, however, a rather marked difference between the upper and lower social classes was apparent. The lower-class Mexican mother was much more pessimistic and fatalistic in her outlook on life.

*Factor 2: Sophisticated Acceptance.* Culture, socioeconomic status, and age of the child all proved to be significant for Factor 2, as did the interaction between culture and social class. In this case, however, it is the American mothers who show a significant social-class difference, while the Mexican mothers do not. Although both upper- and lower-class American mothers have significantly higher scores on Sophisticated Acceptance than do their Mexican counterparts, the upper-class Americans are appreciably higher than the lower-class Americans.

*Factor 3.* Defined largely by items from Hereford's Confidence scale, this minor factor shows only a significant difference between the two cultures and the two social classes, no interaction being apparent. The American mothers received higher scores on Factor 3 than did the Mexican mothers, and the upper-class parents in both cultures obtained higher means than did the lower-class ones.

*Factor 4.* Only culture proved to be significant for Factor 4. The Mexican mothers generally approved of more authoritarian discipline in child-rearing than did the American mothers, who tended to favor laissez-faire approaches to discipline.

## Personal Traits Valued by the Mother

Following the Parent-Attitude Survey, the mother rated the fifteen traits in the Parent Trait Survey according to how highly she valued them as personal traits in her own child. A four-way analysis of variance involving culture, social class, age group, and sex was employed, as in the analysis of items within the parental interview. Most of the significant differences obtained could be attributed to culture, social class, or the interaction of culture and social class. Mean scores for each personal trait as valued by the mother are given in Table 11-4.

The forced-choice nature of the task in rating traits from the most important to the least eliminates any possibility of response set entering into the results except with respect to the rating of 0 for "no importance at all." For this reason any significant differences can be attributed to real differences in the relative value attributed to each of the traits. Where one is valued highly, the forced-choice nature of the task forces others to be valued less highly.

Cross-cultural differences were obtained in all but two of the traits—economy in money matters and good manners. For convenience of interpretation, the traits are arranged in Table 11-4 with the trait valued most highly by lower-class American mothers first, followed by the other traits in descending order. The lower-class American mother stood alone in valuing loyalty to the church most highly. No differences are apparent in the importance ascribed to this trait by mothers in the other three groups. While frankness in dealing with others was valued highly by all four groups of mothers, the upper-class American mother did not rate it as highly as did lower-class American mothers or Mexican mothers. Tolerance was the trait most highly thought of by the upper-class American mothers, who differed greatly from the upper-class Mexicans in this regard.

The least valued traits on the part of Americans were the desire to make a name in the world and strict obedience. It is interesting to note that desire to make a name in the world was the most important trait in the eyes of the Mexican mothers, while at the same time it was the least important as judged by the Americans. Strict obedience was valued only by lower-class Mexican mothers, the other three groups thinking of it as unimportant. Social concern was rated moderately important by all the mothers except the lower-class Americans. Among the Mexican mothers, curiosity

Table 11-4
Mean Scores for Personal Traits in the Child as Valued by the Mother

| Trait | | Lower Class U.S. | Lower Class Mex. | Upper Class U.S. | Upper Class Mex. |
|---|---|---|---|---|---|
| oyalty to the church | (* # †) | 2.57 | 2.08 | 2.08 | 2.07 |
| rankness in dealing with others | (* ††) | 2.30 | 2.32 | 2.03 | 2.42 |
| ood manners | | 2.17 | 2.12 | 2.12 | 1.91 |
| olerance | (** ##) | 2.14 | 1.34 | 2.48 | 1.61 |
| dependence | (** ##) | 1.88 | 1.18 | 2.18 | 1.59 |
| atriotism | (*) | 1.83 | 1.50 | 1.57 | 1.51 |
| onomy in money matters | | 1.75 | 1.76 | 1.53 | 1.71 |
| nowledge of sex hygiene | (** ††) | 1.60 | 1.67 | 1.30 | 1.87 |
| oncentration | (**) | 1.58 | 1.42 | 1.86 | 1.43 |
| ppreciation of art, music, and poetry | (** #) | 1.52 | 1.04 | 1.60 | 1.29 |
| etting very good grades in school | (** ## ††) | 1.38 | 2.21 | 1.29 | 1.47 |
| uriosity | (** ## †) | 1.33 | .67 | 1.86 | .76 |
| cial concern | (** ##) | .99 | 1.45 | 1.50 | 1.66 |
| rict obedience | (** ##) | .87 | 1.35 | .64 | .90 |
| sire to make a name in the world | (**) | .68 | 2.40 | .69 | 2.50 |

NOTE: The higher the score, the more highly valued the trait.
  *: culture significant at .05 level
 **: culture significant ≤ .01 level
  #: social class significant at .05 level
 ##: social class significant ≤ .01 level
  †: culture-by-social-class interaction significant at .05 level
 ††: culture-by-social-class interaction significant ≤ .01 level

was judged to be the least important trait, a value orientation quite different from that expressed by the American mothers, particularly those in the upper class.

Getting very good grades in school was ranked least important by the most affluent group, the upper-class American mothers, and most important by the lower-class Mexican mothers, with the other two groups arrayed consistently in between. This negative relationship between the importance of getting very good grades in school and actual recognized attainment and affluence is consistent with the general idea that people who are deprived value the unattained goal much more highly than those who have achieved it. It may also indicate that education is still perceived by many lower-class mothers as a means to a better life for their children.

Knowledge of sex hygiene was relatively unimportant in the eyes of the upper-class American mother, as compared to the other three groups. Americans of both social classes valued concentration and the appreciation of art, music, and poetry more highly than Mexican mothers of either social class.

Sex differences were also obtained on five of the traits. Frankness in dealing with others is a trait that was valued more for sons than for daughters among the American mothers but not among the Mexicans. Appreciation of art, music, and poetry was valued more for daughters than for sons, a finding that must be qualified, however, by a complex interaction among social class, sex, and age group. Knowledge of sex hygiene was valued more highly for daughters than for sons among lower-class mothers, while no difference is apparent for upper-class mothers in either culture.

Two of the traits that are intellectual in nature, curiosity and getting very good grades in school, also show interactions between sex and another factor. While there were no differences for the youngest children, curiosity was valued more for boys than for girls among the seventh-graders and more for girls than for boys among the tenth-graders. Getting good grades in school was more important among boys than among girls for lower-class mothers, while no sex difference is present for upper-class mothers in either culture.

Several traits also show significant interactions or main effects involving the age of the child. Among the youngest families, there was no difference between upper- and lower-class mothers in the importance they attached to concentration as a trait. In Groups II and III, however, the importance of concentration dropped for the lower-class mothers, while it rose for the upper class. A significant interaction is also apparent for culture and age group. No cross-cultural difference is apparent for this trait in Groups I and II, although in Group III there is a marked difference, with the Mexican mother rating the trait as much more important than the American mother.

---

The many significant cross-cultural differences found for attitudes and personal traits valued by the mothers must be interpreted in light of the other significant differences reported and discussed in Chapters 7–10. The concluding section of the book, Part Four, seeks to accomplish this task. In Chapter 12 the many findings of the study are integrated and their implications are discussed. Chapter 13 deals with a number of issues in culture and personality and states six general hypotheses to account for the major cross-cultural differences found between Mexico and the United States. A brief summary of the project is given in Chapter 14.

# PART FOUR

## Discussion and Conclusions

The mask of an old man is as indecipherable at first glance
as a sacred stone covered with occult symbols. . . . Eventually
these features are seen as a face, and later as a mask,
a meaning, a history.

Octavio Paz

*The Labyrinth of Solitude*
trans. Lysander Kemp

# 12. Synthesis and Interpretation of Major Findings

Cross-cultural and developmental comparisons using large numbers of carefully selected children in the United States and Mexico over a six-year period of repeated testing in both cultures have resulted in literally hundreds of significant findings. These empirical findings have been presented according to the type of psychological measurement involved, one variable at a time, in the preceding chapters. While such a presentation is useful for concentrating upon specific variables of special interest, it is too fragmentary to permit general interpretations about relationships between culture, social class, sex, and the age of the child, on the one hand, and the individual's cognitive, perceptual, and personality characteristics, on the other. The major findings of the study must be summarized and synthesized in a different manner before the broader cross-cultural developmental significance of the findings will be apparent.

The strengths and limitations of any study are largely determined by the manner in which the basic research problem is defined and the way in which the experimental design is formulated and carried out. Before examining the major findings of the study from a broader perspective, it is instructive to recapitulate the essential features of the research method and procedures.

### Essential Features of the Research Design Re-examined

The most significant features of the present research design are the use of two contrasting cultures—Spanish-speaking Mexicans and English-speaking Americans—and the employment of many different types of psychological measures individually administered to large numbers of children of different ages with six years of repeated testing for each child. Starting in the initial year with equal numbers of children drawn from the first, fourth, and seventh grades in school yields an overlapping longitudinal design, so that practice and adaptation effects, as well as minor sampling differences at different age levels, can be isolated and compensated for in the analysis of other major variables. By the fourth year of testing, the original first- and fourth-graders are in the fourth and seventh grades respectively, providing counterparts for comparison with the initial fourth- and seventh-graders, who by then are in the seventh and tenth grades. Similar comparative analyses are possible in the fifth and sixth years of repeated testing as well. Thus one has the advantage not only of cross-sectional comparisons of different age groups but also of the study of developmental trends within the same individuals over a long period of time.

The use of a special matched cross-cultural sample made it possible to control fairly rigorously for five independent variables, which could be studied in their own right as well as for the interactions among them—culture, socioeconomic status of the family, sex of the child, age group in three levels, and year of repeated testing. In addition to complex analyses both cross-culturally and developmentally, a sufficient number of cases—over one hundred in each instance—were obtained in both cultures and in each of the three age groups to permit independent study of interrelationships among variables within each of these large samples. In this sense, the research design can be thought of as a series of six parallel studies, each using precisely the same research procedures—one each in Mexico and the United States for each of the three age groups. Any one of these six developmental studies would have been a major undertaking in its own right. By conducting all six of them concurrently, one increases greatly the power of generalizations that can be made from any statistically significant results.

Culture represents the most difficult of the five independent variables to define in a scientifically valid manner. Even in the case of two urban cultures in adjacent nations that have been studied intensively, it is difficult to pin down the most salient features of the cultures that may be most important for understanding the cognitive and personality development of children who are growing up in them. While it is true that comparisons between Mexican and American cultures as they may influence personality development are hard to interpret because of the many cultural differences operating that could provide alternative explanations of the findings, there is a sufficiently high degree of consistency in the cross-cultural findings of the present study and the anticipated outcomes from an analysis of sociocultural premises underlying the two cultures to be fairly compelling evidence of the way in which culture and personality are inextricably woven together. A detailed analysis of these relationships between culture and personality as they have emerged from the present study, as well as from related evidence from other investigations, is presented in Chapter 13 after a review of the major findings in the present chapter.

The major cultural variable in the study has been defined by the sampling procedures for selecting children to be studied. Austin, Texas, is a sufficiently cosmopolitan city to be representative of "middle America," or what many have referred to as the broad working and middle classes that constitute the majority of American citizens. By restricting the Austin sample to English-speaking white families who seemed likely to remain in Austin for the six years of the study, the American culture was narrowed still further. It seems safe to say that the children and their families comprising the Austin sample are representative of the blue-collar, clerical, skilled-worker, and educated professional classes that comprise the dominant Anglo-American value system characteristic of the American majority.

Mexico City, with its millions of citizens who have migrated from various parts of Mexico to the capital in the past several generations, is clearly the heart of Mexico. By oversampling from the private schools, a proportionately larger number of middle-class children were obtained in Mexico than would be characteristic of the population as a whole. Only in this way was it possible to obtain large numbers of individuals with comparable educational, occupational, and socioeconomic status across the two cultures. As in the case of the American families, only children with native-born parents and with some prospect of residential stability were selected for the developmental study, thereby narrowing the definition of culture to the dominant emerging upper-middle and working classes in highly urbanized Mexico City.

Socioeconomic status proved to be somewhat easier to measure than culture. By using a combination of father's occupation and education, it was possible to derive an index of socioeconomic status that assured comparability across the two cultures in the matched sample. This comparability was achieved at some cost in terms of the reduced number of cases that could be employed in such analyses and the accompanying constriction in the range of socioeconomic status resulting from eliminating extremes of the distribution. The resulting dimension of socioeconomic status could only be divided into two broad categories with any degree of confidence—a lower class consisting mainly of blue-collar, clerical, and working-class families and an upper class comprised mainly of families with fathers who were highly educated professionals or businessmen.

The remaining three independent variables in the design—sex of the child, age and grade of the child at the start of the longitudinal study, and year of repeated testing—were easily defined and are clear in their interpretation.

Another essential feature of the design that limited the scope and variety of psychological data collected from the children and their parents was the decision to employ techniques of psychological assessment that could be repeatedly administered to the same individual with no loss of validity. Furthermore, the measures had to be appropriate for use in both English and Spanish. Only those techniques that could be administered to the child in school or to the mother in her home were employed, for practical reasons. And finally, strong preference was given to those measures that showed promise of yielding reliable quantitative scores of sufficient precision to reflect cross-cultural and developmental trends. While many interesting techniques were eliminated from consideration by these criteria, the scope and variety of measures within the cognitive, perceptual, and personality domains are nevertheless more extensive than in any other cross-cultural studies that have been attempted in the past.

A longitudinal design with repeated measures over many years is by definition conservative in nature. Once an initial decision has been made to collect certain kinds of cognitive, perceptual, and personality measures on children in the first year of the study, one must continue using a major portion of these measures throughout the years of study in order to obtain accurate, quantitative information on change of the traits over time. To be sure, it is still possible to make some changes in the battery of assessment techniques from year to year, incorporating new instruments as they are perfected. But, unless a major effort is made to maintain a core set of measures intact throughout the repeated years of the study, a fundamental purpose of the investigation will be completely thwarted. Fortunately, in the present study, only a few changes would have been made in the basic research design if it had been possible in retrospect to do so.

Every effort was made to eliminate or at least minimize the likelihood that methodological artifacts could account for any obtained results. While cross-cultural matching on socioeconomic status cannot be perfect, because of differences inherent in the two cultures, the pairing of individual children cross-culturally on the index of socioeconomic status proved to be a fairly rigorous method of controlling for this important variable. Preliminary studies in Mexico also revealed that Mexican families with children in the private school system had essentially the same level of father's occupation and education, size and quality of house, and prevalence of radios, television sets, automobiles, and refrigerators as the typical middle-class American family in the Austin sample. Thus one can conclude that cross-cultural differences obtained in the present study are not confounded with social-class differences. In addition, well-trained native examiners were calibrated and measurement techniques were employed that can be defended in both cultures. Special studies were also made of any possible bias due to the inevitable loss of some subjects over the six years of the study. Since no significant biases were found, it can be concluded that the distribution of social, cultural, and personal characteristics within each cell of the design remained constant throughout the six years of the study.

In spite of these many precautions, there may still be some minor differences in test results across the two cultures that arise from the conditions of testing—subtle but unnoticed differences in Mexican and American examiners and scorers, or minor linguistic variations that may still exist between the meaning of a particular technique given in Spanish and the same technique given in English. One can never be sure that one has eliminated all potentially confounding variables in any comparative study of two cultures. For this reason, it is important to examine results from a number of different sources and different approaches to the study of the same data, always searching for consistencies as well as contradictions.

Running through all levels of data, whether collected directly from the child, from interviews with the mother, or from school records, are the major classification variables of culture, socioeconomic status, sex and age of the child. Reviewing all of the major significant findings for each of these independent variables, both in isolation from each other and for any interactions among them, yields considerable insight into the significance of the over-all results.

### Highlights of the Findings

The extensive variety of tests repeatedly used for psychological assessment of the children provided measures of cognitive or mental abilities, perceptual or cognitive style, and personality characteristics or attitudes. The stability or consistency of individual differences across time was measured by computing test-retest reliability coefficients across the years of repeated measurement. Studies of intercorrelations among these many variables at any given point in time yielded a number of major dimensions as well as a wealth of information concerning correlations across the different domains of cognitive, perceptual, and personality development. These intercorrelational studies shed further light on the meaning of the many variables involved in the study.

### Comparison of Stability across Time in the Two Cultures

The stability of most repeated measures was fairly high even across six years, regardless of culture. This general finding is especially impressive when one realizes that much of the testing covered the formative years in the child's development. As one would expect from developmental theory, the degree of stability generally increased with an increase in the age of the child, regardless of the trait being measured. As a child grew older, the rate of growth slowed down, so that the relative amount of change from one year to the next dropped with increasing age.

Another general finding that applies in both cultures is the fact that test-retest stability dropped off in a regular fashion with increasing size of interval between tests. While most of the measures in the present study showed a sufficiently high degree of stability across time to justify their use as predictors of later behavior, this stability was not so high as to suggest any kind of fixed traits that remain relatively invariant as the child grows older.

For many measures, the difference in the degree of stability between Mexican and American children was small or nonexistent. But where cross-cultural differences were present, the Mexican children showed less stability through time than did the Americans. This greater stability for Americans than Mexicans is evident in the test-retest correlations for Reaction Time, Movement, Pathognomic Verbalization, Integration, Hostility, and Barrier from the Holtzman Inkblot Technique. While in some cases this significant cross-cultural difference can be attributed in part to the fact that the variance of inkblot scores is larger in the Austin sample than for the Mexican children, the differences in stability are nevertheless sufficiently great that at least in part they must be viewed as genuine trait differences in the two cultures.

An even more striking cross-cultural difference in the degree of stability was found for Vocabulary, especially for the youngest children in Group I. By contrast, Block Design showed very little difference cross-culturally in its stability, remaining fairly high throughout the six years of repeated testing in both cultures. Likewise, scores from the Human Figure Drawing and the Embedded Figures Test showed high test-retest stability in both cultures. Indeed, the highest stability of any scores in either culture were obtained for mean reaction time to correct solution on the Embedded Figures Test. Since Block Design, Human Figure Drawing, and the Embedded Figures Test yield scores that define a general dimension referred to by Witkin as field independence, or degree of psychological differentiation, it can be concluded that the sta-

296                                          Discussion and Conclusions

bility of this important dimension is very high among American children and only slightly lower among Mexican children of the same age, sex, and social class. This picture of stability is consistent with the findings of Faterson and Witkin (1970) and of Witkin, Goodenough, and S. A. Karp (1967).

The lower stability of measurement through time on many of the variables for the Mexican children is an important finding that cannot be easily dismissed as an artifact of measurement procedures. Is it possible that the lower degree of predictability of individual differences in cognitive, perceptual, and personality development among Mexicans is due at least in part to a greater sensitivity to situational factors at the time of testing? Lower test-retest stability would result if such external factors as specific interpersonal relations and environmental stimuli produced different expressions of personality or role playing more often among Mexican children than among Americans. While the present study does not contain rigorous evidence bearing upon this question, there is sufficient evidence from other studies, as mentioned in Chapter 13, to suggest this hypothesis as a plausible explanation of the frequently lower stability of individual differences through time for the Mexican children.

## Comparison of Major Dimensions and Intercorrelations across the Two Cultures

Correlational studies within each culture ranged from factor analyses of many variables at a given point in time to the intensive examination of a single bivariate relationship replicated many times across groups and years of testing. In most instances the patterns of intercorrelations were similar in both cultures, yielding sets of major dimensions having comparable cross-cultural meaning. Factor analysis of the Holtzman inkblot scores for each of the age groups in each culture revealed five well-defined factors highly similar in each of the six groups. While minor differences were noted in some groups, there was no consistent cross-cultural difference in the patterns of variables defining each factor. Consequently, it can be concluded with some confidence that the major dimensions present in the Holtzman Inkblot Technique are essentially identical in the two cultures.

Dimensions underlying mental abilities also proved to be very similar in the two cultures. Factor analyses of the WISC subtests plus Human Figure Drawing, HIT Movement, and sex of the child yielded almost identical factors for six-year-olds in Mexico and the United States, as indicated in Table 6-7. The first factor in both cultures was similar to the verbal-comprehension factor frequently found in studies of the WISC. Factor 2 was defined in both cultures primarily by the performance subtests, indicating a perceptual-organization factor, consisting primarily of Block Design, Object Assembly, Coding, and Human Figure Drawing. With regard to the loading of the Wechsler subtests, the two factors are similar to those found by Cohen (1959), and by Goodenough and Karp (1961).

In general, these studies are consistent with past findings in the cognitive area. Repeated significant loadings for HIT Movement on factors dealing with the use of imagination provide a strong link between the cognitive domain and the Holtzman Inkblot Technique in both cultures. Another consistent cluster that repeatedly appears involves the Embedded Figures Test, Human Figure Drawing, and several of the WISC subtests, most notably Block Design, thus confirming many earlier studies that define this general dimension of field dependency, regardless of culture.

At the time this study began, in 1962, three main streams of activity concerned with dimensions of perceptual-cognitive style provided a basis for the inclusion of a number of tests for both Mexican and American children. The Embedded Figures Test was used as the best measure of Witkin's field independence, or psychological differentiation. The Object Sorting Test was employed as a measure of Gardner's equivalence range, a cognitive-control principle. Kagan's work on styles of conceptualization was represented by the Conceptual Styles Test and the Visual Fractionation Test. At that time, nearly all the studies of perceptual-cognitive style had been done on Americans, and little was known about the applicability of such tests to individuals from other cultures. In the past ten years, a great deal of work has accumulated on the Embedded Figures Test, indicating its applicability to many different cultures, ranging from isolated Eskimos of remote Alaska to black Africans of Sierra Leone. The same has not proved to be true of the other cognitive style measures, however. In the past ten years most of them have not lived up to their original promise of providing stable relevant measures of important personality traits. With the exception of Witkin's Embedded Figures Test, intercorrelations between the measures of perceptual-cognitive style are generally disappointing. Only occasionally is there a significant correlation worthy of note in either culture.

Factor analysis of the fifteen scales in the Personality Research Form and six other measures yielded strikingly similar results in both cultures. The same seven factors were found for Mexican children as for Americans, lending strong support to the hypothesis that these personality measures have similar meaning and applicability in both cultures.

Intercorrelations among the sixty-eight items in the Parent-Attitude Survey were generally too low in both cultures to yield strong dimensions on which patterns could be classified according to attitude clusters. Only by analyzing intercorrelations for both cultures combined was it possible to obtain several stable factors. While there are striking differences in the response of mothers in the two cultures to most of the items in the survey, no major differences between the two cultures could be discerned in the patterning of relationships among attitude statements.

Correlational studies involving items from the parent interview proved to be even more limited in value than the parent-attitude measures. Only six variables concerning the mother and the home environment were sufficiently comparable cross-culturally to justify correlational analysis with children's test scores. While a number of interesting and highly significant relationships were found between family and home variables and certain performance measures in school for the American children, comparable data were simply not available in most cases for the Mexicans.

Very few correlations across the various domains of measurement proved to be significant in either culture. Most of the major dimensions and many of the specific traits measured within the cognitive, perceptual, or personality domains proved to be fairly independent of one another. While a few interesting and highly significant cross-domain correlations did appear, there was no systematic trend differentiating one culture from the other.

In general, from all of the correlational studies that were carried out, it can be concluded that the major patterns of relationships among variables are essentially the same in both cultures, although minor but important variations are present.

## Cross-Cultural Similarities

For some of the measures in the present study, no cross-cultural differences were found. Table 12-1 contains a listing of all psychological measures from the children and items from the interview with the mother for which no differences were found between Mexicans and Americans. Obviously, far more measures produced significant differences or interactions between culture and other variables than the small number listed in this table. Significant cross-cultural differences were obtained for all the cognitive measures, nearly all of the cognitive-perceptual style variables, and most of the personality and attitudinal measures, as well as most items obtained from interviews with the mothers of the children. On the Holtzman Inkblot Technique, every score yielded main effects or higher-order interactions that involved cross-cultural differences. No differences between Mexican and American children were found for two major personality factors as defined by

Table 12-1
Measures for Which No Differences Were Found between Mexicans and Americans

**Measures on Children**

| | |
|---|---|
| CST | Inferential-Categorical |
| VFT | Correct |
| WAT | Noun Paradigmatic |
| PRF | Achievement |
| PRF | Endurance |
| PRF | Exhibitionism |
| PRF | Aggression |
| OVI | Feel good about doing well |
| OVI | Make a lot of money |
| OVI | Learn about many interesting things |
| OVI | Free to do in your own way |
| OVI | Be doing many different things |
| OVI | Lead other people |
| OVI | Musician or an artist |

**Items from Mothers' Interviews**

Times family meets together routinely
Hours/week child watches TV
Value placed on good manners
Value placed on economy in money matters

the scales from the Personality Research Form, Persistent Achievement Drive (defined by the Achievement and Endurance scales), and Extroversion (defined by Exhibitionism and Aggression). Seven of the fifteen items from the Occupational Values Inventory also showed no cross-cultural differences.

Only four items from the interview with the mother and her scores on the Parent-Attitude Survey and Parent Trait Survey failed to yield some significant cross-cultural difference between the Mexican and American mothers. All four of these items in Table 12-1 are of only minor importance.

Social class, sex, or the age of the child often proved significant as a factor related to the child's performance. In many cases, these independent classification variables interact with culture, while in some instances they do not. Only the significant differences due to social class, sex, age, or the interactions among these three variables are presented here, leaving for a later section any interactions of significance between these variables and culture.

As one would expect, highly significant differences attributable to the age of the child were found for all of the cognitive tests, such as the Wechsler Intelligence Scale for Children, the Harris-Goodenough scoring of Human Figure Drawings, and the Embedded Figures Test, regardless of culture. Only a few scores among the cognitive-perceptual style or personality measures showed strong age trends, and in nearly all these cases the interaction with culture proved highly significant. The scores that increased markedly with increasing age were Arithmetic, Vocabulary, Picture Completion, Block Design, Harris-Goodenough score for Human Figure Drawings, EFT Correct, TET Delay, VFT Correct, Perceptual Maturity Scale, HIT Reaction Time, HIT Form Appropriateness, HIT Movement, HIT Integration, HIT Human, and PRF Impulsivity. Those scores that decreased with increasing age in both cultures were HIT Rejection, HIT Color, OST number of groups, OST number of single items not used, EFT Errors, EFT Time, EFT Re-exams, VFT Trials, VFT Time, PRF Independence, and OVI Esthetics. These trends occurred in both cultures and are in the directions to be expected from earlier studies.

Differences in performance due to social class are generally present only for the Mexican children. Social-class differences for the Americans as they relate to the child's performance only rarely occur. Because of these significant interactions between social class and culture, most of the important findings concerning social class are discussed in a later section. Only three measures from the children showed a clear social-class difference in both cultures and for both sexes. Upper-class children received higher mean scores on TET Delay, indicating that they could estimate more accurately the length of time equivalent to one minute. Lower-class children showed a higher degree of specific anxiety about taking tests and also valued more highly work in which one could make a lot of money. The mothers of upper-class children valued more highly for their children such traits as independence, tolerance, and social concern, while lower-class mothers valued strict obedience. From information collected in the parent interview, it was also apparent that lower-class fathers and children watched television longer hours and lower-class mothers obtained lower scores on most of the parental-attitude scales than did their upper-class counterparts. These findings are completely consistent with earlier studies employing these same measures.

Sex differences in the child's performance and the mother's response to interview items were a bit more prevalent in both cultures. Girls tended to receive higher scores on the first figure for the Human Figure Drawing and higher scores on PRF Nurturance, PRF Harmavoidance and OVI Esthetics. Boys received higher scores on CST Relational, TET Delay, the Perceptual Maturity Scale, HIT Form Definiteness, HIT Movement, HIT Human, HIT Animal, HIT Hostility, and PRF Autonomy. Boys also tended to draw more masculine males in the Human Figure Drawings than did girls. Other sex differences were found in either Mexico or the United States but not in both cultures. These interactions between sex and culture are discussed in a later section.

In only one case is there any interaction between social class and sex that appears in both cultures. For PRF Endurance, upper-class boys and lower-class girls received higher scores than did lower-class boys or upper-class girls.

## Cross-Cultural Differences

Clear and uniform differences were found across the two cultures for many psychological dimensions and test scores, regardless of the sex, age, or socioeconomic status of the child. In many other instances, the significant differences across the two cultures must be qualified, since they were not uniformly present for both boys and girls, for all ages, or for both upper and lower social classes. These interactions are particularly interesting and will be reviewed after first examining the differences that were uniformly present.

At least some measures in each of the domains for which tests were given to the children yielded uniformly significant differences cross-culturally regardless of the social class, sex, or age of the child. These thirty measures are presented in Table 12-2, together with the over-all mean differences between the Mexican and American children. At the risk of oversimplification, a brief interpretive statement concerning the meaning of each cross-cultural difference is also given in Table 12-2. These statements are phrased so that they apply to the Mexican child as compared to the American. They can just as easily be phrased for the American instead, by simply reversing the direction of the statement.

Many differences were also found between the Mexican and American mothers in terms of their responses to items in the parent interview. Table 12-3 summarizes the results where significant differences were obtained between Mexican and American mothers regardless of the social class, sex, or age of the child. The twenty-six significant items from the interview are organized in clusters identical to those employed in the more detailed analysis given in Chapter 10. Since it is believed that the factorially derived scales for the Parent-Attitude Survey are the most appropriate for cross-cultural comparisons, only these four scales are presented. Five of the fifteen personal traits rated by the mother in the Parent Trait Survey produced uniformly significant cross-cultural differences in the relative value assigned to the trait by the mothers. As in the case of the performance measures from psychological testing of the children, a number of items taken from the mother's interview yielded significant interactions between culture and sex or culture and social class. Such results are too complicated for simple summary in tabular form, although many of them are highly important and will be discussed later. The specific meaning of obtained cross-cultural differences and the content of the items in Table 12-3 are fairly self-evident without additional interpretive aids.

## Table 12-2
### Cross-Cultural Mean Comparisons in Which Uniformly Significant Differences Were Obtained for Children

| | Measure | Mexican | American | Interpretation for Mexican |
|---|---|---|---|---|
| WISC | Vocabulary | 28.8 | 36.3 | Lower word knowledge |
| OST | Percent Open | 61.2 | 77.8 | More restrictiveness in classifying concepts |
| EFT | Errors | 11.8 | 8.7 | Greater field dependency |
| EFT | Correct | 7.1 | 8.1 | Greater field dependency |
| CST | Analytical | 10.0 | 6.3 | More analytical basis for associative objects |
| CST | Relational | 3.8 | 6.5 | Less relational basis for associative objects |
| TET | Delay | 110.4 | 143.0 | Time perceived as passing slower |
| VFT | Trials | 2.38 | 3.04 | Faster associative learning |
| VFT | Time | 3.89 | 5.14 | Faster associative learning |
| HFD | Masculinity-Femininity Discrimination | 0.72 | −0.05 | Greater discrimination of male-female traits |
| HIT | Reaction Time | 21.7 | 17.9 | Slower response time to inkblots |
| HIT | Pathognomic Verbalization | 3.1 | 6.4 | Less pathology in fantasy |
| HIT | Location | 43.3 | 33.3 | More small detail areas |
| HIT | Movement | 14.1 | 25.7 | Less movement in fantasy |
| HIT | Integration | 2.0 | 3.3 | Lower integration of parts into whole |
| HIT | Anxiety | 5.6 | 9.1 | Less anxiety in fantasy |
| HIT | Hostility | 6.3 | 10.1 | Less hostility in fantasy |
| PRF | Order | 12.2 | 10.3 | Greater need for neatness and order |
| PRF | Play | 10.6 | 14.1 | Less need to do things just for fun |
| PRF | Social Recognition | 10.8 | 12.5 | Less concern for what others think of them |
| PRF | Affiliation | 12.4 | 16.0 | Less need to seek out others |
| PRF | Autonomy | 8.7 | 7.1 | Greater need for independence |
| PRF | Impulsiveness | 8.9 | 10.5 | Less impulsive |
| PRF | Infrequency | 3.5 | 1.1 | (Response set scale, not interpreted) |
| TASC | Anxiety | 16.8 | 9.8 | More specific anxiety about taking tests |
| TASC | Lie | 4.0 | 2.0 | (Response set scale, not interpreted) |
| TASC | Defensiveness | 10.6 | 9.5 | More likely to be defensive about test taking |
| OVI | Be with people you like | 4.88 | 6.15 | Less desire to be with likeable people |
| OVI | One day become famous | 5.27 | 4.38 | Greater desire to be famous |
| OVI | Always sure of having a job | 4.23 | 5.26 | Less need for job security |

Table 12-3
Cross-Cultural Comparisons in Which Uniformly Significant Differences
Were Obtained for Mothers

| Items from Mothers' Interview | Mexican | American |
|---|---|---|
| Social class and family life style | | |
| Mother's education | some secondary | some college |
| Number of siblings | 3.7 | 2.0 |
| Other relatives present in home | 18% | 3% |
| Religious preference | Catholic | Protestant |
| Attendance at church once a week | 85% | 63% |
| Club activity of mothers | low | high |
| Hours/week father watches TV | 7.0 | 9.7 |
| Mothers working outside home | 9% | 41% |
| Socialization of the child | | |
| Special family recreation | 52% | 67% |
| Parents helping child choose friends | 56% | 32% |
| Children having home chores | 64% | 88% |
| Intellectual stimulation of the child | | |
| No magazines in the home | 45% | 20% |
| Dictionary and encyclopedia in home | 30% | 79% |
| Parents reading regularly to child as preschooler | 13% | 60% |
| Preschool child unable to read, count, or write | 59% | 22% |
| Child now regularly encouraged to read | 30% | 15% |
| Foreign language spoken in home | 49% | 25% |
| Fathers who have had teaching experience | 8% | 16% |
| Parental aspirations for the child | | |
| Minimum educational level most desired | high school | college |
| No preference stated for child's future occupation | 35% | 63% |
| Parental interest in academic progress of the child | | |
| Only mother talks to child about school progress | 50% | 29% |
| Both parents talk to child about school progress | 40% | 66% |
| Child has regular homework | 98% | 58% |
| Parent sometimes helps child with homework | 45% | 69% |
| Mother's assessment of the child | | |
| Judgment of child's rank in class | medium | high |
| Child reads unassigned books | 69% | 93% |
| Parent-Attitude Survey | | |
| Factor 1: Internal Determinism | low | high |
| Factor 2: Sophisticated Acceptance | low | high |
| Factor 3: Confidence | low | high |
| Factor 4: Authoritarian Discipline | high | low |
| Value placed on personal traits of child | | |
| Desire to make a name in the world | 2.45 | 0.68 |
| Appreciation of art, music, and poetry | 1.16 | 1.56 |
| Independence | 1.38 | 2.03 |
| Tolerance | 1.48 | 2.31 |
| Curiosity | 0.71 | 1.60 |

*Cross-Cultural Differences in Developmental Trends,*
*Social Class, and Sex*

Where significant interactions arise between culture and age, it means that the trait in question changed with age in a different manner for Mexican children than for Americans. Among the more interesting of such interactions are those in which the mean difference between Mexican and American children actually reversed itself with increasing age, so that the developmental trend for the Mexican children crosses over the trend for the Americans. This type of interaction was especially common for the cognitive and cognitive-perceptual style domains.

Mexican children in the first grade scored higher than their American counterparts on Arithmetic and Block Design. This trend reversed for the fourth-graders and widened still further for the seventh-graders in the initial year of the study. The Mexican first-graders used more items in the Object Sorting Test and received a higher score on Percent Private than did the American first-graders. The youngest Mexicans also obtained a higher score on the Perceptual Maturity Scale and gave more syntagmatic associations and fewer verb or adjective paradigmatic associations than did the youngest American children. This difference favoring the young Mexicans reversed itself for the older children. In all of these interactions the rate of change for the Americans with increasing age was greater than the rate of change for the Mexicans. Where higher-order interactions were present, as in the case of Vocabulary, the lower-class Mexican girl was placed at an increasingly noticeable disadvantage with increasing age.

It is interesting to note that on the relevant personality measures, interactions between culture and age tended to be the reverse of those found for the cognitive measures. The sixth-grade Americans were higher on PRF Understanding than their Mexican counterparts, a difference that reversed itself for the ninth- and twelfth-graders. The Americans showed a drop between ages eleven and fourteen in the need to understand many areas of knowledge, while the Mexicans showed a comparable increase in need for understanding over this same age period. An identical interaction for OVI Creativity revealed that Mexican children placed an increasingly higher value upon making or inventing new things as age increased from eleven through fourteen to seventeen, while Americans did just the opposite.

When taken together, these interactions between culture and age suggest that, for at least some cognitive functions, the Mexican child develops less rapidly than the American through the school years, even though they may both start out on roughly the same footing. Intellectual stimulation of the child in the American home is generally greater than that in the Mexican household, and American mothers value curiosity in the child much more highly than do Mexican mothers. By the time the Mexican child is well into adolescence, he has a stronger unmet need for understanding, and he values work that involves making or inventing new things more highly than does the American child.

The amount of homework assigned to the child in school and the parent's attitude toward homework may have been significant factors influencing these developmental trends. For the youngest children, homework was a rarity in the American family, although it was universally present in the Mexican home. Even in secondary school, the Mexican child generally had more homework than the American. Where dissatisfaction was expressed by the mother, the American thought her child had too little homework, whereas the Mexican thought her child had too much. Undoubtedly, the type of instruction and the conditions under which learning takes place in the Mexican home and school are different than is the case for the American child, regardless of social class within the narrow range of the present study.

An even more powerful model for the cross-cultural study of developmental trends could be applied to the core measures for which repeated testing on all children was available throughout the six years. Vocabulary and Block Design from the WISC, the Harris-Goodenough developmental score from the Human Figure Drawing, and scores from the Holtzman Inkblot Technique—a total of twenty-four variables—were available for all six years in the overlapping longitudinal design. The developmental trends with increasing age in the same children for the three cognitive tests were essentially the same as those revealed in the case of the analysis of data for only the first year of testing. With only minor exceptions, the growth curves for the three cognitive functions were smooth and highly similar in the two cultures. In the case of the Holtzman Inkblot Technique, however, some practice and adaptation effects were present for Location and Form Definiteness. With repeated testing, the Mexican children tended to increase at a faster rate than the Americans in their use of detailed areas of inkblots rather than use of the entire blot for their percepts, as indicated in Figure 8-6. Mean reaction time increased more rapidly for the Mexicans than for the Americans with increasing age, except for the oldest children, where the two growth curves converged (Fig. 8-8). The younger Mexicans tended to report percepts that fitted the actual form of the inkblot more often than did the Americans (Fig. 8-9), a difference in Form Appropriateness that disappeared by early adolescence. The youngest American children gave considerably more Shading than did the Mexicans (Fig. 8-10), but with increasing age this gap narrowed gradually until it disappeared in early adolescence. The American children also generally gave more Pathognomic Verbalization, with the exception of ages seven, twelve, and fourteen. And, finally, the youngest Americans tended to give more Human responses, as compared to the Mexicans, who gave more Animal content, a difference that also tended to disappear among the older children. When taken together, these developmental trends suggest that in most cases the Mexican children tend to converge upon the Americans with increasing age. It is almost as though socialization in the two cultures and the influences of society, peer groups, and the school, as contrasted to the family, bring the two populations of children closer together on some perceptual and personality characteristics as measured by the Holtzman Inkblot Technique.

Developmental trends as measured by the interaction between culture and age group must be qualified by inclusion of social class or sex in some cases. A number of three-way and even four-way interactions proved to be highly significant for certain of the psychological measures. Developmental trends for several of the items in the parent interview must also be interpreted in the light of social class and sex differences, as well as differences between the two cultures.

The triple interaction of culture, social class, and age group appeared most frequently in the Holtzman Inkblot Technique. The interactions for Color and Pathognomic Verbalization indicate the greatest differences between social classes and across the two cultures for the youngest children. The lower-class American first-graders received the highest mean score on Color, indicating a more impulsive reactive behavior, a finding consistent with other evidence of impulsivity from the Personality Research Form. Lower-class six-year-old Americans also gave more Pathognomic Verbalization than any other group. When coupled with the higher Anxiety and Hostility for Americans, this result indicates that the younger lower-class American boys are more expressive of their fantasies and are more likely to act out impulsively than is the case of the younger Mexican children. Later socialization brings a convergence of the lower- and upper-class Americans until the differences disappear after several years of schooling. Such is not the case, however, for the upper- and lower-class Mexicans, between whom a number of social-class differences continue to persist into later years.

The items from the Occupational Values Inventory concerned with intellectual stimulation also yielded a significant triple interaction involving culture, social class, and age. While no social-class differences were apparent for the American children, the upper-class Mexican eleven-year-olds valued intellectually stimulating work much more highly than did their lower-class counterparts. This difference disappeared for the fourteen-year-olds and reversed itself for the seventeen-year-olds, among whom the lower class actually valued work that was intellectually stimulating more highly than did the upper-class Mexicans. The same triple interaction appeared for one of the items in the parent interview concerned with intellectual stimulation of the child. Nearly all upper-class Mexicans received daily newspapers at home. For the youngest lower-class Mexicans, however, newspapers in the home were uncommon. But, by the time the lower-class Mexicans reached the age of seventeen, nearly all of their families received a daily newspaper at home. Although significant differences persisted in cognitive abilities and school performance between the upper- and lower-class Mexicans as they entered young adulthood, the lower-class Mexicans had a strong desire to improve themselves. It may well be that this new generation of lower-class Mexicans is being

educated and is stimulating the parents to ⌐
newspapers.

In several instances, the sex of the child ɪ
account in order to understand the cross
developmental trends. The complex intera⌐
already been discussed. For the Americans, u⌐
lary between boys and girls and between working-clas⌐
middle-class families failed to appear. For the Mexicans, howᵥ
both sex and social class were significant factors influencing verbal
ability as measured by Vocabulary. Among the Mexican girls, in
particular, as age increased, the gulf between the upper- and
lower-class girls widened appreciably, placing the lower-class Mexican girl at a particularly noticeable disadvantage as contrasted to
Mexican boys of either social class and upper-class Mexican girls.
The youngest lower-class Mexican boys also stood out in several
respects. A significant interaction for OST Number of Groups
arose largely because the youngest lower-class Mexican boys sorted
objects into an unusually high number of categories as compared
to the other children. Their equivalence range tended to be very
low, since they did not see the ways in which most of the objects
belonged together. This social-class difference for Mexican boys
disappeared with increasing age.

In repeated testing for the Embedded Figures Test, the Mexican
boys caught up with the Americans on EFT Time by the age of
thirteen, while the Mexican girls continued to lag behind. The
difference between boys and girls on field dependency for the
Mexicans was much greater than that for the Americans, among
whom only minor differences due to sex were discovered.

Interactions involving culture, age group, and sex were also
found for Autonomy, Impulsiveness, and Harmavoidance, three
scales clustering together as the nonconformity factor in the Personality Research Form. The eleven-year-old Mexican boys showed
the greatest need for independence. The eleven-year-olds as a
whole were less likely to be impulsive than the older adolescents.
Older American boys also tended to be less fearful, while American
girls of all ages were the most fearful and cautious of any groups.
From the Occupational Values Inventory, it is apparent that prestige was more important for boys than girls among upper-class
eleven-year-olds, while the reverse was true for the lower-class

even-year-olds. This interaction between sex and social class was present for eleven-year-olds and to some extent for fourteen-year-olds, but disappeared completely for seventeen-year-olds in both cultures. It should also be noted that in general Mexican children valued prestige more highly than did the Americans, suggesting that young Mexican boys from upper-class families dream of some day becoming famous more often than any other group.

Still another interaction involving age group, culture, and sex was the value placed upon doing the same kind of work that the child's father did, an item in the Occupational Values Inventory. Following in their fathers' footsteps was valued more highly by boys than girls, with the exception of eleven-year-old Mexicans and seventeen-year-old Americans. The American twelfth-graders were ready to move on to some other occupation, while both boys and girls among the Mexican sixth-graders found their fathers' work appealing.

The most significant interaction of all involving culture and sex occurred for the masculinity-femininity ratings of the male and female drawings from Human Figure Drawing. American girls drew more feminine male figures, while American boys tended to draw more masculine female figures than was the case for Mexican girls and boys. The difference score obtained by subtracting the femininity rating for the female drawing from the masculinity rating for the male drawing yields a Masculinity-Femininity Discrimination index. As summarized in Table 12-2, this index clearly shows a greater degree of discrimination on the part of Mexican children than on the part of Americans. These results are not surprising in view of the de-emphasis of sex differences among American boys and girls and the continued emphasis upon accentuating such differences in the Mexican culture. A significant interaction between culture and sex also appeared for several of the scales in the Personality Research Form. American boys were high on Aggression, while American girls were low; no differences between boys and girls were apparent in Mexico. Higher scores for American boys on Aggression are consistent with their higher scores on HIT Hostility. American girls were also highest of all on need for Affiliation from the PRF, as well as Nurturance. No sex differences were obtained for the Mexican children on either Affiliation or Nurturance. The American teen-age girls showed a stronger need than any other group to be especially sympathetic, maternal, and comforting to others in need of help.

The parent interview also revealed some interesting interactions between culture and sex. Three times as many Mexican children had no regular duties in the home as was true for Americans. While there were no sex differences for the Americans, boys were given home chores only rarely, as compared to girls, in Mexico. None of the Mexican girls showed any interest in hobbies or crafts, although one out of seven American girls did. Only the American children showed any strong interest in intellectual activities, according to the mothers who were interviewed. Mexican girls tended to have fewer interests than any other group. Discussion by parents among themselves of how their child was getting along in school was rather rare for lower-class American daughters but very common for lower-class Mexican daughters. With the exception of lower-class boys, Mexican parents discussed among themselves more frequently how their children were getting along in school than Americans did.

Some interesting differences in social class across the two cultures are also apparent from the highly significant culture-by-social-class interactions found for certain of the items in the parent interview, as well as several measures on the children themselves. While no significant differences existed in arithmetic performance between upper- and lower-class Americans, a marked difference was apparent among the Mexicans, where children from working-class families did much more poorly. Special lessons for the child were more frequent among Americans and upper-class Mexicans, lower-class Mexicans rarely having them. Both American and upper-class Mexican fathers share many activities with the child, while the lower-class Mexican father does this less frequently. Social-class differences are also much greater for Mexicans than for Americans with respect to recreation and trips taken together as a family. Such activities are quite common for both upper- and lower-class Americans and to some extent for upper-class Mexicans. These results all point to the relatively wide gulf between working and professional families in Mexico, as contrasted to the United States. At the same time, it is interesting to note that American children in working-class families value job security much more highly than children of professional, educated families, while just the re-

verse is true for the Mexicans, as indicated by the significant culture-by-social-class interaction for OVI Security.

While these many hundreds of significant findings are difficult
to organize and interpret in any simple fashion, several major
trends are apparent in the results. These are summarized next in
the form of general observations or emerging hypotheses about
culture and personality that merit further examination.

## Some Broad Generalizations

Sex and social-class differences in the cross-cultural patterns of
psychological attributes have been adequately summarized in the
previous section. Differences between boys and girls and between
working and professional or business classes are generally more
marked in Mexico than in the United States. The reasons for these
differences have already been discussed. In addition there are three
other topics on which broad generalizations are justified: (*a*) cognitive abilities and intellectual stimulation of the child; (*b*) active
versus passive coping style; and (*c*) field dependency and socialization practices.

### Cognitive Abilities and Intellectual Stimulation of the Child

A major question of great interest in all modern societies concerns the extent to which aspects of a child's environment within
the home, the school, the neighborhood, and the larger cultural
milieu facilitate or impede the development of cognitive or mental
abilities. While one must be careful not to misinterpret associated
events as having direct implications for cause-and-effect relationships, there are nevertheless many findings within the present
study that bear upon this important topic. The subtests of the
Wechsler Intelligence Scale for Children are often thought of as
measures of intelligence, which in turn are related to success and
failure in school performance as well as, to a much lesser extent,
later success in high-prestige professional occupations. What can
be said about the obtained differences and similarities on certain of
the cognitive variables across the two cultures? Do the interactions
with social class, age, and sex provide significant clues to those aspects of the two cultures that are most conducive to a high degree

of cognitive development? Are there related findings from the parent interview, home environment, and school practices that may account for some of the differences noted in the children's performance on cognitive tests?

Among children in the two cultures as they entered the first grade of school, Mexican children performed slightly better than their American counterparts on Arithmetic and Block Design. The American first-graders did better on Vocabulary, Picture Completion, and the Harris-Goodenough Developmental score from the Human Figure Drawings. After several years of schooling, the initial advantage enjoyed by the Mexicans disappeared. By early adolescence, the American children performed significantly better on all the cognitive tests with one exception—associative learning as measured by the Visual Fractionation Test. When considered together with the greater number of analytic responses by Mexican children to the Conceptual Styles Test, this more rapid associative learning suggests a higher motivation to do well and a stronger wish to avoid error on the part of the Mexican children. It is also worth noting that the patterns of relationships among the WISC subtests differ appreciably across the different age groups, indicating that the concept of "general intelligence" is probably not a useful construct for describing the mental abilities of children in the two cultures. The clear separation of verbal and nonverbal factors and the existence of several other independent factors underlying the WISC and associated cognitive tests indicate that it is necessary to postulate a number of dimensions of mental ability in order to understand fully the nature of cognitive performance by children in Mexico and the United States.

Those items from the interview with mothers that are most directly related to intellectual development are clustered together in Table 12-3 under the heading "intellectual stimulation of the child." The cross-cultural differences for these seven items are indeed striking. The Mexican family was less likely to have intellectually stimulating reading material or study aids for the child in the home. Only rarely did the Mexican parents read regularly to the child before the child entered school, while the majority of American parents read to their children on a regular basis. Most of the Mexican children were unable to read, count, or write before they entered school, while most of the American parents took pride in the fact that their child had made significant progress in these cognitive skills prior to school entrance. At the same time, it should be pointed out that, after the child had entered school, the Mexican parents more often encouraged the child to read than did the Americans. This difference probably means that the American child needs less encouragement to read, since nearly all American mothers reported that their children regularly read unassigned books, while only two-thirds of the Mexican mothers reported such unassigned reading.

When it comes to spoken languages, however, the Mexican family showed decided advantages over the American. Foreign languages (usually English in Mexico City) were spoken in half the Mexican homes, encouraging large numbers of Mexican children to broaden their horizons beyond their native language. In addition, it should be pointed out that Mexican families have a custom of regular story-telling to young children rather than reading to them from books. Consequently, one would expect the oral language facility and associated interpersonal relations to be more highly developed among Mexican children, other things being equal, than they would for their American counterparts.

Yet another difference between the Mexican and American samples that should be noted is the larger number of American fathers who had had experience as high-school or college teachers— nearly twice as many as in the case of the Mexican family. This difference may be partly a result of the large concentration of teachers in Austin due to the presence of the state university, a factor that may account in part for some of the more striking differences in the items clustered under intellectual stimulation of the child.

Certain other differences in family characteristics, parental attitudes, and life style may also enter into the picture as influencing the degree of cognitive development of children in the two cultures. Of greatest importance is the fact that the level of the mother's education in Mexico is markedly lower on the average than the level of education for the American mother. In a developing society such as Mexico, where traditional values do not place much emphasis upon the education of women, it is not surprising that highly educated fathers are frequently married to relatively uneducated mothers. The number of children in the typical Mexican family is almost twice as many as in the American family, creating a situation in the lower-class Mexican family where the mother must devote most of her energies simply to managing the household. In the upper-class Mexican family, an uneducated maid often enters the picture as an important caretaker of young children. In both instances, sibling pressures and influences are probably greater in the Mexican family than in the American, where frequently only one or two children are present. Other relatives are also much more likely to be living in the same home with the Mexican child, providing an immediate extended family that increases the degree of affiliative activity while de-emphasizing solitary intellectual pursuits. The American parent is more likely to plan special events, vacation trips, and private lessons aimed at enriching the life of the child. The American parent is more likely to get involved in assisting the child with his school work where necessary. There is also a greater value placed by American mothers on the development of independence and a high degree of intellectual curiosity than is typical of the Mexican mother.

All of these cross-cultural differences in family life style and home environment point toward the greater opportunity, on the average, for the American child, regardless of social class, to be encouraged toward independent thinking and intellectual activities in which individual achievement is stressed rather than interpersonal fulfillment. The gulf between the social classes in the rapidly changing society of Mexico City sharply distinguishes the working-class Mexican family and its traditional orientation from the professional and upper-class Mexican family, which looks increasingly like the American middle-class family with its high achievement values.

While the youngest children in both cultures had similar patterns and levels of most cognitive abilities, after several years of schooling the two cultures diverged considerably, the Mexican children generally falling behind the Americans. Aside from the differences in the degree of intellectual stimulation within the Mexican and American home, there are undoubtedly differences in emphasis and mode of instruction within the schools themselves that can account for these findings. Public education in Austin for the dominant Anglo-American subculture is highly homogeneous, regardless of social class. Special instructional materials, well-trained teachers, and a great deal more capital investment are possible within the American school. By contrast, elementary and secondary education in Mexico is highly heterogeneous, ranging from rather limited, overcrowded public schools to highly enriched upper-class private schools for those who can pay the extra tuition. The increasing divergence between lower- and upper-class Mexican children as they progress through school may be at least in part due to this inequality of opportunity.

Another feature of the Mexican system of education that may be significant in its implications for cognitive development is the stress upon rote learning and homework typical of most Mexican schools, both public and private. This type of passive learning does not encourage independent divergent thinking to the extent that the more active learning characteristic of American schools may do. Failure is more common in the Mexican school, and children are often forced to go back and do a grade level over once again if they are unable to master the curriculum satisfactorily. In some cases, the Mexican child may fall hopelessly behind and drop out of school at an early age. For the American child in the dominant Anglo middle class, such failure is rather rare.

So many variables differ in the two cultures that it is impossible from the present study to pin down more precisely the importance of factors influencing mental development in young children. There is, however, a closely related study undertaken by Mary Tamm in the American School in Mexico City that sheds light on this important question (Tamm 1967a; 1967b). Tamm designed a study involving bilingual Mexican and American children attending the same school. Thirty children in the first, fourth, and seventh grades were tested at six years, eight months, nine years, eight months, and twelve years, eight months of age respectively in order to provide precise parallels to the experimental design employed in the cross-cultural study between the United States and Mexico. One-half of the children were native Mexicans for whom Spanish was the primary language. They generally came from upper-class Mexican families in which there was a strong desire on the part of the parents for their children to obtain an American-style education. The remainder of the children were Americans whose fathers were businessmen or government representatives in

Mexico City. These American families wanted their children to develop bilingual-bicultural skills and attitudes. The curriculum in the American School was taught half in English and half in Spanish.

Tamm administered the Holtzman Inkblot Technique and all the subtests of the Wechsler Intelligence Scale for Children to each of the ninety school children two years in a row. The children's test performance was analyzed in a three-way analysis-of-variance design—by culture, age group, and year of testing.

Of the WISC subtests, only Digit Span proved significant across cultures, the Mexican children doing slightly better than the Americans. The usual developmental differences were clearly apparent in both groups. On the Holtzman Inkblot Technique, however, marked differences were found between the Mexican and American children—differences that in every respect were essentially the same as the major differences found for the HIT in the larger cross-cultural study. The Mexican children used much more small detail, gave less color, less movement, less pathognomic verbalization, less human content, less anxiety, and less hostility than did the American children.

The lack of any notable differences between the Mexican and American children on the intelligence tests in Tamm's study, regardless of the length of time the child had spent in the American School or his age, provides convincing evidence that the combination of home environment and schooling is important in the development of these mental abilities. At the same time, the dramatic differences in personality and perceptual style reflected in the Holtzman Inkblot Technique—differences that are identical to those obtained when Americans in Austin are compared with Mexican children in Mexico City—indicate that fundamental aspects of the American and Mexican personality or "national character" remain intact in spite of common schooling and other forces within the immediate milieu of the children that would tend to produce convergence of the two cultures. The sociocultural premises underlying American and Mexican societies and the basically different styles of coping with the challenges of life in the two cultures provide a key to the interpretation of the above results.

A basic value in Mexico is represented by the saying "As long as our family stays together, we are strong." As A. H. Maslow and Díaz-Guerrero (1960) have pointed out, in its solidarity, the Mexican family tends to shut itself off from the outer world. The child is brought up in the bosom of the family, playing with his siblings rather than with schoolmates or neighborhood children as the American child usually does. Unlike the father in most American families, the Mexican father is the undisputed authority on all family matters, an authority usually obeyed without question. Though she may frequently suffer in silence, the mother is revered as the primary source of affection and care. This emphasis on family affiliation leads the Mexican to say, "I will achieve mainly because of my family, and for my family, rather than myself." By contrast, the self-reliant American would say, "I will achieve mainly because of my ability and initiative and for myself rather than my family."

In general, when faced with the testing situation, the Mexican child is willing to cooperate, although he will seldom take the initiative. He will try to please the adult examiner and will tend to be cautious. By contrast, the American child will see the testing situation as a challenge to be mastered, an opportunity to show how much he can do. Given a common schooling environment, as in Tamm's American School, and achievement-oriented parents for Mexicans as well as Americans, it is easy to understand how such achievement-relevant tests as the WISC subtests would yield essentially the same results for both Mexican and American children in Mexico City. Without such common schooling and achievement-oriented home environments, however, the more passive coping style, affiliative characteristics of the extended family, and strong traditional values of the typical Mexican families in the cross-cultural longitudinal study, especially the lower-class Mexicans, would yield to increasing divergence between the performance of the American children in Austin and their Mexican counterparts in Mexico City. The different sociocultural premises underlying American and Mexican culture are explored thoroughly in Chapter 13, as part of a general discussion of culture and personality. The specific implications of active versus passive coping style for test performance on the cognitive-perceptual style and personality measures in the present study are explored in more detail in the next section.

## Active versus Passive Coping Style

Most of the differences between the Mexican and American children on the Holtzman Inkblot Technique can be understood better in terms of coping style than any other concept. The American child produced faster reaction time, used larger portions of the inkblots in giving his responses, gave more definite form to his responses, and was still able to integrate more parts of the inkblots while doing so. In addition, he incorporated other stimulus properties of the inkblots, such as color and shading, into his responses more often than did the Mexican child and elaborated his responses by ascribing more movement to his percepts. In attempting to deal with all aspects of the inkblots in such an active fashion, however, he failed more often than the Mexican child, that is, the Mexican child gave responses with better form and less often produced responses that showed deviant thinking and anxious and hostile content. In general, the American child tried to deal with the testing situation in a much more active fashion than the Mexican child, even when he was unable to do so successfully.

On the cognitive style tests, the Mexicans showed more restrictiveness in classifying concepts, showed greater field dependency, and perceived time as passing more slowly. From scales on the personality tests, it is apparent that Mexicans generally had a greater need for neatness and order and a lesser need to be spontaneously impulsive or to do things just for the fun of it. Mexican adolescents also showed less concern for what others thought of them and less need to seek out others for companionship than American teen-agers. At the same time, the Mexican adolescent has a greater need for independence, a need growing out of his increasing awareness that he is indeed highly dependent upon others within his extended family and affiliative network.

Given a coping style based more upon passive obedience and desire to please, rather than active independence and struggle for mastery, specific anxieties and defensiveness concerning test-taking are more acute for the Mexican child than for the American. Tests are a necessary hurdle repeatedly demanded of children by society.

An active coping style provides a self-directed means of reducing such anxiety. A passive, obedient coping style leads only to conforming behavior in the face of threatening tests, a form of inactivity that seems only to heighten specific anxieties.

## Field Dependency and Socialization Practices

The concept of field dependence and its converse, field independence, grew out of the early studies by Witkin and others (1954), as a way of explaining consistent patterns of perception in a variety of situations where conflicting perceptual cues make it difficult for some people to extract the embedded figure from its surrounding ground. Although there are a number of experimental perceptual tasks that have been used to measure field dependence, Witkin's Embedded Figures Test has proven most popular because of its ease of administration in a variety of situations. People differ considerably in their ability to extract an embedded figure from its ground. The field dependence-independence dimension refers specifically to this ability to overcome an embedding context, an ability somewhat different from that of overcoming the effects of distracting fields.

Later studies by Witkin and others (1962) broadened the concept of field dependence to embrace the concept of differentiation. Evidence has accumulated from a number of studies that such personality attributes as differentiation of self-concept, articulateness of body image, and method of impulse regulation form an interrelated cluster that includes field independence as measured by Witkin's tests. Such psychological differentiation is closely tied to developmental change from undifferentiated early states to more highly differentiated adult states. At the same time it is clear from these investigations that high or low differentiation (or field dependence) has no relationship to general intelligence, personal maladjustment, or other aspects of the individual often judged to be good or bad within the value system of the culture. Women tend to be more field dependent than men; younger children tend to be more field dependent than older; and nurturant, affiliative, socially sensitive, intuitive individuals tend to be more field dependent than analytical, scientific persons. While many studies have been done in the past decade expanding upon the concept of differentiation (field independence), the studies of greatest relevance to the current investigation are those concerned with cross-cultural comparisons and with the relationship between socialization of the child and later patterns of development as reflected in this dimension.

Many of these cross-cultural studies have been summarized by Witkin and his colleagues (1974) in reviewing the relationship between social conformity pressures in a culture and the degree of psychological differentiation that develops in members of the society. Typical of the earlier studies is the one by John W. Berry (1966), dealing with two very different nonwestern cultures, the Temne villagers of West Africa and Eskimos from Frobisher Bay. These two cultures were selected because of their marked differences in socialization practices and visual environments. The Temne are farmers in a land with a great variety of vegetation and color. The Eskimos are hunters who travel widely on the sea and land and inhabit a world of uniform visual stimulation. Socialization practices among the Temne place great emphasis upon strict discipline and conformity, coupled with affection for the young child, who is not allowed to assert his individuality. By contrast, Eskimo children are encouraged to become individualistic, assertive, and venturesome. Children are treated lovingly, and punishment is avoided wherever possible. Using a variety of tests, Berry confirmed the earlier hypothesis of Witkin concerning the relationship between socialization practices and psychological differentiation. The Temne child-rearing practices and value orientation fostered development of field-dependent individuals, while the Eskimos proved to be highly field independent.

In the more recent study by Witkin and his colleagues (1974) on social conformity and psychological differentiation, two villages were selected from each of three countries (Holland, Italy, and Mexico) because they presented contrasting pictures within each country concerning the degree of emphasis on conformity to family, religious, and political authority. Differentiation was assessed by a battery of tests, including the Embedded Figures Test and Human Figure Drawing. In every comparison of mean test scores between pairs of villages, in each of the three countries children from the village in which social conformity was stressed obtained scores reflecting less differentiated functioning. These cross-cultural studies strongly suggest that greater field independence is likely to be found in cultures that place great emphasis on autonomy in child rearing and are loosely structured. Greater field dependence is likely to be found in cultures that emphasize conformance with adult authority and have a strict hierarchical social organization. Taking the findings for Mexico reported by Witkin and others (1966), together with the results of the present study, we can see that, although Mexican children tend to be more field dependent than their American peers, there is at the same time diversity in extent of field dependence among Mexican children related to diversity in the extent of emphasis on conformity.

A number of findings in the present study concerning attitudes, values, family life style, and socialization practices within the Mexican home closely resemble items employed by R. B. Dyk and Witkin (1965), Dyk (1969), and the cross-cultural studies mentioned above. Each of the following outcomes from the current investigation would foster greater field dependence among Mexican children and greater field independence among American.

1. Mexicans, particularly women, tend to be passive-obedient.

2. Fewer Mexican fathers, particularly from the lower-class group, share activities with their sons. (Previous studies have shown that children, especially sons, of families where the father is absent or distant tend to be relatively field dependent).

3. Mexican children are given less responsibility in the home.

4. Mexican children are more likely to have their friends chosen by their parents.

5. Mexican mothers are more likely to admit to problems in child rearing and to express the attitude that child rearing is difficult.

6. Mexican mothers are less accepting and more controlling of their children.

7. Mexican mothers give their children less freedom to express themselves or to take part in family discussions.

8. Mexican mothers are less tolerant of children's right to engage in activities on their own without including their parents.

9. Mexican mothers tend to be more authoritarian.

10. Mexican mothers are more likely to press their children toward socially favored goals, such as getting good grades in school or making a name for themselves.

11. Mexican mothers, particularly from the lower classes, place higher value on strict obedience in their children.

12. Mexican mothers value independence in their children less than American mothers.

13. Curiosity, which implies looking into things on one's own, is less valued in children by Mexican mothers.

14. The high predominance of Catholicism, frequency of church attendance, and other signs of adherence to traditional values constitute greater social-conformity pressures for the Mexican child.

While all of the above observations concerning differences in the family life styles and socialization practices of Mexicans and Americans lead to the same general conclusion that Mexicans should be more field dependent and Americans more field independent, it should be noted that the actual differences cross-culturally, though highly significant in a statistical sense, are not large. The amount of overlap in the distributions for Mexican and American children on the scores from the Embedded Figures Test is very great, in spite of the fact that the means themselves are different. With increasing age in the longitudinal study, there was sufficient convergence of the two cultures that by year 5 the differences between the Mexican and American children had diminished to the point where they were no longer significant, regardless of the score analyzed. Another word of caution that should be injected in any interpretation of these results concerns the lack of any appreciable relationships between scores on the Embedded Figures Test and specific items from the parent interview within each of the two cultures. Admittedly, few of the items within the parent interview proved to be sufficiently sensitive and robust to permit their inclusion in the correlational studies. It is regretted that more information bearing upon socialization practices was not obtained in a standardized fashion in each culture so that investigation of these other important points could be fully carried out.

---

From differences noted in the two cultures, one would expect that in the traditional, passive, affiliative hierarchy of Mexico, there would be more value placed on affective rather than cognitive aspects of life, coupled with a preference for a static rather than a dynamic approach. The Mexican should be family-centered rather than individual-centered; should prefer love, friendship, and leisure to work; and should prefer external controls to self-directed impulsiveness. At the same time, the Mexican should be somewhat more pessimistic about the hardships of life and passive-obedient rather than active-rebelling in style of coping with stresses in the environment. For the American, on the other hand, the opposite of each of these statements should tend to be true. In Chapter 13, a more detailed analysis of these personality and sociocultural differences will be examined in the larger context of the historical antecedents for existing culture in Mexico and the United States.

# 13. Some Reflections on Culture and Personality

As a formal discipline, the study of culture and personality has been described as the youngest and smallest branch of anthropology (Spiro 1968). Hardly existing until recently outside of the United States, it is a hybrid of anthropology and psychology, with a little sociology frequently added for good measure. In the initial anthropological studies, only psychoanalytic psychology seemed to provide a bridge between field data obtained by anthropologists and theories of personality development that emerged from clinical studies. Testing the universality of Freudian concepts provided a major impetus for anthropologists studying exotic isolated cultures. In the initial studies, prior to World War II, anthropologists had few techniques for the assessment of personality other than depth interviews and systematic observation of family interaction. Projective techniques and other nonverbal psychological methods were also tried in subsequent years with mixed success. In nearly every instance, these personality studies were unsystematic, heavily descriptive, and empirical in nature, usually concentrating upon intensive case studies of a single society.

Serious cross-cultural investigations of culture and personality were initiated only twenty-five years ago by J. W. M. Whiting,

Child, and others working from the Human Relations Area Files
and starting with Murdock's (1949) classification of nearly two
hundred societies as a universe from which to draw appropriate
samples representing wide cultural variation. The inadequacies
of these data in the Human Relations Area Files led to new systematic field studies on child-rearing practices and personality development (B. B. Whiting 1963) in which six different cultures
were studied intensively and concurrently by specially trained
teams of field workers. But even in this pancultural approach, with
a tremendous investment of time and talent, the net result was limited to six extensive, detailed case studies, rich in complexity and
limited in significant generalizations.

Unlike the anthropologists, who were highly sophisticated in
dealing with complex cultural and linguistic variables, the social
psychologists quickly adapted their American-style techniques by
simple translation and replication in other literate societies. The
net result until recently has been a plethora of cross-cultural findings that are uninterpretable because the problems of sampling,
linguistic equivalence of meaning, examiner variability, and cultural variation have been lightly dismissed or ignored. With few
exceptions, cross-cultural psychological studies prior to the 1960's
suffered badly from fatal methodological and theoretical flaws.

In the twelve years since the present cross-cultural developmental study was begun in Mexico and the United States, cross-
cultural psychology has mushroomed into a subdiscipline itself.
Broadly speaking, this subdiscipline involves the psychological
study of individuals, their differences and similarities, in two or
more cultures, using equivalent methods of measurement. Indicative of the burgeoning number of studies in this new field is the
recent extensive review by Harry C. Triandis, Roy S. Malpass, and
Andrew R. Davidson (1971). Within the five-year period up to
late 1970, nearly four hundred studies in cross-cultural psychology
were uncovered by Triandis and his colleagues. Only a small number of these, however, dealt specifically with culture and personality.

While there are still all too many fragmentary studies undertaken in the name of cross-cultural research, an impressive number of investigators are working together across different nations
on major programs. Nearly all of these comparative studies are

cross-sectional in nature, consisting of one sampling point in time rather than the systematic study of change within several societies by repeated measures on the same individuals over a number of years. A cross-cultural longitudinal design like the present one requires unusual resources and financial stability that only rarely exist.

As cultural anthropologists, sociologists, and psychologists have drawn closer together in recent years, a number of new books have appeared that deal with culture, society, and personality. Child (1968) reviewed the culture and personality area; George A. De-Vos and A. A. Hippler (1969) covered the closely related area of cultural psychology; Alex Inkeles and Daniel J. Levinson (1969) examined the theory and methodology concerned with national character; John J. Honigmann (1967) published a book on personality in culture; Douglas R. Price-Williams (1969) compiled selected readings on ethnopsychology, as did Ilisan Al-Issa and Wayne Dennis (1970); Robert B. Edgerton (1971) related aspects of personality to other features of four primitive societies; Michael Cole and others (1971) reported on the relation between culture and cognition; Triandis, Malpass, and Davidson (1971) developed comparative methods for the analysis of subjective culture and applied them in novel ways to a variety of different cultures; Guy J. Manaster and Robert J. Havighurst (1972) published a handbook of how and why to design and perform cross-national research; and Robert A. LeVine (1973) completed his theoretical and methodological review of culture, behavior, and personality—all within the short span of six years, testifying to the greatly increased interest in this interdisciplinary field.

Part of the problem in dealing with culture and personality has been the development of sufficiently precise, operationally defined concepts to delimit the terms *culture* and *personality* in a manner that would stimulate theory and research. After reviewing several hundred definitions of culture, A. L. Kroeber and C. Kluckhohn arrived at a comprehensive formulation that represents a condensation of what most American anthropologists would call culture: "Culture consists of patterns, explicit and implicit, of and for behavior acquired and transmitted by symbols, constituting the distinctive achievement of human groups, including their embodiments in artifacts; the essential core of culture consists of traditional (i.e., historically derived and selected) ideas and especially their attached values; culture systems may, on the one hand, be considered as products of action, on the other as conditioning elements of further action" (1952, p. 181).

The definition of what is meant substantively by personality is even more difficult to establish with any generality. As Calvin S. Hall and Gardner Lindzey point out in their comprehensive review of theories of personality, "the way in which a given individual will define personality will depend completely upon his particular theoretical preference" (1957, p. 9). In other words, personality is defined largely by the specific empirical concepts that are part of the theory of personality explicitly or implicitly employed by the investigator or observer. In spite of the many different theories of personality, there is a general understanding by most cross-cultural psychologists of what is meant by personality. One of the clearest definitions is that given by Ross Stagner:

The definition of personality as an inner system of beliefs, expectancies, desires and values has numerous advantages. From the viewpoint of research, it provides a focus of investigation less convenient than a definition in response terms, but less confusing than a definition in stimulus terms. On logical grounds, it appears to unite successfully these two divergent approaches. One has no difficulty in thinking of an inner structure which determines responses, which in turn influences the judgments of others about us. Furthermore, it resolves certain problems raised by the facts of variable behavior in different social environments and of similar responses which require dissimilar interpretations. (1961, p. 8)

Three basic questions are posed by LeVine (1973) for research on culture and personality. Are there psychological differences between human populations? If so (and there is growing evidence to support such a conclusion), what are the causes in individual development of psychological differences between populations? And finally, how are psychological differences between populations related to the sociocultural environments of these populations? With respect to the present study, the answer to LeVine's first question is clearly positive in one respect and probably negative in another. There are indeed psychological differences between Mexican and American children in terms of their mean scores on a wide variety of cognitive, perceptual, and personality measures.

The amount of diversity within each culture, however, is so great that considerable overlap exists in the distribution of scores in the two cultures. Moreover, the interrelationships of variables and general dimensions underlying the various domains studied are highly similar in the two cultures, suggesting that the underlying psychological processes are identical. While personality differences noted between Mexican and American children can be attributed to recognized differences in the two cultures, such inferences must remain tentative, since they cannot be rigorously demonstrated in terms of cause-and-effect relations.

LeVine goes on to classify existing theoretical conceptions of culture-personality relations into five main groups: (*a*) the anti–culture-personality position, which mainly characterizes outsiders to the field; (*b*) psychological reductionism, in which individual psychological factors are seen as independent causes of cultural and social behavior; (*c*) the personality-is-culture view, or configural approach to culture and personality, in which both *culture* and *personality* refer to configurations of behavior that are manifested and carried by individuals but are characteristic of a group; (*d*) the personality-mediation view, in which personality has both its cultural causes or antecedents and its cultural effects or consequences; and (*e*) the "two-systems" conception, which represents modal personality and sociocultural institutions as two systems interacting with each other. Of these five positions, only the last two are seen by LeVine as representing tenable positions on which to base empirical studies. The conception of personality as a connective or mediator between two aspects of culture is particularly appropriate to employ in the present study of personality development among Mexican and American children.

Formulated first by Abram Kardiner and Ralph Linton, the personality-mediation view was further refined by Whiting and Child. A recent version of the Whiting theory, as formulated by Robert A. and Barbara B. LeVine (1966), is presented in Figure 13-1. Child-rearing practices for socialization of the individual operate within the constraints set by the maintenance system of the culture, which in turn functions for the survival of the society in relation to its external environment. The products or expressive aspects of the culture can be thought of as the projective system. Personality is seen not only as mediating causal influence between

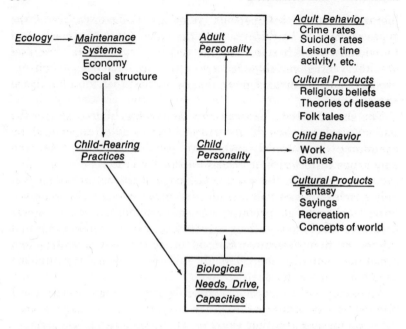

Figure 13-1. The relation of personality to culture. Reprinted from *Nyansongo*, by Robert LeVine and Barbara LeVine (1966), by permission of John Wiley and Sons, Inc.

two aspects of culture but also as actively integrating them with one another.

Granted that biological as well as social factors enter into the development of an individual personality, certain shared attitudes, beliefs, and values within the culture provide a common basis for socialization of the child. These implicit attitudes, beliefs, and values constitute sociocultural premises that are fundamental determinants of shared personality characteristics within a given culture (Díaz-Guerrero 1967*b*). A historic sociocultural premise is a deep-seated belief or assumption about life transmitted from one generation to the next and held by a majority of individuals belonging to a given culture, subculture, or group. While various sayings, beliefs, and world views can be thought of as the cultural products, they are also expressive of the underlying sociocultural premises, which in turn form or govern the feelings, the ideas, the hierarchization of interpersonal relations, the stipulation of the types of roles to be fulfilled, and the rules for the interaction of individuals in such roles. In this respect, sociocultural premises are intervening variables inferred from an analysis of cultural products but understood more deeply in terms of their historical antecedents.

The shared beliefs, expectancies, and values that comprise the sociocultural premises of the culture can be best understood by examining the cultural products in relation to both short- and long-range historical happenings within the culture. Verbal statements or sayings in the natural language of the culture often provide a rich source of cultural products from which to infer underlying sociocultural premises. Such statements reflect logical premises; that is to say, they signify the sources of conclusions and inferences that determine courses of action and modulate and sometimes actually determine the feelings, the thinking, and the behavior of the individual.

An example of an important dimension reflecting a sociocultural premise is the primary dimension underlying the sixty bipolar items comprising the Views of Life Questionnaire (Díaz-Guerrero 1973). Tentatively labeled Affiliative Obedience versus Active Self-Assertion, this general dimension sharply discriminates among four different groups of fourteen-year-old populations, as illustrated in Table 13-1. Several of the pairs of statements making up the subdimension of Authority under this general dimension within the Views of Life Questionnaire are given in Table 13-2, where the results are broken down further to indicate social-class as well as cross-cultural differences. An individual filling out the questionnaire is asked to choose which of the alternatives in each item is closer to his own personal beliefs. The over-all sociocultural-premise dimension of Affiliative Obedience versus Active Self-Assertion is obtained by combining a number of the items into a more abstract scale in accordance with earlier factor analyses of item intercorrelations conducted as part of the Cross-National Study of Coping Styles and Achievement (Peck and associates, forthcoming). While similar data are also available for Japan, Brazil, Italy, and Germany, only data for the two major cultures of the present study and their historical antecedents are summarized in Tables 13-1 and 13-2.

Table 13-1
Differences among Fourteen-Year-Old Boys from Four Cities in
Affiliative Obedience versus Active Self-Assertion

| | Mexico City (%) | Austin (%) | Chicago (%) | London (%) |
|---|---|---|---|---|
| Affiliative Obedience | 60 | 38 | 26 | 15 |
| Active Self-Assertion | 40 | 62 | 74 | 85 |

SOURCE: Taken from data collected in the Cross-National Study of Coping Styles and Achievement in 1968–1969 by K. Miller (London), R. Havighurst (Chicago), R. Peck (Austin), and R. Díaz-Guerrero (Mexico), using the Views of Life Questionnaire. (See Peck and associates, forthcoming.)
NOTE: N = 200 for each percentage.

Table 13-2
Cross-Cultural and Social-Class Differences in the Authority Factor

| Item No. | Mexico City | | Austin | | Chicago | | London | |
|---|---|---|---|---|---|---|---|---|
| | Lower (%) | Middle (%) | Lower (%) | Middle (%) | Lower (%) | Middle (%) | Lower (%) | Middle (%) |
| 22a | 18 | 41 | 52 | 67 | 60 | 72 | 81 | 89 |
| 22b | 82 | 59 | 48 | 33 | 40 | 28 | 19 | 11 |
| 40a | 61 | 40 | 43 | 37 | 29 | 24 | 17 | 17 |
| 40b | 39 | 60 | 57 | 63 | 71 | 76 | 83 | 83 |
| 57a | 65 | 51 | 32 | 34 | 23 | 14 | 11 | 12 |
| 57b | 35 | 49 | 68 | 66 | 77 | 86 | 89 | 88 |

SOURCE: From the Cross-National Study of Coping Styles and Achievement (Peck and associates, forthcoming).
NOTE: Table gives percentages of fourteen-year-old boys from each city and social class who selected each statement in the forced-choice bipolar statement pairs constituting the Authority Factor in the Views of Life Questionnaire. N = 100 for each percentage.

Item Statement Pairs from Authority Factor

22a. When a person thinks his (or her) father's orders are unreasonable, he should feel free to question them.
22b. A father's orders should always be obeyed.
40a. A teacher's orders should always be obeyed.
40b. When a person thinks his (or her) teacher's orders are unreasonable, he should feel free to question them.
57a. A person should not question his (or her) mother's word.
57b. Any mother can make mistakes, and one should feel free to question her word when it seems wrong.

Among the three English-speaking groups, the majority of fourteen-year-old boys subscribe to Active Self-Assertion as a sociocultural premise, while their Mexican counterparts prefer Affiliative Obedience. The four populations are distributed on a continuum ranging from London, which is highly active, through Chicago and Austin, which are moderately active, to Mexico City, which is the least active. The differences among all four groups are statistically significant. As indicated in Table 13-2, the most striking differences among cultures appear for the lower working class rather than the upper middle class, a finding consistent with the social-class-by-culture interactions found repeatedly in the present study. The lower working class, especially in a more traditional society that is still developing toward modern industrialism, tends to be the primary carrier of traditional sociocultural premises inherited from the past.

It is interesting to examine the four variations in culture represented by the four cities. The underlying sociocultural premise represented by the Affiliative Obedience versus Active Self-Assertion dimension is intimately linked to the historical antecedents of contemporary culture in each of the four cities. Let's examine several of the critical historical incidents in the overthrow of absolute, religious, or state authority in each of these cities. London, as the seat of power for British kings over the centuries, laid the groundwork for the development of individual freedoms and the overthrow of absolute authority with the Magna Carta in the thirteenth century, the English Reformation in the sixteenth century, and the execution of Charles I by Parliament in 1649. The first major reformation in Mexico occurred in 1860, a reformation that was not completed until the Mexican Revolution of 1910, only sixty-four years ago. Although Austin and Chicago are both cities within the same nation, unlike Chicago, Austin shares its cultural heritage with Mexico. In addition to their common Anglo-Saxon heritage, the American Revolution of 1776 predated the establishment of both Chicago and Austin as cities. Both Mexico City and London, on the other hand, have existed as metropolitan areas for many centuries. Clearly, the cultural antecedents of all four cities with respect to the handling of authority and related sociocultural premises are different. Let's take a closer look at these cultural antecedents in Mexico and the United States.

*Some Cultural Antecedents of Contemporary*
*Society in Mexico and the United States*

The historical cultural antecedents of contemporary society in
Mexico and the United States have been richly documented and
analyzed by numerous historians, philosophers, and social critics.
To cover in any comprehensive manner this voluminous literature
would be an undertaking far beyond the scope of the present work.
Nevertheless, a brief sketch highlighting some of the important
work in this field, particularly that done in Mexico, which is less
well known elsewhere, may suffice to illustrate the importance
of the historical antecedents of contemporary culture as they influence shared attitudes, beliefs, and values that form an integral
part of individual personality.

In his *Many Mexicos* (1962), L. B. Simpson stressed the great
efforts of Spain, particularly through its friars, to establish the City
of God in Hispanic America. Originating in 400 A.D. in the writings of Saint Augustine, the City of God constituted a utopian
vision that drove the Franciscan and Dominican Friars (followed
later by Augustinians and Jesuits) to build thousands of convents
and churches throughout Spanish America. In Mexico these early
friars were apparently warm and understanding individuals who
tended to the needs of the Indians and in turn exacted work from
them. There are numerous historical testimonies of friars speaking
out for the interest of the Indians against the semifeudal lords who
were first the conquistadors and their descendants and then later
the central government.

Far more common than elsewhere in New Spain was the formation in Mexico of the mestizo family. The union of the male
Spanish conqueror, the powerful, with one or several of the Aztec
or other defeated Indian women, the weak, was the modal pattern
that could easily be responsible for the contemporary Mexican
sociocultural premise that men are superior to women.

Within the utopian vision of the early friars representing the
Catholic kings of Spain, there was a natural necessity to establish
and maintain a hierarchy of absolute power, but love could be
given in equal amounts to everybody. Santa Teresa de Jesús even
attempted to establish equality through the hierarchy. She used
the analogy that there were different glasses of different sizes but

each glass could be filled all the way to the top. As Bernardino de Sahagún pointed out (1938), a hierarchy of power within both the government and the family was also typical of the preconquest Aztecs and their empire, leading naturally to an easy acceptance of the Spanish order for over three hundred years.

Leopoldo Zea, the noted Mexican philosopher, attempted to include in one sweeping synthesis the history of Spanish America face to face with that of Anglo-America. He has the following to say with respect to the choices confronting the liberals and conservatives of Spanish America:

All of Spanish America will divide itself in two groups: The group of those who aspire to convert their countries into modern nations and the group of those that will oppose all transformation, considering that the best form of government is the one they have inherited from Spain; the latter aspire to an order similar to that of Spain, but without Spain.

In their intentions, those in the second group have the greatest advantages. The first group, the revolutionaries, have no other advantage but their audacity and their persistence. The conservative groups count with the sturdy allies of habits and custom imposed by Spain during three centuries. The liberators are soon aware of this fact; to counteract it they do not find any other solution than a species of enlightened despotism; dictatorships for freedom. It was necessary to force the Spanish Americans into entering a new world of freedom, denying them the right of selecting any other road. This was particularly necessary, since the freedom for choice would have no other source of information than the same assemblage of habits and customs which had been originally imposed by force. Only when Spanish Americans should become aware and know their freedom, only then could they be abandoned to their destiny. Meanwhile, the liberators will assume responsibility for these nations; Bolívar made his powers felt to the people, to the nations that he liberated. The same was done by O'Higgins in Chile, Rivadavia in Argentina, and Dr. Francia in Paraguay. But before the dictatorships for freedom, there will rise the forces committed to the restoration of the old order. Liberal dictatorships or conservative dictatorships. (Zea 1956, pp. 26–27, trans. R. Díaz-Guerrero)

Anglo-Americans, born in freedom, have never been able to understand these facts. While Spanish American republics have had scores of revolutions in the space of 150 years, the United States has suffered only one Civil War.

In their study of the changing American character, D. Riesman, N. Glazer, and R. Denney (1950) were concerned with the link between social character and society. While both conformity and creativity are a part of social character, according to Riesman, societies and individuals may live well enough without creativity but they cannot exist without some mode of conformity, even if it be one of rebellion. Societies are divided roughly into three types, depending upon their position on the curve of population growth— tradition-directed people in societies of high growth potential, inner-directed people in societies of transitional population growth, and other-directed people in societies of incipient population decline. To support his macrotheory of society and character, Riesman accumulates an impressive amount of evidence supporting the hypothesis that the United States moved rapidly from a society of high growth potential in its origin to a transitional society with a major emphasis upon inner-directed people who acquired very early in life an internalized set of goals that provided the principal mode of securing conformity: "Such a society is characterized by increased personal mobility, by a rapid accumulation of capital (teamed with devastating technological shifts), and by an almost constant expansion: intensive expansion in the production of goods and people, and extensive expansion in exploration, colonization, and imperialism. The greater choices this society gives—and the greater initiatives it demands in order to cope with its novel problems—are handled by character types who can manage to live socially without strict and self-evident tradition-direction. These are the inner-directed types" (Riesman, Glazer, and Denney 1950, pp. 29–30).

The inner-directed character is bound by traditions that are incorporated into his "psychological gyroscope," which, once it is set upon a certain course through socialization, provides an inner-direction for the individual's later choices and values. While the tradition-directed person hardly thinks of himself as an individual, the inner-directed person has heightened self-awareness and highly values his apparent freedom of choice.

Stabilization of population growth leads to the third type of society, according to Riesman, in which the other-directed character emerges as dominant. Metropolitan America twenty-five years ago was seen as the only illustration of a society in which other-direction was the dominant mode of insuring conformity. More recently, some societies of Western Europe would also be added. The primary characteristic of other-directed people is the strong psychological need for approval from one's contemporaries, who provide the source of direction for the individual. Of course, Riesman recognizes that these idealized "types" hardly exist in reality, being primarily useful for organizing masses of information in simplified form.

Contemporary American society is probably going through yet another major change as an aftermath to the convulsive period of the 1960's. In the early 1960's prior to the assassination of President Kennedy, the optimism of American society seemed boundless. The New Frontier and subsequent Great Society constituted a fulfillment of the American Dream that seemed almost within reach. A rapid succession of assassinations, the rise of terrorism, and the onset of the Vietnam War soon washed away the remnants of the American Dream. A new generation arose in the mid-1960's—a generation defiant of contemporary American values and determined to launch a counterculture to compensate for the perceived excesses of their predecessors. The period of data collection from American children in Austin during the present study covered most of this era, 1962–1968.

Recent studies on the attitudes of American youth by Daniel Yankelovich, Inc., an American opinion-research organization, point to major changes in the complexion and outlook of an entire generation of young Americans (Yankelovich 1972; 1974). Yankelovich interprets this extraordinary pattern of change as due to two unrelated factors, the Vietnam War and the emergence of a new set of postaffluent values. By 1973, the annual surveys by Yankelovich led him to conclude that, while the Vietnam War and youthful values intimately tied to it are now past history, the new values have spread from the minority of college students identified as forerunners to the majority of youth. Religion, patriotism, and the belief that hard work always pays off are no longer seen as very important values by the majority of young Americans. At the same time, there has been a return to traditional career aspirations and a search for economic security. Two motivations are implied by

the new set of postaffluent values, desire for personal self-fulfill-
ment and a new vision of what a just and harmonious society
might be.

These college youth studied across the nation by Daniel Yankelovich, Inc., in annual surveys during 1969–1973 are contemporaries
of the Austin children tested in the present study during the 1960's.
While no similar systematic data are available on a national scale
in Mexico, it can be assumed that cultural change in Mexico, as in
the United States, has been proceeding at a more rapid pace in the
past ten years than ever before. Among high-school students in
Mexico City significant changes away from traditional patterns
in the sociocultural premises underlying male-female and parent-
daughter relations were discovered between 1959 and 1970 (Díaz-
Guerrero 1974).

Results from the present study as reported in the previous chapters, as well as the recent findings of other investigators working in
Mexico and the United States, point to a number of personality
differences closely related to contrasting aspects of the two cultures. Having reviewed the larger context of historical antecedents
for existing cultures in Mexico and the United States, let us turn
now to a more detailed analysis of these personality differences.

## *Major Personality Dimensions Related to*
## *Contrasts in Mexican and American Cultures*

Throughout the preceding chapters, a number of significant
differences were found between Mexican and American children
with respect to cognitive, perceptual, and personality development.
Several broad generalizations were summarized in Chapter 12—
generalizations dealing with the cognitive abilities and intellectual
stimulation of the child, active versus passive coping styles, and the
way in which field dependence or psychological differentiation is
related to socialization practices in the two cultures. Other investigators working with Mexican and American populations have
reported findings highly compatible with the results obtained in
the present study. In some cases a somewhat different conceptualization of a personality dimension has been employed. While none
of these other studies are truly comparable to the present cross-
cultural developmental project, several of them are sufficiently
relevant to the current work to justify further analysis and inte-

gration into a set of major hypotheses concerning personality differences between Mexicans and Americans that can be attributed to recognizable features of the two contrasting cultures. First, each hypothesis will be stated, followed by a summary of evidence bearing upon it.

*Americans tend to be more active than Mexicans in their style of coping with life's problems and challenges.*

An active style of coping, with all of its cognitive and behavioral implications, involves perceiving problems as existing in the physical and social environment. The best way to resolve such a problem is to modify the environment. A passive pattern of coping assumes that, while problems may be posed by the environment, the best way to cope with them is by changing oneself to adapt to circumstances. As indicated in Chapter 12, many of the cross-cultural differences in the present study can be understood in terms of this general dimension of active versus passive coping style. The American child tends to be more actively independent and to struggle for a mastery of problems and challenges in his environment, whereas the Mexican child is more passively obedient and adapts to stresses in the environment rather than trying to change them.

As indicated earlier, the sociocultural premises presented in Table 13-2 dealing with Affiliative Obedience versus Active Self-Assertion are closely related to the active versus passive coping style. It should be pointed out that obedience, as portrayed in these statements, is in clear reference to defined types of figures in authority, the parents and teachers of the child, who not only are highly respected but also play a major role in providing the interdependent affiliation that is a major feature of the Mexican culture. Any fear or anxiety concerning the taking of examinations in school on the part of the Mexican child is not so much a fear of individual failure as it is a fear of failing to support the interdependent system in which the family plays a central role. Even the Spanish language, as contrasted to the English, provides a more passive way of describing a self-initiated event that is potentially traumatic. In Mexico when a child breaks his mother's favorite vase or flowerpot, the child says "se rompió," or, in English, "it broke itself." There simply is no proper grammatical equivalent for the American child in a similar situation, who is expected to respond, "I broke it." Octavio Paz, an intuitive Mexican poet, captured the essence of this cultural characteristic in somewhat extreme form when, in speaking for the Mexican, he said: "There's nothing simpler, therefore, than to reduce the whole complex group of attitudes that characterize us—especially the problem that we constitute for our own selves—to what may be called the 'servant mentality' in opposition to the 'psychology of the master' and also to that of modern man, whether proletarian or bourgeois" (Paz 1961, p. 70).

In unpublished studies of Mexican and American high-school boys who were given the Semantic Differential (Osgood, Suci, and Tannenbaum 1957), Charles E. Osgood and Díaz-Guerrero computed indigenous distance matrices for each culture that contained indices of the distance between concepts in semantic space. Of special interest are the distance measures between ratings of *I myself, most people,* and each of twenty-seven occupations. For Mexicans, the concept of *I myself* was closest in affective meaning to *most people* (0.6), *storekeeper* (0.9), *peasant* (1.0), *servant* (1.0), *teacher* (1.0), and *artist* (1.0), and was most unlike *beggar* (3.9) and *student* (2.4). By contrast, for the Americans, the concept of *I myself* was closest in affective meaning to *soldier* (0.4), *worker* (0.6), *student* (0.7), and *policeman* (1.0), and was most unlike *beggar* (5.6) and *artist* (3.4). These results are remarkably close to the impressionistic observations of Paz noted above and are clearly consistent with the active versus passive coping style found in the present study.

A recent spokesman for the American style of active coping is Amitai Etzioni, a sociologist who has strongly advocated the active society. Etzioni deplores the lingering concept of man as a passive observer in a world not of his making and not under his control. To be active is to be in charge; to be passive is to be under control. "The active orientation has three major components: a self-conscious and knowing actor, one or more goals he is committed to realize, and access to levers (for power) that allow resetting of the social code" (1968, p. 4). Etzioni has a vision of the active society as one that is in charge of itself and can control its own destiny by the appropriate application of collective power.

*Americans tend to be more technological, dynamic, and external than Mexicans in the meaning of activity within subjective culture.*

While interesting in its own right, this hypothesis sheds further light on the meaning of the more general active-passive dimension in Mexico and the United States. The concept of subjective culture as defined by Triandis and associates (1972) concerns the internalized norms, ideals, values, expectations, and other shared attributes of the cognitive structures of entire groups of people rather than specific individuals. The elements of subjective culture are hypothetical constructs that can be inferred only from observation of behavior in a cultural context. Typical of the methods proposed by Triandis for describing subjective culture is the Semantic Differential technique originally developed by Osgood, Suci, and Tannenbaum (1957). Since 1963, Osgood and his colleagues have been undertaking a major cross-cultural project involving more than twenty-five cultural groups and representing the major languages of the world (Osgood 1974; Snider and Osgood 1969). The goal of this monumental work is to produce by 1980 a comprehensive set of publications reporting on affective meaning systems throughout the world.

The Semantic Differential is a flexible technique consisting of a large number of concepts (such as *world, body, I myself,* and *prayer*), rated on a series of seven-point bipolar scales (such as loved-hated, tender-tough, relaxed-tense, and fast-slow). Osgood's earlier studies demonstrated that there are generally three major dimensions underlying the Semantic Differential—evaluation, potency, and activity. In the world-wide study, six hundred concepts are being rated by samples of young male monolinguals in each of the twenty-five cultures. Since data have already been collected for many of these concepts in Mexico in cooperation with Díaz-Guerrero, preliminary results can be used to examine the differences between young men in Mexico City and in Decatur and Rantoul, Illinois.

Table 13-3 contains activity scores for concepts that represent modern, dynamic, machine technology, as well as concepts dealing with static clothing and foods. All of these concepts show a statistically significant difference between Mexicans and Americans. For all but two of the modern technological concepts (*bicycle* and *nuclear submarine*), the Americans received a higher mean activity score than did the Mexicans. Just the reverse was true for the more static concepts, such as *bed, pillow,* or *sweater*, and the food concepts, such as *bread* or *meat*. All but three of these static

Table 13-3
Dynamic Technological Concepts, Static Clothing and Food Concepts, and the
Self as Rated on the Semantic Differential Activity Score by
Mexican and American Men

| Concepts | Mean Activity Score[a] | |
|---|---|---|
| | Mexico | United States |
| Modern, dynamic, technological concepts | | |
| Airplane | 0.8 | 1.9 |
| Automobile | 0.3 | 1.8 |
| Atomic bomb | 0.0 | 2.3 |
| Bicycle | 1.1 | 0.1 |
| Bus | —0.7 | 0.2 |
| Machine | 0.5 | 1.7 |
| Nuclear submarine | 2.0 | 1.5 |
| Radios (pocket) | 1.1 | 1.8 |
| Railroads | —0.2 | 1.2 |
| Space travel | 1.0 | 1.9 |
| Telephone | 1.2 | 1.4 |
| Television | 1.3 | 1.9 |
| Train | —0.6 | 1.7 |
| Self rating | | |
| I myself | 1.1 | 2.1 |
| Static clothing and food concepts | | |
| Bed | 0.2 | —0.5 |
| Chair | —1.0 | —1.9 |
| Pillow | 0.3 | —1.4 |
| Rug | —0.3 | —1.5 |
| Dress | 1.0 | —0.5 |
| Hat | —0.5 | —1.2 |
| Necktie | —0.2 | —1.5 |
| Shoes | 1.1 | —1.1 |
| Sweater | 0.5 | —0.8 |
| Bread | 1.6 | —0.7 |
| Butter | 0.7 | —1.0 |
| Candy | 0.2 | —0.4 |
| Canned food | 0.3 | —0.2 |
| Cheese | 0.3 | —1.5 |
| Coffee | —0.8 | —1.5 |
| Egg | 0.3 | —0.4 |
| Fish | 1.5 | 1.0 |
| Food | 1.3 | 0.1 |
| Fruit | 1.4 | 0.5 |
| Meat | 1.3 | —0.5 |
| Milk | 0.9 | 0.1 |
| Rice | —0.3 | —0.8 |
| Salt | —0.4 | —1.6 |
| Tea | —0.1 | —1.4 |
| Vegetables | 0.7 | 0.2 |
| Water | 1.1 | 0.5 |
| Apple | 0.1 | 1.0 |
| Beer | —0.5 | 0.5 |
| Whiskey | —0.7 | 0.3 |

[a] Scores are standard scores derived from original semantic-differential factor scores that can range from +3.00 (highest activity) to —3.00 (highest passivity); a mean difference of 0.5 is significant at the .05 level.

clothing and food concepts (*apple, beer,* and *whiskey*) were rated higher on activity by the Mexicans than the Americans. The Americans also rated *I myself* much higher on the activity dimension than did the Mexicans, a self rating in line with results obtained elsewhere concerning the relative degrees of activity and passivity in the two cultures.

A third set of concepts for which significant differences were found between Mexican and American men is comprised of parts of the body, both external and internal. Results for these concepts are presented in Table 13-4. Without exception, the four internal parts of the body (*brain, heart, intestines,* and *blood*) were judged to be more active by Mexicans than by Americans. Just the reverse was true, however, for the external parts of the body. Only in the case of *lips* and *hair* did the Mexicans' mean activity score exceed the Americans' where external parts of the body are concerned. The more dynamic external body parts are judged to be more active by the Americans, while the static internal organs are rated more active by the Mexicans.

Still a fourth set of concepts for which semantic-differential ac-

Table 13-4

External versus Internal Parts of the Body as Rated on the Semantic Differential Activity Score by Mexican and American Men

| | Mean Activity Score[a] | |
|---|---|---|
| Concepts | Mexico | United States |
| External parts of the body | | |
| Tooth | −0.2 | 0.8 |
| Face | 0.7 | 1.2 |
| Head | 0.6 | 1.1 |
| Arm | 1.1 | 1.6 |
| Left hand | −0.4 | 0.7 |
| Right hand | 1.1 | 1.6 |
| Fingers | 1.3 | 1.9 |
| Body | 0.3 | 1.8 |
| Hair | 0.4 | −0.1 |
| Lips | 1.4 | 0.8 |
| Internal parts of the body | | |
| Brain | 2.4 | 1.1 |
| Heart | 2.3 | 1.4 |
| Intestines | 1.5 | −0.4 |
| Blood | 1.4 | 0.6 |

[a] A mean difference of 0.5 is significant at the .05 level.

tivity-score ratings are available consists of emotional terms, such as *anger, hate,* and *sympathy.* Results for these concepts are presented in Table 13-5. Of the thirteen emotions that showed a significant difference between Mexican and American activity scores, the Americans rated more highly the dynamic, aggressive-competitive emotions, while the Mexicans rated more highly such static, self-modifying emotions as *devotion, shame,* and *sympathy.* In other words, Americans perceive aggressive, competitive emotions as highly active, while Mexicans tend to see as more active the static, internalized emotions, such as *shame,* which calls for self-modification.

In all four of these sets of cross-cultural differences, the Mexican assigns higher activity than does the American to internal and static clothing and food concepts. By contrast, the American assigns higher activity scores to modern technological, external, and dynamic concepts than does the Mexican. Results from the present study confirm these semantic-differential findings concerning static versus dynamic views of the world. The Mexican child sees less movement in inkblots and has longer reaction times in test situations than the American child. Time passes more slowly

Table 13-5
Cross-Cultural Differences in Mean Activity Score Ratings of Emotional Concepts

| Concepts | Activity Score[a] | |
| | Mexico | United States |
|---|---|---|
| Dynamic, aggressive-competitive emotional concepts | | |
| Being aggressive | —0.2 | 1.6 |
| Anger | —0.6 | 0.6 |
| Contempt | —1.2 | —0.6 |
| Courage | 0.2 | 1.0 |
| Determination | 0.4 | 1.0 |
| Envy | —1.2 | —0.3 |
| Hate | —0.7 | —0.1 |
| Pain | —1.1 | —0.3 |
| Pride | —0.2 | 0.8 |
| Surprise | 0.2 | 1.5 |
| Static, self-modifying emotional concepts | | |
| Devotion | 0.5 | —0.1 |
| Shame | —0.2 | —0.8 |
| Sympathy | 0.5 | —0.8 |

[a] A mean difference of 0.5 is significant at the .05 level.

for the Mexican than the American. Activity has a different meaning for the American than for the Mexican.

*Americans tend to be more complex and differentiated in cognitive structure than Mexicans.*

The Mexican children in the present study tended to develop more slowly, on the average, in terms of their cognitive skills and mental abilities than was generally true for their American counterparts. The American six-year-olds also showed a greater degree of complexity in their cognitive functioning, as evidenced by the fact that more factors were necessary to explain the intercorrelations among the cognitive tests for the Americans than for the Mexicans. In many respects, the rich cluster of significant findings centered around Witkin's Embedded Figures Test and the concept of field dependency, or psychological differentiation, also confirms this general hypothesis. The differences in socialization practices and value orientations related to child rearing among the Mexican families, as compared to the American families, were presented in some detail in Chapter 12 in the discussion of field dependency and socialization of the child.

It is interesting to note that the primary exception to the above generalization is the finding by Tamm (1967a) that bilingual children from upper-class Mexican families do not differ in cognitive development from closely matched American children. In this instance, the Mexican children came from families where there was a strong desire on the part of their parents for them to obtain an American-style education. While there is no way one can separate the biological from the social factors in cognitive development across the two cultures, the evidence thus far strongly suggests that the differences in level and pattern of cognitive development among Mexican and American children are due primarily to differences in the sociocultural premises, value orientations, and environmental milieu—especially family and school—in the two societies.

*Mexicans tend to be more family-centered, while Americans are more individual-centered.*

Social philosophers and poets have often pointed to the extensive kinship patterns and close affiliation of family members in Mexico as a positive quality arising from the combination of Spanish and Indian cultures. Families in Mexico, as well as those in other

Latin American countries, tend to stretch out in a network of relatives that often runs into scores of individuals.

In 1966 an early version of the Views of Life Questionnaire was given to college students in Mexico and the United States. One of the bipolar items consisted of the following pair of statements: (*a*) One must fight when the rights of the family are threatened, or (*b*) One must fight when the rights of the individual are threatened. Only 22 percent of American college students selected the family-centered alternative, the remaining 78 percent selecting the individual-centered alternative. Just the reverse occurred for the Mexicans; 68 percent selected the family version, while only 32 percent preferred the individual one.

*Mexicans tend to be more cooperative in interpersonal activities, while Americans are more competitive.*

While the present data do not bear directly upon this hypothesis, a series of studies by S. Kagan and M. C. Madsen have provided clear evidence that Mexican children tend to be highly cooperative in experimental games, while Anglo-Americans are highly competitive. Typical of their research are their experimental studies of young lower-class children in the urban areas of Los Angeles and in a small Mexican village just south of California (Kagan and Madsen 1971; 1972). In one study, the game consisted of a circle matrix board, on each side of which a child sat, taking turns moving a marker one circle at a time. Completely cooperative behavior occurred when one child would assist the other in moving quickly toward the goal. Completely competitive behavior consisted of opposing children moving the marker back and forth in the center of the board, using up the number of allowed turns without either child reaching a goal. Since there were a number of trials, and toys were offered as rewards to the winning child, complete cooperation was more adaptive in this task (with alternating winners, by mutual consent), while complete competition was maladaptive, since neither child would receive any toys. In between these two extremes were various forms of partial conflict. Among the seven-to-nine-year-old Mexican children, 63 percent exhibited complete cooperation, while only 10 percent of the Anglo-American children were completely cooperative. The great majority of Anglo-Americans exhibited either complete competition or sufficient conflict to be maladaptive. Similar results were obtained with other children,

using different kinds of experimental games for assessing cooperative and competitive tendencies.

From these studies, Kágan and Madsen have concluded that
American children, unlike Mexican children, are reared in a developmental milieu in which competition is rewarded to such an
extent that the competitive strategy is even generalized to situations in which it is nonadaptive. As an interesting side note, it is
worth mentioning that Mexican-American children fell part way
between the extremes of cooperation typical of the Mexicans and
competition characteristic of the Anglo-Americans.

*Mexicans tend to be more fatalistic and pessimistic in outlook
on life than Americans.*

As in the case of internal versus external locus of control, the
primary scale from the Parent-Attitude Survey, Internal Determinism, is also relevant to this hypothesis. A number of the
items in this factorially derived scale reflect either a pessimistic or
an optimistic outlook on life, depending upon the answer given by
the mother. In general, the Mexican mothers tended to appear
more pessimistic, while the Americans were more optimistic in
their general outlook on life.

American society has always been full of hope for the future
and optimism about its destiny, at least until very recently. By
contrast, the history of Mexico has been one of losing external
wars, suffering through devastating internal turmoil until well into
the twentieth century, and being unable to provide opportunities
for personal, economic, and worldly success for the large masses
of its people, at least until recently. It is quite understandable that
such a milieu would induce a pessimistic-fatalistic outlook on life,
especially among the lower classes. Daniel Cosío Villegas describes
the plight of the Mexican as contrasted to the American:

The North American, fabulously rich, is accustomed to count up what
he has, what he makes and what he loses; hence his tendency to base
many of his value judgments on magnitude, on quantity. The Mexican, thoroughly poor as he usually is, has very little or absolutely
nothing to reckon up, and consequently the notion of magnitude or
quantity is somewhat strange to him; for this reason he bases, or
endeavors to base, his judgments on the notion of quality. The North
American, who in his country has natural resources that no other country has known until now (perhaps Russia may have them), has found

through experience that he can do things, and that their accomplishment requires only determination and effort. This makes him naturally active and confident. Mexico is poor in physical resources; for that
reason the Mexican believes that his determination and his effort are
not enough, that before and above man there are given conditions—
providential, he would call them—which are very difficult or impossible to set aside. This makes him a skeptic, distrustful of action, a be-
liever in forces superior to himself, more likely to cavil than to act. He
leaves for tomorrow many of his enterprises, not from laziness or mere
indecision, but because the insufficiency of his resources has taught
him over and over again that you can't make the day dawn any sooner
no matter how early you get up in the morning. (Cosío Villegas 1971)

While a certain Pollyanna character has prevailed until recently
in American culture, the Mexican has more often than not perceived life as something to be endured rather than enjoyed. To the
Mexican, the optimism of the American may even seem to be out
of touch with reality. Although carried to excesses in his poetic
license, Octavio Paz has the following to say: "The North American system only wants to consider the positive aspects of reality.
Men and women are subjected from childhood to an inexorable
process of adaptation; certain principles, contained in brief formu-
las, are endlessly repeated by the press, the radio, the churches
and the schools, and by those kindly, sinister beings, the North
American mothers and wives. A person imprisoned by these
schemes is like a plant in a flowerpot too small for it: he cannot
grow or mature. This sort of conspiracy cannot help but provoke
violent individual rebellions" (Paz 1961, p. 25).

## National Character

Self-conscious awareness of differences among nations has characterized man through the centuries wherever one culture engaged
in commerce with another. For most Europeans, Asians, and Africans, exchanges among nations have been commonplace, leading to
stereotypes and attitudes about enduring personality characteristics
and unique life styles that seem to typify the national character of
entire populations. At least until recently, only the southwestern
part of the United States and the urban and northern parts of
Mexico have had continuous interchanges, while the remaining

sections of both countries have relied chiefly upon secondary sources and stereotypes as a basis for characterizing each other.

The perception of differences across nations has led to a great deal of verbal expression and impressionistic writing, but only in the past thirty years have there been serious efforts to engage in empirical studies of national character. During the period of World War II and immediately thereafter, these empirical studies had to be conducted at a distance and were often based upon fragmentary information and impressions. All too often, these national character studies have attempted to explain behavior on the basis of presumed psychological mechanisms operating within the culture. Tendencies to oversimplify and ignore the range and variability of behavior are common failings in many of these studies of national character, particularly those that are based upon psychoanalytic interpretations. In his concept of modal personality, Linton (1945) emphasized the fact that personality patterns are not invariable, especially in the more complex societies. The concept of modal personality allows for a quantitatively descriptive approach, while recognizing the great range and variety of individual personality configurations found in any culture.

The same precautions should be exercised in interpreting the results of the present cross-cultural longitudinal study of Mexican and American children and their families. While there are definite trends evident in the two societies that can be attributed to noted differences in the two cultures, it is hardly possible at this time to speak of one "national character" that would be appropriate for either Mexico or the United States.

Ten years have gone by since the initial data collection on large numbers of school children in Mexico City and Austin. Both societies have gone through major changes in this same period. Indeed, the amount of change is so great that, if it continues apace for another ten years, both societies and the subjective cultures that comprise the shared personality characteristics within each society will have moved on to a point where many of the observed cross-cultural differences will have been markedly altered, at least among the upper middle classes.

Whether the Mexican elite will gradually take on the characteristics of the modal American personality or the American will shift closer to the Mexican cannot be predicted with any reliability at this time. More likely than not, the subjective culture of both societies will move on to a new order more in keeping with future demands, retaining some common features of the old while establishing new priorities and values. Perhaps it is too much to hope that the more adaptive aspects of the active American society can be fused with the affiliative strengths and interpersonal loyalties of the traditional Mexican society. If such a blending occurred, however, it could only benefit both cultures.

# 14. Summary

By 1962 seven years of research had been completed by the research team at the University of Texas on the development and standardization of the Holtzman Inkblot Technique (HIT), a new inkblot test designed to overcome the psychometric limitations of the Rorschach. During the extensive standardization program, developmental trends across the different normative samples proved particularly interesting. But the limitations inherent in any cross-sectional study, when dealing with developmental trends, led the University of Texas group in 1962 to undertake the present longitudinal study of large, representative samples of normal school children with repeated measurement annually for six years.

Shortly after this program of research began, plans were completed for a cross-cultural replication of the entire study in Mexico City. The close proximity of Texas and Mexico has naturally resulted in considerable professional and scientific interaction over the years among psychologists and other behavioral scientists, particularly between those at the University of Texas and those at the National University of Mexico. The large proportion of Spanish-speaking people of Mexican descent in Texas and the heavy influx to Mexico City of North American ideas, products, tourists, scholars, and businessmen have sensitized both groups to the desirability of conducting cross-cultural research before further diffusion and social changes occur.

An area of great interest to both Mexican and American psychologists was personality development in children. Before their part of the study could begin, however, the Mexicans had to organize a research group, obtain major financial support for a long-range operation, train psychological examiners, translate and adapt test materials, and conduct pilot studies of a statistical and sociological nature to determine demographic background data needed for obtaining samples of Mexican children comparable to those in Austin. Preliminary studies and planning led to a major program aimed at determining the relative importance of cultural factors, school environment, and characteristics of the family and home environment upon the development of cognitive, perceptual, and personality functioning in normal school children from these two contrasting cultures.

An overlapping longitudinal design was employed, so that a span of twelve years of development could be covered in only six calendar years of repeated testing. A three-year overlap between groups made it possible to splice them together into one span of twelve years for determining developmental trends, while at the same time permitting replication and cross-validation of the perceptual-cognitive and personality indices that were found related to different stages of development.

The relatively brief period of data collection and the size of the samples overcame to a great extent the problem of attrition. The inevitable loss of subjects with the passage of time was compensated for in part by the overlap of the three groups. For example, shrinkage in Group I during the last three years of data collection was compensated partially by the initially large size of Group II. It was expected that complete developmental data could be obtained for six hundred children, three hundred in Austin and a comparable number in Mexico City. The final sizes of the three age groups were sufficiently large to permit the application of multivariate analysis for the identification of specific as well as general principles of developmental change.

In Austin, children were drawn mainly from six elementary schools and one junior high school, representing a broad range of

working-class, business, and professional families. Only
English-speaking families were used. The Austin sample p
can be characterized best as middle-class urban childre_ __ ___
fairly stable families that represent the dominant values in American culture.

Defining the sample and selecting children in Mexico City
proved to be more difficult, largely because little previous work
had been done on the social characteristics of Mexican families
and because the organization of education in Mexico is very different from that found in the United States. Considerable information about family structure, parental occupation and education,
size and quality of the home, and possession of radio or television
sets, automobiles, and refrigerators was obtained from interviews
with parents in the preliminary sociological survey. Only children
both of whose parents were born in Mexico of Mexican parents
were included in the sample, to insure that the dominant Mexican
value system and urban life style would be clearly present. The
results of this survey indicated that the Mexican families in the
private school system were very similar in socioeconomic status to
the American families in Austin. Consequently, more children
were drawn from the private system than from the two public
ones. It was estimated that nearly two-thirds of the Mexican and
Austin children could then be used for cross-cultural comparisons
in which important subcultural variations would be matched
across the two samples. The remaining third of the Mexicans
would be too low socioeconomically, while the remaining third of
the Americans would be too high.

The basic test battery included selected cognitive, perceptual,
and personality tests given individually to each child once a year
on the anniversary date of the initial testing. Criteria employed in
deciding whether or not to use a particular test consisted of the
following: (*a*) suitability for individual administration under field
conditions in a school; (*b*) demonstrated reliability and objectivity
from previous studies; (*c*) appropriateness for use throughout the
age span of six to seventeen years; (*d*) relevance  to perceptual-
cognitive development or importance as a measure of significant
personality traits pertinent to developmental stages in children;
and (*e*) feasibility for use in the Spanish and English languages
within Mexican and American cultures, respectively.

It was realized that some important psychological techniques might be suitable for administration once or twice; others would be appropriate for use with young children but inappropriate for older ones or vice versa; and still others might come to our attention as worthy of inclusion after a year or two of testing had been completed. Rather than adhere rigidly to only a fixed set of measures to be applied uniformly in all six years and both samples, provision was made for distinguishing between the basic core battery, which was to be applied uniformly; the partial core battery, which was to be applied uniformly for all children in the second grade or above; the supplementary repeated battery, consisting of tests to be employed two or more successive years though not uniformly; and other measures, which were to be used once or twice but not successively across years.

Principal tests selected for inclusion fall for the most part into three main categories: tests of cognitive-mental abilities, tests of perceptual-cognitive style, and attitudinal-personality measures. The primary measures of mental abilities were from the Wechsler Intelligence Scale for Children (WISC) and the Wechsler Adult Intelligence Scale (WAIS). Other measures included in the core or supplementary test batteries as measures of cognitive or mental abilities included the Goodenough-Harris Human Figure Drawings (HFD), the Embedded Figures Test (EFT), and the Visual Fractionation Test (VFT). Tests primarily of perceptual-cognitive style included the Time Estimation Test (TET), the Perceptual Maturity Scale (PMS), the Object Sorting Test (OST), the Conceptual Styles Test (CST), and the Word Association Test (WAT). Tests yielding personality and attitude variables were the Personality Research Form (PRF), the Test Anxiety Scale for Children (TASC), and the Occupational Values Inventory (OVI). The more "structural" scores from the Holtzman Inkblot Technique (HIT) can be classified as perceptual style variables, while the "content" scores usually are thought of as personality variables. In a similar fashion some of the other tests employed yield measures that can be thought of as falling into more than one category.

In addition, a determined effort was made throughout the years of the study to obtain data about the children and their families from sources other than the children themselves. Different types of data collected can be divided logically into four major categories: (*a*) performance data from children; (*b*) ratings of the children; (*c*) data on the family and home environment; and (*d*) attitudes toward child rearing collected from the children's mothers.

After extensive methodological, psychometric, and intercorrelational studies were carried out on test and interview variables within each culture relevant to cross-cultural comparisons, matched cross-cultural samples from the total set of U.S. and Mexican cases were developed. Matched pairs of subjects—one from each culture—were controlled rigorously for the age, sex, and socioeconomic status of each child, both in analyses of tests given for the first time in each culture and in the analyses of repeated administration of tests through time. The use of such a special cross-cultural sample made it possible to control for five independent variables and the interactions among them, which could then be studied: culture, socioeconomic status of the family, sex of the child, age group in three levels, and year of repeated testing. In addition to complex analyses, both cross-cultural and developmental, a sufficient number of cases were obtained in both cultures and in each of the three age groups to permit independent study of interrelationships among variables within each of these large samples. Thus, the research design can be thought of as a series of six parallel studies, each using precisely the same research procedures—one each in Mexico and the United States involving the six years of development from age six to age eleven, one in each culture for children from nine to fourteen, and one in each culture for children from twelve to seventeen. By conducting six such investigations concurrently, the power of generalizations that were made was increased greatly.

Clear and uniform differences were found across the two cultures for many psychological dimensions and test scores, regardless of sex, age, or socioeconomic status of the child. All the cognitive measures, almost all the cognitive-perceptual style variables, most of the personality and attitudinal measures, and most of the items obtained from interviews with mothers yielded significant cross-cultural differences. On the Holtzman Inkblot Technique, every score revealed main effects or higher-order interactions that involved cross-cultural differences. No such differences were found for a small number of measures employed, however. No differences were found between Mexican and American children for Persistent Achievement Drive and Extroversion from the Personality Research Form; seven of the fifteen items from the Occupational Values Inventory; and four items from the interview and the Parent-Attitude and Parent Trait surveys.

The age, social class, or sex of the child often proved significant as a factor related to the child's performance. In many cases, these variables interacted with culture, while in some instances they did not.

Age naturally was a significant variable for all of the cognitive tests, such as the Wechsler Intelligence Scale for Children, the Harris-Goodenough scoring of the Human Figure Drawings, and the Embedded Figures Test, regardless of culture. Only a few scores among the cognitive-perceptual style or personality measures showed strong age trends; and, in nearly all these cases, the interaction with culture proved highly significant. The measures that increased markedly with increasing age were Arithmetic, Vocabulary, Picture Completion, Block Design, the Harris-Goodenough score for Human Figure Drawings, EFT Correct, TET Delay, VFT Correct, the Perceptual Maturity Scale, HIT Movement, HIT Integration, HIT Human, and PRF Impulsivity. Those measures that decreased with increasing age in both cultures were OST number of groups, OST number of single items not used, EFT Errors, EFT Time, EFT Re-exams, VFT Trials, VFT Time, PRF Independence, and OVI Esthetics. These trends occurred in both cultures and are in the directions to be expected from earlier studies.

Social-class differences generally were present only for the Mexican children, such differences occurring only rarely for the American children. Only three measures showed a clear social-class difference in both cultures and for both sexes: upper-class subjects received higher scores on Time Estimation Delay, indicating that they could estimate more accurately the length of time equivalent to one minute; lower-class children showed a higher degree of specific anxiety about taking tests and also valued more highly work in which one could make a lot of money. The mothers of upper-class children valued more highly for their children such traits as independence, tolerance, and social concern, while lower-class mothers valued strict obedience. From information collected in the parent interview, it was also apparent that lower-class fathers and children watched television longer hours and lower-class mothers obtained lower scores on most of the parental-attitude scales than did their upper-class counterparts.

Sex differences in the child's performance and the mother's response to interview items were a bit more prevalent in both cultures. Girls tended to receive higher scores on the first figure for the Human Figure Drawing, PRF Nurturance, PRF Harma-voidance, and OVI Esthetics. Boys received higher scores on CST Relational, TET Delay, the Perceptual Maturity Scale, HIT Form Definiteness, HIT Movement, HIT Human, HIT Animal, HIT Hostility, and PRF Autonomy. Boys also tended to draw more masculine males in the Human Figure Drawings than did girls. Other sex differences were found in either Mexico or the United States but not in both cultures.

In only one case was there any interaction between social class and sex that appeared in both cultures. For PRF Endurance, upper-class boys and lower-class girls received higher scores than did lower-class boys or upper-class girls.

Of even greater interest than the many significant differences due to culture are the several significant interactions between culture and the other major independent variables studied, especially age. When taken together, the significant interactions between culture and age suggest that for some perceptual-cognitive and personality functions the Mexican and American children started out roughly the same, the Mexican child developing less rapidly than the American through the school years. For other functions the two cultures converged as the children grew older, especially among the upper-middle-class families. It is almost as though socialization in the two cultures and the influences of society, peer groups, and the school, as contrasted to the family, brought the two populations of children closer together on certain psychological characteristics.

In some cases, of course, developmental trends as measured by the interaction between culture and age group must be qualified by inclusion of sex or social class. In general, differences between boys and girls and between working and professional or business classes in Mexico were more marked than in the United States. For example, differences in WISC Vocabulary between American boys and girls and between American working-class and upper-middle-class families failed to appear. For the Mexicans, however, both sex and social class were significant factors influencing verbal ability. Among the Mexican girls, in particular, as age increased, the gulf between the upper- and lower-class girls widened appreciably, placing the lower-class Mexican girl at a particularly noticeable disadvantage as contrasted to Mexican boys of either social class and upper-class Mexican girls. Lower-class Mexican boys also stood out on some measures, but these social-class differences tended to disappear with increasing age.

The most significant interaction of all involving culture and sex occurred for the masculinity-femininity ratings of the male and female drawings from the HFD. American girls drew more feminine male figures, while American boys tended to draw more masculine female figures than was the case for Mexican girls and boys. A Masculinity-Femininity Discrimination index clearly showed a greater degree of discrimination on the part of Mexican than American children.

The findings reported above in some detail are only a few of the many hundreds of significant ones obtained. While difficult to organize and interpret in any simple fashion, they can be summarized in terms of three topics on which broad generalizations are justified: (*a*) cognitive abilities and intellectual stimulation of the child; (*b*) active versus passive coping style; and (*c*) field dependency and socialization practice.

While the youngest children in both cultures had similar patterns and levels of most cognitive abilities, after several years of schooling the two cultures diverged considerably, the Mexican children generally falling behind the American. This finding is seen as due to differences in the degree of intellectual stimulation within the Mexican and American home and to differences in emphasis and mode of instruction within the schools themselves.

Most of the differences between the Mexican and American children on the HIT and some of the cognitive style and personality tests can be understood better in terms of coping style than any other concept. The American child produced faster reaction time, used larger portions of the inkblots, gave more definite form, and integrated more parts of the inkblots while doing so. In addition, he incorporated other stimulus properties into his responses. The Mexican child, on the other hand, gave responses with better form and less often produced deviant, hostile, or anxious content. In general, the American child attempted to cope with the task in a much more active fashion than did the Mexican child, even when he was unable to do so successfully.

A number of findings in the present study concerning attitudes, values, family life style, and socialization practices within the Mexican and American homes would tend to foster greater field dependence among Mexican children and greater field independence among American. From differences noted in the two cultures, one would expect that there would be more value placed on affective, rather than cognitive aspects of life in Mexico, coupled with a preference for a static rather than a dynamic approach to the environment. The Mexican should be more family-centered, prefer leisure to work and external to internal controls. In addition, he should be somewhat more pessimistic about life and passive-obedient in style of coping with his environment. For the American, the opposite of each of these statements should tend to be true.

Following a discussion of several approaches to the study of culture and personality as a formal discipline, several historical antecedents of contemporary society in Mexico and the United States are reviewed and cultural differences described. On the basis of this analysis six major hypotheses concerning personality differences between Mexicans and Americans that can be attributed to recognizable features of the two contrasting cultures are presented, together with data from the current and other related investigations that bear upon their validity: (a) Americans tend to be more active than Mexicans in their style of coping with life's problems and challenges; (b) Americans tend to be more dynamic, technological, and external than Mexicans in the meaning of activity within subjective culture; (c) Americans tend to be more complex and differentiated in cognitive structure than Mexicans; (d) Mexicans tend to be more family-centered, while Americans are more individual-centered; (e) Mexicans tend to be more cooperative in interpersonal activities while Americans are more competitive; and (f) Mexicans tend to be more fatalistic and pessimistic in outlook on life than Americans.

# APPENDIX A
## The Interview Schedule

ID# ——————————

Child's name ————————————— Date ——————————
Parent's name ————————————— Interviewer ——————
Address ————————————————————

Children (from oldest to youngest) (circle subject):

| Name | Age | Sex | Grade Level | Remarks (adopted, half-brother) |
|------|-----|-----|-------------|---------------------------------|
| 1. | | | | |
| 2. | | | | |
| 3. | | | | |
| 4. | | | | |
| 5. | | | | |
| 6. | | | | |

Adults presently living in home (specify if divorced, deceased, etc.):
Father:   Yes (   )   No (   ) ————————————————
Mother:   Yes (   )   No (   ) ————————————————
Other (specify): ——————————————————————

| | Father | Mother |
|-|--------|--------|
| Occupation | | |
| No. years | | |
| Previous work | | |
| Educ. (extent, major) | | |
| Age | | |

How long in present home:———— Own (buying) home: Yes (   )
Lease or rent home: Yes (   )

Cities of residence since marriage: ————————————————
————————————————————————————————————

Schools attended by (child): ————————————————————
————————————————————————————————————

Child's duties in home:
   None ( ) Less than 1 hr./wk. ( ) 1-5 hrs./wk. ( ) More than 5 ( )
Religious affiliation:   Protestant  ( ) (Specify) ————————————
                         Catholic    ( )
                         Jewish      ( )
                         Other       ( ) (Specify) ————————————
Church attendance:
   Never                    ( )    Family                ( )
   Rarely                   ( )    Children only         ( )
   Once or twice a month    ( )    Mother and children   ( )
   Just about every week    ( )    Other ————————————————
   More than once a week    ( )

1. Do you have any form of religious observances in the home—
   daily, weekly, annually?
         *Activity*          *When*              *1. Occas., 2., 3. Very regularly*

2. Does (child) have any special interests or hobbies, pastimes or
   sports in which he is presently active?
         *Nature*      *Duration*      *Level of Interest*[a]      *How Started*

3. Is (child) taking any special lessons or instruction outside of
   school?
         *Nature*      *Duration*      *Level of Interest*      *How Started*

4. Do you get any newspapers or magazines regularly?
   *Names* (check ones used by child):


   Others bought occasionally?

5. Do you or your husband belong to any organizations or clubs?
    *Who*[b]          *Name of Club*         *Level of Activity*[c]

6. Are you or your husband taking any study courses?
    *Who*          *What*         *Why*

7. Do you as a family have any special recreational activities?
    *Nature*          *Frequency*

8. Do you or your husband have any special sports, interests, or hobbies in which you are presently active?
    *Who*          *What*         *Level of Activity*

9. Have you as a family traveled anywhere during the past two years?
    *Where*          *Why*         *Child's Activities*

10. Do you have relatives or friends whom you visit regularly?
    *Who*    *Where*    *How Often*    *Child Included?*

    Relatives or friends who visit you regularly?
    *Who*    *Where*    *How Often*    *Bring Children?*

11. How satisfied or dissatisfied are you with (child's) progress in school in terms of his own ability?
    \_\_\_\_Very dissatisfied
    \_\_\_\_Dissatisfied
    \_\_\_\_Satisfied
    \_\_\_\_Very satisfied

12. Do you and your husband discuss how (child) gets along in school?
    *Frequency*

    *Topics Most Often Discussed*

13. Do you discuss with (child) his progress in school?
    *Frequency*          *Which Parent*

    *Topics Most Often Discussed*

14. How would you compare (child's) progress in school with the other children in the family? With his classmates?

|  | Siblings |  | Classmates |
|---|---|---|---|
| *Grades* | *Ability* | *Effort* | *Grades* |
| ——1. Better | ——1. | ——1. More | ——1. Top third |
| ——2. Same | ——2. | ——2. Same | ——2. Middle third |
| ——3. Not as good | ——3. | ——3. Less | ——3. Lower third |

15. Does (child) have homework?
    - ——1. No
    - ——2. Occasionally
    - ——3. About 30 min./day
    - ——4. About 1–2 hrs./day
    - ——5. More than two hours a day
16. In general, do you think (child) has too much homework or not enough?
    - ——1. Excessive
    - ——2. Appropriate
    - ——3. Insufficient
17. What particular subjects does (child) usually get homework in?

18. Do you or other members of the family assist (child) with his homework?
    *Who Helps*       *How Often*       *Am't Time/Week*

19. What reasons do you give (child) to encourage him to study?

20. Before (child) was able to read, did you or your husband read to him?
    ———1. Only occasionally
    ———2. Fairly regularly
    ———3. Very regularly
21. Did you or other members of the family teach (child) to read or count or write his name before he started school?
    *Who Helped   What Was Learned   How It Was Learned   Age*


22. Would you say that (child) is a reader?   Yes ( )   No ( )
    Does (child) read books, other than assigned ones?
    ———1. Never
    ———2. Less than 1 hr./wk.
    ———3. 1–3 hrs./week
    ———4. About an hour/day
    ———5. More than an hour/day
23. Do you encourage (child) to read any particular types of reading materials?
    *Types                   Manner of Encouragement*


24. Do you have a dictionary or encyclopedia in your home?
    *Name      How Gotten    Use by Child* (1 little, 2, 3 much)


25. Have you or your husband had any experience teaching?
    (Mother, Father)  *Grade Level   Subject(s)   Length of Experience*


26. On the average, how many hours a week does (child) watch television—figuring in week-ends, too?


27. Do you find it necessary to exercise control over what (child) watches, or how much he watches TV?
    —1. Little or none    —2. A fair amount    —3. Very much
28. What are his favorite TV programs?
    *Name              Approve, Disapprove of Any in Particular?*

29. On the average, how many hours a week do you watch TV? Your
    husband?
    _____ Mother            _____ Father
    Favorite programs:


30. Are there any special times during the week when your family is
    together routinely?
    *When*                        *What for*


31. Are there any special activities that your husband shares with
    (child)?


    Are there any special activities that you share with (child)?


32. Do you work at present outside of your home?
    *Type*          *Hours/*        *Time*          *After-School*
    *Work*          *Week*          *of Day*        *Care of Child*


33. Did you work when (child) was a preschooler?
    *Type*          *Hours/*        *Time*      *Type Person Caring*
    *Work*          *Week*          *of Day*         *for Child*


34. Have you had any other work experience?


35. Do you or others in the family ever correct (child's) speech?
    __1. Rarely __2. Sometimes __3. Whenever he makes mistake

36. Do you or others in the family speak any language other than
    English?
    *Language   Who Speaks It   1. Seldom   2. Fair Amount   3. Good Bit*

37. With regard to (child's) education, how much would you like him to receive, ideally?

38. What is the minimum amount of education that you feel he *must* receive?

39. Is there any particular type work that you would like to see him do when he is grown?

40. Is there any particular type work that you would *not* like to see him do when he is grown?

41. How satisfied or dissatisfied would you say your husband is with the work he does?
     \_\_\_\_1. Very dissatisfied
     \_\_\_\_2. Slightly dissatisfied
     \_\_\_\_3. Satisfied
     \_\_\_\_4. Very satisfied

42. Had he previously wanted to do some other type work? \_\_\_\_Yes
     \_\_\_\_No   If so, then what?

43. Do you know any of (child's) present teachers by name?

44. Have you had any contact with his teacher(s) during this school year?
     
     | *Purpose* | *Initiated by* | *How Often* |
     
     Last year?

45. Can you describe (child's) use of his free time—ways of playing?

46. Do you know (child's) best friends in the neighborhood and school? _____ Do you approve of them? _____
Do you help your child in choosing his friends? If so, how?

47. Is there anything in particular about (child)—things he does or certain characteristics—that you approve of or find especially pleasing?

48. How do you and your husband express your approval of him?
   *Mother*                              *Father*

49. Is there anything in particular about (child) that you disapprove or are sorry about or find displeasing?

50. How do you and your husband express your disapproval of him?
   *Mother*                              *Father*

51. Has (child) had any serious illnesses or accidents?
   *Nature of Illnesses*     *Duration*     *Child's Age*

   Has he had medical care over an extended period of time for any particular reason?

52. Have you had to consult a doctor in regard to (child's) health within the last year?
   *General Nature of Problem*     *Frequency of Consultation*

53. Are there any special summer programs, such as summer camp or school, that (child) has participated in?
   *Nature*               *How Initiated*               *Age*

54. That completes this group of questions. Can you think of anything else of importance that we haven't touched on?

55. Additional comments or information:

ᵃ Level of interest:
   1.  Slight interest
   2.  Fair interest
   3.  Great interest
ᵇ Who:
   M  Mother
   F  Father
   B  Both
ᶜ Level of Activity
   1.  Only occasionally active
   2.  Fairly active
   3.  Very active

## NEIGHBORHOOD AND HOME RATINGS

Name _____ Child ID# _____

### *Neighborhood*

| | | | |
|---|---|---|---|
| Traffic: | Light ( ) | Medium ( ) | Heavy ( ) |
| Dwelling units: | Distant ( ) | Well-spaced ( ) | Crowded ( ) |
| Play space for children: | Ample ( ) | Adequate ( ) | None ( ) |
| Condition of neighborhood: | Well-kept ( ) | Average ( ) | Run-down ( ) |

### *The Home*

Type of dwelling unit: House ( )   Duplex ( )   Apartment ( )
Other (specify) _____

| | | | |
|---|---|---|---|
| Condition (inside): | Well-kept ( ) | Average ( ) | Run-down ( ) |
| Yard, lawn, grounds: | Well-kept ( ) | Average ( ) | Run-down ( ) |
| Living space: | Spacious ( ) | Comfortable ( ) | Crowded ( ) |

Comparison with other homes in neighborhood:
    Better ( )      About the same ( )      In worse condition ( )
Additional comments about neighborhood and home:

_____

_____
_____

Interviewer's impression of parent interviewed:
    *Language Usage*        *Above Average*        *Average*        *Below Average*
    Fluency, facility
        of expression:        _____        _____        _____
    Pronunciation:            _____        _____        _____
    Vocabulary:               _____        _____        _____
    Personal Appearance:      Neat ( )   Average ( )   Unkept ( )

# APPENDIX B
## Parent-Attitude Survey and Parent Trait Survey

ID#——————————————— Date——————

## PARENT-ATTITUDE SURVEY

*Instructions*: Most of the following statements concern parents and children. A few deal with life in general. Please indicate your agreement or disagreement with each statement in the following manner:

| | |
|---|---|
| Strongly agree | circle "A" |
| Agree | circle "a" |
| Undecided | circle "u" |
| Disagree | circle "d" |
| Strongly disagree | circle "D" |

For example: If you strongly agree with the following statement, you would mark it in this way:

Boys are more active than girls       (A) a u d D

This survey is concerned only with the attitudes and opinions that parents have; there are no "right" or "wrong" answers. Work just as rapidly as you can—it is your first impression that we are interested in. There is no time limit.

   C:  Item taken from Hereford's Confidence Scale
   Ca: Item taken from Hereford's Causation Scale
   A:  Item taken from Hereford's Acceptance Scale
   U:  Item taken from Hereford's Understanding Scale
   T:  Item taken from Hereford's Trust Scale
   O:  Item taken from CYS Orientation to Society Scale
   R:  Item adapted from Rosen's scales
   D:  Item taken from Díaz-Guerrero's sociocultural premises studies in Mexico

REMEMBER:    A = Strongly agree
             a = Agree
             u = Undecided
             d = Disagree
             D = Strongly disagree

Please go ahead . . .

C   1. Raising children isn't as hard as most parents let on.   A a u d D (1)

Ca  2. When you come right down to it, a child is either good or bad and there's not much you can do about it.   A a u d D (2)

R   3. Nowadays with world conditions the way they are the wise person lives for today and lets tomorrow take care of itself.   A a u d D (3)

A   4. The earlier a child is weaned from his emotional ties to his parents the better he will handle his own problems.   A a u d D (4)

U   5. Family life would be happier if parents made children feel they were free to say what they think about anything.   A a u d D (5)

T   6. Children have no right to keep anything from their parents.   A a u d D (6)

Ca  7. With all a child hears at school and from friends, there's little a parent can do to influence him.   A a u d D (7)

R   8. The secret of happiness is not expecting too much out of life and being content with what comes your way.   A a u d D (8)

A   9. If you put too many restrictions on a child, you will stunt his personality.   A a u d D (9)

U  10. If you let children talk about their troubles they end up complaining even more.   A a u d D (10)

R  11. A good son would try to live near his parents even if it means giving up a good job in another part of the country.   A a u d D (11)

C  12. It's hard to know when to make a rule and stick by it.   A a u d D (12)

Ca 13. Most all children are just the same at birth; it's what happens to them afterwards that is important.   A a u d D (13)

A  14. There is no reason why a child should not learn to keep his clothes clean very early in life.   A a u d D (14)

U 15. Talking to a child about his fears most often makes the fear look more important than it is. A a u d D (15)

Ca 16. Why children behave the way they do is too much for anyone to figure out. A a u d D (16)

R 17. All a man should want out of life in the way of a career is a secure, not-too-difficult job, with enough pay to get by. A a u d D (17)

T 18. More parents should make it their job to know everything their child is doing. A a u d D (18)

C 19. I feel I am faced with more problems than most parents. A a u d D (19)

Ca 20. Most of the bad traits children have (like nervousness or bad temper) are inherited. A a u d D (20)

A 21. A child who wants too much affection may become a "softie" if it is given to him. A a u d D (21)

U 22. Children shouldn't be asked to do all the compromising without a chance to express their side of things. A a u d D (22)

R 23. Nothing is worth the sacrifice of moving away from one's parents. A a u d D (23)

T 24. It is hard to let children go and visit people because they might misbehave when parents aren't around. A a u d D (24)

C 25. It's hard to know what to do when a child is afraid of something that won't hurt him. A a u d D (25)

Ca 26. Some children are just naturally bad. A a u d D (26)

A 27. One thing I cannot stand is a child's constantly wanting to be held. A a u d D (27)

U 28. If a parent sees that a child is right and the parent is wrong, the parent should admit it and try to do something about it. A a u d D (28)

T 29. If rules are not closely enforced children will misbehave and get into trouble. A a u d D (29)

R 30. Planning only makes a person unhappy since your plans hardly ever work out anyway. A a u d D (30)

C 31. Most parents aren't sure what is the best way to bring up children. A a u d D (31)

Ca 32. Some children are so naturally headstrong that a parent can't really do much about them. A a u d D (32)

A  33. A child who misbehaves should be made to feel guilty and ashamed of himself.  A a u d D (33)

U  34. There's a lot of truth in the saying, "Children should be seen and not heard."  A a u d D (34)

T  35. Children have a right to activities which do not include their parents.  A a u d D (35)

C  36. Few parents have to face the problems I find with my children.  A a u d D (36)

R  37. When a man is born the success he is going to have is already in the cards, so he might just as well accept it and not fight against it.  A a u d D (37)

Ca  38. Psychologists now know that what a child is born with determines the kind of person he becomes.  A a u d D (38)

A  39. When a boy is cowardly, he should be forced to try things he is afraid of.  A a u d D (39)

U  40. Most children's fears are so unreasonable it only makes things worse to let the child talk about them.  A a u d D (40)

O  41. These days a person doesn't really know whom he can count on.  A a u d D (41)

T  42. If let alone, a child will usually do the right thing.  A a u d D (42)

C  43. Children don't realize that it mainly takes suffering to be a good parent.  A a u d D (43)

AD  44. If children are to grow up and get somewhere in life, they must be continuously kept after.  A a u d D (44)

T  45. It is hard to know when to let boys and girls play together, when they can't be seen.  A a u d D (45)

Ca  46. If a child is born bad, there's not much you can do about it.  A a u d D (46)

A  47. A child should be weaned away from the bottle or breast as soon as possible.  A a u d D (47)

O  48. In spite of what most people say, the life for the average person is getting worse, not better.  A a u d D (48)

R  49. Much of what a son does should be done to please his parents.  A a u d D (49)

U  50. A child's ideas should be seriously considered in making family decisions.  A a u d D (50)

AD 51. Children who always obey grow up to be best adults. A a u d D (51)

Ca 52. A child is destined to be a certain kind of person no matter what the parents do. A a u d D (52)

T 53. Children who are not watched will get into trouble. A a u d D (53)

A 54. It's a parent's right to refuse to put up with a child's annoyances. A a u d D (54)

O 55. It's hardly fair to bring children into the world with the way things look for the future. A a u d D (55)

C 56. Raising children is a nerve-racking job. A a u d D (56)

D 57. If a person doesn't always get much done but can enjoy life as he goes along, that is the best way. A a u d D (57)

AD 58. Too much freedom will make a child wild. A a u d D (58)

Ca 59. A child that comes from bad stock doesn't have much chance of amounting to anything. A a u d D (59)

C 60. Parents sacrifice most of their fun for their children. A a u d D (60)

A 61. Children should be toilet-trained at the earliest possible time. A a u d D (61)

O 62. When you get right down to it no one is going to care much what is going to happen to you. A a u d D (62)

U 63. Children should have a share in making family decisions just as grown-ups do. A a u d D (63)

D 64. A boss should understand and not penalize a worker who sometimes without warning takes a little time off for fun. A a u d D (64)

AD 65. Strict discipline develops a fine strong character. A a u d D (65)

T 66. Children must be told exactly what to do and how to do it or they will make mistakes. A a u d D (66)

U 67. Family conferences which include the children don't usually accomplish much. A a u d D (67)

T 68. A child should be allowed at times to try out what he can do without the parents watching. A a u d D (68)

## PARENT TRAIT SURVEY

There was a study done of a midwestern town in 1924 concerning many aspects of the life in the town and the people there—how they thought and acted in 1924. The mothers then were asked to fill out a questionnaire about what they thought were the most important traits to be stressed in bringing up their children. We thought it would be interesting to let you fill out the same questionnaire 40 years later, to see what kinds of things have changed, and what kinds of things are pretty much the same.

In the list below, mark the three traits you consider most important with the letter "A". Mark the next 5 traits in importance with the letter "B". Mark any traits of third importance with the letter "C" and those traits which you think have no importance mark with a zero.

———Frankness in dealing with others

———Desire to make a name in the world

———Concentration

———Social concern

———Strict obedience

———Appreciation of art, music, and poetry

———Economy in money matters

———Loyalty to the church

———Knowledge of sex hygiene

———Tolerance

———Curiosity

———Patriotism

———Good manners

———Independence

———Getting very good grades in school

# APPENDIX C
## Interview Schedule Coding Form

|  | DATA CARD 15 |
| ITEM AND DESCRIPTION | COLUMN |
| --- | --- |

Group:                                                                           1

    Group I = 1
    Group II = 2
    Group III = 3

Subject's I.D. number:                                                3, 4, 5

    List number as it appears on schedule.

Subject's sex:                                                        6

    Male ........................................................................1
    Female ...................................................................2

Culture:                                                             8

    Texas .....................................................................1
    Mexico ..................................................................2

Interviewer:                                                    15

    Stitt ......................................................................1
    Williams ................................................................2

Date of interview:                                            16

    Dec. 1964 .............................................................0
    Jan. 1965 ..............................................................1
    Feb. 1965 ..............................................................2
    Mar. 1965 .............................................................3
    Apr. 1965 ..............................................................4
    May 1965 ..............................................................5
    Jun. 1965 ..............................................................6
    Jul. 1965 ...............................................................7
    Aug. 1965 .............................................................8
    Sep. 1965 and after .............................................9

ITEM AND DESCRIPTION

Number of siblings:                                                          19
List the number of brothers and sisters of subject.

Age and sex of siblings:                                                     20
  None ................................................................................0
  Younger brother(s) only .................................................1
  Younger sister(s) only ...................................................2
  Younger brother(s) and sister(s) ................................3
  Older brother(s) only ....................................................4
  Older sister(s) only .......................................................5
  Older brother(s) and sister(s) ....................................6
  Younger and older brother(s) ....................................7
  Younger and older sister(s) .......................................8
  Younger and older brother(s) and sister(s) ..............9

Adults living in the home:                                                   21
  Father and mother ......................................................0
  Mother only ..................................................................1
  Father only ..................................................................2
  Father, mother, and other relatives .........................3
  Father and stepmother ...............................................4
  Mother and stepfather ...............................................5
  Foster parents .............................................................6
  Father and other relative(s) .....................................7
  Mother and other relative(s) ....................................8
  Other relative(s) .........................................................9

Father's occupation:                                                         22
    References to father or mother should always be
    in light of the parent who is the most meaning-
    ful where a choice is between a stepparent and
    a true parent.

    *Farm laborers*: All non-owning, non-renting farm
    workers (except men who work on their own
    father's farm) ...........................................................1

    *Unskilled manual workers*: Garage laborers,
    sweepers, porters, janitors, street cleaners, con-
    struction laborers ...................................................2

    *Semiskilled manual workers*: Truck drivers, ma-
    chine operators, waiters, maintenance, counter-
    men, service-station attendants ............................3

*Skilled manual workers*: Carpenters, machinists, plumbers, masons, printers, barbers, cooks, mechanics (include all foremen) ................................4

*Farm owners or managers*: Any person who owns or manages a farm, ranch, or grove ................5

*White collar*: Clerks and kindred workers, agents, salesmen, semiprofessional workers, policemen, technicians (without college degree), secretary, traffic manager ................................6

*Small-business owners*: Small retail dealers, contractors, proprietors of repair shops employing others (includes both owners and managers) ......7

*Professional*: Physicians, dentists, professors, teachers, ministers, engineers, lawyers, pharmacists, accountants, free-lance writers, army officers, high-level technicians with college degree ................................8

*Large-business owners*: Bankers, manufacturers, large department store owners and managers, large farm and ranch owners ................9

Father's education:      23

Mother's education:      24

No formal schooling ................................0
Six years or less ................................1
Some junior high school ................................2
Finished junior high school (9th grade) ................3
Some high school ................................4
Finished high school (12th grade) ................5
Some college or post high school ................6
College graduate (B.A., B.S., etc.) ................7
Some post college (M.A., M.S., etc.) ................8
Advanced or professional degree (M.D., LL.D., Ph.D.) ................................9

Father's age:      25, 26

Mother's age:      27, 28
List age (if deceased, code 00)

How long in present home:      29, 30
List the number of years. This is to be rated in terms of whole years, i.e., 0 to 18 months is rated as one (01) year, 18 to 31 months is rated as two (02) years, etc.

| ITEM AND DESCRIPTION | | COLUMN |
|---|---|---|
| Buying or renting home: | | 31 |
| Buy/own | 0 | |
| Rent/lease | 1 | |
| Cities of residence since marriage: | | 32 |
| *List number* including city at time of marriage and the present city. | | |
| Schools attended by child: | | 33 |
| *List number* (not to include kindergarten). | | |
| Child's duties in home: | | 34 |
| None | 0 | |
| Less than 1 hour a week | 1 | |
| 1 to 5 hours a week | 2 | |
| More than 5 hours a week | 3 | |
| Religious affiliation of father: | | 35 |
| Religious affiliation of mother: | | 36 |
| Religious affiliation of child: | | 37 |
| Baptist/Church of Christ | 0 | |
| Presbyterian | 1 | |
| Catholic | 2 | |
| Christian/Disciples | 3 | |
| Episcopal | 4 | |
| Lutheran | 5 | |
| Methodist | 6 | |
| Jewish | 7 | |
| Other | 8 | |
| Frequency of church attendance: | | 38 |
| Never | 0 | |
| Rarely | 1 | |
| One to two times a month | 2 | |
| Once a week | 3 | |
| More than once a week | 4 | |
| Who attends church: | | 39 |
| No one | 0 | |
| Father only | 1 | |
| Mother only | 2 | |
| Father and mother only | 3 | |
| Children only | 4 | |
| Father and children | 5 | |
| Mother and children | 6 | |
| Whole family | 7 | |

1. Religious observances in home:          40
   None ........................................................................0
   Grace only ..............................................................1
   Other than grace ..................................................2
   Grace and other ....................................................3

2. (A) Special interests (activities, hobbies, pastimes, sports, etc.) of child:         41
      *List number* ......................................0 to 9

   (B) Variety of special interests:        42
      No special interests ......................................0
      No variety ........................................................1
      Some ..................................................................2
      A great deal ....................................................3

   (C) Who predominantly initiated special interests:   43
      No special interests ......................................0
      Self-initiated ..................................................1
      Parent-initiated ............................................2
      Initiated by others in the family ................3
      Initiated by others outside the family ........4

   (D) Predominant type of special interests:   44
      No interests ....................................................0
      Intellectual ....................................................1
      Hobby, crafts, and mechanics ..................2
      Physical ............................................................3
      Artistic ............................................................4
      Other ................................................................5

   (E) Interest level in special interests:   45
      No special interests ......................................0
      None ..................................................................1
      Slight ................................................................2
      Moderate ..........................................................3
      Great ................................................................4

3. (A) Child's special lessons:   46
      *List number* ........................................0 to 9

   (B) Variety of special lessons:   47
      No special lessons ........................................0
      No variety ........................................................1
      Some ..................................................................2
      A great deal ....................................................3

ITEM AND DESCRIPTION

(C) Who predominantly initiated special lessons:            48
    No lessons ............................................................0
    Self-initiated ......................................................1
    Parent-initiated ................................................2
    Initiated by others in the family ................3
    Initiated by others outside the family ..........4

(D) Type of special lessons:                                49
    No lessons ............................................................0
    Physical ................................................................1
    Intellectual ........................................................2
    Artistic ................................................................3
    Intellectual/artistic ........................................4
    Physical/intellectual/artistic ....................5

(E) Interest level in special lessons:                      50
    No lessons ............................................................0
    None ......................................................................1
    Slight ..................................................................2
    Moderate ............................................................3
    Great ..................................................................4

4. (A) Newspapers received regularly in home:               51
    *List number* ..............................................0 to 9

(B) Does child regularly read newspapers:                   52
    No ........................................................................0
    Qualified answer ..........................................1
    Yes ......................................................................2

(C) Magazines received regularly in home:
    Romance/detective ..........................0 to 9:          53
    Sports/adventure ............................0 to 9:          54
    Fashion/clothes/home ....................0 to 9:          55
    News/general interest ....................0 to 9:          56
    Intellectual/scientific/technical ........0 to 9:          57
    Children's magazines ....................0 to 9:          58

(D) Magazines read by child:
    Romance/detective ..........................0 to 9:          59
    Sports/adventure ............................0 to 9:          60
    Fashion/clothes/home ....................0 to 9:          61
    News/general interest ....................0 to 9:          62
    Intellectual/scientific/technical ........0 to 9:          63
    Children's magazines ....................0 to 9:          64

5. (A) Clubs to which father only belongs:       65
    List number ............................................................0 to 9

  (B) Variety of clubs:       66
    No clubs ................................................................0
    No variety ............................................................1
    Some ......................................................................2
    A great deal ........................................................3

  (C) Type of clubs:
    Religious ......................................0 to 9:   67
    Business/professional ................0 to 9:   68
    Social/fraternal/athletic/charitable/
      service ..................................0 to 9:   69
    Cultural/educational ................0 to 9:   70

  (D) General level of activity in clubs:   71
    No clubs ................................................................0
    None ......................................................................1
    Slight ....................................................................2
    Moderate ..............................................................3
    Great ....................................................................4

CARD NUMBER:       79–80

| ITEM AND DESCRIPTION | Data Card 16 Column |
|---|---|
| Group:<br>  Group I = 1<br>  Group II = 2<br>  Group III = 3 | 1 |
| Subject's I.D. number:<br>  List number as it appears on schedule. | 3, 4, 5 |
| Subject's sex:<br>  Male ................................................................1<br>  Female ............................................................2 | 6 |
| Culture:<br>  Texas ..............................................................1<br>  Mexico ............................................................2 | 8 |
| Interviewer:<br>  Stitt ................................................................1<br>  Williams ........................................................2 | 15 |

ITEM AND DESCRIPTION

| Date of interview: | | 16 |
|---|---|---|
| Dec. 1964 | 0 | |
| Jan. 1965 | 1 | |
| Feb. 1965 | 2 | |
| Mar. 1965 | 3 | |
| Apr. 1965 | 4 | |
| May 1965 | 5 | |
| Jun. 1965 | 6 | |
| Jul. 1965 | 7 | |
| Aug. 1965 | 8 | |
| Sep. 1965 and after | 9 | |

(E) Clubs to which mother only belongs:      19
     *List number* ........................................... 0 to 9

(F) Variety of clubs:      20
     No clubs ........................................... 0
     No variety ........................................... 1
     Some ........................................... 2
     A great deal ........................................... 3

(G) Type of clubs:
     Religious ........................... 0 to 9:    21
     Business/professional ........... 0 to 9:    22
     Social/fraternal/athletic/charitable/
       service ........................... 0 to 9:    23
     Cultural/educational ........... 0 to 9:    24

(H) Level of activity in clubs:      25
     No clubs ........................................... 0
     None ........................................... 1
     Slight ........................................... 2
     Moderate ........................................... 3
     Great ........................................... 4

(I) Clubs to which both parents belong:      26
     *List number* ........................................... 0 to 9

6. (A) Academic/vocational study courses father takes:    27
    (B) Academic/vocational study courses mother takes:    28
    (C) Domestic study courses father takes:    29
    (D) Domestic study courses mother takes:    30
     *List number* ........................................... 0 to 9

7. (A) Recreational activities of family:    31
     *List number* ........................................... 0 to 9

(B) Variety of recreational activities:                    32
    No activities ........ 0
    No variety ........ 1
    Some ........ 2
    A great deal ........ 3

(C) Predominant type of recreational activities:                    33
    No special activities ........ 0
    Intellectual ........ 1
    Hobby, crafts, and mechanics ........ 2
    Physical ........ 3
    Artistic ........ 4
    Other ........ 5

(D) Frequency of recreational activities:                    34
    No activities ........ 0
    Seldom all ........ 1
    Seldom some/Often some ........ 2
    Often all ........ 3

8. (A) Special interests (sports, hobbies) of father:                    35
    *List number* ........ 0 to 9

(B) Variety of special interests:                    36
    No interests ........ 0
    No variety ........ 1
    Some ........ 2
    A great deal ........ 3

(C) Predominant type of special interests:                    37
    No special interests ........ 0
    Intellectual ........ 1
    Hobby, crafts, and mechanics ........ 2
    Physical ........ 3
    Artistic ........ 4
    Other ........ 5

(D) Special interests (sports, hobbies) of mother:                    38
    *List number* ........ 0 to 9

(E) Variety of special interests:                    39
    No interests ........ 0
    No variety ........ 1
    Some ........ 2
    A great deal ........ 3

ITEM AND DESCRIPTION

(F) Predominant type of special interests:                        40
    No special interests ................................0
    Intellectual ...........................................1
    Hobby, crafts, and mechanics ...............2
    Physical ..................................................3
    Artistic ...................................................4
    Domestic ...............................................5
    Other ......................................................6

(G) Special interests (sports, hobbies) shared by
    mother and father:                                          41
    *List number* common to both ...............0 to 9

9. (A) Variety of places visited as a family unit:                42
    No trips ..................................................0
    One or more trips to the same place ............1
    Some variety of places (2 or 3 per year) ......2
    Great variety of places ...........................3

(B) Purpose of trips:                                             43
    No trips ..................................................0
    Visits to friends and/or relatives ...............1
    Recreational .........................................2
    Intellectual/educational ........................3
    Combinations of above ..........................4

10. Was child included in visits to friends or relatives:         44
    Few is to mean four or fewer times a
    year for this item. Seldom means that the
    child was included less than 30 percent
    of the time.
    No visits ................................................0
    Few visits—child seldom or never
      included ...........................................1
    Many visits—child seldom or never
      included ...........................................2
    Few visits—child often or always
      included ...........................................3
    Many visits—child often or always
      included ...........................................4

11. Mother's satisfaction with child's progress in school: 45
    Very dissatisfied .................................................0
    Dissatisfied ...........................................................1
    Satisfied ................................................................2
    Very satisfied ......................................................3

12. (A) Do mother and father discuss together how
    child gets along in school: 46
    Never ......................................................................0
    Seldom ..................................................................1
    Often ......................................................................2
    Very often ............................................................3

    (B) Topics discussed:
    Assignments ....................... No ....0; Yes....1: 47
    Progress/effort of child ....No.....0; Yes.....1: 48
    Relation of child to peers . No ....0; Yes.....1: 49
    Relation of child to teachers/
        school authorities ......... No ... 0; Yes ....1: 50

13. (A) Does parent discuss with child his (her)
    progress in school: 51
    Never ......................................................................0
    Seldom ..................................................................1
    Often ......................................................................2
    Very often ............................................................3

    (B) Which parent discusses progress with child: 52
    Neither ..................................................................0
    Father ....................................................................1
    Mother ..................................................................2
    Both ......................................................................3

    (C) School topics that parent(s) discuss with child:
    Assignments ....................... No ...0; Yes ...1: 53
    Progress/effort of child ... No.....0; Yes.....1: 54
    Relation of child to peers  No ...0; Yes ... 1: 55
    Relation of child to teachers/
        school authorities ......... No ... 0; Yes ... 1: 56

14. (A) How does mother compare child's *grades* in
    school with sibling(s): 57

(B) How does mother compare child's *ability* in
    school with sibling(s):                                      58

(C) How does mother compare child's *efforts* in
    school with sibling(s):                                      59
        No siblings .........................................................0
        Not as good ......................................................1
        Same ...................................................................2
        Better ..................................................................3
        Not as good as————, but better than———— 4

(D) How does mother compare child's class rank
    in school with classmates':                                    60
        Lower third .........................................................0
        Middle third ......................................................1
        Top third ............................................................2

15. Does child have homework:                                61
        No ........................................................................0
        Occasionally ......................................................1
        About 30 minutes a day ............................... 2
        About 1 or 2 hours a day .............................3
        More than 2 hours a day ..............................4

16. Does mother think child has too much school
    homework or not enough:                                     62
        Insufficient ........................................................0
        Appropriate ......................................................1
        Excessive ...........................................................2

17. Subjects mentioned in which child usually has
    homework:
        Math/science ................... No .... 0; Yes ....1:      63
        English/reading/language No ....0; Yes......1:      64
        Social science/history/
          geography ................... No .... 0; Yes.....1:      65
        Religious subjects ............. No.... 0; Yes....1:      66
        Other ................................ No.... 0; Yes....1:      67

18. (A) Who predominantly assists child with school
    homework:                                                    68
    No one ........................................................0
    Doesn't need assistance ...........................1
    Peer ........................................................2
    Sibling ....................................................3
    Grandparent/aunt/uncle .........................4
    Father ......................................................5
    Mother ....................................................6
    Father and mother ................................7
    Other family combination ..................... 8
    Other ......................................................9

    (B) How often is child helped with school
    homework:                                                     69
    Never ......................................................0
    Only occasionally ...................................1
    Fairly regularly ....................................2
    Very regularly ......................................3

    (C) Amount of time child is helped per week with
    school homework:                                              70
    No homework ...........................................0
    Number of hours .........................1 to 9

19. (A) What reasons are given child to encourage
    him to study:                                                 71
    None ........................................................0
    Do not have to, he knows it is expected .......1
    Do not have to, he expects it of himself ...... 2
    Immediate material reward ................... 3
    Future material reward (job preparation) ...4
    To become cultured, valuable to society .....5
    To avoid trouble in the future ...............6

    (B) Reasons given for child to study:                        72
    None ........................................................0
    Immediate ...............................................1
    Future ....................................................2

CARD NUMBER:                                                 79–80

| ITEM AND DESCRIPTION | DATA CARD 17 COLUMN |
|---|---|

Group:                                                                    1
  Group I = 1
  Group II = 2
  Group III = 3
Subject's I.D. number:                                          3, 4, 5
  List number as it appears on schedule.
Subject's sex:                                                            6
  Male ....................................................1
  Female ................................................2
Culture:                                                                   8
  Texas ...................................................1
  Mexico .................................................2
Interviewer:                                                              15
  Stitt .....................................................1
  Williams ...............................................2
Date of interview:                                                       16
  Dec. 1964 ...........................................0
  Jan. 1965 ............................................1
  Feb. 1965 ...........................................2
  Mar. 1965 ...........................................3
  Apr. 1965 ...........................................4
  May 1965 ...........................................5
  Jun. 1965 ...........................................6
  Jul. 1965 ............................................7
  Aug. 1965 ..........................................8
  Sep. 1965 and after ...........................9

20. Before child could read, did mother or father read
    to child:                                                        19
      No ...............................................0
      Only occasionally ......................1
      Fairly regularly .........................2
      Very regularly ..........................3
21. (A) Could child read, count, or write before school:        20
      No ...............................................0
      Read ............................................1
      Count ..........................................2
      Write ...........................................3
      Read and count .........................4
      Read and write .........................5
      Count and write ........................6
      Read, count, and write ...............7

(B) Who taught child to read, count, or write:     21

    Didn't learn any of these ............................................0

    Nurse/maid ............................................................1

    Sibling ..................................................................2

    Father ...................................................................3

    Mother ..................................................................4

    Some combination of family members ........5

    Picked it up himself ..........................................6

    Nursery school ....................................................7

    Other ....................................................................8

22. Does child read unassigned books (excluding

comics):     22

    Never .....................................................................0

    Less than 1 hour a week ..................................1

    1 to 3 hours a week ..........................................2

    1 hour a day ........................................................3

    More than 1 hour a day ....................................4

23. (A) Does mother encourage child to read:     23

(Active encouragement, such as taking the
child to the library, providing special books
for the child as well as verbalized encouragement can be rated. A "conditional answer" would be one where the parent
makes a statement to the effect that, "We
make sure that there are plenty of books
around—he is exposed to them.")

    No ..........................................................................0

    Doesn't need encouragement ........................1

    Conditional answer ...........................................2

    Yes ........................................................................3

(B) In what manner does mother encourage child

to read:     24

    Doesn't encourage .............................................0

    Suggests that he read ........................................1

    Provides material ...............................................2

    Insists that he read ............................................3

    More than one of the above ............................4

    Other ....................................................................5

24. (A) Does home have a dictionary or encyclopedia:     25

    Neither .................................................................0

    Dictionary ...........................................................1

    Encyclopedia .......................................................2

    Both .....................................................................3

ITEM AND DESCRIPTION

(B) Use of dictionary or encyclopedia by child:          26
    None ............................................................0
    Little ...........................................................1
    Some ..........................................................2
    Much .........................................................3

25. (A) Has father or mother had academic or voca-
    tional teaching experience:                          27
    No ...............................................................0
    Father .........................................................1
    Mother .......................................................2
    Both ...........................................................3

(B) Father's teaching grade level:                       28
(C) Mother's teaching grade level:                       29
    (If the answer includes more than one
    level, rate the most advanced level.)
    None ..........................................................0
    Vocational ..................................................1
    Elementary ...............................................2
    Junior high school ....................................3
    High school ...............................................4
    College .......................................................5

(D) Length of father's teaching experience:           30, 31
(E) Length of mother's teaching experience:           32, 33
    List number of years (for none, use 00)

(F) Subjects taught by father:                           34
(G) Subjects taught by mother:                           35
    (For parents who taught in grades 1
    through 6, and who did not state specific
    courses which they taught, rate the grade-
    school category.)
    None ..........................................................0
    Physical education/domestic arts ..............1
    Music/art ...................................................2
    Math/science .............................................3
    English/reading/language .........................4
    Social science/history/geography ..............5
    Technical/vocational .................................6
    Other ..........................................................7
    Combination of above ..............................8
    Grade school .............................................9

26. How many hours a week does child watch
television:          36
       0–2 ............................................................0
       3–4 ............................................................1
       5–9 ............................................................2
       10–14 ........................................................3
       15–20 ........................................................4
       21–25 ........................................................5
       26 and over ............................................6

27. How much control do parents exercise over child's
television-watching:      37
       Little or none ........................................0
       Fair amount ..........................................1
       Very much ..............................................2
       No control needed ................................3

29. (A) Number of hours mother watches television:      38, 39
     (B) Number of hours father watches television:      40, 41
         List number of hours (for none, use 00)

30. Special times that family is together routinely:      42
       None ........................................................0
       Meals ......................................................1
       Other than meals ................................2
       Meals and other ..................................3

31. (A) Activities father shares with child:      43
       None ........................................................0
       Some ......................................................1
       A great many ......................................2

     (B) Types of activities father shares with child:      44
       None ........................................................0
       Physical ................................................1
       Intellectual ..........................................2
       Hobby, crafts, and mechanics ..........3
       Domestic ..............................................4
       Artistic ..................................................5
       Combination of above ......................6

     (C) Activities mother shares with child:      45
       None ........................................................0
       Some ......................................................1
       A great many ......................................2

(D) Type of activities mother shares with child:                    46
      None ............................................................................0
      Physical .....................................................................1
      Intellectual ..............................................................2
      Hobby, crafts, and mechanics ......................3
      Domestic ...................................................................4
      Artistic ......................................................................5
      Combination of above .......................................6

32. (A) How many hours a week does mother work out-
        side the home:                                               47, 48
          List number of hours (for none, use 00)

   (B) What type of work does mother do:                             49
        *Housewife*: No paid work outside the
          home .....................................................................0
        *Semiskilled*: store clerk, telephone operator,
          waitress, saleswoman, factory worker,
          nursery attendant, hospital aide .............1
        *Office work*: legal secretary, legislative sec-
          retary, cashier, stenographer, typist, sta-
          tistical clerk, medical secretary, book-
          keeper ................................................................2
        *Teaching*: public schools, librarian, music
          teacher, substitute teacher, dancing
          teacher ...............................................................3
        *Professional, executive, or self-owned busi-
          ness*: decorator, social worker, nurse,
          sculptor, musician, store buyer, dieti-
          tian, comptroller, researcher, reporter,
          peace-corps director, personnel director ... 4

   (C) Does mother's work take her away while child
        is home:                                                     50
          Does not work outside the home ................0
          Away all of the day while child is home .. 1
          Away part of the day while child is home ... 2
          Not away while child is home ...................... 3

(D) Provision for child care: 51
    Mother does not work outside the home ......0
    No care ...........................................................1
    Does not need care ......................................2
    Relative or friend ........................................3
    Sibling ...........................................................4
    Housekeeper/maid .....................................5
    Hired person especially to care for child ... 6
    Other ...........................................................7

33. (A) How many hours a week did mother work
    when child was a preschooler: 52, 53
    List number of hours (for none, use 00)

(B) What type of work did mother do when child
    was a preschooler: 54
    (Use general criteria listed above.)
    Housewife .................................................... 0
    Semiskilled ...................................................1
    Office work ...................................................2
    Teaching .......................................................3
    Professional/executive/self-owned business ..4

(C) If mother worked when child was a preschooler,
    what provision was made for child care: 55
    Mother did not work outside the home ....... 0
    No care ...........................................................1
    Relative or friend ........................................2
    Sibling ...........................................................3
    Housekeeper/maid .....................................4
    Nursery school/care center .... ................. 5
    Any combination of 2 through 5 .... ........ 6

34. Has mother had other work experience: 56
    (Use general criteria listed above.)
    Housewife ....................................................0
    Semiskilled ...................................................1
    Office work ...................................................2
    Teaching .......................................................3
    Professional/executive/self-owned business 4

| ITEM AND DESCRIPTION | DATA CARD 17 COLUMN |
|---|---|

36. (A) Do family members speak another language:                    57
        No ................................................................0
        French .............................................................1
        German ...........................................................2
        Oriental ..........................................................3
        Scandinavian ...................................................4
        Slavic ..............................................................5
        Spanish/Mexican ..............................................6
        2 of above ........................................................7
        3 or more of above ...........................................8
        Other ..............................................................9
    (B) Who speaks another language:                                 58
        No one ...........................................................0
        Father .............................................................1
        Mother .............................................................2
        Father and mother ............................................3
        Child ................................................................4
        Family combination including child ..........5
        Relative living in home ....................................6
        Person (other than relative) in home ........7
    (C) How much is other language spoken:                           59
        None ...............................................................0
        Seldom ............................................................1
        Fair amount .....................................................2
        A good bit ........................................................3
37. How much education would parent like child to
    receive:                                                          60
38. Minimum amount of education that parent feels
    child must receive:                                               61
        No formal schooling .........................................0
        Six years or less ..............................................1
        Some junior high school ...................................2
        To finish junior high school (9th grade) ...3
        Some high school ............................................4
        To finish high school (12th grade) ............5
        Some college or post high school ..............6
        To graduate college (B.A., B.S., etc.) ..........7
        Some post college (M.A., M.S., etc.) ......... 8
        Advanced/professional degree (M.D.,
            LL.D., Ph.D.) ...............................................9

39. Type of work that parent would like to see child
do when grown:
(Use general criteria listed above.)

(A) If male (leave blank if female):                62
Not specific/no preference stated ................0
Farm laborer ......................................1
Unskilled manual worker ..........................2
Semiskilled manual worker ........................3
Skilled manual worker ............................4
Farm owner or manager ............................5
White-collar worker ..............................6
Small-business owner or manager .................7
Professional .....................................8
Large-business owner or manager ................9

(B) If female (leave blank if male):               63
Not specific/no preference stated ............. 0
General principles of choice ...................1
Mentions specific choice .......................2

40. Type of work that parent would not like to see
child do when grown:

(A) If male (leave blank if female):               64
Nothing specific stated ....................... 0
Manual labor ...................................1
Other general exclusions .......................2
Specific exclusions ............................3

(B) If female (leave blank if male):               65
Nothing specific stated ....................... 0
General exclusions .............................1
Specific exclusions ............................2

41. How satisfied is father with his work:          66
Very dissatisfied ..............................0
Slightly dissatisfied ..........................1
Satisfied ......................................2
Very satisfied .................................3

398

| ITEM AND DESCRIPTION | DATA CARD 17 COLUMN |
|---|---|

42. Had father previously wanted to do another kind
of work (what kind?):  67
    (Use general criteria listed above.)
    No ...... 0
    Farm laborer ...... 1
    Unskilled manual worker ...... 2
    Semiskilled manual worker ...... 3
    Skilled manual worker ...... 4
    Farm owner or manager ...... 5
    White-collar worker ...... 6
    Small-business owner or manager ...... 7
    Professional ...... 8
    Large-business owner or manager ...... 9

44. (A) Has parent had contact with teachers this year:  68
    (B) Did parent have contact with teachers last year:  69
    (C) Did parent have contact with PTA this year:  70
    (D) Did parent have contact with PTA last year:  71
    No contacts ...... 0
    1 contact ...... 1
    2 to 4 contacts ...... 2
    5 or more contacts ...... 3

CARD NUMBER:  79–80

| ITEM AND DESCRIPTION | DATA CARD 18 COLUMN |
|---|---|

Group:  1
  Group I = 1
  Group II = 2
  Group III = 3
Subject's I.D. number:  3, 4, 5
  List number as it appears on schedule
Subject's sex:  6
  Male ...... 1
  Female ...... 2
Culture:  8
  Texas ...... 1
  Mexico ...... 2
Interviewer:  15
  Stitt ...... 1
  Williams ...... 2

Date of interview:                                                    16

   Dec. 1964 ................................................................................0

   Jan. 1965 ................................................................................1

   Feb. 1965 ................................................................................2

   Mar. 1965 ................................................................................3

   Apr. 1965 ................................................................................4

   May 1965 ................................................................................5

   Jun. 1965 ................................................................................6

   Jul. 1965 ................................................................................7

   Aug. 1965 ................................................................................8

   Sep. 1965 and after ................................................................9

45. (A) Child's predominant use of free time:                         19

     No free time ................................................................0

     Mostly alone ................................................................1

     Usually with a friend ................................................2

     Mostly group activities ................................................3

     Other ................................................................4

  (B) Type of child's free time activity:                            20

     No free time ................................................................0

     Physical/social/recreational ................................1

     Intellectual ................................................................2

     Physical and intellectual ................................3

     Other ................................................................4

46. (A) Does parent know child's best friends:                        21

     Doesn't have any ................................................0

     Yes ................................................................1

     No ................................................................2

     Qualified answer ................................................3

  (B) Does parent approve of child's best friends:                   22

     No opinion ................................................................0

     Disapprove ................................................................1

     Qualified approval ................................................2

     Approve ................................................................3

  (C) Does parent help child to choose his friends:                  23

     Yes ................................................................0

     Qualified yes ................................................1

     No ................................................................2

47. Mother's positive comments about the child:                       24

     Not positive ................................................................0

     Positive ................................................................1

     Very positive ................................................................2

| | Data Card 18 |
|---|---|
| ITEM AND DESCRIPTION | Column |

48. (A) How does mother express approval of child:                25
    (B) How does father express approval of child:                26
        Doesn't ................................................................0
        Doesn't warrant any ................................................1
        Physically ..........................................................2
        Verbally ............................................................3
        Material reward ....................................................4
        Combination of above ...............................................5

49. Mother's negative comments about the child:                   27
        Not negative .......................................................0
        Negative ...........................................................1
        Very negative ......................................................2

50. (A) How does mother express disapproval of child:            28
    (B) How does father express disapproval of child:            29
        Doesn't ............................................................0
        Doesn't warrant any ................................................1
        Mild physically ....................................................2
        Severe physically ..................................................3
        Mild verbally ......................................................4
        Severe verbally ....................................................5
        Physically and verbally ............................................6
        Limitation of privileges ...........................................7
        Any combination of 2 through 7 .....................................8

51. Has child had serious illness or accident:                   30
        None ...............................................................0
        Accident ...........................................................1
        Acute illness ......................................................2
        Chronic illness ....................................................3
        Accident and acute illness .........................................4
        Accident and chronic illness .......................................5
        Acute and chronic illness ..........................................6
        Acute and chronic illness and accident .............................7

52. Has parent consulted a doctor in the past year
    regarding child:                                              31
        No .................................................................0
        Routine/minor ......................................................1
        Special/serious ....................................................2
        Chronic care .......................................................3
        Combination of above ...............................................4

53. (A) Special summer programs for child:

Physical/recreational ...............0 to 9     32

Vocational ...............0 to 9     33

Academic/intellectual ...............0 to 9     34

(B) How were special summer programs for child
initiated:     35

No programs ...............0

Self-initiated ...............1

Parent-initiated ...............2

Initiated by others in the family ...............3

Initiated by others outside the family ...............4

54–55. Significant additional
information ...............No......0; Yes......1:     36

*Neighborhood and Home Ratings*

Traffic:     37

Light ...............0

Medium ...............1

Heavy ...............2

Dwelling units:     38

Distant ...............0

Large lots ...............1

Average lots ...............2

Small lots ...............3

Crowded ...............4

Play space for children:     39

Ample ...............0

Adequate ...............1

None ...............2

Type of neighborhood:     40

Established status area ...............0

New status area ...............1

Unpretentious but neat ...............2

Some deterioration ...............3

Run-down ...............4

Type of dwelling unit:     41

House ...............0

Duplex ...............1

Apartment ...............2

Other ...............3

| ITEM AND DESCRIPTION | DATA CARD 18 COLUMN |
|---|---|

Condition inside home:     42
    Well-kept .......... 0
    Average .......... 1
    Run-down .......... 2

Furnishing:     43
    Excellent .......... 0
    Good .......... 1
    Without decor .......... 2
    Just furniture .......... 3

Amount of living space:     44
    Spacious .......... 0
    Comfortable .......... 1
    Crowded .......... 2

Condition of yard, lawn, grounds:     45
    Excellently kept .......... 0
    Well-kept .......... 1
    Average .......... 2
    Irregular maintenance .......... 3
    Run-down .......... 4

Comparison of home with other homes in the
neighborhood:     46
    Better .......... 0
    About the same .......... 1
    Worse condition .......... 2

Parent's grammar-pronunciation:     47
Parent's loquacity:     48
Parent's cordiality:     49
Parent's personal appearance:     50
    Excellent .......... 0
    Above average .......... 1
    Average .......... 2
    Below average .......... 3
    Poor .......... 4

CARD NUMBER:     79–80

# APPENDIX D
## Word Association Test in English and Spanish

Name:————————————————— I.D. #:——————

### WORD-ASSOCIATION TEST

*Instructions*: I am going to read a list of words to you, and I would like for you to tell me the *first* word that you think of when you hear this word.

| Word | RT | Response | Code | Word | RT | Response | Code |
|------|----|----------|------|------|----|----------|------|
| 1. milk | | | | 24. fiddle | | | |
| 2. salt | | | | 25. die | | | |
| 3. ship | | | | 26. jam | | | |
| 4. joy | | | | 27. mask | | | |
| 5. bread | | | | 28. rough | | | |
| 6. shovel | | | | 29. peer | | | |
| 7. whistle | | | | 30. smile | | | |
| 8. ham | | | | 31. green | | | |
| 9. sickness | | | | 32. pail | | | |
| 10. steel | | | | 33. mutton | | | |
| 11. whiskey | | | | 34. dock | | | |
| 12. butterfly | | | | 35. increase | | | |
| 13. stool | | | | 36. tablet | | | |
| 14. glare | | | | 37. foot | | | |
| 15. stomach | | | | 38. pain | | | |
| 16. justice | | | | 39. hit | | | |
| 17. ail | | | | 40. radio | | | |
| 18. discharge | | | | 41. yellow | | | |
| 19. heat | | | | 42. end | | | |
| 20. oil | | | | 43. cast | | | |
| 21. beautiful | | | | 44. street | | | |
| 22. doctor | | | | 45. boy | | | |
| 23. plain | | | | 46. blossom | | | |

| Word | RT | Response | Code | Word | RT | Response | Code |
|------|----|----|----|------|----|----|----|
| 47. lamp | | | | 64. stud | | | |
| 48. calf | | | | 65. bark | | | |
| 49. crow | | | | 66. soft | | | |
| 50. table | | | | 67. rip | | | |
| 51. man | | | | 68. nail | | | |
| 52. shack | | | | 69. black | | | |
| 53. scissors | | | | 70. crate | | | |
| 54. long | | | | 71. thirsty | | | |
| 55. eagle | | | | 72. woman | | | |
| 56. scab | | | | 73. cottage | | | |
| 57. sour | | | | 74. scale | | | |
| 58. tug | | | | 75. sweet | | | |
| 59. tobacco | | | | 76. frigid | | | |
| 60. high | | | | 77. needle | | | |
| 61. strangle | | | | 78. short | | | |
| 62. knife | | | | 79. afraid | | | |
| 63. bitter | | | | 80. eating | | | |

RT: reaction time

### Test de Asociación de Palabras
### Programa de Investigación Sobre el Desarrollo
### de la Personalidad del Escolar Mexicano

Nombre_____ No._____

Escuela_____ Edad_____ Grado _____

Fecha de Aplicación _____ Sistema I_____ II_____ III_____

Aplicación III _____ IV_____ V_____ Examinador_____

Instrucciones: Voy a leerte una lista de palabras y quiero que me
   digas la primera palabra que se te ocurra cuando escuches la palabra que yo te diga.

| Palabra | TR | Respuesta | Código | Palabra | TR | Respuesta | Código |
|------|----|----|----|------|----|----|----|
| 1. leche | | | | 10. acero | | | |
| 2. sal | | | | 11. hermosa | | | |
| 3. barco | | | | 12. doctor | | | |
| 4. alegría | | | | 13. sencillo | | | |
| 5. pan | | | | 14. violín | | | |
| 6. pala | | | | 15. morir | | | |
| 7. silbato | | | | 16. apretar | | | |
| 8. jamón | | | | 17. máscara | | | |
| 9. enfermedad | | | | 18. tosco | | | |

| Palabra | TR | Respuesta | Código | | Palabra | TR | Respuesta | Código |
|---------|-----|-----------|--------|--|---------|-----|-----------|--------|
| 19. camarada | | | | | 50. aceite | | | |
| 20. sonrisa | | | | | 51. carne | | | |
| 21. verde | | | | | 52. muelle | | | |
| 22. dolor | | | | | 53. aumento | | | |
| 23. muchacho | | | | | 54. tableta | | | |
| 24. flor | | | | | 55. pie | | | |
| 25. lámpara | | | | | 56. cubeta | | | |
| 26. becerro | | | | | 57. golpear | | | |
| 27. cuervo | | | | | 58. radio | | | |
| 28. mesa | | | | | 59. amarillo | | | |
| 29. hombre | | | | | 60. fin | | | |
| 30. cabaña | | | | | 61. tirar | | | |
| 31. tijeras | | | | | 62. calle | | | |
| 32. largo | | | | | 63. amargo | | | |
| 33. aguila | | | | | 64. tachón | | | |
| 34. costra | | | | | 65. ladrar | | | |
| 35. agrio | | | | | 66. suave | | | |
| 36. remolcar | | | | | 67. rasgar | | | |
| 37. tabaco | | | | | 68. clavo | | | |
| 38. alto | | | | | 69. negro | | | |
| 39. estrangular | | | | | 70. cesto | | | |
| 40. cuchillo | | | | | 71. sediento | | | |
| 41. wisky | | | | | 72. mujer | | | |
| 42. mariposa | | | | | 73. casucha | | | |
| 43. banquito | | | | | 74. escala | | | |
| 44. brillo | | | | | 75. dulce | | | |
| 45. estómago | | | | | 76. frialdad | | | |
| 46. justicia | | | | | 77. aguja | | | |
| 47. molestar | | | | | 78. corto | | | |
| 48. descargar | | | | | 79. miedo | | | |
| 49. calar | | | | | 80. comiendo | | | |

TR: *tiempo de reacción* (reaction time)

# BIBLIOGRAPHY

Ahumada, I. R. de, R. Ahumada, and R. Díaz-Guerrero. 1967. Consideraciones acerca de la estandarización de pruebas a Latinoamerica, con ilustraciones de la adaptación del WISC a México. In *Aportaciones de la psicología a la investigación transcultural*, ed. C. F. Hereford and L. Natalicio, pp. 410–421. Mexico City: Editorial F. Trillas.

Al-Issa, I., and W. Dennis, eds. 1970. *Cross-cultural studies of behavior.* New York: Holt, Rinehart and Winston.

Anderson, H. H., and G. L. Anderson. 1961. Image of the teacher by adolescent children in seven countries. *American Journal of Orthopsychiatry* 31:481–492.

————. 1962. Social values of teachers in Rio de Janeiro, Mexico City, and Los Angeles County, California: A comparative study of teachers and children. *Journal of Social Psychology* 58:207–226.

Berry, J. W. 1966. Temne and Eskimo perceptional skills. *International Journal of Psychology* 1:207–229.

Breeskin, J. 1966. The development of time estimation in children. Ph.D. dissertation, University of Texas at Austin.

Broverman, D. M. 1964. Generality and behavioral correlates of cognitive styles. *Journal of Consulting Psychology* 28:487–500.

Brown, W. F., and W. H. Holtzman. 1967. *Survey of study habits and attitudes: Forms C and S.* New York: Psychological Corporation.

Campbell, D. T. 1961. The mutual methodological relevance of anthropology and psychology. In *Psychological anthropology*, edited by F. L. K. Hsu, pp. 333–352. Homewood, Ill.: Dorsey Press.

Cattell, R. B., and F. W. Warburton. 1967. *Objective personality and motivation tests.* Urbana: University of Illinois Press.

Child, I. L. 1954. Socialization. In *The handbook of social psychology*, edited by G. Lindzey, II, 655–692. Reading, Mass.: Addison-Wesley.

————. 1968. Personality in culture. In *Handbook of personality theory and research*, edited by E. F. Borgatta and W. W. Lambert, pp. 82–145. Chicago: Rand McNally.

Cohen, J. 1959. The factorial structure of the WISC at ages 7-6, 10-6, and 13-6. *Journal of Consulting Psychology* 23:285–299.

Cole, M., J. Gay, J. A. Glick, and D. W. Sharp. 1971. *The cultural context of learning and thinking: An exploration in experimental anthropology.* New York: Basic Books.

Conners, C. K. 1965. Effects of brief psychotherapy, drugs, and type of disturbance on Holtzman inkblot scores in children. In *Proceedings of the 73rd Annual Convention of the American Psychological Association,* pp. 201–202. Washington, D.C.: APA.

Cosío Villegas, D. 1971. *American extremes.* Austin: University of Texas Press.

Cronbach, L. J. 1970. *Essentials of psychological testing.* 3d ed. New York: Harper and Row.

Currie, S. F., W. H. Holtzman, and J. D. Swartz. 1974. Early indicators of personality traits viewed retrospectively. *Journal of School Psychology* 12:51–59.

Dave, R. H. 1964. The identification and measurement of environmental process variables that are related to educational achievement. Ph.D. dissertation, University of Chicago.

DeVos, G. A., and A. A. Hippler. 1969. Cultural psychology: Comparative studies of human behavior. In *The handbook of social psychology,* edited by G. Lindzey and E. Aronson, 2d ed., IV, 323–417. Reading, Mass.: Addison-Wesley.

Díaz-Guerrero, R. 1965. Socio-cultural and psychodynamic processes in adolescent transition and mental health. In *Problems of youth,* edited by M. Sherif and C. W. Sherif, pp. 129–152. Chicago: Aldine.

———. 1967a. The active and the passive syndromes. *Revista Interamericana de Psicología* 1:263–272.

———. 1967b. Sociocultural premises, attitudes, and cross-cultural research. *International Journal of Psychology* 2:79–87. Also in *Psychology of the Mexican: Culture and personality.* Austin: University of Texas Press, 1975.

———. 1972a. Una escala factorial de premisas histórico-socioculturales de la familia Mexicana. *Revista Interamericana de Psicología* 6:3–4.

———. 1972b. Occupational values of Mexican school children. *Totus Homo* 4:18–26.

———. 1973. Interpreting coping styles across nations from sex and social class differences. *International Journal of Psychology* 8:193–203.

———. 1974. La mujer y las premisas histórico-socioculturales de la familia Mexicana. *Revista Latinoamericana de Psicología* 6:7–16.

Dyk, R. B. 1969. An exploratory study of mother-child interaction in infancy as related to the development of differentiation. *Journal of the American Academy of Child Psychiatry* 8:657–691.

Dyk, R. B., and H. A. Witkin. 1965. Family experiences related to the development of differentiation in children. *Child Development* 30:21–55.

Edgerton, R. B. 1971. *The individual in cultural adaptation.* Berkeley and Los Angeles: University of California Press.

Entwistle, D. R. 1966. *Word associations of young children.* Baltimore: Johns Hopkins Press.

Ervin, S. M. 1964. Language and TAT content in bilinguals. *Journal of Abnormal and Social Psychology* 68:500–507.

Etzioni, A. 1968. *The active society.* New York: The Free Press.

Faterson, H. F., and H. A. Witkin. 1970. Longitudinal study of development of the body concept. *Developmental Psychology* 2:429–438.

Gardner, R. W. 1959. Cognitive control principles and perceptual behavior. *Bulletin of the Menninger Clinic* 23:241–248.

Gardner, R. W., D. N. Jackson, and S. Messick. 1960. Personality organization in cognitive controls and intellectual abilities. *Psychological Issues* 2, no. 4 (whole no. 8).

Goodenough, D. R., and S. A. Karp. 1961. Field dependence and intellectual functioning. *Journal of Abnormal and Social Psychology* 63:241–246.

Hall, C. S., and G. Lindzey. 1957. *Theories of personality.* New York: Wiley.

Haroz, M. M. SEE Tamm, M.

Harris, D. B. 1963. *Children's drawings as measures of intellectual maturity.* New York: Harcourt, Brace and World.

Havighurst, R. J., M. E. Dubois, M. Csikszentmihalyi, and R. Doll. 1955. *A cross-national study of Buenos Aires and Chicago adolescents.* Basel: S. Karger.

Hereford, C. F. 1963. *Changing parental attitudes through group discussion.* Austin: University of Texas Press.

Herron, E. W. 1962. Intellectual achievement-motivation: A study in construct clarification. Ph.D. dissertation, University of Texas at Austin.

———. 1963. Psychometric characteristics of a thirty-item version of the group method of the Holtzman Inkblot Technique. *Journal of Clinical Psychology* 19:450–453.

Hill, E. F. 1972. *The Holtzman Inkblot Technique: A handbook for clinical application.* San Francisco: Jossey-Bass.

Hilton, T. L., and C. Patrick. 1970. Cross-sectional versus longitudinal data: An empirical comparison of mean differences in academic growth. *Journal of Educational Measurement* 7:15–24.

Hobhouse, L. T., G. C. Wheeler, and M. Ginsberg. 1915. *The material culture and social institutions of the simpler peoples: An essay in correlation.* London: Chapman and Hall.

Holtzman, W. H. 1969. Precursors of later personality traits in children. *Proceedings of the 77th Annual Convention of the American Psychological Association* 4:289–290. Washington, D.C.: APA.

Holtzman, W. H., D. R. Gorham, and L. J. Moran. 1964. A factor-analytic study of schizophrenic thought processes. *Journal of Abnormal and Social Psychology* 69:355–364.

Holtzman, W. H., E. C. Moseley, R. C. Reinehr, and E. Abbott. 1963. Comparison of the group method and the standard individual version of the Holtzman Inkblot Technique. *Journal of Clinical Psychology* 19:441–449.

Holtzman, W. H., J. S. Thorpe, J. D. Swartz, and E. W. Herron. 1961. *Inkblot perception and personality.* Austin: University of Texas Press.

Honigmann, J. J. 1967. *Personality in culture.* New York: Harper and Row.

Inkeles, A., and D. J. Levinson. 1969. National character: The study of modal personality and social systems. In *The handbook of social psychology*, 2d ed., edited by G. Lindzey and E. Aronson, IV, 418–506. Reading, Mass.: Addison-Wesley.

Jackson, D. N. 1967. *Manual for the Personality Research Form.* New York: Research Psychologists Press.

Jackson, D. N., and G. M. Guthrie. 1968. Multitrait-multimethod evaluation of the Personality Research Form. *Proceedings of the 76th Annual Convention of the American Psychological Association* 3:177–178. Washington, D.C.: APA.

Jensen, A. R., and J. D. Rohwer. 1966. The Stroop Color-Word Test: A review. *Acta Psychology* 25:36–93.

Kagan, J., H. A. Moss, and I. E. Siegel. 1963. Psychological significance of styles of conceptualization in basic cognitive processes in children. In *Basic cognitive processes in children*, edited by J. C. Wright and J. Kagan, pp. 73–112. Monographs of the Society for Research in Child Development, vol. 28 (whole no. 86).

Kagan, S., and M. C. Madsen. 1971. Cooperation and competition of Mexican, Mexican-American, and Anglo-American children of two ages under four instructional sets. *Developmental Psychology* 5:32–39.

Bibliography 411

————. 1972. Experimental analyses of cooperation and competition of Anglo-American and Mexican children. *Developmental Psychology* 6:49–59.

Kaiser, H. F. 1963. Image analysis. In *Problems in measuring change*, edited by C. W. Harris, pp. 156–166. Madison: University of Wisconsin Press.

Kaplan, B. 1961. Cross-cultural use of projective techniques. In *Psychological anthropology*, edited by F. L. K. Hsu, pp. 235–254. Homewood, Ill.: Dorsey Press.

Koppitz, E. M. 1968. *Psychological evaluation of children's human figure drawings*. New York: Grune and Stratton.

Kroeber, A. L., and C. Kluckhohn. 1952. *Culture: A critical review of concepts and definitions*. Harvard University Peabody Museum of American Archeology and Ethnology Papers, vol. 47, no. 1. Cambridge, Mass.: Peabody Museum.

Laosa, L. M. 1971. Development of word association structures among school children in Mexico and the United States. Ph.D. dissertation, University of Texas at Austin.

Laosa, L. M., J. D. Swartz, and R. Díaz-Guerrero. 1974. Perceptual-cognitive and personality development of Mexican and Anglo-American children as measured by Human Figure Drawings. *Developmental Psychology* 10:131–139.

Laosa, L. M., J. D. Swartz, and L. J. Moran. 1971. Word association structures among Mexican and American children. *Journal of Social Psychology* 85:7–15.

Levine, M., G. Spivak, J. Fuschillo, and A. Tavernier. 1959. Intelligence and measures of inhibition and time sense. *Journal of Clinical Psychology* 15:224–226.

LeVine, R. A. 1973. *Culture, behavior, and personality*. Chicago: Aldine.

LeVine, R. A., and B. B. LeVine. 1966. *Nyansongo: A Gusii community in Kenya*. New York: Wiley.

Lindzey, G. 1961. *Projective techniques and cross-cultural research*. New York: Appleton.

Linton, R. 1945. *The cultural background of personality*. New York: Appleton-Century-Crofts.

Lynd, R. S., and H. M. Lynd. 1937. *Middletown*. New York: Harcourt, Brace.

McClelland, D. C., J. W. Atkinson, R. A. Clark, and E. L. Lowell. 1953. *The achievement motive*. New York: Appleton-Century.

McGaughran, L. S., and L. J. Moran. 1956. "Conceptual level" vs.

"conceptual area" analysis of object-sorting behavior of schizophrenic and nonpsychiatric groups. *Journal of Abnormal and Social Psychology* 52:43–50.

Malinowski, B. 1927. *Sex and repression in savage society.* New York: Harcourt, Brace.

Manaster, G. J., and R. J. Havighurst. 1972. *Cross-national research: Social-psychological methods and problems.* Boston: Houghton Mifflin.

Manuel, H. T. 1966. *Prueba de lectura nivel 1: Primario forma CEs serie interamericana.* Austin, Texas: Guidance Testing Associates.

Marjoribanks, K. 1972. Environment, social class, and mental abilities. *Journal of Educational Psychology* 63:103–109.

Maslow, A. H., and R. Díaz-Guerrero. 1960. Delinquency as a value disturbance. In *Festschrift for Gardner Murphy,* edited by J. Peatman and E. L. Hartley, pp. 228–240. New York: Harper.

Mead, M. 1928. *Coming of age in Samoa.* New York: Morrow.

Mead, M. 1930. *Growing up in New Guinea.* New York: Morrow.

Megargee, E. I. 1966. Relation of response length to Holtzman Inkblot Technique scores. *Journal of Consulting Psychology* 30:415–419.

Messick, S., and N. Kogan. 1963. Differentiation and compartmentalization in object-sorting measures of categorizing style. *Perceptual and Motor Skills* 16:47–51.

Moore, B. M., and W. H. Holtzman. 1965. *Tomorrow's parents: A study of youth and their families.* Austin: University of Texas Press.

Moran, L. J. 1966. *Generality of word-association response sets. Psychological Monographs* 80, no. 2 (whole no. 612).

Moran, L. J., and R. Núñez. 1967. Cross-cultural similarities in association structures. *Revista Interamericana de Psicología* 1:1–6.

Moseley, E. C. 1963. Psychodiagnosis on the basis of the Holtzman Inkblot Technique. *Journal of Projective Techniques and Personality Assessment.* 27:86–91.

Murdock, G. P. 1949. *Social structure.* New York: Macmillan.

Murphy, L. B. 1964. Unpublished study.

Osgood, C. E. 1974. Probing subjective culture. Part I: Cross-linguistic tool-making. *Journal of Communication* 24:21–35.

Osgood, C. E., G. J. Suci, and P. H. Tannenbaum. 1957. *The measurement of meaning.* Urbana: University of Illinois Press.

Paz, O. 1961. *The labyrinth of solitude,* translated by L. Kemp. New York: Grove Press.

Peck, R. F., and R. Díaz-Guerrero. 1963. Two core-culture patterns and the diffusion of values across their borders. In *Proceedings of the*

*Seventh Interamerican Congress of Psychology*, pp. 107–115. Mexico City: Sociedad Interamericana de Psicología. Also in *Psychology of the Mexican: Culture and personality*, by R. Díaz-Guerrero. Austin: University of Texas Press, 1975.

Peck, R. F., and associates. Forthcoming. *Coping styles and achievement: A cross-national study of school children*, vol. 1. Austin, Texas: Research and Development Center in Teacher Education.

Porteus, S. D. 1950. *The Porteus maze test and intelligence*. Palo Alto, Calif.: Pacific Books.

Price-Williams, D. R., ed. 1969. *Cross-cultural studies: Selected readings*. Harmondsworth, England: Penguin Books.

Quereshi, M. Y. 1972. Factorial patterns of the WISC at ages six, ten, and fourteen. *Proceedings of the 80th Annual Convention of the American Psychological Association*. 7:53–54. Washington, D.C.: APA.

Rabin, A. I. 1959. Comparison of American and Israeli children by means of a sentence completion technique. *Journal of Social Psychology* 59:3–12.

———. 1961. Culture components as a significant factor in child development, 2: Kibbutz adolescents. *American Journal of Orthopsychiatry* 31:493–504.

Riesman, D., N. Glazer, and R. Denney. 1950. *The lonely crowd*. New Haven: Yale University Press.

Rosen, B. C. 1964. The achievement syndrome and economic growth in Brazil. *Social Forces* 42:341–354.

Sahagún, B. de. 1938. *Historia de las cosas de la Nueva España*. Mexico City: Editorial Pedro Robredo.

Sanders, J. L., W. H. Holtzman, and J. D. Swartz. 1968. Structural changes of the color variable in the Holtzman Inkblot Technique. *Journal of Projective Techniques and Personality Assessment* 32:556–561.

Sapir, E. 1927. The unconscious patterning of behavior in society. In *The unconscious: A symposium*, edited by E. S. Dummer, pp. 114–142. Chicago: University of Chicago Press.

———. 1932. Cultural anthropology and psychiatry. *Journal of Abnormal and Social Psychology* 27:229–242.

———. 1934. The emergence of the concept of personality in a study of cultures. *Journal of Social Psychology* 5:408–415.

Sarason, S. B., K. S. Davidson, F. F. Lighthall, R. R. Waite, and B. K. Ruebush. 1960. *Anxiety in elementary school children*. New York: Wiley.

Sarnoff, I., F. F. Lighthall, R. R. Waite, K. S. Davidson, and S. B. Sarason. 1958. A cross-cultural study of anxiety among American and English school children. *Journal of Educational Psychology* 49:129–136.

Sears, R. R. 1961. Transcultural variables and conceptual equivalence. In *Studying personality cross-culturally*, edited by B. Kaplan, pp. 445–455. Evanston, Ill.: Row Peterson.

Simpson, L. B. 1962. *Many Mexicos.* Berkeley and Los Angeles: University of California Press.

Snider, J. G., and C. E. Osgood. 1969. *Semantic differential technique: A sourcebook.* Chicago: Aldine.

Spiro, M. E. 1968. Culture and personality. In *International encyclopedia of the social sciences*, edited by D. L. Sills, III, 558–563. New York: Macmillan and the Free Press.

Spivak, G., M. Levine, and H. Sprigle. 1959. Intelligence test performance and the delay function of the ego. *Journal of Consulting Psychology* 23:428–431.

Stagner, R. 1961. *Psychology of personality.* 3d ed. New York: McGraw-Hill.

Stitt, J. D. 1970. Family and social background factors as they influence cognitive and perceptual development in children. Ph.D. dissertation, University of Texas at Austin.

Stroop, J. R. 1935. Studies of interference in serial verbal reactions. *Journal of Experimental Psychology* 18:643–661.

Swartz, J. D. 1967. The roles of culture, age, sex, and father's occupational level in children's responses to the Holtzman Inkblot Technique. In *Aportaciones de la psicología a la investigación transcultural*, edited by C. F. Hereford and L. Natalicio, pp. 130–142. Mexico City: Editorial F. Trillas.

Swartz, J. D., and W. H. Holtzman. 1963. Group method of administration of the Holtzman Inkblot Technique. *Journal of Clinical Psychology* 19:433–441.

Swartz, J. D., L. Lara Tapia, and J. S. Thorpe. 1967. Perceptual development of Mexican school children as measured by responses to the Holtzman Inkblot Technique. *Revista Interamericana de Psicología* 1:289–295.

Tamm, M. [Haroz, M. M.] 1967*a*. El Holtzman Inkblot Test, el Wechsler Intelligence Scale for Children y otros tests en el estudio psicológico transcultural de niños de habla española e inglesa residentes en México. Ph.D. dissertation, Universidad Nacional Autónoma de México.

———. 1967*b*. Resultados preliminares de un estudio transcultural y desarrollo de la personalidad de niños mexicanos y norteamericanos. In *Aportaciones de la psicología a la investigacion transcultural*, edited by C. F. Hereford and L. Natalicio, pp. 159–164. Mexico City: Editorial F. Trillas.

Terhune, K. W. 1963. An examination of some contributing demographic variables in a cross-national study. *Journal of Social Psychology* 59:209–219.

Thorpe, J. S. 1960. Level of perceptual development as reflected in responses to the Holtzman Inkblot Technique. Ph.D. dissertation, University of Texas at Austin.

Thorpe, J. S., and J. D. Swartz. 1965. Level of perceptual development as reflected in responses to the Holtzman Inkblot Technique. *Journal of Projective Techniques and Personality Assessment* 29:380–386.

Triandis, H. C., R. S. Malpass, and A. R. Davidson. 1971. Cross-cultural psychology. In *Biennial Review of Anthropology*, edited by B. J. Siegel, pp. 1–84. Stanford, Calif.: Stanford University Press.

Triandis, H. C., and associates. 1972. *The analysis of subjective culture*. New York: Wiley.

Tylor, E. B. 1889. On a method of investigating the development of institutions; applied to laws of marriage and descent. *Journal of the Anthropological Institute of Great Britain and Ireland* 18:245–269.

Van de Castle, R. L. 1965. Development and validation of a perceptual maturity scale using figure preferences. *Journal of Consulting Psychology* 29:314–319.

Veldman, D. J. 1967. *Fortran programming for the behavioral sciences*. New York: Holt, Rinehart and Winston.

———. 1974. Simple structure and the number of factors problem. *Multivariate Behavioral Research* 9:191–200.

Villegas, D. C. SEE Cosío Villegas, D.

*Webster's seventh new collegiate dictionary*. 1970. Springfield, Mass.: G. and C. Merriam.

Whiting, B. B., ed. 1963. *Six cultures: Studies in child rearing*. New York: Wiley.

Whiting, J. W. M. 1954. The cross-cultural method. In *The handbook of social psychology*, edited by G. Lindzey, I, 523–531. Reading, Mass.: Addison-Wesley.

Whiting, J. W. M., and I. L. Child. 1953. *Child training and personality*. New Haven: Yale University Press.

Witkin, H. A. 1950. Perception of the upright when the direction of the force acting on the body is changed. *Journal of Experimental Psychology* 40:93–106.

Witkin, H. A., R. B. Dyk, H. F. Faterson, D. R. Goodenough, and S. A. Karp. 1962. *Psychological differentiation.* New York: Wiley.

Witkin, H. A., H. F. Faterson, D. R. Goodenough, and J. Birnbaum. 1966. Cognitive patterning in mildly retarded boys. *Child Development* 37:301–316.

Witkin, H. A., D. R. Goodenough, and S. A. Karp. 1967. Stability of cognitive style from childhood to young adulthood. *Journal of Personality and Social Psychology* 7:291–300.

Witkin, H. A., H. B. Lewis, M. Hertzman, K. Machover, P. B. Meissner, and S. Wapner. 1954. *Personality through perception.* New York: Harper and Brothers.

Witkin, H. A., D. Price-Williams, M. Bertini, B. Christiansen, P. K. Oltman, M. Ramírez, and J. van Meel. 1974. Social conformity and psychological differentiation. *International Journal of Psychology* 9:11–29.

Witzke, D. B. 1973. *A program for score estimation for subjects with missing data in repeated measures designs.* Austin, Texas: Research and Development Center for Teacher Education.

Wolf, R. 1964. The identification and measurement of environmental process variables related to intelligence. Ph.D. dissertation, University of Chicago.

———. 1965. The measurement of environments. In *Proceedings of the 1964 invitational conference on testing problems,* edited by C. W. Harris, pp. 93–106. Princeton, N.J.: Educational Testing Service.

Yankelovich, D. 1972. *The changing values on campus.* New York: Washington Square Press.

———. 1974. *The new morality: A profile of American youth in the 70's.* New York: McGraw-Hill.

Zea, L. 1956. *Esquema para una historia de las ideas en Iberoamérica.* Ediciones Filosofía y Letras, vol. 6. Mexico City: Universidad Nacional Autónoma de México.

# INDEX

intellectual stimulation: of the child, 252–256, 357; cognitive abilities related to, 312–319; in cross-cultural comparison, 306, 308, 313; development of, represented in interview, 313. *See also* Intellectual Stimulation score
Intellectual Stimulation score (on OVI), 230–231, 234
Interamerican Tests, Manuel's, 95
Internal Determinism, 58, 281
interview. *See* parent interview
Iowa Tests, 40
IQ scores, 40

Jackson, Douglas N., 33, 144, 146
Jackson Personality Research Form. *See* Personality Research Form

Kagan, Jerome, 29, 92, 346–347. *See also* Conceptual Styles Test; Visual Fractionation Test
Kagan, S., 346–347
Kaiser, Henry F., 57
Kansas studies, 43. *See also* Topeka studies
Kaplan, Bert, 4
Kardiner, Abram, 329
Karp, S. A., 296, 297
Kluckhohn, C., 327
Kogan, Nathan, 181
Koppitz, Elizabeth M., 167–168
Kroeber, A. L., 327

Lambert, William W., 6, 8
languages spoken in the home, 255, 314
Laosa, Luis M., 179
LeVine, Barbara B. 328–329
LeVine, Robert A., 327, 328–329
Levinson, Daniel J., 327
Lie Scale (of TASC), 30, 87–88, 140, 154, 227–228
Lindzey, Gardner, 4, 328
Linton, Ralph, 329, 349
Location variable (of HIT), 35, 55, 67, 80; first-year analysis of, 204; in HIT factors, 99, 102, 105, 106–107; independent variables correlated with, 307; longitudinal analysis of, 213–214; variance proportion of, 100
London: in four-city comparison, 333
longitudinal design of study: age in,

323; complexities of, 95–97; methods of, 354; reason for, 352
Lynd, H. M., 43
Lynd, R. S., 43

McClelland, David C., 11
McGaughram, Lawrence S., 28, 181
Madsen, M. C., 346–347
Malinowski, Bronislaw, 4
Malpass, Roy S., 326, 327
Management score (on OVI), 233
Manaster, Guy J., 327
Manuel, H. T., 95
Manuel's Interamerican Tests, 95
Manuel's Reading Test, 33
*Many Mexicos*, 334
Marjoribanks, Kevin, 40
Masculinity-Femininity Discrimination index, 310, 358
Masculinity-Femininity ratings (on HFD), 196–198
Maslow, A. H., 318
Mazes subtest (of WISC), 109, 110; in cognitive factors, 114, 116
Mead, Margaret, 4
Megargee, E. I., 207
mental-abilities tests, 34–35, 354; in HFD, 179–181; in WISC, 116, 173–179. *See also* cognitive/mental-abilities tests
Messick, Samuel, 181
Metropolitan Achievement Test, 40
Mexico City: in four-city comparison, 333
Michigan State University, 9
"Middletown" studies, 43, 50, 54
Moore, Bernice M., 42
Moran, Louis J., 28, 31, 151, 181. *See also* Word Association Test
Moss, H. A., 181
mother: age of, 240–241; assessment of child by, 267–271; attitudes and values of, 42–44, 171; education of, 239–240, 314; school performance of child assessed by, 268; work outside the home of, 246
Movement variable (of HIT), 55, 67, 141, 151, 153, 297, 300, 301; in cognitive factors, 110–118 passim; in cross-cultural comparison, 319, 344, 356, 357; degree of variance in, 100; HFD correlated with, 149–150; in HIT factors, 99, 101, 106, 148, 206–207, 209; independent variables